TREES
of
MICHIGAN
Including Tall Shrubs

Linda Kershaw

with contributions by

Anton A. Reznicek & Bill Cook

LONE
PINE

Lone Pine Publishing International

Distributed by Lone Pine Publishing
1808 B Street NW, Suite 140
Auburn, WA, USA 98001

Website: www.lonepinepublishing.com

Library and Archives Canada Cataloguing in Publication

Kershaw, Linda J., 1951–

  Trees of Michigan, including tall shrubs / Linda Kershaw.

Includes bibliographical references and index.
ISBN-13: 978-976-8200-07-5
ISBN-10: 976-8200-07-3

  1. Trees—Michigan—Identification. 2. Shrubs—Michigan—Identification.
I. Title.

QK167.K47 2006   582.1609774   C2006-901651-8

Technical Review: Anton A. Reznicek, Bill Cook
Separations & Film: Elite Lithographers Co.

Cover photo by Hans Blohm/Masterfile

The photographs in this book are reproduced with the generous permission of their copyright holders. A full list of photo credits appears on p. 6, which constitutes an extension of this copyright page.

Disclaimer: This guide is not intended to be a "how to" reference guide for food or medicinal uses of plants. We do not recommend experimentation by readers, and we caution that a number of woody plants in Michigan, including some used traditionally as medicines, are poisonous and harmful.

PC: 13

Contents

List of Keys

Acknowledgments

Many people have helped in the preparation and production of this book. In particular, I thank Dr. Tony Reznicek, Curator of the University of Michigan Herbarium in Ann Arbor and Bill Cook, a forester/biologist at Michigan State University Extension in Escanaba. Tony and Bill both reviewed the species list and manuscript and provided valuable criticism and suggestions as the book evolved. Tony also reviewed all of the photos and distribution maps. The knowledge of these two colleagues has been invaluable, and their positive, encouraging feedback was always appreciated.

Photographs and other illustrations add to the beauty and usefulness of the guide. Thanks to Ian Sheldon, whose watercolour paintings illustrate the form of most species. Many people searched through their collections of slides and digital photos and provided excellent images. A full list of photo credits can be found on p. 6.

At Lone Pine, Nicholle Carrière edited the text and coordinated the project, while Carol Woo located and organized scores of photos and Heather Markham and Curtis Pillipow wove text and illustrations together on the final pages. Thanks to everyone at Lone Pine for your hard work and creative ideas.

Photo Credits

Photos are by Linda Kershaw, except the following:

Wasyl Bakowsky: 28b, 29c, 71b, 74b, 79a, 80a, 104c, 110c, 134b, 175b, 176b, 192a, 199a, 200a, 200b, 211a, 239b

Bill Cook: 21a, 21b, 23a, 23b, 24a, 24b, 89b, 89c, 92c, 96c, 112c, 114b, 122c, 127c, 200c, 211b, 247c

Bill Crins: 169a, 175a, 185b, 186b, 189b

Don Doucette: 13

Tamara Eder: 20

Mary Gartshore: 94a, 98b, 188a, 238a, 238b, 238c

Erich Haber: 65c, 66c, 69b, 72a, 89a, 101a, 105a, 112b, 119c, 120c, 122b, 152b, 212a, 214c, 229b, 236c

Alex Inselberg: 5

Glen Lumis: 1, 31b, 32a, 33a, 33b, 33c, 79c, 101c, 107c, 109a, 111b, 120b, 161c, 176a, 189c, 194c, 209a, 211c, 212b, 214b, 217c, 224b, 225c, 231a, 244b, 244c, 245a, 245b

Tim Matheson: 17, 18

Morton Arboretum (Chicago, IL) 76b, 81a, 81b, 81c, 86b, 86c, 106b, 108b, 111c, 113c, 115a, 115b, 115c, 116a, 125b, 133c, 133d, 142b, 151, 166a, 180a, 180b, 189a, 190a, 190c, 191a, 198a, 198c, 202b, 203b, 204, 216a, 216b, 227a, 227b, 228c, 242b, 242c, 243b, 249a

Fred Nation: 138a, 138b

Allison Penko: 19

Tony Reznicek: 91a, 91b, 91c

Robert Ritchie: 15, 16, 188c, 230b

Anna Roberts: 143b

Royal Botanical Gardens (Ontario, Canada) 100b, 100c, 124a, 124b, 124c, 169b, 169c, 172c, 210a, 240c

Don Sutherland: 105b, 172a

Pam Trewatha: 165a, 165b

Pictorial Guide

NEEDLE LEAVES

Balsam fir	Norway spruce	White spruce	Black spruce
p. 64	p. 65	p. 66	p. 67

Tamarack	Eastern hemlock	Eastern white pine	Red pine
p. 68	p. 69	p. 70	p. 71

Scots pine	Jack pine	Eastern red-cedar	Eastern white-cedar
p. 72	p. 73	p. 74	p. 75

ALTERNATE BROAD LEAVES

Small-flower tamarisk	Tulip-tree	Pawpaw	Sassafras
p. 76	p. 78	p. 79	p. 80

Spicebush	American sycamore	American witch-hazel	Elms
p. 81	p. 82	p. 83	pp. 83–89

Pictorial Guide

Hackberries
pp. 90–91

Osage-orange
p. 92

Mulberries
pp. 93–94

Butternut
p. 96

Black walnut
p. 97

Hickories
pp. 98–101

American beech
p. 104

American chestnut
p. 105

Oaks
pp. 106–116

Ironwood
p. 119

Musclewood
p. 120

American hazelnut
p. 121

Birches
pp. 122–125

Alders
pp. 126–128

White poplar
p. 133

Aspens
pp. 134–135

Balsam poplar
p. 136

Cottonwoods
pp. 137–138

Pictorial Guide

Willows
pp. 139–153

Cherries
pp. 161–163, 165–167

Peach
p. 164

Plums
pp. 168–170

Common pear
p. 171

Common apple
p. 174

Crabapples
pp. 172–173

Mountain-ashes
pp. 175–177

Hawthorns
pp. 178–187

Pictorial Guide

Serviceberries
pp. 188–189

Mountain silverbell
p. 190

Black locust
p. 191

Redbud
p. 192

Honey-locust
p. 193

Kentucky coffee-tree
p. 194

Japanese angelica-tree
p. 195

Smooth sumac
p. 197

Shining sumac
p. 198

Poison-sumac
p. 176

Common prickly-ash
p. 200

Castor-aralia
p. 201

European smoketree
p. 202

Common winterberry
p. 203

Common mountain-holly
p. 204

Tree-of-heaven
p. 205

Common hop-tree
p. 206

American basswood
p. 207

Littleleaf linden
p. 208

Russian-olive
p. 209

Pictorial Guide

ALTERNATE BROAD LEAVES

Black tupelo
p. 210

Glossy buckthorn
p. 211

European buckthorn
p. 212

Alternate-leaf dogwood
p. 214

OPPOSITE BROAD LEAVES

Gray dogwood
p. 216

Eastern flowering
dogwood, p. 217

Eastern wahoo
p. 218

European spindle-tree
p. 219

American bladdernut
p. 220

Horsechestnut
p. 221

Ohio buckeye
p. 222

Sugar maple
p. 224

Maples
pp. 225–232

Maples
pp. 225–232

Pictorial Guide

Common lilac
p. 234

European privet
p. 235

Ashes
pp. 236–240

Ashes
pp. 236–240

Common elderberry
p. 242

Amur honeysuckle
p. 243

Nannyberry
p. 244

Wayfaring-tree
p. 245

American highbush-
cranberry, p. 246

Northern catalpa
p. 247

Silver buffaloberry
p. 248

Buttonbush
p. 249

Michigan would be a quite different place without trees. Each spring, trees bring a flush of green to the landscape, often accompanied by sprays of fragrant flowers. In summer, trees shade our parks and yards, giving shelter from hot sun or drenching downpours and providing homes for birds, squirrels and other animals. In autumn, the red and golden leaves of some trees create a beautiful patchwork of color, and the fruits of others provide delicious treats. In winter, evergreen trees shelter us from wind and snow and add color to a drab landscape.

Trees are our largest plants, and they dominate many ecological systems. Some plants require the shelter of a forest canopy for survival, while others need the partial protection of open-grown trees in sunnier sites to become established. Beneath the canopy, light levels are lower, humidity is higher and the immediate impacts of wind and rain are muted.

Trees are also important ecosystem producers. They create large quantities of carbohydrates and oxygen, and they store huge amounts of nutrients in their trunks and branches. Their leaves, flowers, fruits, bark and twigs provide food for insects, birds and mammals, and their trunks and boughs provide shelter and nesting sites.

Through the ages, trees have also been important to human survival. Bark has been used for covering canoes, roofs and walls, for tanning leather, for making dyes and even for producing soft fibers that could be woven into blankets and clothing. Sap has provided food, glue, caulking and water-proofing. Fruits and nuts are still an important source of food, and many parts of different trees have been used as medicines. Fine roots have been split and spun to make thread and cord, and the knees and elbows of some larger roots were highly valued in shipbuilding. Most notably, however, trees have provided wood. This strong, versatile material is still widely used for building homes and other structures; for making boats, tools, utensils and other small items; for carving works of art; for producing paper, cellophane, turpen-tine, charcoal and countless other products; and for fuel. Without the food, shelter and fuel provided by trees, settlement in Michigan would have been difficult at best.

Many collections of trees have been established in parks and gardens throughout Michigan. An **arboretum** is a place where trees and other plants are cultivated for their beauty and for scientific and educational purposes. If you would like to learn more about trees by viewing living specimens, try visiting some of the collections listed in the appendix (p. 250).

Plants can also be studied using dried, pressed specimens. An **herbarium** is a large collection of such specimens that have been mounted, labeled and filed systematically. See the appendix (p. 251) for the names and locations of herbaria in Michigan.

What Is a Tree?

Most of us have a fairly clear idea of what a tree is. Trees are tall, long-lived plants with stout, woody trunks and spreading canopies. A giant sugar maple or perhaps a towering white pine might come to mind with the word "tree." Many small trees, however, fall into the gray area between trees and shrubs. Robust specimens might be considered trees, but younger or less robust individuals would be called shrubs. These species have also been included in this guide in an effort to include all species that could possibly be viewed as "trees."

For the purposes of this guide, a tree or tall shrub is defined as an erect, perennial, woody plant reaching **over 15' in height**, with a distinct crown and with a trunk (one or more of the trunks on a multi-stemmed specimen) reaching at **least 3" in diameter**. The trunk diameter is the DBH (diameter at breast height), measured 4½' from the ground.

Some definitions stipulate that a true tree must have a single trunk that divides into branches well above the ground, so that the tree has a clearly defined bole (main stem). However, many trees, such as some willows, have trunks that divide at or near the ground. Other species, such as birches, oaks and basswood, often coppice (form bushy clumps from sprouting stumps).

Trees are some of our longest-lived and largest organisms. Most live 100–200 years, but some survive much longer. For example, eastern white-cedar can live from 600 to almost 1000 years. Many smaller trees are relatively short-lived, typically surviving 60–80 years. Most trees reach 50–80' in height, but some grow even taller. For example, eastern white pine can reach 200' and tulip-tree and white oak may tower to 170' and 134' respectively. At the other end of the spectrum, pussy willow, mountain maple and poison-sumac rarely exceed 16'.

In order to support the large trunks and branches of a tree, many cells are gradually transformed into nonliving supportive tissues, such as wood and cork. These dead cells account for about 80% of a mature tree, and the remaining 20% are live cells that maintain vital functions.

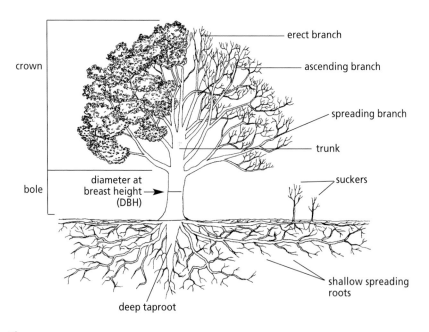

crown

erect branch

ascending branch

spreading branch

trunk

bole

diameter at breast height → (DBH)

suckers

shallow spreading roots

deep taproot

Trunks

The sturdy, woody trunk of a tree supports the weight of the aboveground mass, and it carries water and nutrients from the ground and food from the leaves to the living tissues. A trunk is made up of several distinct layers, each with a different function.

The outermost layer is the bark. Tree bark forms a protective, waterproof layer that can shield the tree from fire damage, insect or fungal attack and the stress of sudden temperature changes. Not all types of bark offer the same protection. For example, trees with thick, corky bark may survive a fire that would seriously damage or kill trees with thin or papery bark.

All bark has small, round or vertically or horizontally elongated pores called **lenticels**, which allow the trunk to breathe. Lenticels are often difficult to see, but in some trees they are very conspicuous and distinctive, with raised edges that roughen the bark. Often, trees with thin, smooth bark (e.g., birches, cherries) have large, conspicuous lenticels.

Acer saccharum, sugar maple

Bark is sometimes very distinctive (e.g., in paper birch, beech and sycamore), but differences between related species are often subtle. Bark characteristics can also change greatly with age. Young bark is usually smooth with visible pores, but as a tree ages, its bark becomes thicker and rougher, and the pores are obscured in many corky layers.

Bark cells grow from a special thin layer of living cells on the inner side of the bark, called the **cork cambium** or bark cambium. Each year, the cork cambium lays down another successive layer of bark to cover the ever-expanding trunk or branch. As growth continues, the oldest, outermost layers of bark are forced either to split into corky ridges or scales (as in maple bark) or to peel away from the tree (as in birch bark).

To the inner side of the cork cambium lies the **phloem** or bast. This thin, inconspicuous layer of cells is very important to the tree because it carries the food (carbohydrates) produced by the leaves to all the tree's living tissues. A tree can be killed by "girdling," i.e., removing or cutting through the bark, cork cambium and phloem in a complete band around the trunk. The roots of a girdled tree no longer receive food and eventually die, along with the rest of the tree. Some roots may persist for a time using stored reserves, but the final effect of girdling is inevitable.

Trunk cross-section

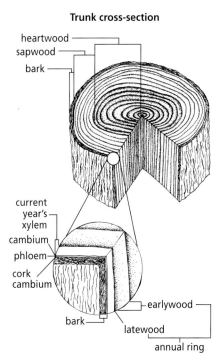

heartwood
sapwood
bark

current year's xylem
cambium
phloem
cork cambium
bark
earlywood
latewood
annual ring

Fagus grandifolia, American beech

time, these may gradually become plugged with resins, tannins and other compounds and eventually cease to transport fluids altogether, but by then many younger xylem cells have been laid down around them to take their place. As long as xylem cells continue to transport fluids, they are part of the tree's **sapwood**, but once they clog and cease to function, they become part of the **heartwood**. Heartwood is often darker and harder than sapwood because of the resins and other compounds that fill its cells. Heartwood helps support the trunk but otherwise is not important to the general health of the tree. A tree's heartwood can burn or rot away almost completely, leaving a hollow trunk, while the branches and leaves continue to flourish.

Trees growing in temperate regions, where there are definite seasonal changes in growth, develop patterns in their wood called **annual rings**. Each year, after the first flush of spring growth, the trees set down large, relatively thin-walled, light-colored xylem cells. As the season progresses, growth slows and the xylem cells become smaller and thicker-walled. Eventually, trunk growth stops almost completely in late summer, as trees begin to store nutrients for the coming winter and following spring. Consequently, the ring of wood that is laid down each year gradually changes from pale, large-pored **earlywood** or springwood to harder, darker, small-pored **latewood** or summerwood. The following spring, a new layer of pale springwood is laid down, often in sharp contrast to the darker adjacent summerwood of the previous season. As a result, each year's growth forms a distinct annual ring. The rings can be observed as concentric circles across a log or stump when a tree is cut down, or as a series of light and dark bands along a cylinder when a core is taken from the trunk.

Close examination of annual rings reveals much about the history of a tree. Because a new ring is created each year, counting the rings reveals the age of the tree. We can also learn much about the tree's health and environment because many factors affect the growth rate and subsequent ring widths of a tree. Drought, unusually cold years, flooding, insect infestations, diseases and pollution can all make a tree

On the inner side of the phloem lies an even narrower ring of cells, too thin to see, called the **cambium**. The cambium is responsible for increases in the diameter of a trunk or branch. Cambium cells produce phloem cells along the outer surface of the ring and xylem cells along the inner surface. The **xylem** transports water and nutrients up from the roots to the branches and leaves, where the tree produces its food. The thick-walled, cylindrical cells of the xylem join end to end, forming thousands of capillary tubes that extend up the trunk like tiny, elongated drinking straws. The xylem cells soon die, but their firm hollow tubes continue to function, often for many years.

Within its bark, then, the trunk of a tree has a thin outer ring of living tissue composed of the phloem and cambium, and a narrow ring of living xylem. Most of the rest of the trunk, which we call **wood**, is made up of dead xylem cells. With

produce narrow annual rings. Alternatively, increased light (perhaps as a result of an opening in the canopy), influxes of nutrients and unusually warm or wet years can result in wider annual rings. Scars from forest fire or insect damage may eventually be overgrown by new wood, but will remain hidden in the trunk as a permanent record of the event. In many parts of the world, information gleaned from the study of tree rings has been used to map ancient forest fires and to assess prehistoric climate change.

Branches and Twigs

Branches develop the same woody structure as trunks. In young twigs, however, the soft central core of early growth, called the **pith**, is more obvious. In some trees, the pith is quite distinctive. For example, in pawpaw twigs, the pith is marked with horizontal bands, and in hackberry twigs, it has a series of horizontal chambers; both patterns are visible in longitudinal section (cut lengthwise down the middle of the twig). In oaks,

Acer rubrum, red maple

the pith is five-pointed when viewed in cross-section (cut across the twig).

Unlike the trunk, branch tips and twigs grow in length as well as width. The history of recent growth can often be observed through a series of leaf or bud scars on young branches. Each summer, small branches produce buds along their lengths and (usually) at their tips. By autumn, each bud contains all the rudimentary cells necessary to produce a new structure. The **tip bud** or terminal bud is often much larger than the lower **side-buds** or lateral buds, and it produces a new extension of the shoot the following year. Most side-buds produce leaves and sometimes flowers, but a few send out new branches.

Buds develop gradually over the summer. Usually they are covered by one or more tough, overlapping **bud scales**, which protect the tender, developing tissues from insect and fungal attacks and from drying out. A few trees have **naked buds**, which lack bud scales.

Each bud contains embryonic tissues of the part that it will produce the following year. These tissues remain dormant over winter, but in spring, rapid growth resumes, and the new shoots, leaves and flowers expand to emerge from their buds. As the buds open, the scales are shed, but scars remain to show where the scales were attached to the branch. Buds at the twig tips are encircled by scales, which leave a ring of scars around the

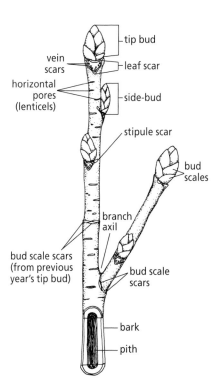

tip bud
vein scars
leaf scar
horizontal pores (lenticels)
side-bud
stipule scar
bud scales
branch axil
bud scale scars (from previous year's tip bud)
bud scale scars
bark
pith

Picea glauca, white spruce

outer leaf tissues. The leaf then uses the trapped energy in a process called **photosynthesis** to combine carbon dioxide and water and produce sugars (the direct or indirect source of energy for animals) and oxygen (also essential to plant and animal life).

Most trees that have needle-like leaves are **evergreen**, shedding some leaves each year but always retaining some green needles for photosynthesis. In Michigan, most trees have broad, **deciduous** leaves, which are produced each spring and shed each autumn.

Leaves breathe through many tiny pores called **stomata**. During the day, leaves take in carbon dioxide and give off moisture and oxygen through their stomata. At night, photosynthesis stops, but the tree continues to respire, consuming oxygen and expelling carbon dioxide. On broad, deciduous leaves, stomata are usually concentrated on the lower surface of the leaf, and a thin, waxy coating called the **cuticle** protects the upper surface and reduces water loss. On evergreen needles, all sides of the leaf are coated with a cuticle, and the stomata are scattered over the needle surface or concentrated in bands or lines on the lower side. The more extensive cuticle of evergreen needles helps to reduce water loss in winter, when below-freezing temperatures limit water supply.

twig, and each successive ring or **annual node** along a branch indicates one year's growth.

Leaves

Leaves come in all shapes and sizes, from the tiny, simple scales on cedar boughs to the giant, compound leaves a yard long on the Kentucky coffee-tree. (See pp. 38–42 for further discussion of leaf shapes, structures and arrangements.)

Leaves house the food factories and breathing devices of the tree. A leaf produces food by first capturing the sun's energy with the green pigment **chlorophyll**, which is concentrated in the

Reproductive Structures

All tree species can reproduce sexually, but the reproductive structures are not always present on

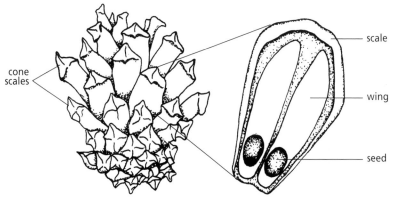

cone scales

scale

wing

seed

every tree. Male and female structures are produced on mature trees in cones or in flowers. In **cones**, these parts are hidden behind protective scales, but in most Michigan trees male and/or female structures are readily visible in flowers.

Flowers may consist of several series of structures. Usually the female organs, or **pistil**(s), are at the center, surrounded by a ring of male organs, or **stamens**, and then rings of floral leaves (petals and sepals). **Petals**, which collectively form the **corolla**, are usually much larger and showier than sepals. Most showy tree flowers in Michigan have white petals, but some are brightly colored or marked with contrasting spots or stripes. **Sepals**, which collectively form the outer ring or **calyx**, tend to be small and green, serving primarily to protect immature flowers in much the same way as bud scales. Sometimes the petals and sepals look alike and all are then called **tepals**.

When all four sets of organs are present, the flower is called **complete**, but in most cases, one or more sets of organs are absent. **Bisexual** or perfect flowers have both female and male organs (pistils and stamens); unisexual flowers have either male or female parts. Unisexual flowers of each sex may be borne on the same **(monoecious)** or separate **(dioecious)** trees.

A flower's main function is to transfer viable **pollen** from its **anthers** (pollen-producing organs of the stamens) to the receptive **stigma**

Malus cultivar, crabapple

(pollen-receiving organ of the pistil) of another flower, preferably on another plant. When transfer to another plant succeeds, **cross-pollination** occurs.

Many tree flowers are small, greenish and inconspicuous, with minute petals or no petals at all. These flowers usually appear early in the year and are wind pollinated (the pollen is carried from one flower to another by the wind). Other

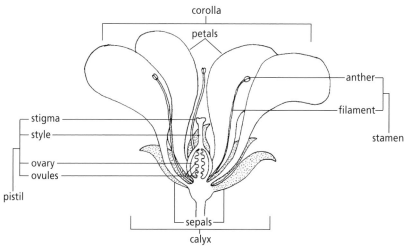

19

Acer ginnala, Amur maple

ovaries produce **aggregate fruits**. Occasionally, compact flower clusters produce very dense clusters of fruits (e.g., mulberries). These **multiple fruits** resemble aggregate fruits, but each part of the group is produced by an individual flower.

Fruits can serve many functions, including protecting the seeds, aiding in seed dispersal and providing moisture and nutrients for the developing seedlings. Fleshy fruits such as **drupes** (cherries, plums), **pomes** (apples, serviceberries, mountain-ash fruits) and true **berries** (pawpaw fruits) are often juicy and rich in sugars. These fruits attract birds and mammals that swallow the seeds along with the flesh and later deposit the seeds in their droppings at new sites. Similarly, many animals eagerly seek the oil-rich meat of **nuts** (walnuts, butternuts, hickory nuts, oak acorns). In fleshy fruits, the edible part is outermost, enclosing one or more seeds that are often protected by woody or bony structures (e.g., cores or stones). In nuts, the edible part of the fruit is encased in a hard shell, and the seed within lacks a protective inner covering.

Many animals also feed on nonfleshy fruits, but these fruits often have special structures that promote seed dispersal without animal assistance. Trees such as ashes, maples and elms produce **samaras** with broad wings that help to carry the seeds through the air or on water to new sites. **Capsules** (willows, American witch-hazel, common lilac) and **legumes** (redbud, honey-locust, Kentucky coffee-tree, black locust) are all dry fruits with protective coverings that eventually dehisce (split open) to release the seeds.

Seeds vary greatly in size from one species to the next, but all have a dry, often hard covering, the **seed coat**, which protects the developing **embryo** and its food reserves. Seeds with thin, papery seed coats usually germinate as soon as they are shed, whereas those with thick, hard seed coats may persist for several years before developing. Many Michigan trees have seeds that must experience a cold, dormant period before they can germinate. Once germination begins, food reserves in the seed sustain the seedling while it develops roots and leaves for producing its own food. Large seeds, such as those of walnuts and

trees have insect-pollinated flowers, with showy petals that attract insects and sometimes provide them with handy landing platforms. Often flowers have special glands called **nectaries**, which produce a sugary liquid **(nectar)** that attracts numerous insects. Many flowers also produce strong odors. Usually these are sweet and fragrant, attracting bees and other nectar-seeking insects, but sometimes flowers have a fetid odor that is irresistible to flies in search of carrion. When an insect visits a flower, it is first directed over the stigma, where it deposits pollen from the previous flower, and then past the anthers, where it picks up pollen to carry to the next blossom.

When pollen fertilizes an **ovule** in a female cone or flower, the ovule develops into a **seed**. In conifers, the seeds are naked but remain protected behind the scales of the cones. Other trees produce flowers with ovules in **ovaries**, which develop into **fruits**. Fruits generally have a protective outer skin, but the inner layer surrounding the seeds can vary from thick and fleshy to dry and fibrous or even hard and bony. In most cases, **simple fruits** are produced from the fertilization of a single ovary. However, in some trees (e.g., tulip-tree), dense clusters of many fertilized oaks, may have enough stored energy to allow the seedling to survive for many days. Small seeds have limited reserves, so the seedlings must develop quickly.

Although trees may produce many thousands of seeds each year, very few survive predation and disease, and even fewer find their way to suitable sites where they can grow into new trees.

Michigan's Ecoregions & Forest-type Distribution

Michigan without forests is almost unimaginable. Native Americans lived with the forests they found and used them to survive. The legacy of that use can still sometimes be found. As Euro-American settlers poured into the new State of Michigan, the forests were so vast that people thought the supply of timber was inexhaustible. Large tracts of forest fell to farmers and logging barons, and the millions of acres of wildfire that followed. These settlement practices forever changed the forests.

A growing number of far-sighted people began to fear a forest-less Michigan and brought conservation to the state. Today, we might look back

to the early 1900s as the darkest days of Michigan's forests, and most of the ancient or old-growth forests are gone. Yet, the incredibly diverse and productive forests we currently enjoy are legacies of those days. The second-growth forest offers an amazing array of opportunities and uses. Change, including catastrophic disturbance, has always been a part of forest ecology. That change continues, from both natural and human influences. Our forests also serve as testimony to the management careers of hundreds of foresters and conservationists.

Forests cover slightly more than half of Michigan, although the distribution is uneven. Nearly half the forest acreage and volume lies in the Upper Peninsula, one of the most heavily forested regions in the United States. In the Lower Peninsula, 70% of the forest lies north of a line extending west from Saginaw. The forests of the south have largely been converted to agricultural and urban land uses.

Michigan can be divided into four major ecoregions (Albert, 1995). These regions can be roughly described as the Western Upper Peninsula, the Eastern Upper Peninsula, the Northern Lower Peninsula and the Southern Lower Peninsula. Variables used to define these regions include veg-

Paper birch, white pine and balsam fir forest

Baraga County

Escanaba

MICHIGAN

Saginaw

Grand Rapids

★Lansing

Ann Arbor • Detroit

MICHIGAN ECOREGIONS

- Western Upper Peninsula
- Eastern Upper Peninsula
- Northern Lower Peninsula
- Southern Lower Peninsula

etation, soils, landforms, geology, glacial history and climate. The forests that grow across these regions, along with other land cover, provide a complex mosaic of vegetation and habitats.

The **Western Upper Peninsula** is underlain by ancient Precambrian bedrock, often exposed as outcrops and cliffs. Soils are generally thin, with glacial landforms interspersed throughout the region. A heavily forested region, over half the forest in the Western Upper Peninsula consists of northern hardwoods, some of which are among the best in the world. These hardwoods are dominated by sugar maple. There are also significant amounts of swamp conifer and aspen forest in the region.

Bedrock in the **Eastern Upper Peninsula** consists mostly of sandstone and limestone, evidenced by cliffs along both Lake Superior and Lake Michigan. Much of the Eastern Upper Peninsula was once inundated by glacial lakes, and many wetlands remain, such as Seney National Wildlife Refuge. Extensive outwash plains and moraines can also be found here. The forests of the this region are dominated by northern hardwood stands and extensive conifer swamps. The northern hardwoods have a strong beech component not found in the Western Upper

Sturgeon River Gorge

Paint River

Peninsula. Nearly half of Michigan's cedar swamps are found in the Eastern Upper Peninsula.

The **Northern Lower Peninsula** has large lakeplains, ancient sand dunes and numerous

glacial deposits with much deeper soils. While the proportion of forested acres is much smaller than in the Upper Peninsula, northern hardwoods continue to dominate. Mixes of oak, cherry and other more southern species become increasingly common to the south. There are also large areas of jack pine, red pine and aspen in the Northern Lower Peninsula. The jack pine plains in this region harbor one of Michigan's most well-known endangered species, the Kirtland's warbler.

The **Southern Lower Peninsula** is dominated by farms and cities. Only about 20% of the land is forested. Ground moraines and lakeplains provide rich soils that have been converted to agricultural land. Many of the wetlands have been drained to acquire additional arable acres. In the remaining forested areas, northern hardwoods are most common, typically dominated by red maple. Stand composition includes many tree species that are uncommon farther north, such as sweetgum, sassafras, hickories and some oaks. Oak-hickory and swamp hardwood forests are also well represented in the forest remnants of the Southern Lower Peninsula.

cedar habitat (above), Tahquamenon Falls (below)

Rare Species

Some of Michigan's native tree and tall shrub species are rare, threatened or endangered in the state and/or in the country. The Endangered Species Program of the Michigan Department of Natural Resources and the Michigan Natural Features Inventory has produced a list of Michigan's rare plants, but the status of these species is continually changing. The center's natural features inventory maintains computerized databases and supporting files with information on rare species, plant community occurrences and natural areas in the state. Up-to-date information about rare, threatened and endangered species and spaces is accessible through the Michigan State University web site at http://web4.msue. msu.edu/mnfi/. Lists and information about the Endangered Species Program are available from the Endangered Species Coordinator online, via regular mail (Wildlife Division, Michigan Department of Natural Resources, P.O. Box 30028, Lansing, MI 48909) or by phone (517-373-1263).

Employing methods developed by The Nature Conservancy, global ranks (GRANKs) and state ranks (SRANKs) are assigned for each species in the state. These ranks are not legal designations, but they are used to assess species' rarity and conservation status and thereby assist in setting protection priorities for species and natural communities. Occurrence information is gathered only for those species and communities deemed rare or extirpated in the state, i.e., ranked S1, S2, S3, SH or SX.

Although a number of factors are considered in assigning a rank, the most important single factor is the estimated number of occurrences. Definitions for the rank levels are provided below. For more information on global and sub-national ranks, consult either the Michigan State University Extension web site (given above) or the NatureServe web site (http://www.natureserve.org/).

The number in each rank denotes the following:
1 Extremely rare; usually 5 or fewer occurrences or very few remaining individuals; often especially vulnerable to extirpation

2 Very rare; usually between 5 and 20 occurrences or with many individuals in fewer occurrences; may be at risk of extirpation
3 Rare to uncommon; usually between 20 and 100 occurrences; may have fewer occurrences, but with a large number of individuals in some populations; may be susceptible to large-scale disturbances
4 Common and apparently secure; usually with more than 100 occurrences
5 Very common and demonstrably secure
? If a question mark follows a ranking (e.g., S3?), the rank is questionable owing to insufficient information.

If two ranks are given (e.g., G3G5), it means the rank falls between these two categories. Occasionally, a letter (rather than a number) is used to assign an S or G rank:
H Historically known from Michigan, but not verified recently (typically not recorded in the state in the last 20 years); however, suitable habitat is thought to remain in the state and there is reasonable expectation that the species may be rediscovered
Q Questionable taxonomic status
X Apparently extirpated from Michigan, with little likelihood of rediscovery; typically not seen in the state for many decades, despite searches at previously noted sites.

Invasive Exotic Species

Some of the worst invaders of natural habitats in Michigan are trees and large shrubs that have escaped from cultivation. Most of these produce fruits that are dispersed by birds, and most are usually found in or near cities and towns. However, as more wild populations become established, these species could easily spread farther afield. Most tend to invade disturbed habitats, but some also become established in natural ecosystems. Some species can grow so thickly in woodlots as to render the understory virtually impenetrable. This dense growth makes it difficult for native species to grow and reproduce, affecting both

Introduction

Rare or Threatened Trees and Tall Shrubs in Michigan

Scientific Name	Common Name	State	Global	Page
Betula murrayana	Murray birch	S1		122
Castanea dentata	America chestnut	S1S2	G4	105
Celtis tenuifolia	dwarf hackberry	S3	G5	91
Crataegus douglasii	black hawthorn	S3S4	G5	179
Euonymus atropurpurea	eastern wahoo	S3	G5	218
Fraxinus profunda	pumpkin ash	S2	G4	238
Gymnocladus dioicus	Kentucky coffee-tree	S3S4	G5	194
Morus rubra	red mulberry	S2	G5	94
Populus heterophylla	swamp cottonwood	S1	G5	138
Prunus alleghaniensis var. davisii	Alleghany plum	S3	G4T3Q	168
Quercus shumardii	Shumard oak	S2	G5	114
Salix pellita	satiny willow	S2	G5	140
Viburnum prunifolium	smooth blackhaw	S3	G5	244

Source: Michigan Natural Features Inventory (Michigan Department of Natural Resources Endangered Species Program 2000), http://web4.msue.msu.edu/mnfi/data/specialplants.cfm.

Invasive Trees and Tall Shrubs in Michigan

Scientific Name	Common Name	No. of Counties	Page
Acer ginnala	Amur maple	5	231
Acer platanoides	Norway maple	18	226
Acer pseudoplatanus	sycamore maple	1	226
Aesculus hippocastanum	horsechestnut	8	221
Ailanthus altissima	tree-of-heaven	21	205
Alnus glutinosa	European alder	2	128
Betula pendula	European white birch	11	125
Elaeagnus angustifolia	Russian-olive	9	209
Elaeagnus umbellata	autumn-olive	16	209
Euonymus alata	winged burning-bush	7	219
Euonymus europaea	European spindle-tree	7	219
Euonymus hamiltoniana	Japanese spindle-tree	2	219
Frangula alnus	glossy buckthorn	25	211
Ligustrum vulgare	European privet	15	235
Lonicera maackii	Amur honeysuckle	12	243
Maclura pomifera	Osage-orange	9	92
Morus alba	white mulberry	36	93
Picea abies	Norway spruce	3	65
Pinus sylvestris	Scots pine	6	72
Populus alba	white poplar	33	133
Prunus domestica	garden plum	11	170
Prunus persica	peach	8	164
Pyrus calleryana	ornamental pear	1	171
Pyrus communis	common pear	14	171
Rhamnus cathartica	European buckthorn	20	212
Rhamnus utilis	Chinese buckthorn	1	212
Robinia pseudoacacia	black locust	40	191
Tamarix parviflora	small-flower tamarisk	2	76
Ulmus pumila	Siberian elm	20	77
Viburnum lantana	wayfaring-tree	6	245
Viburnum opulus opulus	European highbush-cranberry	7	246

Source: Anton Reznicek (personal communication); Invasive and Exotic Species website, http://www.invasive.org/weeds.cfm (Douce et. al 2005).

wildflower displays and the natural development of forest communities.

This guide includes only native and naturalized trees and tall shrubs—species that are known to grow wild in Michigan. However, there are many other cultivated trees and shrubs that self sow readily in arboreta, parks and gardens, and these may also eventually spread. Some likely candidates to watch include goldenrain-tree (*Koelreuteria paniculata*), corktrees (*Phellodendron* spp.), evodias (*Tetradium* spp.) and various pears (*Pyrus* spp.), apples (*Malus* spp.) and cherries/plums (*Prunus* spp.).

About This Guide

This guide includes all of Michigan's native trees as well as many introduced species that have escaped cultivation and therefore could be mistaken for wild native trees. Assume each species is native to Michigan unless otherwise specified.

tree shape

leaf and flower detail

bark colour and texture

When identifying a tree, be sure to look carefully for all available clues, both on the tree and on the ground nearby. Large features such as tree size and shape, bark patterns and leaf dimensions may be clearly visible at a glance, but a 10x hand lens can come in handy for examining smaller features such as leaf hairs, flower structures and bud scales.

The main information sources used for compiling the species descriptions in this guide are Elias (1989), Gleason and Cronquist (1991) and Voss (1972, 1985, 1996). Additional sources of information are included in the reference list (pp. 260–261).

Keys

The guide presents several illustrated keys to each genus based on different tree features: leaves (pp. 38–42), flowers and young cones (pp. 43–46), fruits and mature cones (pp. 47–50), and winter characteristics (twigs and buds, pp. 51–54). These keys are followed by a broader, conventional key (pp. 55–60) that uses combinations of characteristics (e.g., leaves and fruits) to identify all families and some genera. Throughout the rest of the book, large families are prefaced with a key for identifying each genus, as well as keys to the species for large genera. (The terms family, genus and species are discussed in the next section, "Organization.")

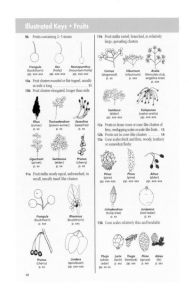

Gymnosperms (conifers or softwoods)

Angiosperms (flowering trees or hardwoods)

If you are a novice botanist, don't feel intimidated by the keys. Once you have used keys a few times, they become invaluable aids to identification. You may want to start with the illustrated keys, which are more user-friendly for beginners. All of the keys in this book are **dichotomous**— that is, they provide mutually exclusive, paired descriptions (e.g., 1a and 1b). Each choice leads either to another dichotomy or to the name of the group (family, genus or species) to which the tree belongs. Whenever possible, keys use everyday language and focus on readily recognizable features. Consult the glossary (pp. 252–259) for explanations of any unfamiliar terms.

Organization

Trees can be divided into two main groups— the gymnosperms in Division Pinophyta and the angiosperms in Division Magnoliophyta.

Gymnosperm trees are also called **conifers** or **softwoods**, because they produce cones rather than flowers and fruits, and because their wood is typically softer than that of the flowering trees. The name gymnosperm ("naked seed") refers to the bare seeds produced at the base of protective scales in cones. All gymnosperms in Michigan have needle-like leaves and most are evergreen. Some people mistakenly use "conifer" and "evergreen" interchangeably, but tamarack (p. 68) is a conifer with deciduous leaves.

alternate branching   opposite branching

All the **angiosperm** trees in Michigan except *Tamarix* bear **deciduous** leaves with broad, flat blades—hence the name **broad-leaved trees**. Broad-leaved evergreens grow elsewhere in the world (e.g., arbutus trees along the Pacific Coast) but are not part of the Michigan flora. Angiosperm ("enclosed seed") trees are also called **flowering trees** or **hardwoods**. All species in this large, highly variable group produce flowers with ovules (immature seeds) protected by ovaries, which eventually develop into fruits. In a few cases, the flowers are reduced to tiny structures behind protective scales in cone-like clusters, but most flowers have visible petals and/or sepals as well as stamens and/or pistils. Although broad-leaved trees produce the hardest, heaviest wood, the general label "hardwood" can be misleading, because the wood of many angiosperms (e.g., willows, poplars, basswoods) is softer than that of some softwoods (e.g., some pines).

The families, genera and species in this guide have been organized in a roughly systematic order, in an attempt to place the most similar, closely related species together. Minor deviations from the taxonomic sequence allow the angiosperms to be divided into two convenient groups: species with **alternate branching** (only one leaf or branch at each node) and those with **opposite branching** (two leaves or branches at each node).

Within the three broad groups—needle-leaved, alternate broad-leaved and opposite broad-leaved—trees are further divided into a hierarchy of taxonomic groups, beginning with **families**, such as the rose family (Rosaceae). Families are then divided into **genera** (plural of **genus**); for example, the rose family is made up of several genera including *Amelanchier* (serviceberries), *Prunus* (cherries, plums) and *Sorbus* (mountain-ashes). Genera, in turn, are divided into **species**; for example, the mountain-ash genus, *Sorbus*, includes species such as *Sorbus aucuparia* (European mountain-ash) and *Sorbus decora* (showy mountain-ash).

Some species can be divided further into forms, varieties and subspecies, but these taxa are not usually described in this guide. Species in some groups of plants (e.g., spruces, poplars, willows, ashes) frequently cross-pollinate to produce **hybrids** with characteristics of both parents. In some cases (e.g., hawthorns), hybridization is so common and the characteristics of offspring are so variable that the entire genus might be best described as a highly variable complex. This

NEEDLE LEAVES

ALTERNATE BROAD LEAVES

OPPOSITE BROAD LEAVES

FAMILY
e.g., Rose Family (Rosaceae)

GENERA

Sorbus
mountain-ash

Malus
apple

SPECIES

Sorbus decora
showy mountain-ash

Sorbus aucuparia
European mountain-ash

guide mentions a few hybrids, but they are not described in separate entries. Similarly, horticultural variants or **cultivars**, developed by plant breeders, are also mentioned in some species accounts but are not described separately.

Species Entries
NAMES

Each species entry provides the scientific name (usually derived from Latin or Greek and always italicized), as well as one or more common names. The preferred or most frequently used common name is presented first, but additional common names and scientific **synonyms** (other scientific names under which the species is known or has been known in other works) can be found under the heading "Also Called."

Although common names may seem easiest to use at first, they can present problems. Most species have many common names, some unique to different regions. Because common names originate through local usage, it is also possible for the same name to apply to different trees in different regions.

Scientific names, on the other hand, aspire to be worldwide standards and are the same in all languages and throughout the range of the species. All must be published in taxonomic works, which clearly describe the plant being named. If study of a group results in a taxonomic revision, and the name of a species is changed, this change is typically justified carefully in print so that it can be evaluated and accepted by the scholarly community. However, taxonomists, have been known to disagree, and in some cases, the same plant is classified in different ways and thus has different names in different works. Occasionally, older names are also found, requiring a name change. Fortunately, because all name changes must be published, it is possible to trace synonyms and reduce confusion.

Though unfamiliar to the ear at first, scientific names are much more consistent than common ones and provide a reference point for finding and exchanging information in Michigan and around the world. The scientific names used in this guide follow treatments of the Integrated Taxonomic Information System (ITIS 2003), Voss (1972,

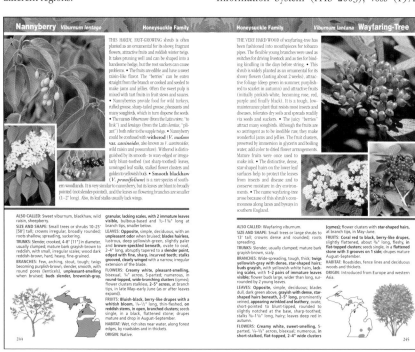

Nannyberry *Viburnum lentago* — Honeysuckle Family

THIS HARDY, FAST-GROWING shrub is often planted as an ornamental for its showy, fragrant flowers, attractive fruits and reddish winter twigs. It takes pruning well and can be shaped into a handsome hedge, but the root suckers can cause problems. • The fruits are edible and have a sweet raisin-like flavor. The "berries" can be eaten straight from the branch or cooked and seeded to make jams and jellies. Often the sweet pulp is mixed with tart fruits in fruit stews and sauces. • Nannyberries provide food for wild turkeys, ruffed grouse, sharp-tailed grouse, pheasants and many songbirds, which in turn disperse the seeds. • The names *Viburnum* (from the Latin *viere*, "to link") and *lentago* (from the Latin *lentus*, "pliant") both refer to the supple twigs. • Nannyberry could be confused with witherod (*V. nudum* var. *cassinoides*, also known as *V. cassinoides*, wild raisin and possumhaw). Witherod is distinguished by its smooth- to wavy-edged or irregularly blunt-toothed (not sharp-toothed) leaves, unwinged leaf stalks, stalked flower clusters and golden to yellowish buds. • **Smooth blackhaw** (*V. prunifolium*) is a rare species of southern woodlands. It is very similar to nannyberry, but its leaves are blunt to broadly pointed (not slender-pointed), and the leaves on flowering branches are smaller (1–2" long). Also, its leaf stalks usually lack wings.

ALSO CALLED: Sweet viburnum, blackhaw, wild raisin, sheepberry.
SIZE AND SHAPE: Small trees or shrubs 10–25' [50'] tall; crowns irregular, broadly rounded; roots shallow, spreading, suckering.
TRUNKS: Slender, crooked, 4–8" [11"] in diameter; usually clumped; mature bark grayish-brown to reddish, with small, irregular scales; wood dark reddish-brown, hard, heavy, fine-grained.
BRANCHES: Few, arching, stout, tough; twigs becoming purplish-brown, slender, smooth, with round pores (lenticels), unpleasant-smelling when bruised; buds slender, brownish-gray, granular, lacking scales, with 2 immature leaves visible, bulbous-based and ¹/₂–1¹/₈" long at branch tips, smaller below.
LEAVES: Opposite, simple, deciduous, with an unpleasant odor when bruised; blades hairless, lustrous, deep yellowish-green, slightly paler and brown-speckled beneath, ovate to oval, 2–4" long, abruptly tapered to a slender point, edged with fine, sharp, incurved teeth; stalks grooved, clearly winged with a narrow, irregular extension of the blade.
FLOWERS: Creamy white, pleasant-smelling, bisexual, ¹/₄" across, 5-parted; numerous, in round-topped, wide-branching clusters (cymes); flower clusters stalkless, 2–5" across, at branch tips, in late May–early June (as or after leaves expand).
FRUITS: Bluish-black, berry-like drupes with a whitish bloom, ¹/₄–¹/₂" long, thin-fleshed, on reddish stems, in open, branched clusters; seeds single, in a black, flattened stone; drupes mature and drop in August–September.
HABITAT: Wet, rich sites near water, along forest edges, by roadsides and in thickets.
ORIGIN: Native.

244

Wayfaring-Tree *Viburnum lantana* — Honeysuckle Family

THE VERY HARD WOOD of wayfaring-tree has been fashioned into mouthpieces for tobacco pipes. The flexible young branches were used as switches for driving livestock and as fire for binding kindling in the days before string. • This shrub is widely planted as an ornamental for its showy flowers (lasting about 2 weeks), attractive foliage (deep green in summer, purplish-red to scarlet in autumn) and attractive fruits (initially pinkish-white, becoming rose, red, purple and finally black). It is a tough, low-maintenance plant that resists most insects and diseases, tolerates dry soils and spreads readily via seeds and suckers. • The juicy "berries" attract many songbirds. Although the fruits are so astringent as to be inedible raw, they make wonderful jams and jellies. The fruit clusters, preserved by immersion in glycerin and boiling water, add color to dried flower arrangements. Mature fruits were once used to make ink. • The distinctive, dense, star-shaped hairs on the lower leaf surfaces help to protect the leaves from insects and disease and to conserve moisture in dry environments. • The name wayfaring-tree arose because of this shrub's commonness along lanes and byways in southern England.

ALSO CALLED: Wayfaring viburnum.
SIZE AND SHAPE: Small trees or large shrubs to 13' tall; crowns dense and rounded; roots spreading.
TRUNKS: Slender; usually clumped; mature bark grayish-brown, scaly.
BRANCHES: Wide-spreading, tough, thick; twigs yellowish-gray with dense, star-shaped hairs; buds grayish, with yellowish-white hairs, lacking scales, with 1–2 pairs of immature leaves visible; flower buds large, wider than long, surrounded by 2 young leaves.
LEAVES: Opposite, simple, deciduous; blades dull, dark green above, grayish with dense, star-shaped hairs beneath, 2–5" long, prominently veined, appearing wrinkled and leathery, ovate, short-pointed to blunt-tipped, rounded to slightly notched at the base, sharp-toothed; stalks ³/₈–1¹/₈" long, hairy; leaves deep red in autumn.
FLOWERS: Creamy white, sweet-smelling, 5-parted, ¹/₄–³/₈" across, bisexual; numerous, in short-stalked, flat-topped, 2–4" wide clusters (cymes); flower clusters with star-shaped hairs, at branch tips, in May–June.
FRUITS: Coral red to black, berry-like drupes, slightly flattened, about ³/₈" long, fleshy, in flat-topped clusters; seeds single, in a flattened stone with 3 grooves on 1 side; drupes mature August–September.
HABITAT: Roadsides, fence lines and deciduous woods and thickets.
ORIGIN: Introduced from Europe and western Asia.

245

1985, 1996), Gleason and Cronquist (1991) and Kartesz and Meacham (1999).

A scientific name is often followed by the name, often abbreviated, of the **author** (person or persons) who coined the species epithet or who transferred it to the current genus. In this book, authors can be found in the index.

NOTES

The paragraph at the top of each entry provides special points of interest for each species. The content of the notes varies from one species to the next. Ethnobotanical information is usually provided, indicating how a tree has been and is important to people. You may also find points of historical interest and notes about propagating and cultivating certain species. Trees are very important components of natural systems, and ecological factors such as common diseases and pests and the importance of trees to wildlife may be noted here. Also look for the derivation (etymology) of common and scientific tree names. Names often have an interesting history that can help you to understand and remember them. Finally, one or more secondary species closely related to the primary species may be described in this section. Taxonomic problems may also be addressed, particularly if the trees are sterile or frequently hybridize, and tips are provided to help distinguish commonly confused species.

Gymnocladus dioicus, Kentucky coffee-tree

ILLUSTRATIONS

Each primary species is illustrated with one or more color photos or drawings showing diagnostic characteristics. Secondary species mentioned in the notes section may also be illustrated with photos. A color illustration at the bottom of the page shows the overall shape of the primary species.

DESCRIPTIONS

The lower section of each account presents a detailed description of the tree and its parts. Diagnostic or key features are highlighted in bold text. Descriptions include size ranges based on information from Michigan or occasionally from elsewhere in North America. Most trees that you come across in the field should fall within these ranges.

Acer saccharum, sugar maple

Prunus pensylvanica, pin cherry

In most descriptions, the typical range of tree height or trunk diameter is followed by the height/diameter of the largest tree in Michigan (shown in square brackets). For more information about Michigan's "Champion Trees," check http://www.michbotclub.org/big_trees/champion_list.htm.

Tree characteristics are described under the following headings:

Size and Shape. In addition to describing the size and shape of the tree as a whole, this section may also include the depth and expanse of the roots. Tree heights in this section reflect the usual size for the species. However, many trees can reach even greater heights, given ideal growing conditions and/or nurturing care. When available, the height of Michigan's largest, champion tree is included in square brackets after the typical size range.

Trunks. Here you will find information on trunk shape, diameter and orientation, as well as bark characteristics. When available, the diameter of Michigan's champion tree is included in square brackets after the typical size range. Because bark can change dramatically with age, young bark and

Juglans nigra, black walnut

old bark are often presented separately. Bark descriptions usually focus on color, texture and thickness. Although bark is not always a reliable feature for identifying trees, some groups of trees (e.g., birches, sycamores, beech) have very distinctive bark, and in some genera (e.g., ashes), bark characteristics can be useful in distinguishing species.

The wood of different species may be recognizably distinct under a compound microscope, but wood is seldom used for identifying trees in the field. Many people, however, consider wood the most important part of the tree. Wood descriptions usually include color, hardness, weight and strength. In this book, some of these features may be mentioned in the notes section of an entry, along with a discussion of how the wood has been used.

Amelanchier laevis, smooth serviceberry

Branches. This section begins with a description of the size, orientation and arrangement of the main branches. Spines or thorns are important diagnostic features for some species. Twigs are often very different from the larger branches and can provide helpful clues for identifying a tree. Twig descriptions usually include color, texture, hairiness and occasionally pith characteristics (when viewed in cross- or long-section) or general twig shape (e.g., round or square). Buds can help you identify a tree during the winter, when leaves, fruits and flowers are absent (see the illustrated twig key, pp. 51–54). Important bud characteristics vary with the species, but they may include color, texture, hairiness, size, number of scales, arrangement of buds and their scales and the presence of sticky or fragrant resins.

Viburnum lantana, wayfaring-tree

Leaves. Of all the parts of a tree, the leaves are the most widely used for identifying species (see the illustrated leaf key, pp. 38–42). The leaf descriptions in this guide usually begin with the arrangement of leaves on the branch (opposite, whorled, alternate, spiral) and the type of leaf (simple or compound; deciduous or evergreen). In some cases, care must be taken not to confuse compound and simple leaves. The long, firm central axes of some large compound leaves (e.g., Kentucky coffee-tree) could be mistaken for a small branch and the leaflets for simple leaves.

Gymnocladus dioicus, Kentucky coffee-tree

Liriodendron tulipifera, tulip-tree

Leaflets of a compound leaf are always attached to a herbaceous (not woody) main stalk that lacks buds. Most branchlets, on the other hand, have developed buds in the leaf axils by midsummer. Definitions and illustrations of leaf shapes and arrangements are presented in the glossary (pp. 252–259).

Leaf characteristics can vary greatly with age and environment, so when choosing a representative sample for identification, look for healthy, mature leaves on normal branches in full sun. Disease, insect infestations, adverse weather conditions, low light levels and rapid growth spurts can all produce abnormal leaves. Some trees are more changeable than others. The hawthorns are extremely variable, but aberrations are greatest on vegetative shoots, so choose leaves from flowering or fruiting shoots.

The most obvious part of a leaf is the blade. Important blade characteristics include size, color (above and beneath), texture (thin, leathery, fleshy), shape (linear, oblong, round, widest above or below the middle) and edges (smooth, toothed, lobed). Leaf stalks are described separately, because they are often quite different from the blades in color and hairiness. Some leaf stalks have distinctive characteristics such as unusual shapes (e.g., distinctly flattened), length (e.g., as long as the blade) or glands (usually near the junction with the blade), whereas others have stipules at the stalk base. Leaf scars can also be useful diagnostic features, especially when identifying trees in winter (see twig key, pp. 51–54). Important leaf scar characteristics include shape, size and arrangement on the branch, as well as the number and arrangement of vein scars within the leaf scars.

The leaf section may also contain a few notes about seasonality (e.g., leaf color in fall, winter persistence).

Reproductive structures. Cones, flowers and fruits are often much less variable than vegetative parts such as leaves and branches, and consequently, reproductive parts may offer more reliable features for identifying trees. Unfortunately, not all trees have reproductive structures at any given time. Many species don't begin to produce seed until they are 30 years old, and even then, they may not flower every year. Diseases, insect infestations, drought and other environmental stresses can all prevent trees from flowering. In most cases, only healthy, mature trees have the reserves necessary to produce abundant seed crops.

Cones are the reproductive structures of the first trees in the guide, the gymnosperms (see the illustrated keys on pp. 43–50). Although male and female cones usually appear on the same tree, they are very different in appearance and position, so they are described separately. Male (pollen) cones are small and soft, whereas female (seed) cones are relatively large and woody when mature. Important characteristics include color, texture, shape, size and arrangement on the branches. The scales of female cones are sometimes also described. The cone section ends with a short description of seasonality (the timing of cone growth and changes at maturity).

Most Michigan trees are flowering plants (angiosperms) whose reproductive structures are true flowers, not cones. Flowers can be very distinctive and can provide essential clues to a tree's identity (see the illustrated flower key, pp. 43–46). Unfortunately, flowers are often high in the canopy and inaccessible or very short-lived, soon dropping off and developing into fruit. Occasionally, the structure of a faded flower can be reconstructed through careful observation of parts that persist on the fruits. The flower section of the tree description indicates color, texture, shape, size, fragrance and sexuality (e.g., bisexual or unisexual). Most flowering trees in Michigan have unisexual flowers, so male flowers and female flowers and their clusters are often described separately. Diagnostic flower parts such as petals, sepals, stamens and stigmas are sometimes described in detail, but in many cases these components are too small or are not sufficiently distinctive to warrant description. The flower section also describes the arrangement of flowers and types of inflorescences or flower clusters (e.g., racemes, panicles, corymbs, umbels; see glossary, p. 255), and the timing of their development (seasonality).

Ligustrum vulgare, European privet

Fruits are usually more useful than flowers in tree identification, because they tend to last longer. Many fruits can be found throughout the year, either on branches or on the ground nearby, providing valuable clues to the identity of the tree (see the illustrated fruit key, pp. 47–50). The fruit section describes the color, texture, shape, size and type of fruit (e.g., drupes, capsules, nuts, samaras; see glossary, pp. 256–257). The number, size and shape of the seeds are usually described separately. The fruit section also describes the arrangement of the fruits (hanging vs. erect; cluster shape and size) along with the characteristics of mature fruit (e.g., color changes, dehiscence).

Habitat. This section describes the types of sites where a tree species is usually found. Habitat information, combined with the distribution (shown on the accompanying map), gives a general idea where to look for the tree. Almost all trees grow best on rich, deep, well-drained soils with adequate moisture, but some also do well on open, disturbed sites, and others require the shade and humidity of an established forest.

Carya ovata, shagbark hickory

Trees that move in to colonize recently disturbed areas are sometimes called **pioneer species**, and those that require the protection of a forest canopy are called **climax species**. In the absence of repeated disturbances, sun-loving pioneer species are gradually replaced by shade-tolerant climax species, which eventually create relatively stable, self-perpetuating ecosystems. However, the equilibrium can be upset by disturbances such as fire, windfall or insect attacks, and then the canopy opens and the cycle begins again.

DISTRIBUTION

The distributions of tree species are presented graphically in maps. These range maps are based on information from the University of Michigan Online Atlas of Michigan Plants (Reznicek et. al. 2004) and the Flora of Michigan (Voss 1972, 1985, 1996). The range of the primary species discussed on each page is shown in bright green, and if an additional species is mentioned in the notes section, its range may be shown on the same map in pink (where sufficient information is available). Areas where the two species overlap are indicated in dark green. Occasionally a third species is shown on the map in dark pink (darker green where its range overlaps that of the primary species).

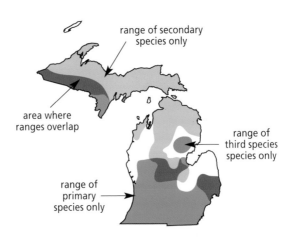

range of secondary species only

area where ranges overlap

range of third species species only

range of primary species only

Illustrated Keys

IT'S EASY TO IDENTIFY TREES using the 4 illustrated keys based on leaf, flower, fruit and twig features. Simply work your way through a key, choosing between paired alternatives. Try the leaf key with a red maple, for example. The leaves have broad blades, so at lead **1** choose **1b**. This takes you to **4**. Your leaf is simple, so choose **4b** and go to **9**. Palmately lobed, toothed edges take you to **9a, 10a, 11a** and finally **12b**. This brings you to the end of your search—a group of illustrations. Choose the best fit, and go to the page or pages indicated for more information.

Leaf Key to Genus

1a Leaves narrow, either needle-like or scale-like
.... **2**
1b Leaves broad, with definite blades **4**

2a Leaves needle-like **3**
2b Leaves scale-like

Juniperus
(red-cedar)
p. 74

Thuja
(white-cedar)
p. 75

Tamarix
(tamarisk)
p. 76

3a Needles in pairs, whorls, tufts or bundles

Juniperus
(red-cedar)
p. 74

Larix
(larch)
p. 68

Pinus
(pine)
pp. 70–73

3b Needles single, alternate

Abies (flat)
(fir)
p. 64

Tsuga (flat)
(hemlock)
p. 69

Picea (3–4-sided)
(spruce)
pp. 65–67

4a Leaves divided into leaflets (compound) **5**
4b Leaves simple **9**

5a Leaves pinnately compound **6**
5b Leaves palmately compound or trifoliate

Ptelea
(hop-tree)
p. 206

Staphylea
(bladdernut)
p. 220

Aesculus
(buckeye)
pp. 221–222

6a Leaves once divided **7**
6b Leaves 2–3 times divided into leaflets

Aralia
(angelica-
tree)
p. 195

Aralia
(Hercules-
club)
p. 195

Gleditsia
(honey-
locust)
p. 193

**Gymno-
cladus**
(coffee-tree)
p. 194

7a Leaves alternate **8**
7b Leaves paired (opposite)

Fraxinus
(ash)
pp. 236–240

Acer
(maple)
pp. 224–232

Sambucus
(elder)
p. 242

8a Leaf edges smooth, without teeth or with 1–2 basal lobes

Toxicodendron
(poison-sumac)
p. 199

Robinia
(locust)
p. 191

Ailanthus
(tree-of-
heaven)
p. 205

Rhus
(sumac)
p. 197–198

8b Leaf edges toothed or many-lobed

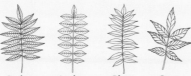

Sorbus
(mountain-ash)
pp. 175–177

Juglans
(walnut)
pp. 96–97

Rhus
(sumac)
pp. 197–198

Carya
(hickory)
pp. 98–101

9a Leaf edges toothed or lobed **10**
9b Leaf edges smooth, without teeth or lobes **27**

10a Leaves lobed, with or without teeth **11**
10b Leaf edges toothed but not lobed **15**

11a Leaves pinnately lobed **12**
11b Leaves palmately lobed **14**

12a Lobes pointed, edged with sharp teeth **13**
12b Lobes blunt, smooth or edged with rounded teeth

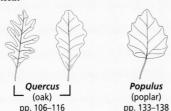

Quercus
(oak)
pp. 106–116

Populus
(poplar)
pp. 133–138

13a Lobes cut less than halfway to the midvein

Crataegus
(hawthorn)
pp. 178–187

Corylus
(hazelnut)
p. 121

Alnus
(alder)
pp. 126–128

Acer
(maple)
pp. 224–232

Malus
(crabapple)
pp. 172–174

Betula
(birch)
pp. 122–125

13b Lobes cut more than halfway to the midvein

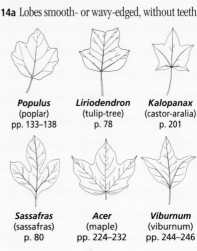

Crataegus
(hawthorn)
pp. 178–187

Quercus
(oak)
pp. 106–116

14a Lobes smooth- or wavy-edged, without teeth

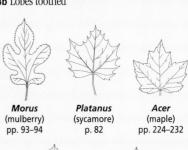

Populus
(poplar)
pp. 133–138

Liriodendron
(tulip-tree)
p. 78

Kalopanax
(castor-aralia)
p. 201

Sassafras
(sassafras)
p. 80

Acer
(maple)
pp. 224–232

Viburnum
(viburnum)
pp. 244–246

14b Lobes toothed

Morus
(mulberry)
pp. 93–94

Platanus
(sycamore)
p. 82

Acer
(maple)
pp. 224–232

Viburnum
(viburnum)
pp. 244–246

Crataegus
(hawthorn)
pp. 178–187

15a Leaves alternate **16**
15b Leaves opposite or whorled

Euonymus
(euonymus)
pp. 218–219

Viburnum
(viburnum)
pp. 244–246

Rhamnus
(buckthorn)
p. 212

16a Leaf bases symmetrical **17**
16b Leaf bases clearly asymmetrical

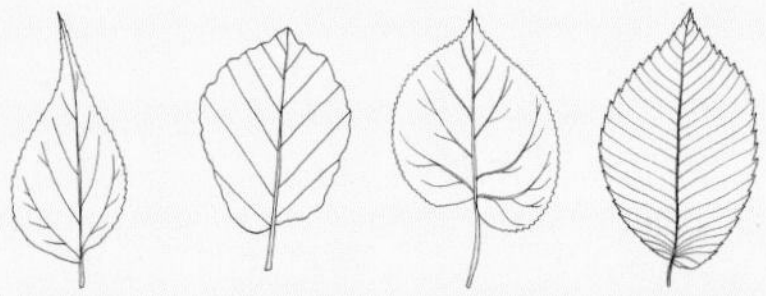

Celtis
(hackberry)
pp. 90–91

Hamamelis
(witch-hazel)
p. 83

Tilia
(basswood)
pp. 207–208

Ulmus
(elm)
pp. 85–89

17a Leaf blades broad, mostly less than twice as
long as wide **18**
17b Leaf blades narrower, mostly at least twice as
long as wide **24**

18a Leaf blades approximately as long as wide,
broadly rounded to squared or notched at
the base **19**
18b Leave blades ovate to broadly elliptic, longer
than wide, rounded to wedge-shaped at the
base **22**

19a Leaf blades rounded to heart-shaped **20**
19b Leaf blades roughly triangular, with squared
bases

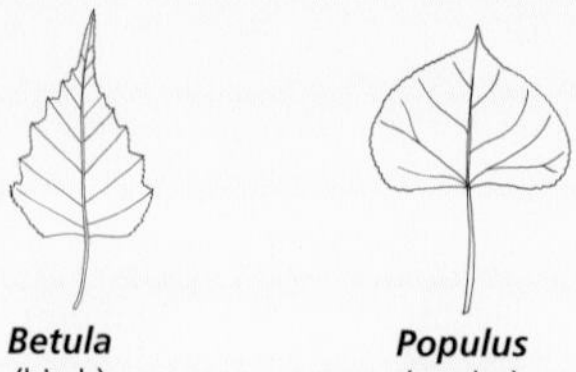

Betula
(birch)
pp. 122–125

Populus
(poplar)
pp. 133–138

20a Teeth double and/or coarse **21**
20b Teeth fine, single

Populus
(poplar)
pp. 133–138

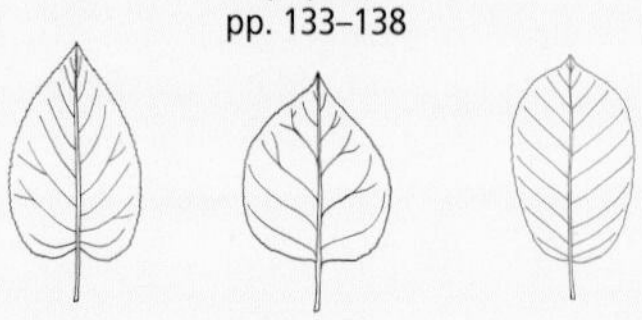

Pyrus
(pear)
p. 171

Prunus
(cherry, etc.)
pp. 161–170

Frangula
(buckthorn)
p. 211

21a Teeth single

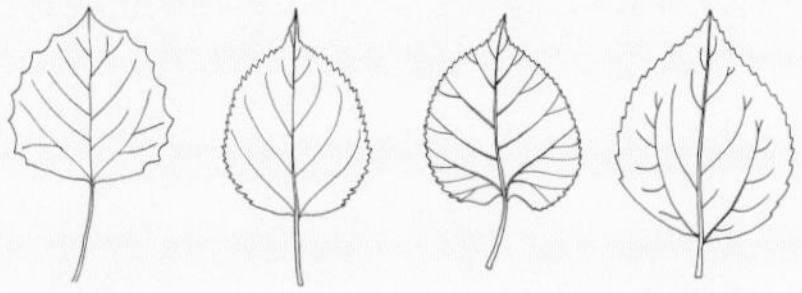

Populus
(poplar)
pp. 133–138

Morus
(mulberry)
pp. 93–94

Tilia
(basswood)
pp. 207–208

Celtis
(hackberry)
pp. 90–91

21b Teeth double

Crataegus
(hawthorn)
pp. 178–187

Corylus
(hazelnut)
p. 121

Betula
(birch)
pp. 122–125

22a Leaves finely and regularly toothed **23**
22b Leaves sharply and irregularly toothed

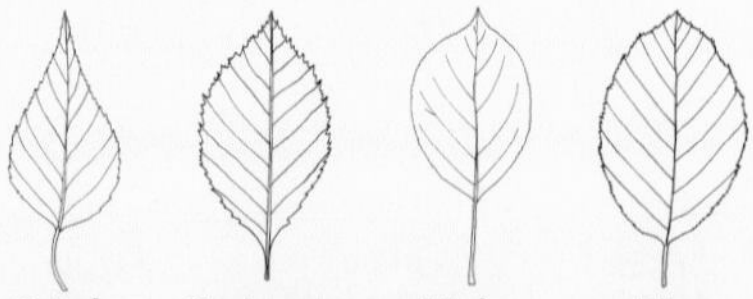

Betula
(birch)
pp. 122–125

Crataegus
(hawthorn)
pp. 178–187

Malus
(crapapple)
pp. 172–174

Alnus
(alder)
pp. 126–128

23a Blades widest above the middle

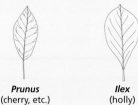

Prunus
(cherry, etc.)
pp. 161–170

Ilex
(holly)
p. 203

23b Blades widest at or below the middle

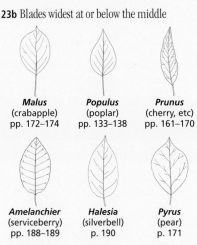

Malus
(crabapple)
pp. 172–174

Populus
(poplar)
pp. 133–138

Prunus
(cherry, etc)
pp. 161–170

Amelanchier
(serviceberry)
pp. 188–189

Halesia
(silverbell)
p. 190

Pyrus
(pear)
p. 171

24a Leaf edges more finely toothed **25**
24b Leaf edges coarsely toothed, usually 1 tooth
per vein

Fagus
(beech)
p. 104

Nemopanthus
(mountain-holly)
p. 204

Quercus
(oak)
pp. 106–116

Castanea
(chestnut)
p. 105

25a Leaf edges with finer or more rounded, teeth
relatively regular **26**
25b Leaf edges sharply, often irregularly
saw-toothed

Ulmus
(elm)
pp. 85–89

Carpinus
(blue-beech)
p. 120

Ostrya
(hop-hornbeam)
p. 119

Betula
(birch)
pp. 122–125

26a Blades widest above the middle

Prunus
(cherry, etc)
pp. 161–170

Ilex
(holly)
p. 203

Frangula
(buckthorn)
p. 211

26b Blades widest at or below the middle

Prunus
(cherry, etc)
pp. 161–170

⌊ **Salix** ⌋
(willow)
pp. 139–153

Populus
(poplar)
pp. 133–138

Halesia
(silverbell)
p. 190

27a Leaf blades broad, clearly less than twice as
long as wide **28**
27b Leaf blades narrower, usually at least twice
as long as wide **31**

28a Leaves alternate **29**
28b Leaves opposite

Catalpa
(catalpa)
p. 247

Cornus
(dogwood)
pp. 214–217

Syringa
(lilac)
p. 234

Cephalanthus
(buttonbush)
p. 249

29a Leaf tips pointed **30**
29b Leaf tips blunt

Cotinus
(smoketree)
p. 202

Frangula
(buckthorn)
p. 211

41

30a Main side veins strong and parallel

Cornus
(dogwood)
pp. 214–217

Frangula
(buckthorn)
p. 211

Nyssa
(tupelo)
p. 210

30b Main side veins less distinctive, more
delicate and repeatedly branched

Cercis
(redbud)
p. 192

Celtis
(hackberry)
pp. 90–91

Sassafras
(sassafras)
p. 80

31a Leaves relatively broad, elliptic to ovate **32**
31b Leaves narrowly oblong to linear

Salix
(willow)
pp. 139–153

Elaeagnus
(oleaster)
p. 209

Shepherdia
(buffaloberry)
p. 248

32a Leaf blades widest at or below the middle **33**
32b Leaf blades widest above the middle

Asimina
(pawpaw)
p. 79

Nyssa
(tupelo)
p. 210

Lindera
(spicebush)
p. 81

Frangula
(buckthorn)
p. 211

33a Leaves mostly 1–3" long

Lonicera
(honeysuckle)
p. 243

Nemopanthus
(mountain-holly)
p. 204

Ligustrum
(privet)
p. 235

Frangula
(buckthorn)
p. 211

33b Leaves mostly 3–7" long

Maclura
(Osage-orange)
p. 92

Quercus
(oak)
pp. 106–116

Flower and Young Cone Key to Genus

1a Reproductive parts tiny, concealed in cones; male cones soft and relatively small; female cones usually with larger, firmer scales **2**

1b Reproductive parts in true flowers **3**

2a Receptive female cones small, <³/₈" long

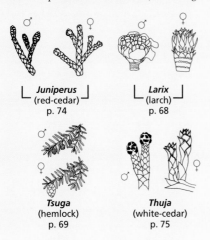

Juniperus	Larix
(red-cedar)	(larch)
p. 74	p. 68

Tsuga	Thuja
(hemlock)	(white-cedar)
p. 69	p. 75

2b Receptive female cones larger, > ³/₈" long

| Pinus |
| (pine) |
| pp. 70–73 |

Picea	Abies
(spruce)	(fir)
pp. 65–67	p. 64

3a Flowers short-stalked or stalkless in dense clusters, tiny, inconspicuous, usually greenish **4**

3b Flowers clearly stalked, usually larger (>¹/₄" across) and showier **9**

4a Flowers unisexual; male and female flowers in separate clusters **5**

4b Flowers bisexual, with both male and female parts

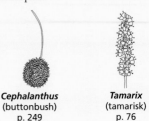

Cephalanthus	Tamarix
(buttonbush)	(tamarisk)
p. 249	p. 76

5a Flowers (at least male flowers) in spherical clusters **6**

5b Flowers (at least male flowers) in elongated clusters (catkins) **7**

6a Flower clusters short-stalked or stalkless

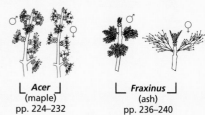

Acer	Fraxinus
(maple)	(ash)
pp. 224–232	pp. 236–240

6b Flower clusters clearly stalked, often hanging

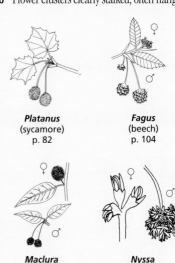

Platanus	Fagus
(sycamore)	(beech)
p. 82	p. 104

Maclura	Nyssa
(Osage-orange)	(tupelo)
p. 92	p. 210

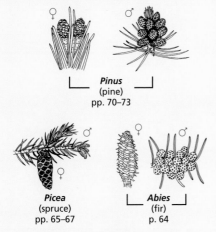

7a Male and female flowers on the same tree **8**

7b Male and female flowers on separate trees

Populus
(poplar)
pp. 133–138

Salix
(willow)
pp. 139–153

Morus
(mulberry)
pp. 93–94

8a Female flowers few, in small, inconspicuous clusters of 1–7

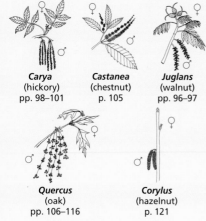

Carya
(hickory)
pp. 98–101

Castanea
(chestnut)
p. 105

Juglans
(walnut)
pp. 96–97

Quercus
(oak)
pp. 106–116

Corylus
(hazelnut)
p. 121

8b Female flowers numerous, usually 15 or more per cluster

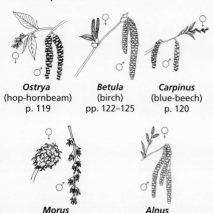

Ostrya
(hop-hornbeam)
p. 119

Betula
(birch)
pp. 122–125

Carpinus
(blue-beech)
p. 120

Morus
(mulberry)
pp. 93–94

Alnus
(alder)
pp. 126–128

9a Flowers small, <³/₄" across, inconspicuous or in showy clusters **10**

9b Flowers large and showy, usually >1" across **21**

10a Flowers small, inconspicuous, greenish or yellowish, single or in small, usually tassel-like clusters; petals tiny or absent **11**

10b Flowers relatively showy, with noticeable petals or petal-like sepals **13**

11a Flower clusters unbranched **12**

11b Flowers in branched, often elongated clusters

Acer
(maple)
pp. 224–232

Ulmus
(elm)
pp. 85–89

Kalopanax
(castor-aralia)
p. 201

12a Flowers single

Celtis
(hackberry)
pp. 90–91

Nemopanthus
(mountain-holly)
p. 204

12b Flowers in tassel-like clusters

Ulmus
(elm)
pp. 85–89

Frangula
(buckthorn)
p. 211

Rhamnus
(buckthorn)
p. 212

Shepherdia
(buffaloberry)
p. 248

Lindera
(spicebush)
p. 81

Ilex
(holly)
p. 203

13a Flower clusters branched **14**
13b Flower clusters unbranched

Elaeagnus
(oleaster)
p. 209

Cercis
(redbud)
p. 192

Prunus
(cherry, etc.)
pp. 161–170

Lonicera
(honeysuckle)
p. 243

14a Flower clusters flat-topped or rounded
(corymbs, cymes, umbels) **15**
14b Flower clusters more elongated, clearly
longer than wide (panicles, racemes) **17**

15a Flowers bisexual... **16**
15b Flowers unisexual, greenish, about $1/4$–$1/2$"
across, in rounded clusters

Ptelea
(hop-tree)
p. 206

Sassafras
(sassafras)
p. 80

Acer
(maple)
pp. 224–232

16a Flowers small (mostly <$3/8$"), white, in
showy, many-branched clusters 2–6" across

Viburnum
(viburnum)
pp. 244–246

Sorbus
(mountain-ash)
pp. 175–176

Cornus
(dogwood)
pp. 216–217

16a (continued)

Acer
(maple)
pp. 224–232

Sambucus
(elder)
p. 242

Aralia
(Hercules-club)
p. 195

16b Flowers at least $3/8$" across, usually in tassel-
like or few-branched clusters

Tilia
(basswood)
pp. 207–208

Euonymus
(euonymus)
pp. 218–219

Prunus
(cherry, etc.)
pp. 161–170

Crataegus
(hawthorn)
pp. 178–187

Viburnum
(viburnum)
pp. 244–246

17a Flower clusters roughly cylindrical, with an
unbranched main axis (central stalk) **18**
17b Flower clusters widest near the base, with
some side-branches again divided.............. **19**

18a Flowers pea-like or bell-shaped; petals
dissimilar or not clearly separate

Robinia
(locust)
p. 191

Staphylea
(bladdernut)
p. 220

18b Flowers star-like; petals similar and clearly separate

Gleditsia
(honey-locust)
p. 193

Amelanchier
(serviceberry)
pp. 188–189

Gymnocladus
(coffee-tree)
p. 194

Acer
(maple)
pp. 224–232

Prunus
(cherry, etc.)
pp. 161–170

19a Flowers white, pink or purple **20**
19b Flowers yellow to greenish-yellow

Ailanthus
(tree-of-heaven)
p. 205

Rhus
(sumac)
pp. 197–198

Toxicodendron
(poison-sumac)
p. 199

20a Flowers 4-petaled, funnel-shaped

Syringa
(lilac)
p. 234

Ligustrum
(privet)
p. 235

20b Flowers 5-petaled, star-shaped

Gymnocladus
(coffee-tree)
p. 194

Sambucus
(elder)
p. 242

Aralia
(Hercules-club)
p. 195

Cotinus
(smoke-tree)
p. 202

21a Flowers (or flower-like clusters) single or in clusters of 2–3 .... **22**
21b Flowers in clusters of 4 or more **23**

22a Petals and sepals in multiples of 3; stamens numerous

Asimina
(pawpaw)
p. 79

Liriodendron
(tulip-tree)
p. 78

22b Petals, petal-like bracts and sepals 4; stamens 4–16

Cornus
(dogwood)
pp. 214–217

Halesia
(silverbell)
p. 190

Hamamelis
(witch-hazel)
p. 83

23a Flowers cupped to star-shaped, with 5 showy, white or pinkish petals

Amelanchier
(serviceberry)
pp. 188–189

Malus
(crabapple)
pp. 172–174

Pyrus
(pear)
p. 171

Prunus
(cherry, etc.)
pp. 161–170

Crataegus
(hawthorn)
pp. 178–187

23b Flowers bell-shaped, trumpet-shaped or pea-shaped, variously colored

Aesculus
(buckeye)
pp. 221–222

Catalpa
(catalpa)
p. 247

Robinia
(locust)
p. 191

Halesia
(silverbell)
p. 190

Fruit and Mature Cone Key to Genus

1a Fruits or cones with a fleshy (juicy to mealy) outer layer covering a stone or several seeds; fruit types include berries, drupes and pomes **2**

1b Fruits or cones dry; fruit types include capsules, nuts and achenes (rarely slightly fleshy) **12**

2a Fruits apple-like with a core containing 1 to several seeds **3**

2b Fruits drupes, berries or fleshy cones; not pomes **4**

3a Fruits single or in small, unbranched clusters, 1–4" long (some crabapples may be smaller)

Malus
(crabapple)
pp. 172–174

Pyrus
(pear)
p. 171

3b Fruits few to many in branched clusters, ¹/₄–¹/₂" long

Amelanchier
(serviceberry)
pp. 188–189

Crataegus
(hawthorn)
pp. 178–187

Sorbus
(mountain-ash)
pp. 175–177

4a Fruits numerous, stalkless, in dense, head-like clusters (clusters may be stalked) **5**

4b Fruits stalked, single or variously clustered; single fruits sometimes short-stalked **6**

5a Fruits numerous, in dense, head-like clusters

Maclura
(Osage-orange)
p. 92

Morus
(mulberry)
pp. 93–94

5b Fruits 2–6 (rarely more), in small clusters at the tips of longer stalks

Nyssa
(tupelo)
p. 210

Cornus
(dogwood)
pp. 216–217

Lonicera
(honeysuckle)
p. 243

6a Fruits small, typically ¹/₄–⁵/₈" long (sometimes larger in domestic cherries) **7**

6b Fruits large (1–4" long) and juicy

Asimina
(pawpaw)
p. 79

Prunus
(plum)
pp. 168–170

Prunus
(peach)
p. 164

7a Fruits single or paired (sometimes 3) **8**

7b Fruits in clusters of 4 or more **10**

8a Fruit stalks (fruit cluster stalks in *Nyssa*) 1.2–4 times as long as the fruit **9**

8b Fruit stalks equal to or shorter than the fruit

Elaeagnus
(oleaster)
p. 209

Shepherdia
(buffaloberry)
p. 248

Frangula
(buckthorn)
p. 211

Ilex
(holly)
p. 203

Juniperus
(red-cedar)
p. 74

9a Fruits containing a single stone

Celtis
(hackberry)
pp. 90–91

Nyssa
(tupelo)
p. 210

Elaeagnus
(oleaster)
p. 209

Prunus
(cherry)
pp. 161–167

9b Fruits containing 2–5 stones

Frangula
(buckthorn)
p. 211

Ilex
(holly)
p. 203

Nemopanthus
(mountain-holly)
p. 204

10a Fruit clusters rounded or flat-topped, usually as wide as long **11**
10b Fruit clusters elongated, longer than wide

Rhus
(sumac)
pp. 197–198

Toxicodendron
(poison-sumac)
p. 199

Sassafras
(sassafras)
p. 80

Ligustrum
(privet)
p. 235

Sambucus
(elder)
p. 242

Prunus
(cherry)
pp. 161–167

11a Fruit stalks nearly equal, unbranched, in small, usually tassel-like clusters

Frangula
(buckthorn)
p. 211

Rhamnus
(buckthorn)
p. 212

Prunus
(cherry)
pp. 161–167

Lindera
(spicebush)
p. 81

11b Fruit stalks varied, branched, in relatively large, spreading clusters

Cornus
(dogwood)
pp. 214–217

Viburnum
(viburnum)
pp. 244–246

Aralia
(Hercules-club, angelica tree)
p. 195

Sambucus
(elder)
p. 242

Kalopanax
(castor-aralia)
p. 201

12a Fruits in dense cones or cone-like clusters of firm, overlapping scales or scale-like fruits **13**
12b Fruits not in cone-like clusters **14**

13a Cone scales thick and firm, woody, leathery or somewhat fleshy

Pinus
(pine)
pp. 70–73

Alnus
(alder)
pp. 126–128

Liriodendron
(tulip-tree)
p. 78

Juniperus
(red-cedar)
p. 74

13b Cone scales relatively thin and bendable

Thuja
(white-cedar)
p. 75

Larix
(larch)
p. 68

Abies
(fir)
p. 64

Picea
(spruce)
pp. 65–67

Tsuga
(hemlock)
p. 69

14a Fruits stalkless or short-stalked, in dense, head-like or cylindrical clusters (clusters may be stalked) **15**

14b Fruits clearly stalked, single or loosely clustered.. **16**

15a Fruit clusters round

Platanus
(sycamore)
p. 82

Cephalanthus
(buttonbush)
p. 249

15b Fruit clusters roughly cylindrical, clearly longer than wide

Carpinus
(blue-beech)
p. 120

Ostrya
(hop-hornbeam)
p. 119

Betula
(birch)
pp. 122–125

Populus
(poplar)
pp. 133–138

Salix
(willow)
pp. 139–153

Tamarix
(tamarisk)
p. 76

16a Fruits without wings **17**
16b Fruits winged nutlets (samaras)

Acer
(maple)
pp. 224–232

Fraxinus
(ash)
pp. 236–240

Ailanthus
(tree-of-heaven)
p. 205

Ptelea
(hop-tree)
p. 206

Ulmus
(elm)
pp. 85–89

Halesia
(silverbell)
p. 190

17a Fruits round to egg-shaped or bell-shaped.. **18**

17b Fruits elongated, often laterally compressed pods, usually linear to narrowly oblong

Catalpa
(catalpa)
p. 247

Gleditsia
(honey-locust)
p. 193

Robinia
(locust)
p. 191

Cercis
(redbud)
p.192

Gymnocladus
(coffee-tree)
p. 194

18a Fruits relatively small nuts, nut-like drupes, capsules or pods **19**

18b Fruits large (mostly 1–2 ¹/₂"), round to pear-shaped nuts or capsules containing large nuts or nut-like seeds within an outer husk

Juglans
(walnut)
pp. 96–97

Carya
(hickory)
pp. 98–101

Aesculus
(buckeye)
pp. 221–222

Castanea
(chestnut)
p. 105

19a Fruits not splitting open when mature (nuts or nut-like capsules) **20**

19b Fruits splitting open when mature to release nutlets or seeds (capsules) **21**

20a Fruits single or in compact, short-stalked clusters of 2–5

Corylus
(hazelnut)
pp. 96–97

Quercus
(oak)
pp. 106–116

20b Fruits few to many in elongated, often branched clusters

Tilia
(basswood)
pp. 207–208

Cotinus
(smoketree)
p. 202

21a Mature capsules membranous, 3-4 lobed, inflated and hollow, or with seeds embedded in a fleshy aril

Euonymus
(euonymus)
pp. 218–219

Staphylea
(bladdernut)
p. 220

21b Mature capsules woody, tipped with a single point (before opening)

Hamamelis
(witch-hazel)
p. 83

Fagus
(beech)
p. 104

Syringa
(lilac)
p. 234

Winter Key to Genus
(excluding characteristics of persistent fruits)

1a Leaves evergreen needles or scales **2**
1b Leaves deciduous, absent in winter **3**

2a Leaves small, flat-lying scales

Juniperus   **Thuja**
(red-cedar)   (white-cedar)
p. 74   p. 75

2b Leaves needle-like

Juniperus   **Tsuga**   **Abies**
(red-cedar)   (hemlock)   (fir)
p. 74   p. 69   p. 64

Picea   **Pinus**
(spruce)   (pine)
pp. 65–67   pp. 70–73

3a Branches and bud scars opposite **4**
3b Branches and bud scars alternate **7**

4a Buds covered by 3 or more scales **5**
4b Buds covered by 1 or 2 scales, naked (with 2 exposed, immature leaves) or embedded in bark and too tiny to see

   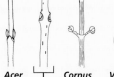 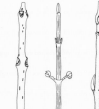

Salix   **Acer**   **Cornus**   **Viburnum**
(willow)   (maple)   (dogwood)   (viburnum)
pp. 139–153 pp. 224–232 pp. 214–217 pp. 244–246

Cephalanthus (buttonbush) p. 249

5a Leaf scars small, with 1–3 dots (vein scars), or absent **6**
5b Leaf scars large, often horseshoe-shaped, usually with several dots (vein scars)

Aesculus   **Catalpa**   **Fraxinus**   **Sambucus**
(buckeye)   (catalpa)   (ash)   (elder)
pp. 221–222   p. 247   pp. 236–240   p. 242

6a Leaf scars with 3 dots (vein scars)

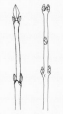  

Acer   ⌐**Rhamnus**⌐   **Staphylea**   **Lonicera**
(maple)   (buckthorn)   (bladdernut)   (honeysuckle)
pp. 224–232   p. 212   p. 220   p. 243

6b Leaf scars with a single dot (vein scar)

Euonymus   **Syringa**   **Ligustrum**
(euonymus)   (lilac)   (privet)
pp. 218–219   p. 234   p. 235

7a Branches armed with thorns or spine-tipped twigs **8**
7b Branches lacking spines or thorns **9**

51

8a Branches armed with true thorns

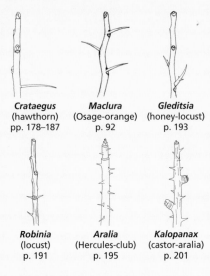

Crataegus
(hawthorn)
pp. 178–187

Maclura
(Osage-orange)
p. 92

Gleditsia
(honey-locust)
p. 193

Robinia
(locust)
p. 191

Aralia
(Hercules-club)
p. 195

Kalopanax
(castor-aralia)
p. 201

8b Branches armed with spine-tipped branches or sharp, dwarf side-branches

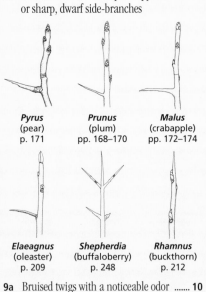

Pyrus
(pear)
p. 171

Prunus
(plum)
pp. 168–170

Malus
(crabapple)
pp. 172–174

Elaeagnus
(oleaster)
p. 209

Shepherdia
(buffaloberry)
p. 248

Rhamnus
(buckthorn)
p. 212

9a Bruised twigs with a noticeable odor **10**
9b Bruised twigs with no noticeable odor **11**

10a Bruised twigs or inner bark sweet-smelling

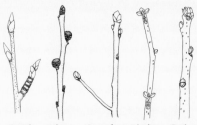

Betula
(birch)
pp.
122–125

Ulmus
(elm)
pp.
85–89

Sassafras
(sassafras)
p. 80

Lindera
(spice-
bush)
p. 81

Cotinus
(smoke-
tree)
p. 202

10b Bruised twigs or inner bark foul-smelling

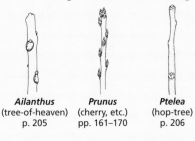

Ailanthus
(tree-of-heaven)
p. 205

Prunus
(cherry, etc.)
pp. 161–170

Ptelea
(hop-tree)
p. 206

11a Pith of twigs solid and uniform, not chambered or banded **12**
11b Pith of twigs chambered or banded

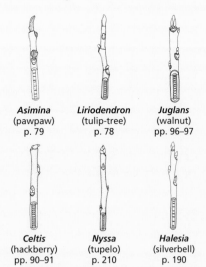

Asimina
(pawpaw)
p. 79

Liriodendron
(tulip-tree)
p. 78

Juglans
(walnut)
pp. 96–97

Celtis
(hackberry)
pp. 90–91

Nyssa
(tupelo)
p. 210

Halesia
(silverbell)
p. 190

12a Buds protected by scales or tiny and
embedded in bark **13**

12b Buds without scales, so immature leaves
exposed

Hamamelis	**Frangula**	**Rhus**
(witch-hazel)	(buckthorn)	(sumac)
p. 83	p. 211	pp. 197–198

13a Buds with 1 or 2–6 equal (not overlapping)
scales, or buds too tiny to see scales
clearly **14**

13b Buds with 3 or more overlapping scales **15**

14a Buds covered by 1 scale or buds tiny on very
slender twigs and difficult to see (*Tamarix*)

Platanus	**Salix**	**Tamarix**
(sycamore)	(willow)	(tamarisk)
p. 82	pp. 139–153	p. 76

14b Buds covered by 2–6 scales

Tilia	**Alnus**	**Carya**
(basswood)	(alder)	(hickory)
pp. 207–208	pp. 126–128	pp. 98–101

Castanea	**Cornus**	**Nemopanthus**
(chestnut)	(dogwood)	(mountain-holly)
p. 105	pp. 214–217	p. 204

15a Buds arranged in 2 vertical rows; twigs
somewhat zigzagged, lacking a true terminal
(tip) bud (sometimes with a pseudo-
terminal bud very near the tip) **16**

15b Buds arranged in 3 or more vertical rows;
twigs tipped with a bud **17**

16a Leaf scars with 4 or more dots (vein scars)

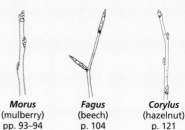

Morus	**Fagus**	**Corylus**
(mulberry)	(beech)	(hazelnut)
pp. 93–94	p. 104	p. 121

16b Leaf scars with 3 dots (vein scars)

Carpinus	**Cercis**	**Betula**
(blue-beech)	(redbud)	(birch)
p. 120	p. 192	pp. 122–125

Ostrya	**Ulmus**
(hop-hornbeam)	(elm)
p. 119	pp. 85–89

17a Twigs lacking short, dwarf side-branches..... **18**

17b Twigs with short, dwarf side-branches tipped with leaf, cone or flower buds

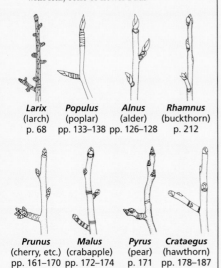

Larix (larch) p. 68

Populus (poplar) pp. 133–138

Alnus (alder) pp. 126–128

Rhamnus (buckthorn) p. 212

Prunus (cherry, etc.) pp. 161–170

Malus (crabapple) pp. 172–174

Pyrus (pear) p. 171

Crataegus (hawthorn) pp. 178–187

18a Leaf scars with 1 or 3 dots (vein scars)

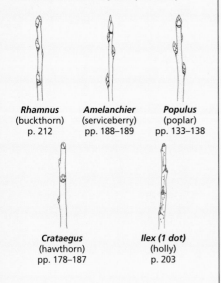

Rhamnus (buckthorn) p. 212

Amelanchier (serviceberry) pp. 188–189

Populus (poplar) pp. 133–138

Crataegus (hawthorn) pp. 178–187

Ilex (1 dot) (holly) p. 203

18b Leaf scars with 5 to many dots

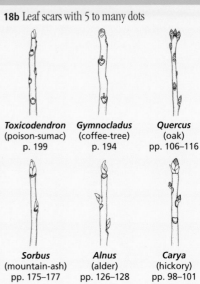

Toxicodendron (poison-sumac) p. 199

Gymnocladus (coffee-tree) p. 194

Quercus (oak) pp. 106–116

Sorbus (mountain-ash) pp. 175–177

Alnus (alder) pp. 126–128

Carya (hickory) pp. 98–101

THE EASIEST WAY TO IDENTIFY A TREE IS BY USING A KEY. It takes a long time to flip through every page in this guide, and many trees look very similar at first glance. A key provides you with a logical way to evaluate the most important characteristics of a tree and to rapidly narrow your choices.

This guide contains several different keys. All are dichotomous—that is, they present you with pairs of descriptions, only one of which will apply to your specimen. Simply work your way through the key choosing one of the two alternatives and then moving to the next set of choices, as indicated by the number at the end of the line. When the line ends in a name (rather than a number), you have found the name of your tree or the group to which it belongs.

The key below will help you identify the major groups (families and genera) of trees in Michigan. It may appear a bit long and intimidating at first, but remember, you don't have to read every pair of choices. For example, choice **1b** takes you to lead **4**, **4b** takes you to lead **17**, and **17b** takes you to lead **27**, over halfway through the key. For large families, you may be directed to other keys farther along in the guide. For example, **3b** leads you to the pine family keys on pp. 62–63.

1a	Leaves reduced to needles or scales, usually evergreen	2
1b	Leaves broader, not needle-like, deciduous	4

2a Trees producing true (though very tiny) flowers; seeds borne in small (¹⁄₁₆" long) capsules that split in 3–4 parts to release many tiny seeds; leaves scale-like, deciduous, forming feathery sprays .... **Tamaricaceae, Tamarisk Family (*Tamarix*, tamarisk, p. 76)**
2b Trees not producing true flowers; seeds borne in cones; leaves various **3**

3a Female cones small (<⅝"), sometimes berry-like, with whorled or paired scales; leaves usually scale-like, opposite or whorled .... **Cupressaceae, Cypress Family**
  i Cones dry, ¼–½" long, with thin, woody or leathery scales spreading to open at maturity; branchlets flattened, forming horizontal sprays .... ***Thuja*, white-cedar (p. 75)**
  ii Cones berry-like, ⅛–¼" long, with fleshy scales fused together at maturity; branches scarcely flattened, if at all .... ***Juniperus*, red-cedar (p. 74)**
3b Female cones usually larger, never berry-like; leaves needle-shaped, bundled, spirally arranged or alternate .... **Pinaceae, Pine Family** (keys to genera and species, pp. 62–63)

4a	Leaves divided into leaflets (compound)	5
4b	Leaves smooth-edged, toothed or lobed, but not divided into leaflets (simple)	17

5a	Fruits winged samaras	6
5b	Fruits not winged samaras	9

6a	Leaves alternate; samaras with the seed near the center	7
6b	Leaves opposite; samaras with the seed near one end	8

Pine Family		Cypress Family	

Scots pine p. 72	jack pine p. 73	eastern red-cedar p. 74	eastern white-cedar p. 75

7a Leaves with 3 leaflets (trifoliate); samaras round and flat
.... **Rutaceae, Rue Family (*Ptelea*, hop-tree,** p. 206)
7b Leaves pinnately divided into 11–41 leaflets; samaras oblong, twisted, with a seed near the center .... **Simaroubaceae, Quassia Family (*Ailanthus*, tree-of-heaven,** p. 205)

8a Samaras single .... **Oleaceae, Olive Family** (keys to genera and species, p. 233)
8b Samaras paired .... **Aceraceae, Maple Family (*Acer*, maple,** key to species, p. 223)

9a Fruits thick-husked capsules containing a nut or large, nut-like seed **10**
9b Fruits otherwise **11**

10a Leaves opposite, palmately divided in to 5–9 leaflets
.... **Hippocastanaceae, Horsechestnut Family (*Aesculus*, buckeye,** pp. 221–222)
10b Leaves alternate, pinnately divided into 11–23 leaflets
................................**Juglandaceae, Walnut Family** (keys to genera and species, pp. 96–97)

11a Fruits plump to dry capsules or pods **12**
11b Fruits somewhat fleshy pomes or drupes **15**

12a Fruits inflated, thin-walled, 3-pointed pods that persist well into winter
.... **Staphyleaceae, Bladdernut Family (*Staphylea*, bladdernut,** p. 220)
12b Fruits otherwise **13**

13a Fruits small (³⁄₁₆"), round capsules with firm, pitted walls that split open along one side (follicles) .... ***Zanthoxylum*, prickly-ash** (p. 200)
13b Fruits elongated, pea-like pods **14**

14a Leaves once-divided .... **Fabaceae, Pea Family (*Robinia*, locust,** p. 191)
14b Leaves twice-divided .... **Caesalpiniaceae, Cassia Family**
   i Branches usually thorny; leaflets up to ¹⁄₂" wide; flowers in compact, elongated clusters (racemes) .... ***Gleditsia*, honey-locust** (p. 193)
   ii Branches without thorns; leaflets ¹⁄₂–1¹⁄₂" wide; flowers in widely branched clusters (panicles) .... ***Gymnocladus*, coffee-tree** (p. 194)

15a Fruits small pomes (like tiny apples) in rounded to flat-topped clusters (corymbs)
....**Rosaceae, Rose Family** (keys to genera and species, pp. 154–160)
15b Fruits fleshy drupes **16**

16a Leaves once-pinnate .... **Anacardiaceae, Cashew Family** (keys to genera and species, p. 196)
16b Leaves twice-pinnate .... **Araliaceae, Ginseng Family (*Aralia*, aralia,** p. 195)

17a Leaves and branches paired (opposite) or whorled **18**
17b Leaves and branches single (alternate) **27**

Maple Family	Walnut Family	Cassia Family	Rose Family
silver maple p. 227	shagbark hickory p. 99	honey-locust p. 193	European mountain-ash p. 177

18a Fruits pairs of winged keys; leaves palmately veined and lobed
.... **Aceraceae, Maple Family (*Acer*, maple,** key to species, p. 223)
18b Fruits and leaves otherwise **19**

19a Fruits tiny capsules in dense, elongated clusters (catkins); buds covered by a single scale
.... **Salicaceae, Willow Family (*Salix*, willow,** key to species, pp. 129–131)
19b Fruits and buds otherwise **20**

20a Leaves toothed **21**
20b Leaves smooth-edged (not toothed) **23**

21a Fruits 4-lobed capsules .... **Celastraceae, Staff-tree Family**
    ia Twigs edged with 4 conspicuous corky wings; leaves essentially stalkless, bright red in
      autumn .... ***Euonymus alata*, winged burning-bush** (p. 219)
    ib Twigs without wings; leaves clearly stalked, not turning bright red .... **ii**
    iia Lower leaf surfaces finely hairy; flowers purplish-maroon; fleshy arils red;
       plants native ....***E. atropurpurea*, eastern wahoo** (p. 218)
    iib Lower leaf surfaces hairless; flowers greenish- to yellowish-white; fleshy arils orange;
       uncommon garden escapes .... **iii**
    iiia Leaves 1¹/₂–4¹/₂" long; anthers yellow
       .... ***E. europaea*, European spindle-tree** (p. 219)
    iiib Leaves 4–5" long; anthers purple
       ....***E. hamiltoniana*, Japanese spindle-tree** (p. 219)
21b Fruits berries or berry-like drupes **22**

22a Flowers 5-parted; flowers and fruits paired in leaf axils or numerous, in branched clusters at
    branch tips ..... **Caprifoliaceae, Honeysuckle Family** (keys to genera and species, p. 241)
22b Flowers 4-parted; flowers and fruits few, in small unbranched clusters (umbels)
    from leaf axils .... **Rhamnaceae, Buckthorn Family (*Rhamnus*, buckthorn,** p. 212)

23a Flowers large (¹/₂–2³/₄" long) funnel-shaped, numerous, in showy, branched clusters (pani-
    cles); fruits not juicy and berry-like; leaves heart-shaped **24**
23b Flowers small (to ¹/₄" long), whitish, 4-parted; leaves elliptic to oval **25**

24a Fruits bean-like pods, 10–20" long
    .... **Bignoniaceae, Trumpet-creeper Family (*Catalpa*, catalpa,** p. 247)
24b Fruits short (³/₈–¹/₂" long), pointed, leathery to woody capsules
    .... **Oleaceae, Olive Family (*Syringa*, lilac,** p. 234)

25a Flowers with petals fused into a funnel shape; fruits reddish-green to brownish,
    pyramidal capsules, ¹/₄" long; flowers/fruits in long-stalked, spherical heads
    .... **Rubiaceae, Madder Family (*Cephalanthus*, buttonbush,** p. 249)
25b Flowers with petals separate; fruits juicy, berry-like drupes ¹/₄–³/₄" across **26**

26a Flowers and fruits in small, unbranched clusters (umbels) in leaf axils, unisexual with male and
    female flowers on separate plants; branches thorny; leaves oblong, blunt tipped, silvery with star-
    shaped hairs .... **Elaeagnaceae, Oleaster Family (*Shepherdia*, buffaloberry,** p. 248)
26b Flowers/fruits in open, branched clusters or in stalkless heads surrounded by showy bracts
    (pseudanthia), bisexual; branches without thorns; leaves elliptic to oval, pointed, lacking star-
    shaped hairs .... **Cornaceae, Dogwood Family (*Cornus*, dogwood,** key to species, p. 213)

27a Leaves smooth-edged (not toothed) **28**
27b Leaves toothed **40**

28a Flowers single, relatively large and showy; fruits large (>³⁄₄") berries or cone-like clusters of overlapping pods **29**
28b Flowers usually in clusters of 2 or more, relatively small; fruits small (<³⁄₄") drupes (occasionally forming large, round masses), berries, pods, capsules or nuts **30**

29a Flowers dull purple; fruits large, sweet-pulpy berries with many large seeds; leaves widest above the middle, not dotted .... **Annonaceae, Custard-apple Family (*Asimina*, pawpaw,** p. 79)
29b Flowers yellowish-green, often with yellow or orange markings; fruits numerous, forming dense, cone-like clusters; leaves with tiny, transparent dots
.... **Magnoliaceae, Magnolia Family (*Liriodendron*, tulip-tree,** p. 78)

30a Fruits small, fleshy, numerous, in large (4–5¹⁄₂"), round, pulpy aggregates resembling lumpy oranges; branches thorny with milky juice
.... **Moraceae, Mulberry Family (*Maclura*, Osage-orange,** p. 92)
30b Fruits and branches otherwise **31**

31a Fruits fleshy berries or drupes **32**
31b Fruits dry capsules, pods, nuts, nutlets or dry drupes **37**

32a Leaf surfaces silvery above and below with dense, star-shaped hairs; drupes silvery, mealy
.... **Elaeagnaceae, Oleaster Family (*Elaeagnus*, oleaster,** p. 209)
32b Leaves and fruits not silvery; fruits crimson, dark blue or purplish-black **33**

33a Flowers ¹⁄₄–³⁄₈" across, yellow, 6-lobed; bark, twigs and wood spicy-fragrant
.... **Lauraceae, Laurel Family**
  i Leaves unlobed, ovate, pinnately veined; flower/fruit clusters stalkless, scattered along branchlets; fruits red .... ***Lindera*, spicebush** (p. 81)
  ii Leaves typically 2–3-lobed, palmately veined; flower/fruit clusters on stalks at branch tips; fruits blue .... ***Sassafras*, sassafras** (p. 80)
33b Flowers tiny (about ¹⁄₈" long), greenish to cream, with 3–5 sepals and petals (sometimes lacking petals); leaves not lobed; trees not spicy-fragrant **34**

34a Flowers borne on long, slender stalks, single or in tassel-like clusters from leaf axils; fruits 1 per stalk **35**
34b Flowers in dense clusters at the tips of long stalks; fruits usually 2 or more per stalk **36**

35a Flowers unisexual, single from leaf axils; winter buds with scales
.... **Aquifoliaceae, Holly Family (*Nemopanthus*, mountain-holly,** p. 204)
35b Flowers bisexual, in small tassel-like clusters from leaf axils
.... **Rhamnaceae, Buckthorn Family (*Frangula*, glossy buckthorn,** p. 211)

36a Flowers bisexual, with 4 stamens and 4 petals; sepals minute; fruits fleshy, red to purplish-black
.... **Cornaceae, Dogwood Family (*Cornus*, dogwood,** key to species, p. 213)
36b Flowers unisexual, with 5 evident sepals and 5–8 minute petals; fruits oily, blue-black, plum-like drupes, usually in spreading pairs at the stalk tip
.... **Nyssaceae, Sourgum Family (*Nyssa*, tupelo,** p. 210)

37a Fruits acorns (1-seeded nuts with the base enclosed in a distinctive cup of overlapping bracts)
.... **Fagaceae, Beech Family (*Quercus*, oak,** key to species, pp. 102–103)
37b Fruits otherwise **38**

38a Flowers showy, pink, pea-like, in small, tassel-like clusters along branches; fruits flattened pods (legumes); leaves heart-shaped
.... **Caesalpiniaceae, Cassia Family (*Cercis*, redbud,** p. 192)

38b Flowers tiny, without obvious petals **39**

39a Flowers/fruits in compact, elongated clusters (catkins); fruits short-stalked capsules containing many fluffy-parachuted seeds; leaves not aromatic
.... **Salicaceae, Willow Family** (keys to genera and species, pp. 129–132)

39b Flowers/fruits in airy, many-branched clusters (panicles); fruits dry drupes on long, slender stalks with many feathery hairs; leaves aromatic, smelling of orange peels
.... **Anacardiaceae, Cashew Family (*Cotinus*, smoketree,** p. 202)

40a Branches spiny or thorny **41**

40b Branches without spines or thorns **42**

41a Flowers relatively large (>1/2" across), with showy, white to pink petals; fruits various
.... **Rosaceae, Rose Family** (keys to genera and species, pp. 154–160)

41b Flowers tiny, about 1/16" across; fruits small, berry-like drupes **43**

42a Flowers and fruits in large (12–24" wide), twice-branched clusters of 50-flowered, 1–2" wide tassel-like clusters (umbels) at the tips of long branches in umbel-like panicles; leaves maple leaf–like, 5–10" across .... **Araliaceae, Aralia Family (*Kalopanax*, castor-aralia,** p. 201)

42b Flowers and fruits in simple, compact, tassel-like clusters (umbels) in leaf axils; leaves ovate to elliptic, 1–2" across, often opposite
.... **Rhamnaceae, Buckthorn Family (*Rhamnus*, buckthorn,** p. 212)

43a Flowers and fruits in small, flat-topped clusters on slender stalks from the middle of strap-like, membranous bracts; leaves usually unevenly heart-shaped
.... **Tiliaceae, Linden Family (*Tilia*, basswood,** pp. 207–208)

43b Fruits, flowers and leaves otherwise **44**

44a Flowers tiny, without petals or sepals, unisexual; male flowers numerous, in dense heads or catkins **45**

44b Flowers not in dense heads or catkins **49**

45a Male and female flowers in spherical heads; leaves with 3–5 broad, palmate lobes
.... **Platanaceae, Plane-tree Family (*Platanus*, sycamore,** p. 82)

45b Male flowers (and sometimes female also) in elongated clusters (catkins) **46**

46a Fruits tiny, short-stalked capsules in catkins; seeds tipped with a tuft of long, silky down; buds often covered by 1 scale .... **Salicaceae, Willow Family** (keys to genera and species, pp. 129–132)

46b Fruits otherwise; seeds not tipped with silky hairs; buds never 1-scaled **47**

Beech Family	Dogwood Family	Holly Family	Willow Family

bur oak
p. 107

gray dogwood
p. 216

common mountain-holly
p. 204

pussy willow
p. 152

47a Fruits large, single nuts seated in a scaly cup or in a bristly husk .... **Fagaceae, Beech Family** (keys to genera and species, pp. 102–103)

47b Fruits small, numerous, in dense clusters **48**

48a Fruits tiny, winged nutlets, protected by dry bracts in scaly or woody catkins .... **Betulaceae, Birch Family** (keys to genera and species, pp. 117–118)

48b Fruits tiny nutlets, each surrounded by fleshy, swollen sepals, forming compact, often blackberry-like clusters .... **Moraceae, Mulberry Family** (*Morus*, mulberry, pp. 93–94)

49a Leaves asymmetrical, with one edge longer than the other at the base **50**

49b Leaves with symmetrical bases **51**

50a Flowers showy, with 4 slender yellow petals, appearing in autumn; fruits woody, 2-seeded capsules; leaves wavy-toothed .... **Hamamelidaceae, Witch-hazel Family** (*Hamamelis*, witch-hazel, p. 83)

50b Flowers inconspicuous, greenish, lacking petals, appearing in spring; fruits round, winged samaras or red to blackish drupes; leaves sharply toothed .... **Ulmaceae, Elm Family** (keys to genera and species, p. 84)

51a Flowers white, pink, blue or violet, relatively large (>$\frac{1}{2}$") and showy, 4–5 petals, 8–16 stamens; fruits various, but drupes 1-seeded **52**

51b Flowers yellowish-green, <$\frac{1}{4}$" across, 4–8 petals, 4–10 stamens; fruits various, but drupes 2–5-stoned **53**

52a Flowers bell-shaped, with fused petals; fruits dry drupes, 1–4-stoned .... **Styracaceae, Snowball Family** (*Halesia*, silverbell, p. 190)

52b Flowers cupped or saucer-shaped, with separate petals; fruits various, usually fleshy, 1-seeded if drupes .... **Rosaceae, Rose Family** (keys to genera and species, pp. 154–160)

53a Flowers unisexual with male and female flowers on separate plants or bisexual; bisexual flowers with a long, slender style tipped with a stigma; unisexual flowers with split styles and 2 stigmas .... **Rhamnaceae, Buckthorn Family**
   i Winter buds protected by scales; flowers bisexual, with undivided styles ....**Rhamnus**, buckthorn (p. 212)
   ii Winter buds lacking scales; flowers unisexual, with styles split $\frac{1}{3}$ of their length ....**Frangula**, glossy buckthorn (p. 211)

53b Flowers unisexual with male and female flowers on separate plants; styles short, stigmas almost sessile .... **Aquifoliaceae, Holly Family**
   i Flowers white, with petals joined at the base; leaves lacking a short, sharp point at the tip, edged with teeth (coarse and spiny to shallow and rounded) .... **Ilex**, holly (p. 203)
   ii Flowers yellow, with separate petals; leaves tipped with a short, sharp point, smooth edged or with a few small sharp teeth ....**Nemopanthus**, mountain-holly (p. 204)

Holly Family	Elm Family	Witch-hazel Family	Beech Family

common winterberry
p. 203

American elm
p. 85

American witch-hazel
p. 83

American beech
p. 104

Needle Leaves

Key to Genera in the Pine Family (Pinaceae)

1a Needles in clusters of 2 or more; branches with dwarf shoots.. **2**

1b Needles single, spirally arranged; branches lacking dwarf shoots... **3**

2a Needles drop each autumn (deciduous), numerous, in dense clusters at the tips of stubby dwarf branches.. *Larix*, **larch** (p. 68)

2b Needles evergreen, in bundles of 2–5 along branches
.... *Pinus*, **pine** (key to species, below)

3a Needles 4-sided, easily rolled between fingers, spirally arranged like bristles on a bottle brush; twigs rough with persistent woody needle bases; cones hanging
.... *Picea*, **spruce** (key to species, p. 63)

3b Needles flat, with 2 white lines on the lower surface, generally twisted to lie flat in 2 rows along the twig.. **4**

4a Seed cones erect, gradually shedding their scales while on the tree; leaves attached directly to the branch, leaving a smooth, round scar when shed... *Abies*, **fir** (p. 64)

4b Seed cones hanging, falling with scales intact; leaves attached to elevated woody bases, leaving twigs rough when shed.. *Tsuga*, **hemlock** (p. 69)

Pinus strobus, eastern white pine

Key to the Pines (Genus *Pinus*)

1a Needles soft and slender, in bundles of 5; seed cone scales thin and flexible, without spiny, thickened tips .... ***P. strobus*, eastern white pine** (p. 70)

1b Needles firmer, thicker, in bundles of 2–3; seed cone scales thickened and rather woody **2**

2a Needles ³/₄–3" long, usually twisted lengthwise or with spreading pairs **3**

2b Needles 3–6" long, straight **4**

3a Needles 1¹/₂–3" long, spirally twisted (both sides visible at once), not noticeably spreading; bark of older branches orange-brown .... ***P. sylvestris*, Scots pine** (p. 72)

3b Needles ³/₄–1¹/₂" long, only slightly twisted (only 1 side visible), spread in a "V"; bark of older branches not orange-brown .... ***P. banksiana*, jack pine** (p. 73)

4a Needles stiff, snapping readily when bent in half; seed cones reddish-brown, stalkless when shed; buds chestnut brown .... ***P. resinosa*, red pine** (p. 71)

4b Needles flexible, not snapping when bent in half; seed cones shiny brown, shed with stalks; buds with whitish resin .... ***P. nigra*, Austrian pine** (p. 72)

Key to the Spruces (Genus *Picea*)

1a Young twigs and buds with many short, fine hairs .... ***P. mariana*, black spruce** (p. 67)

1b Young twigs and buds hairless (or essentially so) **2**

2a Seed cones 1–2³/₈" long with smooth-edged scales; branchlets spreading, rarely hanging .... ***P. glauca*, white spruce** (p. 66)

2b Seed cones 4–7" long, with irregularly toothed scales; branchlets typically hanging .... ***P. abies*, Norway spruce** (p. 65)

Pinus glauca, white spruce

BALSAM FIR'S regular, conical shape and its fragrant, persistent needles make it a popular Christmas tree.
• Balsam fir wood is not commonly used for lumber (occasionally in crates, doors and woodenware), but it is an important source of pulp. Although balsam fir is an important timber species in many parts of North America, it is of minor economic value in Michigan.
• The resin, known as Canada balsam, is used in mounting microscope specimens, in making glue and as a fragrance in perfumes, deodorizers, candles and soaps. It was widely used in folk medicine as an antiseptic. • Although this tree lives 70–100 years, it doesn't produce significant amounts of seed until it is 20–30 years old, and growth often declines after 50–70 years. Dense, pure fir stands protect steep slopes from erosion and provide food and cover for wildlife. Multitudes of shade-tolerant seedlings often make walking difficult.
• This shallow-rooted tree is commonly toppled by high winds and heavy, wet spring snow. Because of its thin bark, it is easily killed by fire. Balsam fir is susceptible to attacks by eastern spruce budworm (*Choristoneura fumiferana*), hemlock looper (*Lambdina fiscellaria fiscellaria*), balsam woolly adelgid (*Adelges piceae*) and heart-rot.

ALSO CALLED: Canada balsam, Canada fir, balsam, eastern fir.

SIZE AND SHAPE: Coniferous trees 35–80' [89'] tall, narrowly cone-shaped; **crowns spire-like;** roots usually shallow.

TRUNKS: Straight, 8–20"[22"] in diameter; young bark thin, smooth, with **blister-like pockets of aromatic resin;** mature bark brownish, irregularly scaly; wood soft, light, somewhat brittle.

BRANCHES: Spreading; **twigs slender, smooth,** yellow-green to grayish, **hairy;** buds dark

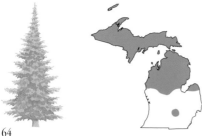

orange-green, lustrous, broadly egg-shaped, 1/8–1/4" long, usually resinous.

LEAVES: Shiny, dark green, **flat, evergreen needles,** with **2 white bands on the lower surface;** 1/2–1 1/8" long on lower branches, 3/8–1/2" on upper, aromatic, blunt or notched, stalkless; spirally attached but **twisted into 2 rows on one plane;** leaf scars flat and round; needles persist 8–10 years.

CONES: Male and female cones on the same tree; male cones yellow, about 1/4" long; female cones **dark purple, erect, barrel-shaped,** 1 1/2–4" long when mature, resinous; seeds purple to brown, 1/8–1/4" long with a shiny, light brown wing 3/8–1/2" long, abundant; seed cones usually mature in first September; both scales and seeds are shed, but **erect cores (axes) persist** on branches for several years.

HABITAT: Low, swampy ground to well-drained hillsides; needs moist soil and air.

ORIGIN: Native to eastern North America.

THIS SPRUCE has 2 forms: the "brush" form, with bunched shoots typical of spruce trees; and the "comb" form, with sparser, upcurved branches from which smaller side branches hang in lines, like teeth on a comb.

• Norway spruce is one of the most important timber trees in central and northern Europe. The timber, known as "whitewood" or "deal," is used in roofing, in house interiors and as a source of pulp. In Britain, Norway spruce is the traditional Christmas tree, and in Germany, turpentine is extracted from the trunks for use in tanning leather.

• Norway spruce is widely planted as an ornamental tree and windbreak in temperate North America. It has also been cultivated here for Christmas tree purposes and has been used in many reforestation projects in eastern Canada and the northeastern U.S. The trees are hardy enough to survive in regions north of Lake Superior, but they are often stunted by winter frosts near their northern limit. • Plant breeders have developed more than 100 cultivars of Norway spruce, in many shapes and sizes, but only a few are commonly cultivated.

ALSO CALLED: Common spruce • *P. excelsa.*

SIZE AND SHAPE: Coniferous trees 50–80' [98'] tall (to 200' in Europe); crowns cone-shaped.

TRUNKS: Tall, 12–40" [46"] in diameter; bark reddish-brown, smooth to shredding; mature bark dark purplish-brown with small, rounded scales; wood white, strong, fine-grained.

BRANCHES: Drooping; twigs hairless, creamy green to **light orange-brown,** rough with small peg-like, leaf-bearing bumps; buds pale to reddish-brown, 1/4–3/8" long, blunt, not resinous.

LEAVES: Dark green, 4-sided, evergreen needles, 1/2–1" long, **sharp-pointed;** spirally arranged but curved upward and forward; needles persist 5–7 years.

CONES: Male and female cones on the same tree; male cones red to yellow, 3/4–1" long; female cones grayish- or reddish-brown when mature, **cylindrical,** tapered at the tip, **4–7" long,** hanging near branch tips; scales thin, flat, tapered to a slightly toothed tip; seeds 1/8" long, long-winged, 2 behind each scale; seed cones drop in first autumn to winter.

HABITAT: Varied, but prefers shaded or partially shaded sites with deep, rich, moist soils.

ORIGIN: Introduced from northern and central Europe and Asia; occasionally **grows wild near parent stands.**

WHITE SPRUCE is an important timber tree in northern North America. The wood is used extensively by the pulp and paper industry and for making boxes, shipping crates and lumber. • White spruce typically lives 150–200 years. Most trees start producing seeds at 20–40 years of age, with heavy crops every 2–5 years. Exceptionally large trees have been found on northern rivers, where tiers of adventitious roots have built up with alternating layers of river sediment. In the absence of fire, it can gradually replace other trees in the canopy. • Native peoples split the tough, pliable roots to make cords for lacing bark canoes and baskets. • This hardy, attractive tree is often used in landscaping and reforestation. • White spruce provides food and shelter for grouse, seed-eating birds, red squirrels, porcupines and black bears. Red squirrels nip off the cones and young shoots. Porcupines often deform spruce trunks when they eat the bark. Black bears can also damage trees when they strip off the outer bark to get at the sweet inner bark. • White spruce needles often drop prematurely as a result of infection by rust diseases. Eastern spruce budworm (*Choristoneura fumiferana*) and spruce sawflies (various species) are also serious pests.

ALSO CALLED: Cat spruce, skunk spruce, pasture spruce, Canadian spruce, single spruce.

SIZE AND SHAPE: Coniferous trees 50–80' [102'] tall; crowns narrowly (northern) to broadly (southern) cone-shaped; roots shallow to moderately deep.

TRUNKS: Straight, 12–24" [33"] in diameter; mature bark dark gray, with thin, scaly plates; newly exposed bark pinkish; wood light, soft and straight-grained.

BRANCHES: Bushy, spreading to drooping, up-curved at the tips; **twigs pale greenish-gray to orange-brown, hairless** (seedling twigs may be hairy), with many small, peg-like, leaf-bearing bumps; buds blunt, 1/8–1/4" long, with tight, ragged, hairless scales not projecting beyond bud tips.

LEAVES: Straight, stiff, **4-sided, evergreen needles;** needles green, **often with a grayish bloom,** white-lined on all sides, 1/2–7/8" long, aromatic; spirally arranged but curved upward and crowded on the upper side; needles persist 7–10 years.

CONES: Male and female cones on the same tree; male cones red to yellow, 1/2–3/4" long; female cones pale brown when mature, **1–2 3/8" long, cylindrical, resilient,** stalkless, hanging near branch tips; **scales thin, smooth-edged, close-fitting;** seeds pale brown, about 1/8" long with a wing 1/8–3/8" long, 2 behind each scale; seed cones mature in first autumn, shed seeds, then **drop over winter.**

HABITAT: Wide range of soils and climates but prefers rich, moist soil.

ORIGIN: Native.

BLACK SPRUCE is a medium-sized tree that is used for pulp and fuel. • This spruce often lives 200–250 years, but stands usually start to decline after 100 years. Healthy trees are prolific seed producers from about 10 years of age, with good crops every other year. Cones can persist for many years in dense clusters on uppermost branches. Fire stimulates cones to open and shed seeds onto newly exposed soil. • When lower branches touch the ground, they often develop roots and send up shoots. This process, called "layering," produces small clumps of young trees around parent trees. In habitats where seed success is limited (e.g., cold, wet, acidic sites), layering is often the main means of regeneration. • Red squirrels nip the tips off cone-bearing branches to gather the cones and eat the seeds. This pruning can result in a dense mass of branches in the upper crown with a bare stretch of trunk immediately underneath. • This shallow-rooted tree is susceptible to damage from high winds, flooding and fire. Black spruce buds open 1–2 weeks later than those of white spruce, so black spruce is less likely to be damaged by late spring frosts.

ALSO CALLED: Bog spruce, swamp spruce, water spruce, shortleaf spruce • *P. nigra.*

SIZE AND SHAPE: Coniferous trees, **columnar** and often stunted on poorly drained sites, cone-shaped and up to 50' [80'] tall on upland sites; **crowns dense, often club-shaped;** roots shallow.

TRUNKS: Straight, 4–12" [15"] in diameter; mature bark dark grayish-brown with thin, irregular scales; **newly exposed bark olive- or yellowish-green;** wood yellowish-white, soft, light.

BRANCHES: Short, spreading to drooping, upturned at tips; **twigs dull orange- to yellowish-brown,** with peg-like, leaf-bearing bumps; **new twigs minutely reddish-hairy;** buds gray-brown, hairy, blunt, 1/8–1/4" long, with **grayish, finely hairy, slender-pointed scales projecting beyond the tips.**

LEAVES: Stiff, **straight, 4-sided, evergreen needles;** needles grayish-green, sometimes with a whitish bloom, 1/4–3/4" **long;** spirally arranged, spreading in all directions, some curved upward; needles persist 7–10 years.

CONES: Male and female cones on the same tree; male cones red to yellow, about 1/2" long, numerous; female cones dull grayish- to **purplish-brown,** rigid, 3/4–1 1/8" **long,** hanging on scaly, curved, **short stalks** near branch tips; scales thin, stiff, brittle, roughly toothed, close-fitting and firmly attached; seeds about 1/8" long with a 3/8–1/2" wing, 2 per scale; seed cones mature in first September, **shed seeds over 1–2 (up to 30) years** or quickly after fires.

HABITAT: Usually in cool, damp sites (e.g., bogs, fens and swamps), but occasionally on well-drained ridges and shores in the north.

ORIGIN: Native.

THOUGH TAMARACK wood is not valued for lumber, it is used in rough construction and as poles, piers and railroad ties, and can also make beautiful paneling. • Tannin-rich tamarack bark was used traditionally for tanning leather. • This relatively short-lived tree usually survives about 150 years, with peak seed crops at 50–75 years of age. In cold, nutrient-poor environments, tamarack often becomes stunted and produces small needles and narrow-scaled cones. • In early fall, red squirrels strip off the cones and eat the seeds. Chipmunks, mice and red crossbills also gather the seeds. White-tailed deer sometimes browse on young shoots, and porcupines often kill tamarack trees by stripping off the outer bark to feed on the sweeter inner bark. • Tamarack is relatively free of serious infection by fungal diseases, but its foliage is sometimes damaged severely by larch sawfly (*Pristiphora erichsonii*). • **European larch** (*L. decidua* or *L. europaea*) is often planted in eastern North America as an ornamental or for forestry purposes, and it occasionally escapes cultivation near parent stands. It is readily distinguished by its large (³/₄–1³/₈" long) cones, which have more than 30 finely hairy scales.

ALSO CALLED: American larch, hackmatack, eastern larch, Alaska larch.

SIZE AND SHAPE: Coniferous trees 40–65' [89'] tall, roughly cone-shaped, irregular with age; roots shallow, wide-spreading.

TRUNKS: Usually straight, 12–24" [35"] in diameter; young bark gray, smooth, thin; mature bark light reddish-brown, with narrow, peeling scales; **newly exposed bark reddish-purple;** wood heavy, strong, durable.

BRANCHES: Of 2 types: long, **slender, spreading branches** with scattered leaves, often gracefully curved; and **stubby, dwarf side-branches** (spur branches) elongating slowly over many years; buds brown to dark red, hairless or ringed by hairs.

LEAVES: Bright green, **soft, slender, deciduous needles,** ³/₄–1" long; tightly spiralled **in clusters** of 10–20 or more at tips of stubby side-shoots; **needles yellow when shed each autumn.**

CONES: Male and female cones on the same tree; male cones small, yellow; female cones yellow-green or reddish when young, pale brown when mature, ³/₈–³/₄" **long,** on short, curved stalks at tips of leafless, stubby side-branches; **scales 10–20, stiff, hairless, longer than wide;** seeds light brown, ¹/₈" long with a ¹/₄" wing; seed cones mature in mid-August, soon shed seeds, often persist through the year.

HABITAT: Usually cold, wet sites such as bogs, fens and swamps, but grows well on moist, well-drained upland sites.

ORIGIN: Native.

EASTERN HEMLOCK wood tends to separate along radial lines and between annual rings, making it brittle and easily split. However, the knots are very hard and can dull saw blades and deflect nails. The poor-quality lumber is sometimes used in construction, crates or cabinets. When burned as firewood, eastern hemlock tends to "pop," sending sparks flying. • Hemlock bark was once gathered commercially for leather tanning, leaving behind many bare, decaying logs. • This tree adapts to different soils and responds to pruning, so it is planted as an ornamental and in windbreaks. Fallen twigs and leaves increase soil acidity, discouraging competition from other plants. • Eastern hemlock often lives 400–500 years, and some trees reach almost 1000 years of age. Young trees produce seed after 20–40 years, with heavy crops every 3–4 years. • Hemlocks provide dense cover and food for white-tailed deer, snowshoe hares, porcupines, ruffed grouse and wild turkeys. After deep snowfalls, white-tailed deer take shelter in hemlock stands, heavily browsing the lower branches. In years when cones are plentiful, songbirds such as black-capped chickadees, pine siskins and crossbills descend en masse to feast on the oil-rich seeds.

ALSO CALLED: Canada hemlock, hemlock spruce.

SIZE AND SHAPE: Coniferous trees 65–100' [121'] tall, densely conical when young, irregular with age, **tipped with a nodding leader;** roots shallow, wide-spreading, fibrous.

TRUNKS: Straight, 12–48" [52"] in diameter; young bark reddish-brown, scaly; mature bark dark reddish-brown or gray, furrowed, broadly ridged; **inner bark bright reddish-purple;** wood light orange-yellow to reddish-brown, lightweight, brittle.

BRANCHES: Slender, flexible, **irregular,** spreading, with drooping tips; **forming flat, horizontal sprays;** twigs hairy, with tiny, leaf-bearing bumps; buds reddish-brown, finely hairy, ¹/₁₆" long.

LEAVES: Flat, flexible, evergreen needles, dark yellowish-green and grooved above, with 2 whitish bands within green margins beneath; ¹/₄–¹/₂" **long,** blunt or notched, edged with tiny teeth; spirally attached by short, thread-like stalks, **twisted into 2 rows on one plane;** needles persist about 3 years.

CONES: Male and female cones on the same tree, near branch tips; male cones yellowish, round; female cones light brown and dry when mature, ¹/₂–³/₄" **long,** hanging on slender, hairy, ¹/₈" long stalks; scales few, thin, the **exposed part of middle scales wider than long,** smooth-edged or faintly toothed; seeds light brown, ¹/₈" long with a ¹/₄–³/₈" wing; seed cones shed seeds from autumn to early winter, but persist 1 year.

HABITAT: Cool, moist, shady, protected sites.

ORIGIN: Native.

THIS MAJESTIC SOFT PINE is Michigan's state tree and was once one of eastern North America's most commercially valuable trees. Michigan's first economic boom, the lumbering era of the late 1800s, stripped northern regions of their extensive pine forests. Eastern white pine stands contained an estimated 900 billion board feet of lumber, but most were cut in the 1700s and 1800s. The tall, straight trunks made excellent ship masts. • The wood is moderately strong and easily worked, with uniform texture and low shrinkage. It has been used in construction, interior and exterior finishing, furniture, cabinets and carvings. • Eastern white pine trees live 200–300 years (sometimes over 450 years) and produce seed regularly after 20–30 years. Seed production fluctuates, with good crops every 3–5 years and little or no production in between. Seedlings can persist in the understory for up to 20 years. The bark resists fire well, and after forest fires, surviving trees readily shed their seed over freshly exposed ground. • This attractive, fast-growing tree has been used in landscaping and reforestation projects. • White pine is seldom planted commercially because it is very susceptible to white pine blister rust (*Cronartium ribicola*) and white pine weevil (*Pissodes strobi*).

ALSO CALLED: Northern white pine, Weymouth pine, soft pine, cork pine.

SIZE AND SHAPE: Coniferous trees 65–100' [201'] tall; crowns conical when young, becoming **irregular (often lopsided) with age** in open sites; roots wide-spreading, very wind-firm.

TRUNKS: Tall, straight, 24–40" [59"] in diameter; young bark grayish-green, thin, smooth; **mature bark dark grayish-green,** 3/4–2" thick, with broad ridges of purple-tinged scales; wood pale brown, soft, lightweight, straight-grained.

BRANCHES: Stout, irregular, horizontal to ascending; twigs flexible and rusty-hairy (1st year) to brownish and hairless (2nd year); buds slender, 1/4–1/2" long, red- to yellow-brown, with overlapping scales.

LEAVES: Light **bluish-green, soft, slender, straight, flexible, evergreen needles; needles 2–6" long,** 3-sided, finely toothed; **bundled in 5s** and sheathed with membranous scales at the base; needles persist 1–4 years.

CONES: Male and female cones on the same tree; male cones yellow, small, clustered at the base of current year's growth in midcrown; female cones light brown and woody when mature, **cylindrical,** often curved, **3–10" long,** hanging on 3/4" long stalks at branch tips in upper crown; scales 50–80, exposed portions thin, rounded, lacking prickles; seeds mottled reddish-brown, about 1/4" long with a 1/2–3/4" wing, 2 per scale; seed cones mature in 2–3 years, drop soon after shedding seeds.

HABITAT: Dry, rocky ridges and dunes to moderately drained loams to swamps; does best on cool, humid sites with well-drained soil.

ORIGIN: Native.

RED PINE is an important timber and pulp tree, the most extensively planted species in Michigan. The moderately hard wood readily absorbs preservatives, making it useful for structural beams, bridges, piles and railroad ties. • Red pine has relatively little genetic variation, so it has a fairly consistent form and growth rate. It is often used in reforestation projects, tree plantations, parks and windbreaks. • This tree usually lives 200–250 years, but some trees have survived for over 300 years. It is slow growing at first, but once established, it can shoot up at a rate of 12" per year. Most red pine trees produce seed consistently at 15–25 years of age, with good crops every 3–7 years. • Red pine requires sunny sites, and it grows well on open sites with thin, infertile soils, where its deep roots help it withstand strong winds. Natural stands usually establish when fire removes competing plants and insect pests, leaving an open seedbed for the wind-borne seeds. • Many songbirds eat red pine seeds, red squirrels harvest the ripening cones from the trees, and chipmunks, mice and voles gather seeds on the ground.

ALSO CALLED: Norway pine (possibly from Norway, Maine).

SIZE AND SHAPE: Coniferous trees 65–100' [154'] tall; crowns conical when young, **rounded and irregular with age**.

TRUNKS: Tall, straight, 24–32" [39"] in diameter; young bark reddish to pinkish-brown, scaly; mature **bark reddish, flaky, with broad, scaly plates,** 1–1¹⁄₂" thick, fire-resistant; wood pale to reddish-brown, lightweight, close-grained.

BRANCHES: Spreading or drooping (lower) to upcurved (upper), in annual false-whorls; twigs stout, ridged; **buds resinous,** ¹⁄₂–³⁄₄" long, red-brown, with white-fringed scales.

LEAVES: Shiny, dark green, evergreen needles; **needles straight, 4–7" long, brittle** (snap easily), finely sharp-toothed; **bundled in 2s** with persistent membranous sheaths; crowded toward branch tips; needles persist 4–5 years.

CONES: Male and female cones on the same tree; male cones small, purple to yellow, clustered at the base of new shoots; female cones light chestnut brown, woody, **1¹⁄₂–2³⁄₄" long,** stalkless, hanging at upper branch tips; **scales only slightly thickened, concave,** tipped with a **spineless bump;** seeds mottled chestnut brown, with a ³⁄₈–⁵⁄₈" wing, 2 per scale; seed cones mature in 2–3 years, shed seeds in autumn, usually drop within the year.

HABITAT: Acidic, sandy or rocky areas; grows best in dry to moist areas with light, sandy loam but is outcompeted by hardwoods.

ORIGIN: Native.

SCOTS PINE is the world's most widely distributed pine and was one of the first trees introduced to North America. Its great variability reflects genetic and habitat differences as well as damage from diseases and pests. In the northern and mountainous regions of Europe, Scots pine is commonly tall and straight trunked with high-quality wood. In contrast, trees from southern Europe tend to have crooked trunks with numerous, spreading branches and poor-quality wood. Unfortunately, these are the trees that were first to arrive in North America, owing in large part to poor seed selection when the species was introduced. Because of its inferior wood quality, Scots pine was often abandoned in favor of other species for lumber, shelterbelts and erosion control. • Scots pines are widely planted as ornamentals and as Christmas trees. Old plantations sometimes appear to be stands of native trees.

• Another introduced species, **Austrian pine** (**P. *nigra***), is a 2-needle pine with straight (not spirally twisted), dark green (not blue-green) needles. This tall (to 100') tree with long (3–6"), flexible (not easily snapped) needles is widely planted as an ornamental and occasionally escapes from cultivation near parent stands.

ALSO CALLED: Scotch pine.

SIZE AND SHAPE: Coniferous trees 35–60' [64'] tall, often shrubby; crowns cone-shaped when young, rounded and irregular with age; roots wide-spreading, with a distinct taproot when young.

TRUNKS: Short and crooked with large branches, rarely straight and branch-free, 8–20" [59"] in diameter; **young bark orange-red, papery,** peeling in strips; mature bark grayish-brown to orange-brown, in irregular, loose plates; inner bark brownish-red; wood reddish-brown, strong, light, straight-grained.

BRANCHES: Irregular, spreading; twigs reddish- to grayish-brown, hairless, ridged; buds red-brown, sharp-tipped, 1/4–1/2" long, with some loose-tipped lower scales.

LEAVES: Slender, **stiff, spirally twisted, dark blue-green, evergreen needles; needles 1 1/2–3" long,** sharp-pointed, finely toothed; **bundled in 2s** with persistent, membranous sheaths about 1/4" long; needles persist 3–4 years.

CONES: Male and female cones on the same tree; male cones small, yellow, clustered at the base of new shoots; female cones usually in 2s or 3s, woody, yellowish- to purplish-brown, 1–3" long, often asymmetrical and **bent backward on the branch; scales flattened, tipped with a 4-sided, (usually) spineless bump;** seeds dark reddish-brown, about 1/8" long, the 3/8–3/4" wing soon lost, 2 per scale; seed cones mature in second autumn, shed seeds over winter and spring, often long-persistent.

HABITAT: Upland sites and pine plantations, preferably with sandy loam soils.

ORIGIN: Introduced from Europe; can become an aggressive invader of sites with sandy, acidic soils.

72

JACK PINE wood provides mine timbers, railroad ties, poles, pilings, lumber and wood fiber for pulp and paper. • This relatively short-lived tree lives 80–100 years and usually declines after about 70 years. Mature cones can remain closed on the tree for many years, until heat from fire or from sunlight on hot days, melts the resin that seals the scales shut, allowing the cones to pop open. Fire produces a favorable seedbed, free of competing plants and disease. However, repeated burns at intervals of less than 15 years will destroy the seed supply. • White-tailed deer browse on new growth, snowshoe hares eat seedlings and porcupines often eat the bark. Intensive browsing can deform trees, particularly young trees. Red squirrels, chipmunks, white-footed mice and birds such as goldfinches, grackles and robins eat large quantities of fallen seeds. • The globally endangered Kirtland's warbler (*Dendroica kirtlandii*), also called the jack pine warbler, requires large (more than 75 acres), pure stands of small (less than 20' tall) jack pine trees. It is known to nest only in northern and north-central Michigan, where controlled fires and plantings have produced dense stands of young jack pines.

ALSO CALLED: Black pine, scrub pine, Banksian pine, gray pine, Hudson Bay pine • *P. divaricata*.

SIZE AND SHAPE: Small coniferous trees, usually 35–50' [84'] tall; crowns cone-shaped, open.

TRUNKS: Straight, 8–12" [30"] in diameter; young bark reddish- to grayish-brown, thin, flaky; mature bark dark brown, 3/8–1" thick, with irregular, narrow, rounded ridges; wood light brown, soft, close-grained.

BRANCHES: Spreading to ascending, often arched; twigs yellowish-green to purplish-brown, slender, flexible, ridged; buds cinnamon brown, resinous, 1/4–1/2" long.

LEAVES: Stout, stiff, yellowish-green, evergreen **needles**, 3/4–11/2" **long, straight or slightly twisted**, sharp-pointed, finely toothed; **bundled in 2s** with spreading tips and sheathed bases; needles persist 2–3 years.

CONES: Male and female cones on the same tree; male cones yellow, 1/2–3/4" long, clustered at the base of new shoots; female cones yellowish-brown when mature, shiny, woody, usually **asymmetrical**, 1–3" long, **pointing toward**

branch tips, mostly in 2s and 3s near branch tips; scales serotinous (glued shut with resin), their tips thick, **smooth or with a tiny spine;** seeds dark, 1/8" long with a pale, 3/8" wing, 2 per scale; seed cones mature in 2–3 years but most remain closed for many years or until opened by fire.

HABITAT: Dry, infertile, acidic, often on sandy or rocky soils in glacial outwash plains.

ORIGIN: Native.

EASTERN RED-CEDAR is the most widespread and drought-resistant conifer in eastern North America. It is becoming increasingly common as more and more forests are removed or disturbed by human activities. Breeders have developed many cultivars for use in landscaping. • The beautiful, reddish wood resists decay, is easily worked and takes a fine finish. It has been used for interior trim, sills and posts. Its aromatic oils repel insects, so cedar chests have traditionally been used for storing woolens. Cedar oil, distilled from the wood, has been used as perfume. • Eastern red-cedar lives 200–350 years. Mature females produce some seed every year but bear large crops every 3 years or so. • Many birds use eastern red-cedar for food and cover. Game birds such as quail, grouse, pheasant and wild turkey as well as many songbirds feed on the "berries." Seed-eating birds (especially cedar waxwings) readily disperse the seeds, so that trees often grow in isolated places along bird migration routes. • The French name for this tree, *baton rouge* or "red stick," was given to the capital city of Louisiana.

ALSO CALLED: Northern red-cedar, red-cedar juniper, red juniper, juniper, savin.

SIZE AND SHAPE: Small coniferous trees up to 35' [66'] tall; **crowns conical to almost cylindrical,** irregular with age, highly variable; roots very fibrous and deep.

TRUNKS: Irregular, often buttressed at base, 8–12" [36"] in diameter, branched to near base; bark light reddish-brown, 1/8–1/4" thick, peeling in long, narrow strips; wood reddish, aromatic, brittle, weak, fine-grained.

BRANCHES: Spreading to ascending; twigs light green to reddish-brown, slender, 4-sided.

LEAVES: Evergreen, dark bluish-green (yellowish-brown in winter), of **2 types:** on mature branches, **flat-lying scales** 1/16" **long,** convex, **in overlapping pairs;** and on young branches, **sharp needles** 1/4–1/2" **long,** spreading to erect; both leaf types sometimes on one branch; needles persist 5–6 years.

CONES: Male and female cones usually **on separate trees;** male cones yellowish, 1/8" long; **female cones berry-like, deep blue with a whitish bloom** when mature, 1/8–1/4" long, firm, resinous, aromatic, not splitting open, short-stalked at twig tips; scales thick, fleshy, eventually fused; seeds 1–2 per "berry," light brown, grooved, pitted, about 1/8" long; **"berries" (seed cones) ripen first autumn.**

HABITAT: Dry, open, rocky or sandy sites and abandoned fields.

ORIGIN: Native.

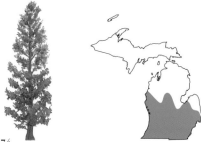

ALTHOUGH CEDAR WOOD is known for its resistance to rot, the trunks of living trees are often hollow from heart-rot. Cedar wood is commonly used for construction in and near water—in cedar-strip canoes, boats, fence posts, shingles and dock posts. The wood also splits easily and has provided rails for many split-rail fences. • This attractive, versatile species provides dense growth in foundation plantings, hedges and windbreaks on both wet and dry sites. Many cultivars are available. • Eastern white-cedar has maximum cone production at 75–150 years of age, with large crops every 3–5 years. Some stunted northern white-cedar trees on limestone cliffs in Ontario, Canada, are over 700 years old, and a 1200-year-old tree was discovered along the St. Lawrence River. • Red squirrels eat cedar buds in spring and later store cone-laden branches in winter caches. The plentiful seeds provide food for pine siskins, goldfinches, redpolls and other winter finches. White-tailed deer occasionally eat the tender branch tips, but the importance of the cedar swamps for wildlife lies mainly in the shelter they provide during severe winters. • Native peoples used northern white-cedar to prevent scurvy and taught this practice to French settlers, giving rise to the name arborvitae, or "tree of life."

ALSO CALLED: Eastern arborvitae, northern white-cedar, eastern thuja, swamp-cedar, tree-of-life, white arborvitae.

SIZE AND SHAPE: Coniferous trees 35–50' [113'] tall; crowns steeple-shaped, compact and "neatly trimmed" (open-grown) to irregular (forest); roots shallow, spreading.

TRUNKS: Often buttressed, knobby and/or curved, 12–24" [86"] in diameter; **mature bark reddish-brown to gray,** 1/4–1/2" thick, **shredding in narrow, flat strips;** wood pale yellowish-brown, fragrant, lightweight, soft.

BRANCHES: Short, wide-spreading, gradually upturned; twigs many, soft, **forming flat, fan-shaped sprays;** buds tiny, protected by leaves.

LEAVES: Dull yellowish-green (sometimes bronze in winter), **scale-like,** evergreen; leaves near branch tips **about** 1/8" long, gland-dotted, overlapping, opposite, **in 4 longitudinal rows** with side leaves folded lengthwise and upper/lower leaves flattened; leaves on older branches lance-shaped, about 1/4" long, glandless; needles persist 1–2 years.

CONES: Male and female cones on the same tree; male cones yellowish, 1/16" long; female cones dry, pale red-brown, 1/4–1/2" long, upright at branch tips; **scales in 4–6 overlapping pairs,** middle ones producing 2–3 seeds; seeds light brown, about 1/8" long, with 2 narrow wings about 1/2 as long as the body; seed cones produced in April–May, release seeds that autumn, drop over several months.

HABITAT: Swampy ground to dry limestone outcrops; prefers **cool, humid habitats** with high snowfall and calcium-rich soils; very shade tolerant.

ORIGIN: Native.

TAMARISKS are easily recognized as a group, but species classification is complex and often controversial. Of the deciduous tamarisks introduced to North America, trees with 5-parted flowers belong to a complex of several salt-cedar species (generally called **T. ramosissima**), and trees with 4-parted flowers are *T. parviflora*. In land management, deciduous tamarisks are usually treated as a group. • These hardy, attractive shrubs have been widely planted as ornamentals for their unusual foliage and springtime haze of profuse flowers. Tamarisks are also hardy subjects for windbreaks and erosion control. They are relatively long-lived, spreading rapidly via massive quantities of seeds and sprouting stem fragments. Once established, they tolerate drought and saline soils (though small-flowered tamarisk is less salt tolerant). Such hardy, prolific trees can become aggressive invaders, especially where human activities have altered flooding, salinity, soil texture and vegetation. In the western U.S., up to 1 million acres have been invaded by tamarisk. Tamarisk escapes only occasionally in Michigan, but it should be carefully monitored. • Historically, tamarisks are best known for the ability of some species (not *T. parviflora*) to exude sugary sap when punctured by insects. This sweet gum is believed to be the Biblical manna. It can be gathered by shaking branches over sheets and is used as a sweetener.

ALSO CALLED: Salt-cedar.

SIZE AND SHAPE: Tall shrubs or small trees 10–20' tall; crowns broad to sprawling; deep taproot.

TRUNKS: Clumped, slender; mature bark brown to dark purplish with horizontal pores (lenticels).

BRANCHES: Few, arching, twiggy, **feathery** in appearance; twigs purple, as **fine as thread and very wiry**, completely covered by scale-like leaves.

LEAVES: Alternate, deciduous, scale-like, lance-shaped, about 1/8" long, with thin, membranous edges, **overlapping, sheathing,** forming feathery sprays; leaves faded green to yellow in fall.

FLOWERS: Pale pink, bisexual, tiny; 4-parted (4 sepals, 4 petals, 4 stamens); petals separate, about 1/16" long, often persistent on fruits; ovaries single, with the stamens, nectary disc, petals and sepals attached at the base; flowers in enormous numbers, borne in elongated clusters (racemes) 3/4–2" long, grouped in **feathery, branched clusters** (panicles), appear in early May–early June (may be found at any time of year in some regions).

FRUITS: Cone-shaped capsules, about 1/8" long, splitting into 3–4 parts (valves), fairly inconspicuous; seeds numerous, tiny, **tipped with a tuft of tiny, 1-celled hairs;** capsules faded green to slightly yellow in autumn.

HABITAT: Dry roadsides; low areas near shores and wetlands farther west.

ORIGIN: Introduced from the northeastern Mediterranean region.

Alternate Broad Leaves

TULIP-TREE is a valuable hardwood timber tree in the U.S. The easily worked wood has been used in interior finishing, cabinet making, construction and pulp and paper, as well as for making furniture, musical instruments and plywood. • Native peoples used the tall, straight trunks to make large canoes, some capable of carrying 20 people or more, and used the sharp-tasting roots to treat rheumatism and fevers. • This large, fast-growing, attractive tree is occasionally used in landscaping in areas beyond its normal range, but it needs plenty of open space to flourish. • Tulip-tree lives about 150 years and usually begins producing flowers and seed when it is 15–20 years old. • Bees gather considerable amounts of nectar from the large flowers. Quail, finches, cardinals, rabbits, red squirrels, gray squirrels, mice and deer eat the abundant seeds. White-tailed deer and rabbits browse on saplings and young trees. • This massive hardwood is sometimes called "Apollo-of-the-woods." Its flowers resemble those of tulips, hence the common name "tulip-tree" and the scientific name *Liriodendron*, from the Greek *leirion*, "lily," and *dendron*, "tree." The specific epithet *tulipifera* means "tulip-bearing."

ALSO CALLED: Tulip-poplar, yellow-poplar, tulip-magnolia, whitewood, Apollo-of-the-woods.

SIZE AND SHAPE: Trees 50–115' [171'] tall; crown compact, cone-shaped; roots deep, spreading.

TRUNKS: Tall, straight, 24–48" [60"] in diameter, 2/3 or more branch-free; young bark with conspicuous, white vertical pores (lenticels); **mature bark ash gray to brown,** with **intersecting, rounded ridges;** wood pale yellow, fine-grained, lightweight.

BRANCHES: Stout; twigs smooth, brittle; **buds**

dark red, flat, duckbill-shaped, with 2 scales meeting at the edges, **about 1/2" long** at twig tips (smaller below), powdery.

LEAVES: Alternate, simple, deciduous; blades bright green above and paler beneath, 2 3/4–6" long, with **squared, notched tips** and 2–3-lobed sides; stalks often longer than blades; stipules large (in spring), leaving a thin scar encircling the twig; leaves yellow in autumn.

FLOWERS: Showy, tulip-shaped, 1 1/2–2" wide, single at branch tips, bisexual; petals 6, **pale greenish-yellow with orange bases,** erect, each 1 1/2–2 3/8" long and 3/4–1 1/8" wide; sepals 3, large, green; stamens many, flattened; carpels pale yellow, numerous, in a "cone" at the flower's center; flowers in May–June (after leaves expand).

FRUITS: Dry, **green to straw-colored,** long-winged, 1–2-seeded nutlets (samaras), 1 1/8–2" long, overlapping in **cone-like clusters 2–3" long;** most fruits drop in autumn, leaving erect central stalks at branch tips.

HABITAT: Sheltered sites with deep, rich, moist but well-drained soils.

ORIGIN: Native.

THIS SMALL TREE is occasionally planted for its attractive form, large leaves, unusual (though fetid) flowers and juicy fruits. Pawpaw thrives in rich, moist soils along rivers and at the edges of wetlands. It often forms dense colonies from suckers and is easily propagated from root cuttings. The dark color and foul fragrance of the flowers suggest that flies are its chief pollinators. • Native peoples gathered the fleshy, edible fruits, but pawpaws are seldom eaten today. The flavor varies greatly from site to site, deteriorating gradually from south to north. It has been likened to that of bananas, pineapples, apples, custard, cream and even eau-de-cologne and turpentine. Pawpaws with orange flesh are said to be more flavorful than yellow-fleshed varieties. • Early settlers used the ripe pulp for making a yellow dye. • Ripe pawpaw fruits can be hard to find, because many animals, including raccoons, opossums, squirrels, bears (historically) and wild turkeys, enjoy the sweet, juicy flesh. • The generic name *Asimina* was taken from a Native name for pawpaw, *assimin*. The specific epithet *triloba* means "3-lobed" and refers to the flower parts, which are grouped in 3s.

ALSO CALLED: Common pawpaw, Michigan banana, false banana, pawpaw custard-apple, tall pawpaw.

SIZE AND SHAPE: Large shrubs or small trees 10–25' [48'] tall; crowns broad; spreading roots sprout to form colonies.

TRUNKS: Single, short, 2–8" [11"] in diameter; mature bark blotched, thin, with warty bumps; wood pale yellow, often red- or brown-streaked, lightweight, soft.

BRANCHES: Straight, spreading; twigs rusty-hairy when young, slender, zigzagged; pith banded (in long-section); **buds reddish-hairy, lacking scales, flattened,** about 1/8" long; tip bud 1/4–3/8" long.

LEAVES: Alternate, simple, deciduous; **blades 4–12" long, hanging near branch tips,** green above, paler with reddish-brown veins beneath, foul-smelling (like motor oil) when crushed, **widest toward tips, tapered to bases,** with **prominent veins looped to adjacent veins at their tips; stalks** 1/4–3/4" **long,** grooved; leaf scars crescent-shaped around a bud.

FLOWERS: Reddish-purple or maroon to pale greenish-yellow, fetid-smelling, 11/8–11/2" wide, broadly bell-shaped, single or in small clusters, bisexual; petals 6 (3 large, 3 small), veiny; sepals 3; flowers in May–June (before or as leaves expand).

FRUITS: Large berries 11/2–6" **long,** yellowish at first, **dark brown with soft, yellow to orange flesh when ripe,** fragrant, cylindrical to pear-shaped, hanging along year-old twigs; **seeds bean-like,** dark brown, flattened, 1/2–11/8" long, several in 1–2 rows; fruits mature in September–October.

HABITAT: Floodplains, dunes and moist woodlands with moist sandy or clayey soils.

ORIGIN: Native.

THE LIGHT, BRITTLE WOOD OF SASSAFRAS has no commercial value, but the bark produces an orange dye and the roots yield aromatic "oil of sassafras," which has been used as a fragrance in soaps and perfumes. • Sassafras bark was traditionally used to make a fragrant, invigorating tea and to flavor root beer. It was also added to some patent medicines. Sassafras roots were once believed to have great healing powers, but these claims proved false. **Caution:** Dried sassafras bark, available in health-food and gourmet stores, should be used with extreme caution, if at all. It contains safrole, a carcinogenic compound banned for use in foods in the U.S. and Canada. • This moderately fast-growing tree can flower after only 10 years, with good seed crops every 2–3 years. Sassafras often forms dense colonies by sending up new shoots (suckers) from underground runners. Such vegetative reproduction, as well as seed dispersal (usually by birds), allows

sassafras to quickly colonize disturbed habitats such as abandoned fields. • Wild turkeys, bobwhites, squirrels, black bears and foxes occasionally feed on the fruits of sassafras.

ALSO CALLED: White sassafras, cinnamonwood, greenstick, mitten-tree, benzoin tree.

SIZE AND SHAPE: Large shrubs or small to medium trees 15–50' [78'] tall; crowns cylindrical, flat-topped; roots wide-spreading.

TRUNKS: Branched from near base, 8–24" [58"] in diameter, **zigzagged; bark fragrant,** dark brown, with **corky ridges;** wood fragrant, orange-brown to yellow, soft, light, coarse-grained, weak.

BRANCHES: Crooked, wide-spreading with upturned tips, corky-ridged; twigs glossy purplish

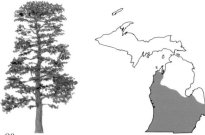

or light green, brittle, **often with side-shoots longer than branch tips;** buds greenish, plump, several-scaled, 1/4–1/2" long at twig tips (smaller below).

LEAVES: Alternate, simple, deciduous, fragrant; blades bright green, **ovate or broadly 2- or 3-lobed** (all 3 shapes usually present), **3–8" long,** 2–4" wide; **leaves yellow to pink or red in autumn.**

FLOWERS: Greenish-yellow, about 1/4" across, inconspicuous; unisexual with male and female flowers usually on separate trees; tepals 6; flowers in loose, **stalked clusters** at the base of new shoots, in late May (with leaves).

FRUITS: Dark blue, berry-like drupes, 3/8–1/2" across, each sitting in a bright red cup at the tip of a **club-shaped, red, 1 3/8–1 1/2" long stalk;** seeds single, large, brown stones; drupes ripen September–October.

HABITAT: Dry to moderately moist, open, usually disturbed sites such as fence lines, old pastures and roadsides, mostly on sandy, acidic soils.

ORIGIN: Native.

ALL PARTS OF SPICEBUSH, especially the bark and berries, have an agreeable spicy fragrance and flavor. During the Revolutionary War (1775–83), the fruits were dried and powdered as a substitute for allspice, which had previously been imported from England. Similarly, people in the blockaded South used spicebush leaves and twigs as a substitute for foreign teas during the Civil War (1861–65). In spring, the flowers added extra sweetness. • Pioneers used the aromatic oil in liniments for treating bruises, sore muscles, aching joints and neuralgia. In the 1800s, spicebush leaves and berries were sold as a stimulant and tonic for treating fevers, colds, coughs, indigestion and general aches and pains, as well as for expelling intestinal worms. Although there is little to validate medicinal claims, bark extracts have been shown to inhibit *Candida albicans* (the yeast-like fungus that causes thrush and yeast infections). • The specific epithet *benzoin* refers to the plant's distinctive aroma, which is similar to the vanilla-like fragrance of benzoin tree (*Styrax benzoin*), an Asian plant that was the major source of benzoin. • This hardy native is an excellent ornamental, valued for its showy, early spring flowers, yellow autumn leaves and bright red "berries." • Caterpillars of the lovely promethea moth (*Callosamia promethea*) and the green-clouded swallowtail (*Pterourus troilus*) feed on spicebush and sassafras (p. 80) leaves.

ALSO CALLED: wild-allspice, spicewood, fever-bush, snap-bush, Benjamin-bush • *Benzoin aestivale.*

SIZE AND SHAPE: Aromatic shrubs up to 15' [23'] tall; crowns round to flat-topped, open; roots shallow.

TRUNKS: Several, clumped, up to 3" in diameter; bark thin.

BRANCHES: Numerous, arched; twigs slender, brittle, aromatic, green to olive brown, with pale, corky pores (lenticels); buds small, green, egg-shaped, placed one above another at joints, absent at branch tips; flower bud clusters conspicuous in fall and winter.

LEAVES: Alternate, simple, deciduous, variable in size, usually largest at branch tips; blades light green above, paler beneath, thin, hairless, with prominent veins, **ovate to elliptic, usually broadest above the middle,** 2–6" long, pointed, tapered to a wedge-shaped base, **smooth-edged;** stalks 1/4–3/4" long; leaves yellow in autumn.

FLOWERS: Honey yellow, fragrant, 1/4–3/8" across, with **male and female flowers on separate trees;** tepals 6, soon shed; flowers numerous, on short stalks in **dense,** 3/4" **wide clusters** at joints on previous year's twigs, in March–May (before leaves expand).

FRUITS: Bright red, spicy-smelling, berry-like drupes, football-shaped, 1/4–1/2" long; seeds single, in small stones; **drupes in small, compact clusters,** mature September–November.

HABITAT: Rich, moist deciduous forests and deciduous swamps.

ORIGIN: Native.

AMERICAN SYCAMORE wood has been used for cabinet making, furniture, boxes, interior trim and butchers' chopping blocks. Early French settlers hollowed out large sycamore trunks to make barges capable of carrying several tons of freight. • American sycamore lives up to 250 years. This fast-growing tree is among the largest in the eastern deciduous forest. It can reach 65–80' in height by 20 years of age and may eventually exceed 115'. Trunks can reach 15' in diameter. • The small, stiffly hairy seeds are carried to new sites by wind and water. American sycamore is moderately shade-tolerant, but the seeds require light to germinate. • Seed-eating birds seldom feed on sycamore seeds, but some small rodents gather them. • American sycamore is sometimes planted as an ornamental shade tree, often outside its natural range. The London plane (*Platanus acerifolia* or *P. hybrida*, most likely a hybrid of *P. occidentalis* and *P. orientalis*) is more widely used in cities because it tolerates pollution and can grow with limited root space. The London plane is distinguished by its more deeply lobed leaves and by its paired flower and fruit clusters. It does not grow wild in Michigan.

ALSO CALLED: Sycamore, buttonball-tree, buttonwood, American plane-tree.

SIZE AND SHAPE: Trees 60–115' tall; crowns irregular, with **massive, crooked branches;** roots wide-spreading.

TRUNKS: Straight, 40–80" in diameter; **bark mottled,** reddish-brown, **jigsaw-like scales flaking off to expose pale inner bark;** wood light reddish-brown, hard, coarse-grained, weak.

BRANCHES: Stout, spreading; twigs slender, zig-zagged; buds shiny reddish-brown, 1/4–3/8" long, **1-scaled**, none at twig tips, covered by leaf stalk bases.

LEAVES: Alternate, simple, deciduous; **blades 4–8" long, slightly wider and bright green above,** paler beneath, hairless (except lower veins), maple leaf–like, **shallowly 3–5-lobed,** coarsely and irregularly toothed; stipules prominent in spring, stipule scars encircling twigs; leaf scars narrow, encircling buds; **leaves orange to orange-brown in autumn.**

FLOWERS: Tiny, in dense heads; unisexual with **male and female flower clusters on separate branchlets of same tree;** male flowers yellowish-green, in "balls" 1/4–3/8" across, along second-year twigs; female flowers dark red, in "balls" 3/8–1/2" across, near older twig tips; flowers in May (with leaves).

FRUITS: Yellowish, seed-like achenes about 3/8" long, brownish-hairy, club-shaped, in **solitary "balls" 3/4–1 3/8" across, on slender stalks 2 3/4–6" long;** fruits mature by October and break apart slowly, some remaining through winter.

HABITAT: Low, wet areas such as floodplains and lakeshores; also on moist, disturbed, upland sites.

ORIGIN: Native.

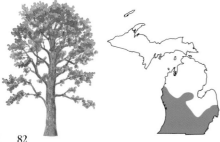

ALTHOUGH THE TRUNKS are too small to provide lumber, evenly forked witch-hazel branches have been used as divining rods for locating underground water and minerals. • Witch-hazel oil, extracted from leaves, twigs and bark, is said to have astringent and sedative properties and to stop bleeding. This volatile oil has been used in liniments, medicines, eyewashes, aftershave lotions and salves for soothing insect bites, burns and poison ivy rashes.

• This slow-growing shrub is sometimes used in landscaping because of its showy, fragrant flowers and interesting, persistent fruits. Unlike other Michigan trees and shrubs, witch-hazel blooms in autumn.

• The name "witch-hazel," suggesting magical powers, probably originated with the divining powers attributed to the branches. The "hazel" in the name refers to the similarities between witch-hazel and the true hazels of the genus *Corylus* (p. 121). The name "snapping-hazel" alludes to the sound the capsules make when they shoot seeds up to 40' from the parent shrub. "Spotted-alder" and "striped-alder" indicate that the bark resembles that of alders (pp. 126–28).

ALSO CALLED: Snapping-hazel, spotted-alder, striped-alder, winterbloom • *H. macrophylla*.

SIZE AND SHAPE: **Shrubby trees** or large, spreading shrubs 12–25' [43'] tall; crowns broad, rounded.

TRUNKS: Usually **2 or more**, crooked, 2–4" [5"] in diameter; bark light brown or grayish, often mottled, thin, with horizontal pores (lenticels); inner bark reddish-purple; wood light brown, hard, heavy.

BRANCHES: Slender; twigs zigzagged; **buds flattened, stalked**, curved, with **dense reddish- to yellowish-brown hairs, lacking scales**, ³/₈–¹/₂" long at twig tips (smaller below).

LEAVES: Simple, alternate, deciduous; blades 2³/₈–6" long, dark green above, paler beneath, hairless (except lower veins), with **asymmetrical bases, wavy-scalloped**, sometimes coarsely toothed, with **5–7 straight, parallel, ascending veins per side;** leaves yellow in autumn.

FLOWERS: Fragrant, small but showy, bisexual; **petals 4, bright yellow, twisted, ribbon-like,** ¹/₂–³/₄" **long;** sepals 4, orange-brown, hairy; in **flowers in 3s** along twigs, in **October–November** (as or after leaves fall).

FRUITS: **Short, thick, 2-beaked capsules** ³/₈–¹/₂" long, light brown and **woody when mature;** seeds 2 per capsule, black, shiny, ¹/₄–³/₈" long; capsules mature the following summer and shoot seeds from capsule tips; **empty capsules often persist** several years.

HABITAT: Moist, shady sites with deep, rich soil to open woodlands with dry, sandy soil.

ORIGIN: Native.

Key to Genera in the Elm Family (Ulmaceae)

1a Leaf blades with 3 main veins at the base; fruits berry-like drupes with thin flesh; branches with chambered pith... *Celtis*, **hackberry** (key to species, below)

1b Leaf blades with many conspicuous pinnate veins; fruits thin samaras; branch pith not chambered... *Ulmus*, **elm** (key to species, below)

Key to the Hackberries (Genus *Celtis*)

1a Leaves distinctly toothed to well below midblade; fruit stalks longer than adjacent leaf stalks; fruits usually purplish-black when ripe; stones to $3/8$" long, conspicuously pitted .... *C. occidentalis*, **common hackberry** (p. 90)

1b Leaves smooth-edged or with scattered teeth above midblade; fruit stalks equal to or slightly shorter than adjacent leaf stalks; fruits brownish when ripe; stones to $1/4$" long, obscurely shallow-pitted.. *C. tenuifolia*, **dwarf hackberry** (p. 91)

Key to the Elms (Genus *Ulmus*)

1a Leaves small ($1^1/8$–$2^3/4$" long), single-toothed, with mostly symmetrical bases .... *U. pumila*, **Siberian elm** (p. 88)

1b Leaves usually larger (often > $2^3/4$" long), double-toothed, with asymmetrical bases **2**

2a Samaras fringed with hairs; leaves relatively smooth on the upper surface, mostly with 15 pairs of side veins.. **3**

2b Samaras not fringed with hairs; leaves very rough on the upper surface, mostly with fewer than 15 pairs of veins **4**

3a Flowers/fruits in tassel-like clusters; samara wings hairless (except for fringe along the edges) .... *U. americana*, **American elm** (p. 85)

3b Flowers/fruits in elongated, branched clusters; samara wings hairy .... *U. thomasii*, **rock elm** (p. 89)

4a Leaves mostly with 12 pairs of side-veins; samaras hairless, about $1/2$" wide, with notch at the tip extending almost to the seedcase...*U. procera*, **English elm** (p. 87)

4b Leaves mostly with 15 pairs of side-veins; samaras hairy or more than $1/2$" wide **5**

5a Leaves 3–6" long, hairless along edges, often 2-lobed near tip, with larger basal lobe curled over stalk; samaras hairless, $3/4$–1" long .... *U. glabra*, **wych elm** (p. 87)

5b Leaves 4–8" long, fringed with fine hairs, neither lobed near tip nor with basal lobe curled over stalk; samaras $3/8$–$1/2$" long, with hairy seedcases .... *U. rubra*, **slippery elm** (p. 86)

ELM WOOD is tough and flexible and keeps well in water, so it has been used to make wharves, boat frames, wheel hubs and spokes, hockey sticks, tool handles, furniture and paneling. Because it is relatively odorless, the wood was used to make crates and barrels for cheeses, fruits and vegetables. Elm wood is seldom used for firewood because it is difficult to split. • This graceful tree was common in parks and along roads and fence lines until Dutch elm disease decimated stands across eastern North America. Caused by the fungi *Ophiostoma ulmi* and *O. novo-ulmi*, this plague arrived in the U.S. in 1930 in infected logs. The fungal spores are carried from tree to tree by small beetles (*Scolytus multistriatus* and *Hylurgopinus rufipes*), which tunnel under the bark to breed. The fungus blocks the flow of water in the trunk, killing the tree within a few years. Many methods have been tested to control Dutch elm dis-

ease, but all have proven either ineffective or too expensive and labor intensive. Attempts to breed disease-resistant trees have had some success, and clones of these trees are available for landscaping.

ALSO CALLED: White elm, gray elm, soft elm, swamp elm, water elm.

SIZE AND SHAPE: Stately trees 65–100' [140'] tall; fan-, umbrella- or **vase-shaped;** crowns broadly rounded.

TRUNKS: Typically with **V-shaped crotches** below crown and buttressed at base, 20–48" [68"] in diameter; bark grayish, with coarse, oblique ridges of **alternating corky, thin, pale layers and thicker, dark layers;** wood pale yellowish-brown, hard, heavy, strong.

BRANCHES: Gracefully arched, often weeping; twigs zigzagged, rarely corky-winged; **buds 6–9-scaled,** reddish-brown, slightly hairy, **lying flat in 2 rows,** absent at twig tips.

LEAVES: Alternate, simple, deciduous, **in 2 vertical rows;** blades 4–6" long, **thick,** usually **slightly rough above, oval,** abruptly pointed, with **rounded, asymmetrical bases;** veins 30–40, **prominent, straight,** ending in sharp double teeth, **0–3 veins with forks;** leaves yellow in autumn.

FLOWERS: Small, bisexual; petals absent; sepals tiny, 6–9; anthers red; pistil single, tiny; flowers hang in **tassel-like clusters** along year-old twigs, appear in March–April (before leaves).

FRUITS: Dry, oval, flat-winged nutlets (samaras) 1/4–1/2" long, with a **membranous wing around a seedcase, deeply notched at the tip, hairy along edges only, hanging on slender stalks in clusters;** samaras drop in May (before leaves expand fully).

HABITAT: Moist bottomlands and protected slopes; also in disturbed, open sites such as pastures and roadsides.

ORIGIN: Native.

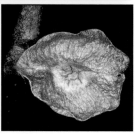

SLIPPERY ELM wood is sometimes sold as American elm but is considered inferior. It has been used to make furniture, paneling, boxes and crates. • This moderately fast-growing species has a life span of about 200 years. Young trees usually start to flower at 15–20 years and produce good seed crops every 2–4 years. • Some tribes used slippery elm bark to cover canoe shells when birch bark was unavailable. Early adventurers chewed the slippery inner bark to relieve thirst. The inner bark was also commonly used in traditional medicine. It was boiled, dried and then ground into a powder, which was used in teas for treating fevers, sore throats and various urinary-tract problems. The slippery juice was sometimes used illegally by baseball players as a lubricant for throwing "spitballs." • Slippery elm seeds provide food for finches and grouse, as well as for chipmunks, squirrels and other small rodents. White-tailed deer and rabbits sometimes browse the twigs. • This elm is less susceptible to Dutch elm disease than the more common American elm (p. 85), but some slippery elm trees still die each year from infection. • The specific epithet *rubra* means "red" and describes the reddish-brown bark and buds.

ALSO CALLED: Red elm, budded elm, moose elm, gray elm, slippery-barked elm, soft elm, sweet elm • *U. fulva.*

SIZE AND SHAPE: Trees 50–80' [90'] tall; somewhat umbrella-shaped; crowns broad, flat-topped; roots wide-spreading.

TRUNKS: Straight, with **U-shaped crotches** below the crown, 12–24" [30"] in diameter; bark reddish-brown, 3/4–1" thick, with irregular ridges of **uniformly brown, corky layers; inner bark fragrant, slimy;** wood reddish-brown, hard, heavy.

BRANCHES: Gradually spreading to arched; **twigs hairy, not corky,** often zigzagged; **buds dark brown, rusty-hairy, blunt,** about 1/4" long, in 2 rows, absent at twig tips.

LEAVES: Alternate, simple, deciduous; blades 4–8" long, **fragrant, thick,** dark green and **very rough above,** paler beneath, **hairy on both sides,** abruptly **long-pointed,** with sharp double teeth and **rounded, asymmetrical bases; veins** prominent, **straight, forked near leaf edge; leaf stalks** 1/4–3/8" **long,** hairy; leaves yellow in autumn.

FLOWERS: Small, bisexual (usually); petals absent; sepals tiny, 5–9, fused in a bell-shaped calyx; anthers dark red, 5–9; pistil single with 2 red stigmas; short-stalked, in **dense, tassel-like clusters** on year-old twigs; flowers in March–April **(before leaves expand).**

FRUITS: Dry, flat, green, winged nutlets (samaras) 3/8–1/2" long, with a membranous wing surrounding each seedcase, **rusty-hairy on seedcases only, shallowly notched at tips,** in **tight clusters;** samaras drop in May (before leaves expand fully).

HABITAT: Moist, fertile sites on low hills and river flats; occasionally on rocky ridges; often on calcium-rich soils.

ORIGIN: Native.

THIS LARGE, SPREADING TREE was introduced in colonial times and is now widely planted across eastern North America. The hard, heavy wood resists splitting and wetting. • "Wych" (pronounced "witch") comes from an Old English word meaning "weak," referring to this tree's branches. The specific epithet *glabra* means "smooth" and refers to the bark, which is smooth even on quite large branches and trunks. The leaves, on the other hand, are relatively harsh and hairy. • Wych elm is very similar to **English elm** (*U. procera*), and some taxonomists believe that these two trees belong to the same species. English elm is distinguished by smaller (³/₈–⁵/₈") fruits, which are notched almost to the seedcase, and leaves with 10–12 (rather than 15) veins per side and smaller basal lobes that do not conceal the stalk. Also, English elm has flowers with shorter (¹/₃₂") stalks and twigs that are often corky-winged. English elm is widely planted in eastern North America and is naturalized in several nearby states and provinces, but not in Michigan. • Wych elm is also similar to slippery elm (p. 86), but slippery elm has smaller (³/₈"), hairy fruits and larger (6–8") leaves, with hairy (not smooth) edges, pointed (not 3-lobed) tips and rounded, asymmetrical bases that do not conceal the leaf stalks.

Photo, bottom right: *U. procera*

ALSO CALLED: Scotch elm • *U. campestris*.

SIZE AND SHAPE: Trees up to 130' tall; crowns broad, oval.

TRUNKS: Straight; bark gray, relatively smooth (for an elm), eventually brownish-gray with fissures and rectangular plates; wood hard, heavy.

BRANCHES: Spreading; twigs reddish-brown, hairy, often zigzagged; **buds hairy, triangular, blunt,** ³/₁₆–¹/₄" long, arranged in **2 rows.**

LEAVES: Alternate, simple, deciduous; **blades thick,** 3¹/₈–6¹/₄" long, deep green and **very rough above,** paler and **hairy beneath, often with a lobe to each side of the pointed tip,** bases rounded and **strongly asymmetrical with 1 side curled over the stalk,** edged with **hairless, sharp, double teeth; veins straight,** prominent; **stalks short, almost concealed.**

FLOWERS: Small, bisexual; petals absent; sepals tiny; stamens 3–5; borne on ¹/₁₆–¹/₈" long stalks, in **dense,** ³/₈" long, tassel-like clusters on year-old twigs; flowers in March (**before leaves expand**).

FRUITS: Greenish to pale brown, **hairless,** dry, flat, winged nutlets (samaras) ³/₄–1" long, with a **broad, membranous wing** around a seedcase, notched at tips, in **tassel-like clusters;** drop in July.

HABITAT: Moist sites along roadsides and forest edges.

ORIGIN: Introduced from Europe and western Asia.

THIS FAST-GROWING, moderately long-lived tree was introduced to North America from eastern Asia in the 1860s and now grows wild in most states and provinces across the continent. These hardy trees are capable of surviving extreme cold and long summer droughts, so they were often planted as windbreaks on the Great Plains. Siberian elm is also highly resistant to Dutch elm disease. On the negative side, these trees shed dead branches throughout the year and their limbs snap easily under the weight of ice or heavy snow. Also, Siberian elms are highly susceptible to attacks from elm leaf beetles (*Pyrrhalta luteola*). • This tree is readily identified by its small (1¹/₈–2³/₄"), single-toothed, almost symmetrical leaves. • Siberian elm is sometimes called Chinese elm, but that name correctly applies to another Asian tree, *U. parvifolia*, which is rarely planted in Michigan. The leaves of these 2 species are somewhat similar, but those of Chinese elm remain green later in the autumn and have more-rounded teeth. Also, Chinese elm produces flowers and wingless fruits in autumn (rather than spring), and it has relatively smooth (not furrowed), platy bark.

ALSO CALLED: Chinese elm (in error).

SIZE AND SHAPE: Shrubby trees 35–80' [122'] tall; crowns irregular, domed; roots wide-spreading.

TRUNKS: Short, 12–24" [71"] in diameter; **bark dark gray,** rough, deeply fissured between broad, interlacing ridges, **inner layers orange,** outer layers solid brown; wood hard, heavy.

BRANCHES: Large, wide-spreading, often dead within the crown; **twigs brittle,** slender, green to gray, zigzagged; buds ¹/₁₆–¹/₈" long, dark reddish-brown, with hairs along scale edges, in 2 rows, absent at twig tips.

LEAVES: Alternate, simple, deciduous; blades lustrous dark green, **hairless** except on veins underneath, ³/₄–2³/₄" **long,** elliptic, **nearly symmetrical,** edged with sharp, mostly **single teeth;** veins prominent, straight, about 10–12 per side, a few forked; **stalks about** ¹/₈" **long;** leaves yellow in autumn.

FLOWERS: About ¹/₈" wide on very short stalks, bisexual (mostly); petals absent; sepals tiny, fused in bell-shaped calyxes; stamens 4–5, purple; flowers in **compact tassel-like clusters** on year-old twigs, in March–April (before leaves expand).

FRUITS: Round, greenish, **hairless, winged nutlets** (samaras), ³/₈–¹/₂" across, in dense, tassel-like clusters; nutlets with a broad, membranous wing **tipped with a deep, closed notch;** samaras drop in April–May (before leaves expand fully).

HABITAT: Disturbed, open sites such as roadsides, fence lines and abandoned lots.

ORIGIN: Introduced from Siberia and northern China; widely spreading from cultivation in Michigan.

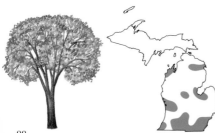

ROCK ELM has the heaviest, toughest wood of any elm. In the 1800s, it was exported to England for use in ship-building. It was also used for auto-mobile chassis and plows before steel became widely used. In North America, rock elm has been used for con-struction and in furniture, piano frames, tool handles and hockey sticks. Unfortunately, this strong, hard wood is no longer readily available. • This moderately fast-growing tree lives 125–300 years. It begins to flower after 20–25 years and pro-duces good seed crops every 2–3 years. Regeneration in the wild is slow. Seedlings can tolerate some shade, but they need full sunlight to grow quickly. Saplings may persevere for several decades in the forest understory, waiting to fill new openings in the canopy. • Rock elm seeds provide food for many birds, including pheasants, grouse and wood ducks. Beavers and muskrats sometimes eat the bark, and white-tailed deer, squirrels, chipmunks and other small mam-mals feed on the twigs, buds and seeds. • Like most elms, rock elm is vulnerable to Dutch elm disease.

ALSO CALLED: Cork elm, winged elm
• *U. racemosa*.

SIZE AND SHAPE: Rough, shaggy-looking trees 50–80' [117'] tall; crowns narrow, oblong, rounded; roots wide-spreading.

TRUNKS: Straight, undivided, 12–24" [64"] in diameter; bark shaggy, with interlacing, **corky ridges of alternating layers of thin, pale scales and thicker, dark scales;** wood light brown, fine-grained, hard, heavy, strong.

BRANCHES: Short, almost horizontal, often drooping, gnarled and **corky-ridged;** twigs develop 2–4 corky, wing-like ridges in first year; **buds chestnut brown, sharp-pointed,** about 1/4" long, **pointing outward** in 2 rows, with fringed scales.

LEAVES: Alternate, simple, deciduous; blades 2–51/2" long, **thick, shiny, dark green above,** paler and somewhat hairy beneath; **tips abruptly pointed, rounded and asymmetrical;** veins about 40, **rarely forked,** ending in sharp, **incurved teeth; stalks about 1/4" long;** leaves bright yellow in autumn.

FLOWERS: Reddish-green, small, bisexual (mostly);

petals absent; sepals tiny, 7–8; flowers borne on year-old twigs, hang in **small clusters with slender central stalks,** in April–May **(before leaves expand)**.

FRUITS: Dry, flat, hairy, indistinctly winged nut-lets (samaras) 3/8–3/4" long, tapered to both ends, shallowly notched at the tip; samaras hang in elongated clusters, drop by May (before leaves expand fully).

HABITAT: Varied, ranging from moist, well-drained forests to drier sites with calcium-rich soils.

ORIGIN: Native.

THIS HARDY NATIVE TREE, with its broad crown and spreading branches, is used as a shade tree in landscaping in some areas. Common hackberry usually grows as a tree and lacks the shrubby stage, except under unusual conditions. It is easily transplanted and readily sends up suckers after cutting or burning. • Common hackberry can live 150–200 years. The tiny, wind-pollinated flowers produce good crops of fruit most years. • Hackberry wood has an attractive grain, but it is weak and has little commercial value. Settlers in Illinois used it to produce a medicine for treating jaundice. • The small, somewhat acidic "berries" are edible but are not widely used by people. Instead, they are usually eaten by game birds and small mammals. • Common hackberry is quite susceptible to attack by parasites, especially in late summer. Leaves are often deformed by nipple-galls or turn prematurely brown from lace-bug (Tingidae spp.) infestations. The caterpillars of three butterflies (*Asterocampa celtis, A. clyton* and *Libytheana bachmannii*) commonly feed on the leaves. • The largest common hackberry tree in the U.S. is a Michigan specimen from Wayland in Allegan County. This giant is 118' tall, with a crown 104' across.

ALSO CALLED: Northern hackberry, sugarberry, western hackberry, bastard-elm, nettle-tree, American hackberry.

SIZE AND SHAPE: Small trees 15–65' (rarely to 110') tall; crowns broad, rounded.

TRUNKS: Short, forked, 8–24" in diameter; bark pale brown to silver gray, with **wart-like bumps on irregular corky ridges;** wood brown, heavy, coarse-textured, weak.

BRANCHES: Ascending to spreading, often with drooping tips; twigs slender, zigzagged, finely hairy; pith banded with cavities visible in long-section;

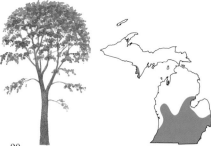

buds 1/8–1/4" long, 5–6-scaled, pointed, flattened, **in 2 rows** (absent at twig tips).

LEAVES: Alternate, simple, deciduous; blades 1 1/2–4 3/4" long, **bluish-green, smooth to slightly roughened above,** paler and hairy on **lacy network of veins** beneath, papery, bases **asymmetrical,** tips tapered to abruptly curved, **15–40 coarse, sharp teeth per side;** leaves light yellow in autumn.

FLOWERS: Small, greenish; unisexual with male and female flowers on the same tree; petals absent; sepals 4–5; male flowers 4–5-stamened, clustered below new shoots; female flowers with 1 pistil, 1–3 in new leaf axils; flowers in April–May (as leaves expand).

FRUITS: Dark olive-purple to purplish-black, **berry-like drupes** about 1/4" long, on slender stalks 5/16–9/16" long, wrinkled and prune-like with age; seeds single, in slightly egg-shaped, pitted (dimpled) stones; drupes mature and drop in September–October.

HABITAT: Moist, shady sites along rivers and streams; often associated with periodic flooding; rarely in upland sites.

ORIGIN: Native.

THIS SMALL, SHRUBBY TREE is one of our rarest and most easily overlooked woody plants. Dwarf hackberry is primarily a southern shrub ranging from Texas and Florida to Illinois and Pennsylvania, but rare, disjunct populations have been found in northern Indiana, southern Michigan, northern Ohio and southern Ontario. It was first discovered in Michigan in 1971, but several additional populations have been found in the state. • Mite (*Eriophyes* spp.) infestations combined with powdery mildew (*Sphaerotheca phytophila*) produce bushy growths (witch's brooms) that are easily recognized in winter. • In the past, dwarf hackberry was considered a variety of common hackberry. However, when the two grow together, the plants remain distinctive, without integration, supporting their classification as two species. • Many features distinguish dwarf hackberry from common hackberry (p. 90). Dwarf hackberry is a bushy, irregular shrub with short, stiff, intertwined twigs that often have spine-like tips (not a symmetrical tree with few, lax branches). Its leaves are leathery, ovate, slender-pointed, equal to slightly asymmetrical at the base, impressed with veins and often partly or entirely smooth-edged (not papery, lance-shaped, with a slender abruptly curved tip, a strongly asymmetrical base, relatively smooth surfaced and uniformly toothed). Also, dwarf hackberry fruits are pink-tinged, smooth and sweet with smooth, round pits (not purple-tinged, puckered and tasteless to slightly bitter, with angled, ridged pits).

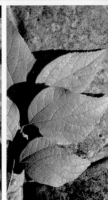

ALSO CALLED: Small sugarberry, monkey nuts, Georgia hackberry, upland hackberry • *C. georgiana.*

SIZE AND SHAPE: Tall shrubs or occasionally small trees, 4–20' (rarely to 65') tall; **crowns irregular.**

TRUNKS: Usually 2 or more; bark pale brown to grayish, with **wart-like bumps and corky ridges;** wood brown, heavy, coarse-textured, weak.

BRANCHES: Widely spreading, numerous; twigs stiff, spreading and intertwined, **somewhat spine-like at tips;** pith banded with cavities, (visible in long-section); buds ¹/₈–¹/₄" long, 5–6-scaled, flattened, **in 2 rows** (absent at twig tips).

LEAVES: Alternate, simple, deciduous; blades 3¹/₂–6¹/₄" long, leathery, **with impressed veins above,** paler and hairy beneath, ovate, **bases symmetrical or slightly uneven,** tips tapered to pointed, **smooth-edged to partly or entirely sharp-toothed;** leaves light yellow in autumn.

FLOWERS: Small, greenish; unisexual with male and female flowers on the same tree; petals absent; sepals 4–5; male flowers 4–5-stamened, clustered below new shoots; female flowers with 1 pistil, 1–3 in new leaf axils; flowers in April–May (as leaves expand).

FRUITS: Salmon-colored to brownish, **berry-like drupes** about ¹/₄" long, on stalks ¹/₈–¹/₄" long, **smooth with age;** seeds single, in smooth, round stones; drupes mature late, often persist to early spring.

HABITAT: Dry upland sites on moraines, dunes and limestone outcrops; common in old fields, hedgerows and roadsides.

ORIGIN: Native.

THE TOUGH, DURABLE WOOD of the Osage-orange has little commercial value because the trunks are small. The wood does, however, make excellent fuel, and the Osage people used it for making bows. The roots and bark have been used to produce a yellow dye for coloring baskets, cloth and leather. The bark is also rich in tannins and has been used in tanning leather. The strong-smelling fruits can be uses as a cockroach repellent.
• This attractive, shade-intolerant tree thrives in a broad range of environments, often surviving stressful conditions. It was once widely planted as an ornamental and in windbreaks and hedgerows in eastern North America. • Once established, Osage-orange spreads readily from sprouting roots and can be difficult to eradicate. The juicy fruits resemble green oranges, but they are not edible. Cleaning up the heavy, fleshy fruits can be a messy chore each year. The tree's sap may cause skin reactions. • Despite its sizable fruits, this tree is of little importance to wildlife. Squirrels and foxes may occasionally tear apart the pulpy balls to eat the seeds, but most animals avoid this messy snack.
• The specific epithet *pomifera* means "apple-bearing" and refers to the large, apple-shaped fruits.

ALSO CALLED: Hedge-apple, bodark, bowwood.

SIZE AND SHAPE: Small, **thorny trees** 15–40' [50'] tall, with **milky sap;** crowns irregular, rounded; roots wide-spreading, deep, with **peeling, orange bark.**

TRUNKS: Soon branched, 12–24" [53"] in diameter; bark orange-brown, irregularly ridged; **wood bright orange,** heavy, hard.

BRANCHES: Stout, few, curved; twigs green to light orange-brown, zigzagged, slender, soon armed with **stout thorns; buds tiny,** brown, partly embedded in twigs, none at branch tips.

LEAVES: Alternate, simple, deciduous; blades 2³/₈–4³/₄" long, 2–2³/₄" wide, **thick, shiny, dark green above,** paler beneath, slender-pointed, **smooth-edged;** stalks slender, 1¹/₈–2³/₈" long; leaves yellow in autumn.

FLOWERS: Tiny, without petals; **in dense, round clusters** at the tips of slender stalks; unisexual with male and female flowers on separate trees; male clusters 1–1¹/₂" across; female clusters ³/₄–1" across; flowers in May–June.

FRUITS: Green, 4–5¹/₂" wide, dimpled, fleshy or pulpy aggregates of many tiny fruits (achenes), containing bitter, milky juice; seeds small, flattened, embedded in flesh; fruits mature in September–October.

HABITAT: Prefers lowland sites with rich, deep soils but tolerates a wide range of conditions including hedgerows.

ORIGIN: Introduced from south-central U.S.; usually in former hedgerows, with limited spread by seed.

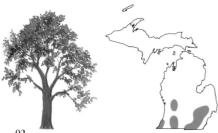

THE LEAVES of white mulberry are the main source of food for silkworms in eastern Asia. The milky juice is rich in rubber-like compounds said to add strength to the silk fibers spun by the worms. The silk industry has been especially important in China, and in that country, white mulberry has been cultivated for thousands of years. In order to accommodate the silkworms, the trees are repeatedly pruned back to the trunk (pollarded), in order to stimulate a dense head of leafy shoots. • Mulberry shrubs were first brought to North America along with silkworms, in an attempt to establish a western silk industry. This ambitious under-

taking failed, but these hardy trees have thrived and spread across eastern and southern North America. • White mulberry grows well in urban centers, and it is often used for landscaping. 'Pendula,' an attractive cultivar with drooping branches, is especially popular as an ornamental. • The Chinese and Japanese use white mulberry wood for decorative carving. In North America, this wood has also been used to make fences and boats. • The genus name *Morus* is derived from *morea*, the classical Latin name for these trees. The specific epithet *alba* means "white" and refers to the whitish fruits.

SIZE AND SHAPE: Small trees 15–50' [76'] tall, with **milky sap; crowns bushy,** spreading; roots wide-spreading.

TRUNKS: Short, 8–36" [60"] in diameter; mature bark pale grayish to yellowish-brown with **orange inner layers,** furrowed.

BRANCHES: Stout, spreading; **twigs slender, light orange-brown;** buds plump, red-brown, about ⅛" long, in 2 rows along twigs.

LEAVES: Alternate, simple, deciduous; blades light green, **lustrous, essentially hairless, coarsely toothed, unlobed to variously lobed,** 2–4" long, widest below the middle, curved to a broad, wedge-shaped tip; leaves yellow in autumn.

FLOWERS: Tiny, without petals, green; unisexual with male and female flowers in separate clusters on the same tree (usually) or on separate trees; male clusters loose and elongated; female clusters short, dense and cylindrical; flowers in May–June.

FRUITS: White, reddish or purplish to blackish, rounded, **blackberry-like; clusters** (multiple fruits) ⅜–¾" **long,** composed of tiny seed-like fruits (achenes) each surrounded by a small, juicy segment; fruits mature June–July.

HABITAT: Open, upland sites, along streams, fences and railroads and in woods.

ORIGIN: Introduced from eastern Asia; grows wild in much of the eastern U.S.

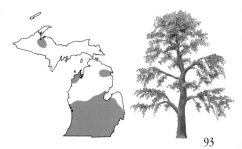

93

RED MULBERRY is rare in Michigan and Ontario, where it reaches the northern limit of its range. It is the only mulberry native to the state. In some nearby regions (e.g., southern Ontario), red mulberry frequently hybridizes with its European cousin, white mulberry (p. 93). Under these circumstances, genetic alteration is probably the single greatest threat to the species. Hybrids are often difficult to identify. • Mulberry wood is very durable, so it has been used to make fence posts and barrels. • The sweet, juicy, ripe fruits are best fresh (though some people find them seedy), but they can also be baked in pies and cakes. • **Caution:** Green mulberry fruits cause stomach upset. Some people develop skin reactions from contact with mulberry leaves and branches.

• Many birds and small mammals such as raccoons and squirrels feed on mulberries and help to disperse the seeds.

• This attractive, fast-growing species could be planted as an ornamental or fruit tree but requires sufficient space to accommodate its spreading branches.

• At first glance, these trees, with their mostly unlobed leaves and relatively few fruits, might not be recognized as mulberries. The leaves are very similar to those of American basswood (p. 207), but basswood leaves have hairless, clearly asymmetrical blades.

SIZE AND SHAPE: Small trees with **milky sap,** 15–35' [56'] tall, up to 60' in forests; crowns dense, broad and rounded.

TRUNKS: Short, 4–14" [55"] in diameter; **mature bark dark reddish-brown, thin, with long, flaky strips;** wood pale orange, soft, weak, light.

BRANCHES: Spreading, stout; twigs green to gray-brown or reddish-brown; buds plump, about ¼" long, lustrous brown, in 2 rows along twigs, none at branch tips.

LEAVES: Alternate, simple, deciduous; blades thin, **dull yellowish-green and sandpapery above, soft-hairy beneath, unlobed to broadly 2–5-lobed,** 2¾–5" long, abruptly tapered to a long-pointed tip, notched and **3-veined at the base,** coarsely sharp-toothed; leaves yellow in autumn.

FLOWERS: Tiny, green, without petals; unisexual with male and female flowers in separate clusters on separate trees, on the same tree or mixed in the same cluster (occasionally); male clusters loose, elongated, ¾–2" long; female clusters dense and short, about ¾" long; flowers in May–early June (before or with leaves).

FRUITS: Red to dark purple or almost black, cylindrical, blackberry-like clusters (multiple fruits) ¾–1⅛" long, composed of tiny seed-like fruits (achenes), each surrounded by a small, juicy segment; fruits mature July.

HABITAT: Moist, rich sites on floodplains and in valleys.

ORIGIN: Native.

Key to Genera in the Walnut Family (Juglandaceae)

1a Leaflets usually 5–9, with the tip leaflet largest; branch pith uniform, lacking horizontal partitions (in long-section); fruit husks splitting into 4 parts
.... *Carya*, **hickory** (key to species, below)

1b Leaflets usually at least 11 (except *J. regia*), those near midleaf largest; branch pith with horizontal partitions (visible in long-section); fruit husks not splitting open
.... *Juglans*, **walnut** (key to species, below)

Key to the Hickories (Genus *Carya*)

1a Bud scales 2–4, bright yellow, paired, not overlapping; leaflets usually at least 9; fruit husks prominently keeled along sutures .... *C. cordiformis*, **bitternut hickory** (p. 101)

1b Bud scales up to 12, tan to brown, overlapping; leaflets usually 5–7; fruit husks lacking prominent keels **2**

2a Branch-tip buds $1/2$–1" long; fruits large (often >$1^3/8$" long), with $1/8$–$1/2$" thick husks soon splitting almost to the base to reveal a 4–6-sided nut **3**

2b Branch-tip buds rarely more than $3/8$" long; fruits smaller (mostly <$1^3/8$"), with thin (<$3/16$" thick) husks **4**

3a Leaflets 5 (rarely 7), fringed with hairs when young, essentially hairless beneath when mature but the teeth often tipped with tiny tufts of hair; fruits $3/4$–$1^1/2$" (rarely 2") long, single or paired
.... *C. ovata*, **shagbark hickory** (p. 99)

3b Leaflets 7 or 9, with permanently hairy lower surfaces; fruits $1^1/2$–$2^3/4$" long, in small clusters
.... *C. laciniosa*, **shellbark hickory** (p. 98)

4a Leaf blades and stalks hairless or blades hairy beneath, along the veins; leaflets 5 (rarely 7); twigs reddish-brown, hairless; mature bark close (not shaggy); fruit husks shiny, dark brown, sometimes slowly splitting open along 1–2 lines (if at all)
.... *C. glabra*, **pignut hickory** (p. 100)

4b Leaves and twigs scurfy, with yellowish scales; leaflets usually 7; mature bark often shaggy in small plates; fruit husks dull pale brown, promptly splitting in 4
.... *C. ovalis*, **red hickory** (p. 100)

Key to the Walnuts (Genus *Juglans*)

1a Leaves with 5–9 smooth-edged leaflets; introduced tree, occasionally escaped from cultivation
.... *J. regia*, **English walnut** (p. 97)

1b Leaves with 11–22 finely toothed leaflets; native tree **2**

2a Leaf stalks, young twigs and fruits sticky-downy; fruits oblong-egg-shaped and somewhat pointed; twig pith chocolate brown..................... *J. cinerea*, **butternut** (p. 96)

2b Leaf stalks, young twigs and fruits finely short-hairy or slightly downy, but scarcely sticky; fruits almost spherical; twig pith tan to cream-colored............... *J. nigra*, **black walnut** (p. 97)

BUTTERNUTS are difficult to shell, and resins in the husks stain hands and clothing, but the sweet, oily kernels are delicious. They are eaten like walnuts—either alone (plain, salted, hickory-smoked) or added to candies and baked goods. Some tribes boiled butternut kernels and skimmed off the oil to use like butter. The remaining kernels were dried and ground into a rich meal for adding to cornmeal mush. • The nut husks and root bark produce an orange or yellow dye. Butternut bark and nut husks were used (without a mordant) to dye uniforms for foot soldiers during the Civil War (1861–65). The leaves, with an alum mordant, produce a brown to bronze dye. • The outer bark was once used in medicinal teas for treating toothaches and dysentery, and dried inner bark was taken as a purgative • This fast-growing, relatively short-lived tree can survive about 80 years. The leaves, bark and nuts contain toxins that inhibit the growth of other plants nearby. • In some parts of North America, including Michigan,

butternut is disappearing rapidly, as trees succumb to butternut canker disease, which was introduced from Asia. Infected trees develop black, oozing cankers and eventually die.

ALSO CALLED: White walnut, lemon walnut, oilnut.

SIZE AND SHAPE: Trees 40–65' [96'] tall; crowns irregular, open, rounded; roots deep, spreading.

TRUNKS: Short, soon forked, 12–40" [57"] in diameter; mature bark rough with flat-topped, intersecting ridges; wood light brown to reddish-brown, light, soft, weak.

BRANCHES: Few, stout, ascending; twigs orange-yellow, **rusty-hairy, sticky;** pith dark **brown, banded** with cavities (visible in longsection); buds hairy, mainly small, rounded and brownish, but **large (¹/₂–³/₄")** and pale yellow at twig tips.

LEAVES: Alternate, deciduous, **12–30" long, aromatic,** sticky when young; compound, **pinnately divided into 11–17 leaflets** that are yellowish-green and rough above, paler and **thickly hairy beneath,** finely toothed, almost stalkless, 2–4³/₄" long, the **3 tip leaflets equal-sized,** gradually smaller downward; **leaf scars prominent,** with 3 vein scars, **downy-hairy across the flat top.**

FLOWERS: Tiny, green, without petals; unisexual with male and female flowers on the same tree; male flowers hang in catkins 2³/₈–5¹/₂" long; female flowers about ¹/₄" long, 1–7 in erect clusters (catkins); flowers in May (with leaves).

FRUITS: Lemon-shaped, green nuts, 1 to few together, 1¹/₂–2³/₈" long, with firm, sticky, hairy husks over hard, oblong, **irregularly jagged-ridged shells;** oily seed kernel inside shell has 2 irregular lobes (cotyledons); nuts mature in October and drop.

HABITAT: Dry, rocky, limestone slopes to moist, rich floodplains; usually with maples.

ORIGIN: Native.

BLACK WALNUT is one of North America's most highly prized hardwoods. Standing trees have fetched $5000 at auction. The lustrous, rich chocolate brown wood has a beautiful grain, stains and polishes well, is easily worked and doesn't shrink or warp. It is used for rifle butts and stocks, high-quality furniture, veneers and boats. • Most of the original black walnut stands have been cut, but this valuable tree has been reintroduced to some regions. These attractive nut trees are also planted as ornamentals. • The sweet, oily kernels can be used like domestic walnuts and butternuts. They are difficult to shell and the husks stain hands and clothing, but cultivars with larger, thinner-walled nuts are being developed. • Walnut husks are rich in tannins and toxins. Ground husks have provided insecticides, fish poison and black dye. • The toxin juglone is exuded from the roots and leached from decaying leaves, preventing other broad-leaved plants (including walnut seedlings) from taking root and providing competition. • **English walnut** (*J. regia*), shown in pink (with arrow) on the map, was introduced from Europe and Asia and occasionally escapes from cultivation. It is readily distinguished by its leaves, with 5–9 hairless, smooth-edged leaflets, and by its large, easily shelled nuts—the commercially available walnut. English walnut trees in Michigan are usually smaller and scruffier than the native black walnut.

ALSO CALLED: American walnut, American black walnut, eastern black walnut.
SIZE AND SHAPE: Trees 65–100' [119'] tall; crowns open, rounded; roots deep, spreading.
TRUNKS: Straight, 24–48" [74"] in diameter; mature bark almost black, with rounded, intersecting ridges; wood dark brown (heartwood) to almost white (sapwood), hard, heavy, strong, decay-resistant, straight-grained.
BRANCHES: Few, large, ascending; twigs orange-brown, **faintly hairy, not sticky;** pith cream-colored, banded with cavities (visible in long-section); buds small, pale gray-brown, slightly hairy, largest (¹/₄–³/₈") at twig tips.
LEAVES: Alternate, deciduous, **8–24" long, aromatic;** compound, **pinnately divided into 13–23 leaflets** that are yellowish-green, smooth above, paler and **faintly hairy below,** finely toothed, short-stalked, 2–4" long, middle leaflets largest, **tip leaflet small or absent; leaf scars heart-shaped, not hairy;** leaves yellow in autumn.
FLOWERS: Green, tiny, without petals; unisexual with male and female flowers on the same tree; male flowers in hanging catkins 2–4³/₄" long; female flowers about ¹/₄" long, in erect clusters of 1–4; flowers in May (with leaves).
FRUITS: Round, yellow-green to brown, aromatic nuts 1¹/₂–2³/₈" across, with a hard, **irregularly smooth-ridged shell** in a firm, slightly hairy husk, hanging in clusters of 1–3; oily seed kernel inside shell has 2 irregular lobes (cotyledons); nuts mature in October and drop.
HABITAT: Deep, well-drained, fertile lowlands.
ORIGIN: Native.

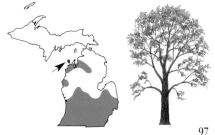

97

SHELLBARK HICKORY has tough, strong wood that makes excellent tool handles, ladders, baskets and fuel. • This tree produces large nuts, with good crops every 1–3 years. The sweet, edible kernels are encased in thick, hard shells within thick, woody husks, so some effort is required to extract them. However, like pecans, they are delicious raw or in baked goods. • The thick green husks were sometimes ground and used as a fish poison. • Foxes, black bears, deer, hares, rabbits, raccoons, muskrats, squirrels and chipmunks all seek out these nuts. Even ducks, wild turkeys and quail occasionally eat hickory nuts. The nuts are dispersed by animals and by flowing water. They can remain viable for several years. • Historically, **mockernut** hickory (*C. alba*, also called *C. tomentosa*) was reported from southern Michigan, but all the old reports have proved false. Mockernut resembles shellbark hickory but has more densely woolly leaf stalks, dark brown twigs, smaller (¹/₂–1¹/₈"), more spherical nuts and tight, ridged (not shaggy) bark. • Hickories are highly variable, and identification can be difficult. Shellbark hickory also resembles shagbark hickory (p. 99), but shellbark hickory is a larger tree with larger leaves, buds, twigs and nuts.

ALSO CALLED: Big shellbark hickory, kingnut hickory, big shagbark hickory, bigleaf, bottom shellbark.

SIZE AND SHAPE: Trees 50–80' [96'] tall; crowns narrow, open; taproot.

TRUNKS: Straight, 24–32" [34"] in diameter; **mature bark gray, in shaggy, 3–4' long strips;** wood dark brown, heavy, hard, elastic.

BRANCHES: Short, spreading; **twigs stout, buff to pale orange-brown** (usually); **pith solid; buds dark brown, ³/₄–1¹/₈" long** at twig tips.

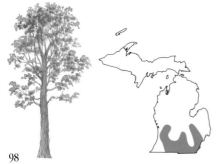

LEAVES: Alternate, deciduous, 10–20" long, **aromatic;** compound, **pinnately divided into 7 (sometimes 9, rarely 5) leaflets** that are dark yellowish-green above, paler and **soft-hairy below,** finely toothed, edges hairless or with non-tufted hairs, **leaflets 5–8¹/₂" long, largest at leaf tips, much smaller downward;** leaf scars conspicuous, raised; leaves often drop leaflets before main stalk.

FLOWERS: Tiny, green, without petals; unisexual with male and female flowers on the same tree; male flowers yellow-green, in 4³/₄–8" long catkins that hang in 3s; female flowers about ¹/₈" long, in erect clusters of 2–5; flowers in May–early June (with leaves).

FRUITS: Compressed, greenish-brown, aromatic nuts 1¹/₂–2³/₄" long, somewhat wedge-shaped at base, usually 1–2 hanging, with a thick, hard, **4-ridged shell** within a woody, ¹/₄–¹/₂" thick **husk that splits to the base along 4 lines;** seed kernel inside shell has 2 large, irregular lobes (cotyledons); nuts mature in October and drop.

HABITAT: Rich, moist to wet sites, usually on floodplains or in swamps.

ORIGIN: Native.

OF ALL OUR NATIVE HICKORIES, shagbark hickory has the best-quality wood and is the most important source of edible hickory nuts. The sweet, walnut-like kernels can be eaten alone or used in recipes.
• Shagbark hickory nuts were a staple food for many tribes and remain the main hickory nut of commerce. Traditionally, the kernels were ground and boiled in water to produce a milky, oil-rich liquid that was used in cornbread and cornmeal mush. The sweet-tasting sap was boiled down to make syrup. Some isolated northern stands may have originated from nuts carried there by Native peoples. • The strong, resilient wood has been used to make wheel spokes, tool handles, plowing instruments and machine parts. It also makes excellent fuel. A cord produces almost as much heat as a ton of anthracite coal. Shagbark hickory wood is used for smoking meat (ham, bacon) and for producing high-quality charcoal. • The inner bark produces a yellow dye, which was patented in the 18th century, but more intense yellows were available, so there was limited demand. • The nuts are an important food source for squirrels. • One look at a mature tree, with its peeling sheets of rough bark, explains the common name.

ALSO CALLED: Upland hickory, scalybark hickory.

SIZE AND SHAPE: Trees 50–70' [76'] tall; crowns somewhat open and narrow; taproot.

TRUNKS: Straight, 12–24" [43"] in diameter; **mature bark dark gray, shaggy,** with peeling plates 12–36" long; wood hard, heavy, fine-grained.

BRANCHES: Short, stout, few; twigs stout, reddish-brown to grayish, shiny; pith solid; **buds greenish-brown, $1/2$–$3/4$" long at twig tips, upper (inner) scales hairy,** loosely overlapping, lower 2–4 scales paired, with abutting edges.

LEAVES: Alternate, deciduous, 6–12" long, aromatic; compound, **pinnately divided into 5 (occasionally 7) leaflets** that are yellowish-green above, paler and **almost hairless beneath,** fine-toothed, **fringed with 2–3 white tufts per tooth** (especially when young), essentially stalkless, 3–7" long, **largest at leaf tip;** leaf scars conspicuous, raised; leaves golden yellow in autumn.

FLOWERS: Tiny, green, without petals; unisexual with male and female flowers on the same tree; male flowers in catkins 4–5" long, hanging in 3s; female flowers about $1/4$" long, in small, erect clusters of 2–5; flowers in May–early June (as leaves expand).

FRUITS: Round, greenish- to dark reddish-brown, **aromatic nuts, shorter than wide,** $3/4$–$1$$1/2$" **(rarely 2") long,** with a hard, 4-angled shell within a thick, **woody husk that splits in 4 to the base;** seed kernel inside shell has 2 large, irregular lobes (cotyledons); nuts single or paired, mature in October and drop.

HABITAT: Moderately dry to moderately moist sites, mixed with other broad-leaved trees, usually in upland forests.

ORIGIN: Native.

PIGNUT HICKORY is highly variable, and its relationship to **red hickory** (*C. ovalis*, also called *C. glabra* var. *odorata*) is unclear. Some taxonomists do not consider red hickory a separate species and treat it as *C. glabra* var. *odorata*. Of those who recognize two species, some say the range of red hickory extends north into Canada and others consider it a more southern species found in the eastern U.S. Pignut hickory and red hickory are distinguished, respectively, on the basis of their twigs (smooth reddish-brown vs. yellowish-scurfy); leaflets (usually 5 vs. usually 7); bark (close and shallowly ridged vs. often shaggy with peeling plates); nut kernels (astringent vs. sweet); nut shells (slightly or not at all compressed and not angled vs. compressed and strongly angled above); and fruit husks (dark shiny brown and splitting slowly or not at all vs. dull, warty, light brown and promptly splitting to the base). However, these features often intergrade, and both "species" have been reportedly been observed on a single tree. • The nutmeats are usually bitter and inedible, and are best left to pigs and wild animals.

ALSO CALLED: Sweet pignut hickory, false shagbark hickory, black hickory, broom hickory, smoothbark hickory • *C. leiodermis.*

SIZE AND SHAPE: Trees 50–65' [70'] tall; crowns narrow, irregular; taproot.

TRUNKS: Straight, 12–32" [46"] in diameter; young bark thin, gray, with pale **crisscross markings;** mature bark rough with **rounded ridges;** wood hard, heavy, strong.

BRANCHES: Short, crooked; **twigs slender, shiny,** reddish-brown to gray, often long-ridged;

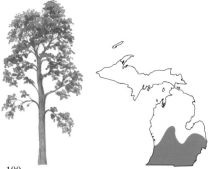

pith solid; buds light brown or gray, 1/4–1/2" long at twig tips, smaller below, upper scales hairy and overlapping, **lower 2–4 scales paired and soon shed.**

LEAVES: Alternate, deciduous, 6–12" long, **aromatic;** compound, **pinnately divided into 5 (sometimes 7, rarely 9) leaflets** that are lustrous, dark yellow-green above, paler and hairless below (except on main veins), thick, **finely sharp-toothed, largest (3–6" long) at the tip,** much smaller below.

FLOWERS: Tiny, green, without petals; unisexual with male and female flowers on the same tree; male flowers in catkins 3–7" long, hanging in 3s; female flowers about 1/4" long, in erect clusters of 2–5; flowers in May–June (as leaves expand).

FRUITS: Pear-shaped, yellowish-brown to dark brown, **aromatic nuts 1/2–1 1/8" (rarely 1 3/4–2") long,** with a hard, **thin, slightly flattened, smooth to 4-lobed shell** within a thin, 4-ridged **husk that usually splits to the base along 4 lines;** seed kernel inside shell has 2 large, irregular lobes (cotyledons); nuts hang in small clusters, mature in October and drop.

HABITAT: Dry, open, well-drained upland forests.

ORIGIN: Native.

BITTERNUT HICKORY is Michigan's only pecan hickory. "Pecan hickories" differ from "true hickories" in their distinctive buds (without overlapping scales), thin, 4-ridged fruit husks and larger number of leaflets. The sulfur yellow buds of bitternut hickory are easily identified year-round.

• Bitternut hickory wood is brittle compared to that of other hickories, but amazingly shock-resistant. It has been used in wooden wheels, tool handles, sporting goods, paneling and furniture. As fuel, it burns intensely, leaving little ash. Bitternut hickory is favored for smoking ham, bacon and other meats because it imparts a distinctive flavor.

• Bitternut hickory kernels are relatively easy to extract from their thin husks and shells, but they are also extremely bitter. Even squirrels eat them only as a last resort.

• The genus name *Carya* comes from the Greek *karuon*, an ancient name for a close relative, the walnut. Walnuts and hickories are distinguished, respectively, by the pith of their twigs (banded or chambered vs. solid), their fruit husks (remaining whole vs. splitting into 4) and their wood (light to dark brown vs. white to reddish-brown).

ALSO CALLED: Swamp hickory, yellowbud.

SIZE AND SHAPE: Trees 50–80' [101'] tall; crowns short, broad, rounded; taproot.

TRUNKS: Straight, slender, 6–12" [54"] in diameter; young bark gray, smooth, with pale, vertical lines; mature bark with flat, shallow, grayish ridges (not shaggy); wood hard, heavy, close-grained.

BRANCHES: Slender, ascending, stiff; twigs shiny, greenish- to grayish-brown and slender; **pith solid; buds sulfur yellow** to bright orange-yellow, with **2–4 large, abutting scales,** flattened and $^3/_8$–$^3/_4$" **long at twig tips,** smaller and 4-sided below.

LEAVES: Alternate, deciduous, 6–12" long, aromatic; compound, **pinnately divided into 7–9 (usually 9, rarely 5 or 11) leaflets** that are shiny, dark green above, **paler, hairy and dotted with glands below, slightly curved,** toothed, 4–6" long, **uppermost largest;** leaves bright gold in autumn.

FLOWERS: Tiny, green, without petals; unisexual with male and female flowers on the same tree; male flowers in catkins 2$^3/_4$–4" long, hanging in 3s from a slender stalk; female flowers hairy, about $^1/_8$" long, erect, 1–5 in compact clusters; flowers in May–early June (as leaves expand).

FRUITS: Round to broadly egg-shaped, greenish-brown, **aromatic nuts,** sharp-tipped, $^3/_4$–1$^3/_8$" long, with smooth, **thin shells** enclosed in thin, **yellow-felted, 4-ridged husks that split in 4 to the middle; reddish-brown seed kernel** inside shell has 2 large, irregular lobes (cotyledons); nuts hang singly or in pairs, mature in October and drop.

HABITAT: Cool, moist, rich sites in hardwood forests, along streams and also on drier sites.

ORIGIN: Native.

101

Key to Genera in the Beech Family (Fagaceae)

1a Fruit a single nut seated in a cup of firm, overlapping scales (acorn); leaves usually lobed, veins not extending beyond the lobe/tooth tips .... *Quercus*, **oak** (key to species, below)

1b Fruits with 1–4 (rarely 5) nuts enclosed in a prickly, bur-like covering that splits open along as many lines as there are nuts; leaves coarsely toothed; leaf veins various **2**

2a Nuts sharply triangular, usually 2 in burs $3/4$–$1^1/8$" wide; leaves oblong-ovate, shallowly toothed, with veins not extending beyond the teeth; bark smooth, pale gray .... *Fagus*, **beech** (p. 104)

2b Nuts flattened on 1 or 2 sides, 2–4 in burs 2–$2^3/4$" wide; leaves coarsely sharp-toothed, with veins extending beyond the tips of the teeth; bark rough, grayish-brown .... *Castanea*, **chestnut** (p. 105)

Key to the Oaks (Genus *Quercus*)

Oaks are generally divided into 2 main groups: white oaks and red and black oaks. White oaks have smooth-edged to blunt-toothed or round-lobed leaves that lack bristle tips; sweet, edible acorns that ripen in one season; acorn shells with smooth inner surfaces; and scaly bark. White oak, bur oak, swamp white oak, chestnut oak, chinquapin oak and dwarf chinquapin oak all belong to this group.

Red and black oaks have smooth-edged, sharp-toothed or sharp-lobed leaves with bristle-tipped points; bitter acorns that ripen in two years; acorn shells with hairy inner surfaces; and non-scaly bark. Black oak, red oak, scarlet oak, pin oak, northern pin oak, Shumard oak and shingle oak all belong to this group.

Oaks are notorious for having little or no barrier to reproduction among species in the same group. Although hybrids are found only occasionally in the field, when you find a puzzling individual that does not seem to "fit," it may be a hybrid.

1a Leaves smooth edged, not lobed, bristle-tipped .... *Q. imbricaria*, **shingle oak** (p. 116)

1b Leaves lobed or toothed, with or without bristle tips **2**

2a Leaves with sharp, bristle-tipped lobes; acorns maturing in the second year, woolly on the inner surface of the shell **3**

2b Leaves with rounded to slightly pointed lobes or teeth, never bristle-tipped; acorns maturing in the first year, hairless on the inner surface of the shell **8**

3a Mature leaves woolly with star-shaped hairs beneath and often along the upper midvein; acorn cups downy on the inner surface and sometimes fringed .... *Q. velutina*, **black oak** (p. 111)

3b Mature leaves essentially hairless (sometimes with tufts in vein axils); acorn cups hairless or with a few hairs around the scar, never fringed **4**

4a Length of largest leaf lobes (on leaves growing in full sun) equal to or slightly greater than width of the middle part of the leaf (between opposing notches) .... *Q. rubra*, **red oak** (p. 112)

4b Largest leaf lobes much (up to 3 times) longer than width of the middle part of the leaf **5**

5a Acorns large and round, usually ³/₄–1" across ....*Q. shumardii*, **Shumard oak** (p. 114)

5b Acorns smaller, ³/₈–³/₄" across **6**

6a Acorns round, ³/₈–¹/₂" across, with saucer-like cups covering ¹/₄–¹/₃ of the nut .... *Q. palustris*, **pin oak** (p. 113)

6b Acorns ellipsoid-cylindrical, ³/₈–³/₄" long, with deeper cups covering ¹/₃–¹/₂ of the nut................. **7**

7a Leaf stalks >¹/₃₂" wide; acorns tipped with rings; acorn cups ⁵/₈–³/₄" wide .... *Q. coccinea*, **scarlet oak** (p. 115)

7b Leaf stalks <¹/₃₂" wide; acorns lacking rings at their tips; acorn cups ³/₈–⁵/₈" wide .... *Q. ellipsoidalis*, **northern pin oak** (p. 114)

8a Leaves coarsely toothed, with 3–14 teeth per side, indented less than ¹/₃ of the way to the midrib; lower leaf surfaces densely covered with whitish, star-shaped hairs............................**9**

8b Leaves with 1–5 distinct lobes per side, indented more than ¹/₃ of the way to the midrib; lower leaf surfaces various **12**

9a Acorns single or paired on long (³/₄–4") stalks; cup scales swollen, with pointed, recurved tips.. *Q. bicolor*, **swamp white oak** (p. 108)

9b Acorn stalks absent or shorter than leaf stalks; cup scales only slightly swollen and lacking recurved tips **10**

10a Leaf teeth blunt and rounded; acorn cups ³/₄–1" wide; lower leaf surfaces sparsely hairy .... *Q. prinus*, **chestnut oak** (p. 109)

10b Leaf teeth tipped with a firm, projecting point (callus); acorn cups ¹/₂–⁵/₈" wide; lower leaf surfaces woolly-hairy..**11**

11a Leaves small (usually 1¹/₂–4" long) with 4–9 main veins per side; shrubby, rarely the size of a small tree... *Q. prinoides*, **dwarf chinquapin oak** (p. 110)

11b Leaves larger (about 4–7" long) with 8–15 main veins per side; tall shrub or medium-tall tree................................... *Q. muehlenbergii*, **chinquapin oak** (p. 109)

12a Mature leaves essentially hairless... *Q. alba*, **white oak** (p. 106)

12b Mature leaves hairy beneath **13**

13a Leaves shallowly and irregularly lobed; acorns on long (>³/₄") stalks; acorn cups not fringed with bristles; first-year twigs usually hairless .... *Q. bicolor*, **swamp white oak** (p. 108)

13b Leaves deeply notched below the middle and broadly lobed at the tip; acorns on short (<¹/₄") stalks; acorn cups distinctly fringed with bristles; first-year twigs hairy .... *Q. macrocarpa*, **bur oak** (p. 107)

BEECH WOOD has been used for spindles, rungs, inexpensive furniture, handles, utensils, containers, flooring, plywood, railroad ties, barrels and casks. Because of its elastic qualities, it was once used to make all-wood clothespins. • Beech nuts are best after the first frosts. They make a tasty trail nibble but should be eaten in moderation because large amounts can cause intestinal inflammation. Dried, roasted and ground beech nuts make a traditional coffee substitute that can be mixed with coffee, milk or chocolate and sweetened with honey. Early settlers gathered beech nuts to extract the oil, which is similar to olive oil and was used as both food and lamp oil. • Beech nuts are eagerly sought by many birds and mammals, which then disperse the seeds. These fat-rich nuts are an important food for muskrats, squirrels, chipmunks, black bears and birds such as grouse, wood ducks and wild turkeys. • Beech bark disease, which is caused by fungus (three *Nectria* species), is killing many beech trees, especially those weakened by beech scale, an introduced, sucking insect (*Cryptococcus fagisuga*). Porcupines also kill beech trees by girdling the trunks.

ALSO CALLED: Red beech.

SIZE AND SHAPE: Trees 60–80' [98'] tall; crowns rounded; roots wide-spreading.

TRUNKS: Often sinuous, 20–40" [61"] in diameter; **mature bark silvery gray, thin, smooth,** sometimes with dark markings; wood reddish-brown, heavy, hard, tough, but not durable.

BRANCHES: Slender, smooth, crooked; twigs shiny, light olive-brown, slender, slightly zigzagged; **buds cigar-shaped,** reddish- to grayish-brown, ³/₈–1" **long,** pointing outward, in 2 vertical rows.

LEAVES: Alternate, simple, deciduous; blades 2–6" long, firm, dark bluish-green above, paler and lustrous below, leathery, narrowly oval, with **9–14 straight, parallel veins per side, each ending in a coarse tooth;** leaf scars small, semicircular; leaves on lower branches or saplings **occasionally persisting** into winter.

FLOWERS: Tiny, yellowish-green, without petals; unisexual with male and female flowers on the same tree; male flowers clustered in dense, ³/₄–1" heads hanging on slender stalks; female flowers about ¹/₄" long, erect, in compact clusters of 2–4; flowers in April–May (as leaves expand).

FRUITS: Small **burs, with pairs of sharply 3-angled,** ³/₈–³/₄" **long, smooth-shelled, reddish-brown nuts** enclosed in a prickly, greenish- to reddish-brown husk that splits in 2–4; seeds single kernels inside each nut; burs split open in September–October.

HABITAT: Hardwood forests on moist slopes and in bottomlands.

ORIGIN: Native.

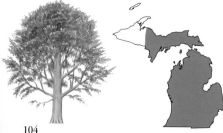

ALTHOUGH AMERICAN CHESTNUT originally grew only in the southeastern corner of Michigan, this attractive tree was also widely planted, and it often escaped to grow wild outside its native range. • Chestnut blight was introduced from Asia in 1904, and by 1937, it had eliminated 99% of the chestnut trees in North America. This fungal disease commonly infects Eurasian chestnuts, but the New World species have almost no resistance. A few trees persist by sprouting from stumps, but shoots usually succumb to the blight before they reach 35' in height. Very few American chestnut trees produce seed before dying. A less virulent strain of the fungus was introduced to compete with the deadly blight, but with limited success. Today, Michigan has one of the few remaining stands of large chestnut trees. • American chestnut was an important commercial tree in the 19th century, valued for its durable wood and its large, sweet, edible nutmeats. • Settlers boiled the leaves to make a jelly for treating burns and sweaty feet. A tea of the bark was taken (with honey) to cure whooping cough and was gargled to soothe inflamed tonsils. • A relatively blight-resistant horticultural species, **Chinese chestnut** (*C. mollissima*, also called *C. bungeana* and *C. formosana*), was introduced from Korea and China. It resembles American chestnut, but its leaves are woolly-hairy beneath.

ALSO CALLED: Sweet chestnut.

SIZE AND SHAPE: Trees 10–35' [110'] tall, from sprouting stumps; taproot.

TRUNKS: Straight, up to 6" [64"] in diameter; young bark dark brown, smooth; mature bark with low, broad, flat-topped ridges; wood reddish-brown, straight-grained, hard, resistant to decay.

BRANCHES: Stout; twigs shiny reddish-brown, stout; **pith 5-pointed** in cross-section; buds greenish-brown, hairless, egg-shaped, about ¼" long, 2–3-scaled.

LEAVES: Alternate, simple, deciduous; blades yellowish-green, smooth, **narrowly oblong, 6–10" long; veins straight, parallel, 15–20 per side, ending in coarse, bristle-tipped teeth;** stalks short, finely hairy.

FLOWERS: Tiny, creamy white, fragrant; unisexual with male and female flowers on the same tree; male flowers in stiff, **semi-erect catkins 4¾–8" long; female flowers about ⅛" long, 1–3 at the base of smaller (2⅜–5⅛" long),** mainly male catkins near branch tips; flowers in June–July (immediately after leaves expand).

FRUITS: Large burs **(chestnuts)** 2–2¾" across, with 1–3 (rarely 4–5), brownish, pointed, smooth-shelled nuts enclosed in a greenish- to reddish-brown, **prickly husk that splits in 4;** seeds single kernels inside nuts; chestnuts mature in September–October, drop after first frost.

HABITAT: Usually in oak-hickory forests on acidic, well-drained soils.

ORIGIN: Native.

WHITE OAK is an important hardwood. The strong, durable wood is amazingly elastic. Before the widespread use of steel, oak was the mainstay of shipbuilding and was also used in automobile and airplane frames and in plows. White oak wood is still used for cabinets, floors, paneling, veneer, plywood, support timbers, caskets, pianos and organs. This wood is famous for its use in watertight barrels, which give aged whiskey and wine a special color and flavor. • Boiled bark tea was once used for treating diarrhea, intestinal inflammation and bleeding gums. Such medicinal uses are not advised, because the concentrated tannins may be **toxic** and **carcinogenic**. • White oak acorns were an important source of food for many tribes. The edible, somewhat sweet kernels can be eaten raw, but traditionally they were usually dried, ground into meal and made into cakes or used to thicken soups. Acorns were also roasted in coals or boiled, then peeled and eaten as a vegetable or snack, often with suet. • Dark-roasted, ground kernels are said to make an excellent, caffeine-free coffee substitute. Acorn flour adds an interesting flavor to breads, muffins and cakes.

ALSO CALLED: Northern white oak, stave oak, barrel oak.

SIZE AND SHAPE: Trees 50–80' [134'] tall; crowns broad, full; taproot plus deep, spreading roots.

TRUNKS: Short, straight, 24–48" [68"] in diameter; **mature bark pale gray,** often red-tinged, variable, coarsely flaky or with low, flat ridges; wood light brown, hard, heavy, water-impermeable, decay-resistant.

BRANCHES: Wide-spreading, gnarled with age; twigs greenish and woolly to reddish and finally **smooth ash gray; pith 5-pointed** in cross-section;

buds reddish-brown, about ⅛" long, with **broad, hairless scales;** buds at twig tips clustered, side-buds spreading.

LEAVES: Alternate, simple, deciduous; blades 4–8" long, bright green above and paler beneath, firm, **hairless when mature, deeply pinnately lobed; lobes rounded, 5–9;** leaves brownish- to reddish-purple in autumn, a few may persist in winter.

FLOWERS: Tiny, without petals; unisexual with male and female flowers on the same tree; male flowers many, yellowish, in hanging catkins 2–3" long; female flowers reddish, about ⅛" long, usually in clusters of 2–4; flowers in May–June (as leaves expand).

FRUITS: Elongated nuts (**acorns**) ½–¾" long, single or paired, with leathery shells; tips rounded with a small, abrupt point, **lower ¼ seated in a cup of overlapping, knobbly scales, not fringed;** seeds single **white kernels;** acorns remain in cup, mature in first autumn.

HABITAT: Commonly in oak-hickory forests on rich, moderately to well-drained soils.

ORIGIN: Native.

BUR OAK is one of North America's most common and widespread white oaks. With its thick bark and deep roots, it is fire and drought resistant enough to grow in grasslands, but it can also tolerate periodic flooding and thrive in seasonally wet lowlands. In moister areas, bur oak often hybridizes with swamp white oak (p. 108).
• Bur oaks are slow-growing trees that typically produce fruit after about 30–35 years. However, they are also long-lived and can generate abundant crops of acorns every 2–3 years over a life span of 200–300 years. • Bur oak wood, acorns, bark and leaves are similar to those of white oak (p. 106) and have been used in the same ways, with the same limitations.
• This attractive tree is often planted in parks, gardens and boulevards as a shade-giving ornamental. It tolerates air pollution in urban centers, but its deep taproot can make it difficult to transplant. • Bur oak acorns provide food for a wide range of animals, including white-tailed deer, squirrels, rabbits, mice, wood ducks and wild turkeys. • The species name *macrocarpa* comes from the Greek *makros*, "large," and *karpos*, "fruit," in reference to the unusually large acorns.

ALSO CALLED: Mossycup oak, blue oak, mossy oak, over-cup oak, scrubby oak.

SIZE AND SHAPE: Trees 40–80' [110'] tall; crowns broad, full; taproot deep.

TRUNKS: Straight, 24–48" [85"] in diameter, often with small branches from dormant buds; mature bark gray, often reddish-tinged, with thick, irregular, scaly ridges; wood hard, heavy, water-impermeable, decay-resistant.

BRANCHES: Spreading to ascending; twigs thick, woolly-hairy, **often corky-ridged; pith 5-pointed** in cross-section; **buds hairy**, about 1/8" long, **flat-lying**, broad-scaled with a few **loose, slender basal scales.**

LEAVES: Alternate, simple, deciduous; blades shiny, dark green above, paler and white-hairy beneath, firm, 4–10" long, deeply **pinnately lobed; lobes rounded,** with 2–4 (sometimes 6–8) small lobes below a broad, coarse-toothed upper lobe; some leaves may persist in winter.

FLOWERS: Tiny, without petals; unisexual with male and female flowers on the same tree; male flowers yellowish-green, hairy, in hanging catkins 4–6" long; female flowers reddish, hairy, about 1/8" across, in clusters of 1–5; flowers in May–June (as leaves expand).

FRUITS: Round nuts **(acorns)** 1/2–11/8" long, usually single; tips rounded with a small, abrupt point, **the lower 1/2–3/4 or more in a conspicuously fringed cup of overlapping, knobbly, pointed scales;** seeds single **white kernels;** acorns remain in cup, mature in first autumn.

HABITAT: A wide range of habitats from deep, rich bottomlands to prairie "oak openings" and rocky uplands, usually mixed with other trees.

ORIGIN: Native.

SWAMP WHITE OAK wood is similar to, and sometimes sold as, white oak wood, but the swamp type is knottier and of poorer quality. Still, it has been used in barrels, furniture, cabinets, interior finishing, veneers and construction. • The sweet, edible acorns can be used like those of white oak for food. • This tree can live 300 years or more, but its shallow roots and relatively thin, scaly bark make it susceptible to fire damage. Swamp white oak usually begins to flower at about 25–30 years of age, and it produces large acorn crops every 3–5 years. • With a magnifier you may be able to see the star-like shapes of some hairs on the velvety undersides of the leaves. The specific epithet *bicolor* means "two-colored" and refers to the contrasting shiny green upper and fuzzy white lower leaf surfaces. The genus name *Quercus* means "tree above all others" and was the traditional Latin name for oak. It may have been derived from the Celtic *quer cuez*, meaning "fine tree." • This oak often crosses with bur oak (p. 107) to produce hybrids (*Q.* x *schuettei*) with intermediate characteristics.

ALSO CALLED: Blue oak, swamp oak.

SIZE AND SHAPE: Trees 40–65' [144'] tall; crowns broad, irregular and rounded, **untidy below;** roots shallow.

TRUNKS: Straight, 24–40" [74"] in diameter; young bark reddish-brown, scaly, peeling; mature bark grayish-brown, flat-ridged; wood light brown, hard, heavy, close-grained, water-impermeable, decay-resistant.

BRANCHES: Ascending to spreading, with **crooked, hanging branchlets** on lower branches; twigs stout; **pith 5-pointed** in cross-section;

buds reddish-brown, hairy, about ⅛" long, tip bud in a cluster.

LEAVES: Alternate, simple, deciduous; blades 4¾–8" long, **shiny, dark green above, pale and white-woolly beneath,** firm, widest above the middle, **shallowly pinnately lobed** to coarsely wavy-toothed, with 4–6 main veins per side, each ending in a rounded lobe/tooth; leaves yellowish-brown to orange in autumn, some may persist.

FLOWERS: Tiny, without petals; unisexual with male and female flowers on the same tree; male flowers yellowish-green, hairy, in hanging catkins 2¾–4" long; female flowers hairy, reddish, about ⅛" across, in stalked clusters of 1–5; flowers in May–June (as leaves expand).

FRUITS: Round nuts **(acorns)** with leathery shells, ¾–1⅛" long, **1–2 on stalks ¾–4" long;** tips rounded with a small point, ¼–½ of the base in a cup of thick, overlapping scales with outcurved tips; seeds single white kernels; acorns mature in first autumn.

HABITAT: Rich, **wet sites** on floodplains and in swamps.

ORIGIN: Native.

CHINQUAPIN OAK wood is sometimes sold as white oak. Although strong and durable, it has little commercial value, largely because of limited supply. It has been used for construction, railroad ties, split-rail fences and fuel. • The sweet, edible acorns are milder than those of most other oaks. They can be eaten fresh from the tree or prepared like white oak acorns. • This tree is sometimes planted as an ornamental. • **Chestnut oak** (*Q. prinus* or *Q. montana*), shown in dark green on the map, is a species of the eastern U.S. that may be confused with chinquapin oak. Chestnut oak is distinguished by its sparsely hairy lower leaf surfaces and rounded (not bristle-tipped) leaf teeth. Also, its acorns are slightly larger, with cups $3/4$–1" wide. Chestnut oak is very rare in Michigan. A single colony has been found at the Waterloo Recreation Area, and it may have originated from a planted tree. • The name "chinquapin" is a Native word for the American chestnut tree (p. 105). The yellowish-green young leaves of chinquapin oak and this tree's similarity to chestnut oak have given rise to another common name, "yellow chestnut oak."

ALSO CALLED: Chinkapin oak, yellow oak, yellow chestnut oak, rock oak.

SIZE AND SHAPE: Trees 40–50' [120'] tall (tallest in forests); crowns narrow, rounded.

TRUNKS: Straight, 12–24" [68"] in diameter, often enlarged at the base; **mature bark pale grayish, thin-scaled, flaky;** wood brown, hard, heavy, close-grained, decay-resistant.

BRANCHES: Short; twigs green to grayish-brown or orange-brown, stiff, slender; **pith 5-pointed** in cross-section; buds pale reddish-brown, hairless, $1/8$–$1/4$" long, buds at twig tips clustered.

LEAVES: Alternate, simple, deciduous; **blades 4–7" long,** widest above the middle, glossy yellowish-green to deep green above, paler and densely hairy with star-shaped hairs beneath, firm, with **8–15 straight, parallel veins per side** ending in large, pointed (sometimes slightly rounded), **minutely bristle-tipped teeth;** some leaves may persist in winter.

FLOWERS: Tiny, without petals; unisexual with male and female flowers on the same tree; male flowers hairy, yellow, in hanging catkins $2 3/4$–4" long; female flowers silver-woolly, reddish,

about $1/8$" across, in compact clusters of 1–5; flowers in May–June (as leaves expand).

FRUITS: Slightly elongated, leathery-shelled nuts **(acorns)** $1/2$–$3/4$" long, single or paired; tips rounded with a small, abrupt, white-downy point, **lower $1/3$–$1/2$ in a cup of silvery-hairy, overlapping, slightly thickened scales;** seeds single white kernels; acorns mature in first autumn.

HABITAT: Dry, basic sites such sand dunes and rocky (especially limestone) ridges and slopes; occasionally in moist bottomlands on neutral to basic soils.

ORIGIN: Native.

DWARF CHINQUAPIN OAK is well named. It is a true dwarf tree, capable of producing acorns when it is scarcely 3' tall. It bears large crops of sweet, edible acorns annually or every other year. • Like most oaks, dwarf chinquapin oak produces hard, dense, high-quality wood, but its trunks are too small to be of any commercial value. • This sun-loving shrub often produces colonies on exposed hillsides by sending up suckers from widely spreading roots. When an old stem dies, its roots may remain alive and sprout a ring of vigorous shoots around the base of the dead trunk. • Dwarf chinquapin oak is a smaller, shrubbier version of chinquapin oak (p. 109). It also differs from its larger cousin in its smaller leaves (mostly 1½–4" long rather than 4–7" long), which have fewer (4–9 rather than 10–15) veins and teeth per side. In Michigan, large specimens of dwarf chinquapin oak (those taller than 7–10') are usually the product of hybridization with chinquapin oak or other white oak species. The blending of characteristics from both parents makes identification difficult. • Dwarf chinquapin oak, chinquapin oak (p. 109), chestnut oak (p. 109) and swamp white oak (p. 108) are sometimes classified as "chestnut oaks." Trees in this group have toothed to shallowly lobed leaves, unlike the deeply lobed leaves usually associated with oaks.

ALSO CALLED: Dwarf chinkapin oak, dwarf chestnut oak.

SIZE AND SHAPE: Small trees (occasionally) or spreading shrubs (usually), **3–10' [46'] tall**, rarely reaching 15'; crowns scruffy, rounded; roots deep, spreading.

TRUNKS: Short, crooked, usually leaning and clumped, 3–5" [7"] in diameter; **mature bark pale brown, thin-scaled, flaky;** wood hard, heavy, close-grained, decay-resistant.

BRANCHES: Spreading; twigs reddish-brown to pale gray, smooth, slender, brittle; **pith 5-pointed**

in cross-section; buds light brown, about ⅛" long, buds at twig tips clustered.

LEAVES: Alternate, simple, deciduous; **blades 1½–4¾" (rarely to 6")** long, widest above the middle, shiny, bright yellowish-green above, densely hairy with white, star-shaped hairs beneath, firm, with **3–9 (usually 6) straight, parallel veins per side ending in large teeth which vary** from long and pointed to shallow and blunt; some leaves may persist in winter.

FLOWERS: Tiny, without petals; unisexual with male and female flowers on the same tree; male flowers yellow, hairy, in hanging catkins 1–2¾" long; female flowers yellowish-red, stalkless, 1–2 per cluster; flowers in May (as leaves expand).

FRUITS: Slightly elongated, **chestnut brown,** leathery-shelled nuts (**acorns**) ⅜–¾" **long,** single or paired; tips rounded with a small, abrupt point, lower ⅓–½ in a **downy-lined cup** of hairy, overlapping, slightly thickened scales; seeds single **white kernels;** acorns mature in first autumn.

HABITAT: Dry, open sites, especially on sandy or gravelly soils.

ORIGIN: Native.

THE THICK, TANNIN-RICH INNER BARK of black oak was sometimes used for tanning leather. It contains the yellow pigment quercitron, which became a popular dye in Europe and was sold commercially until the late 1940s. • White-tailed deer, small mammals, wild turkeys, jays and grouse all eat the bitter acorns and help to disperse the seeds.

• This highly variable oak hybridizes with northern red oak (p. 112) and northern pin oak (p. 114), further complicating identification. Generally, black oak is distinguished from other species with bristle-pointed leaves (the red and black oaks) by its woolly, 4-angled buds (vs. shiny, egg-shaped buds), the star-shaped hairs on the undersides of its leaves (vs. hairless leaves), the loose (vs. compact) scales of its fringed (vs. nonfringed) acorn cups and its bright yellow-orange (vs. usually reddish) inner bark.

• The species name *velutina* means "like velvet," a reference to the silvery-woolly buds and hairy leaves. • This long-lived, shade-intolerant tree is considered a good indicator of sites with dry to very dry conditions.

ALSO CALLED: Yellow-barked oak, yellow oak, quercitron oak.

SIZE AND SHAPE: Trees 50–80' [131'] tall; crowns open, irregular; roots deep (taproot), spreading.

TRUNKS: Straight, 12–48" [79"] in diameter; mature bark dark grayish-brown to blackish, deeply **cracked into rectangles; inner bark yellow to yellowish-orange;** wood light brown, hard, heavy.

BRANCHES: Horizontal to ascending, with irregular branchlets; **twigs stout, stiff, dark reddish-brown, becoming hairless; pith 5-pointed** in cross-section; **buds gray- to white-woolly, 4-angled,** pointed, $1/4$–$3/8$" long.

LEAVES: Alternate, simple, deciduous; blades 4–8" long, **glossy, dark green above, dull yellowish-brown beneath** with **star-shaped hairs on veins and in vein axils,** deeply pinnately lobed; **lobes 5–7, parallel-sided,** perpendicular to main axis; teeth few, coarse, bristle-tipped; **notches U-shaped.**

FLOWERS: Tiny, without petals; unisexual with male and female flowers on the same tree; male flowers hairy, in hanging catkins 4–6" long;

female flowers reddish, about $1/4$" long, in small clusters; flowers in May (as leaves expand).

FRUITS: Round, reddish-brown, leathery-shelled nuts **(acorns)** $1/2$–$3/4$" **long,** single or paired, **lower $1/3$–$1/2$ in a dull brown, slightly fringed cup of thin, loose, overlapping scales;** tips with a small, abrupt point; seeds single yellow kernels; acorns mature in second autumn; both large (second-year) and small (first-year) acorns usually present.

HABITAT: Dry, well-drained sites with sandy or gravelly soils, often mixed with pine or hickory.

ORIGIN: Native.

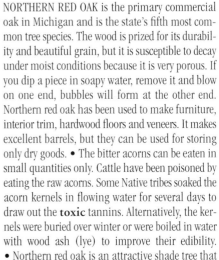

NORTHERN RED OAK is the primary commercial oak in Michigan and is the state's fifth most common tree species. The wood is prized for its durability and beautiful grain, but it is susceptible to decay under moist conditions because it is very porous. If you dip a piece in soapy water, remove it and blow on one end, bubbles will form at the other end. Northern red oak has been used to make furniture, interior trim, hardwood floors and veneers. It makes excellent barrels, but they can be used for storing only dry goods. • The bitter acorns can be eaten in small quantities only. Cattle have been poisoned by eating the raw acorns. Some Native tribes soaked the acorn kernels in flowing water for several days to draw out the **toxic** tannins. Alternatively, the kernels were buried over winter or were boiled in water with wood ash (lye) to improve their edibility. • Northern red oak is an attractive shade tree that transplants readily and grows quickly. Introduced to Europe in 1724, it now grows wild in European forests. • Small mammals such as raccoons and squirrels, as well as white-tailed deer, black bears, wild turkeys and blue jays, eat the acorns. Deer also browse on the young twigs in winter.

ALSO CALLED: Red oak, gray oak • *Q. borealis.*

SIZE AND SHAPE: Trees 65–100' [115'] tall; crowns broad, round; roots deep (taproot), spreading.

TRUNKS: Straight, 12–40" [65"] in diameter; young bark smooth, slate gray; mature bark with long, low, pale gray ridges, eventually checkered; inner bark pinkish-red; wood pinkish to reddish-brown, hard, heavy, coarse-grained.

BRANCHES: Spreading; **twigs reddish-brown and hairless; pith 5-pointed** in cross-section; **buds shiny reddish-brown,** mostly hairless, pointed, about 1/4" long, often clustered at branch tips.

LEAVES: Alternate, simple, deciduous; **blades firm, 4–9" long, deeply pinnately lobed** to shallowly lobed on lower branches or simply toothed on young trees, dull, dark yellowish-green above, paler beneath, vein axils often hairy-tufted; **lobes 5–11, roughly triangular;** teeth few, coarse, **tipped with bristles;** notches rounded, V-shaped; leaves red in autumn.

FLOWERS: Tiny, without petals; unisexual with male and female flowers on the same tree; male flowers hairy, yellowish-green, in hanging catkins 4–5" long; female flowers hairy, bright green, about 1/8" long, usually single or paired; flowers in May–June (as leaves expand).

FRUITS: Round, reddish-brown, leathery-shelled nuts **(acorns)** 1/2–11/8" long, single or paired, lower 1/4 (rarely 1/3) **in a saucer-shaped cup of thin, hairless, reddish-brown scales;** tips rounded with a small, abrupt point; seeds single yellowish kernels; **acorns mature in second autumn;** both large (second-year) and small (first-year) acorns generally present.

HABITAT: Well-drained, upland forests in a wide range of sites, from cool, moist maple-beech stands to warmer, drier, oak-hickory woodlands.

ORIGIN: Native.

THIS ATTRACTIVE, SYMMETRICAL TREE provides checkered shade in many parks and gardens. Pin oak is shallow-rooted and easily transplanted, and it is capable of tolerating urban conditions in areas well outside its natural range. • Because of taxonomic confusion, trees sold as pin oak may be northern pin oak (p. 114) or scarlet oak (p. 115) • The knotty, poor-quality wood is coarse-grained and ring-porous, with a distinct ring of large pores laid down each spring. Pin oak wood is sometimes sold as red oak for construction, fence posts and firewood. • This fast-growing tree is among the first oaks to bloom each spring. It can live 100–200 years. • White-tailed deer, small mammals, wild turkeys and waterfowl eat the bitter acorns. • Two explanations have been suggested for the derivation of the common name. "Pin oak" could refer to the stiff, persistent, "pin-like" branchlets that often project from the trunks and lower branches of larger trees. The name has also been attributed to the many tiny dots or "pin-knots" that speckle lumber cut from the wood of this species. These tiny knots are created by the abundant, persistent side-branches.

ALSO CALLED: Swamp oak, Spanish oak, water oak.

SIZE AND SHAPE: Trees 35–65' [106'] tall; crowns compact, cylindrical to pyramidal; roots shallow.

TRUNKS: Straight, 12–24"[50"] in diameter; mature bark grayish-brown, **smooth or with small, inconspicuous ridges; inner bark reddish;** wood light brown, hard, heavy.

BRANCHES: Slightly drooping (lower) to ascending (upper) with many short, spur-like side-branches; dead branches often persist; twigs reddish-brown, slender, soon becoming hairless; **pith 5-pointed** in cross-section; buds light chestnut brown, about 1/8" long, essentially hairless.

LEAVES: Alternate, simple, deciduous; blades 2¾–6" long, **shiny, dark green above,** paler beneath, with hair tufts in main vein axils, **deeply pinnately lobed; lobes 5–7,** each 3 times as long as the width between opposite notches, **wide-spreading, upper sides perpendicular to the midvein;** teeth few, coarse, each with **bristle at tip;** notches widely U-shaped; stalks slender; leaves bright red in autumn.

FLOWERS: Tiny, without petals; unisexual with male and female flowers on the same tree; male flowers yellowish, numerous, in hanging, hairy catkins 2–4" long; female flowers woolly, reddish, about 1/8" long, in clusters of 1–4 on short, hairy stalks; flowers in May (as leaves expand).

FRUITS: Round, leathery-shelled nuts **(acorns)** 3/8–1/2" long, 1–3 together, **lower 1/4 in a finely hairy, reddish-brown, saucer-shaped cup** of thin, pointed scales; tips rounded with a small, abrupt point; seeds single, yellow to pale brown kernels; acorns mature and separate from cup in second autumn.

HABITAT: Low, flat, poorly drained sites that are seasonally wet, such as wetlands and streamsides.

ORIGIN: Native.

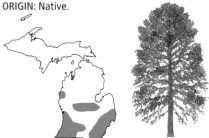

NORTHERN PIN OAK resembles pin oak (p. 113) but prefers upland sites, rather than low, wet habitats. Also, it has slightly elongated acorns with deep cups, rather than round acorns with saucer-shaped cups. It often hybridizes and could be confused with black oak (p. 111), but northern pin oak has smaller leaves, pale yellow (not bright yellow) inner bark and persistent "pin-like" branchlets on its trunks plus larger branches (both absent on black oak). • **Shumard oak** (*Q. shumardii*), shown in pink/dark green on the map, is rare in Michigan. Shumard oak has been confused with black oak and northern red oak (p. 112) or placed among the hybrids of those species. It is distinguished by its more deeply indented leaves and its preference for moist, clayey soils rather than sandy sites. Shumard oak is native to Illinois, Indiana and Ohio, and it has recently been discovered in swamp forests on the Lake Erie–Lake St. Clair lakeplain in Michigan. Look for a large (65–130' tall) tree with large (4–8") leaves each with 7–11 relatively broad lobes. Also, Shumard oak has large ($^1/_2$–$1^1/_8$"), round acorns with tam-shaped cups that enclose $^1/_3$ of the nut.

ALSO CALLED: Hills oak, jack oak, upland pin oak, scrub oak.

SIZE AND SHAPE: Trees 50–65' [103'] tall; crowns narrow, cylindrical, rounded; taproot.

TRUNKS: Straight, 12–24" [44"] in diameter, with many stubby branches persisting below the crown; mature bark dark grayish-brown, with **shallow, narrow ridges; inner bark light yellow;** wood pale reddish-brown, hard, heavy.

BRANCHES: Spreading to ascending; twigs bright reddish-brown and hairy when young, soon grayish-brown and hairless; **pith 5-pointed** in cross-section; buds shiny reddish-brown, $^1/_8$–$^1/_4$" long.

LEAVES: Alternate, simple, deciduous; **blades 3–5" long, shiny, bright green above,** paler with hairy-tufted vein axils beneath, **deeply pinnately lobed; lobes 5–7,** each 3 times as long as the width between opposite notches, **wide-spreading, upper lobes perpendicular to the midvein;** teeth few, **bristle-tipped;** notches widely U-shaped; stalks slender, hairless; leaves bright red in autumn.

FLOWERS: Tiny, without petals; unisexual with male and female flowers on the same tree; male flowers hairy, in hanging catkins 1–$2^3/_4$" long; female flowers red, hairy, about $^1/_8$" long, in compact clusters of 1–3; flowers in spring (as leaves expand).

FRUITS: **Ellipsoidal to almost round,** light brown, leathery-shelled nuts **(acorns)** $^1/_2$–$^3/_4$" **long,** single or paired, **lower $^1/_3$–$^1/_2$ in cup of finely hairy, light brown, thin scales;** tips abruptly small-pointed; seeds single yellow kernels; acorns mature in second autumn.

HABITAT: Heavy soils in swampy forests; elsewhere in dry upland sites.

ORIGIN: Native.

WITH ITS RAPID GROWTH, broad, open crown and bright red autumn leaves, scarlet oak is a popular ornamental tree. It is often cultivated as a hardy shade tree in parks and gardens. • Scarlet oak is closely related to northern pin oak (p. 114), and some taxonomists feel that both belong in a single species complex, grading from scarlet oak in the south to northern pin oak in the north. Scarlet oak is distinguished by its white (rather than yellow) nut kernels, hairy-tipped (rather than hairless) buds and clear trunks (lacking persistent branch stubs almost to the ground). Hybridization with other species such as black oak (p. 111) and northern red oak (p. 112) further confuses the picture, along with a similar north–south species gradation between black oak and red oak. • Large, round galls called "oak apples" appear on the leaves of many oaks. These growths are caused by a substance that certain insects (e. g., wasps) release when they lay eggs in the leaves. The substance causes cells to undergo unusually rapid growth, and the leaf lays down more and more tissue around the egg. Inside the galls, the eggs hatch, and the young larvae find themselves surrounded by protective layers of nutritious leaf cells. Most larvae spend their entire cycle inside the gall and then pupate to emerge as adult insects.

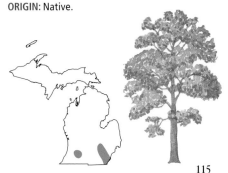

ALSO CALLED: Red oak, black oak.

SIZE AND SHAPE: Trees 50–65' [117'] tall; crowns open, broad, rounded; taproot.

TRUNKS: Straight, 12–24" [77"] in diameter; **mature bark dark grayish-brown, thin, smooth to scaly; inner bark reddish;** wood light reddish-brown, hard, heavy.

BRANCHES: Slender; twigs slender, hairy and green at first, soon becoming hairless and light brown; **pith 5-pointed** in cross-section; buds dark reddish-brown, about ¼" long, hairy toward the tips.

LEAVES: Alternate, simple, deciduous; **blades 3–6" long and almost as wide, firm, shiny green above,** paler beneath, **deeply pinnately lobed; lobes 5–9,** wide-spreading; teeth few, coarse, each with **bristle at tip;** notches widely U-shaped; stalks slender; leaves scarlet in autumn.

FLOWERS: Tiny, without petals; unisexual with male and female flowers on the same tree; male flowers reddish-hairy with yellow anthers, numerous, in hanging catkins 2¾–4" long; female flowers woolly, bright red, about ⅛" long, in clusters of 1–4 on short, hairy stalks; flowers in May (as leaves expand).

FRUITS: Round, pale reddish-brown, leathery-shelled nuts **(acorns)** ½–¾" **long, 1–3 together, lower ½ in a finely hairy, reddish-brown to orange cup** of thin, pointed scales; tips rounded, usually with concentric rings around a small, abrupt point; seeds single whitish kernels; acorns mature and separate from cup late in second autumn.

HABITAT: Dry, well-drained sites (sometimes seasonally wet but then droughty) with sandy soils, usually mixed with other oaks and hickories.

ORIGIN: Native.

115

SHINGLE OAK was known to pioneers for its heavy, straight-grained wood, which could be split into thin sheets and used as clapboard, shakes and shingles. This gave rise to the common name, "shingle oak," and the scientific name *imbricaria*, "overlapping." Today, shingle oak is occasionally cut in mixed stands and marketed as "red oak." • This attractive, relatively fast-growing oak is sometimes used as an ornamental. It is rarely grown in Europe, but in North America it has been planted as a shade tree and also in hedges and windbreaks. Unlike most oaks, shingle oak often holds its dry, brown leaves in winter. • The bitter acorns are eaten by deer, squirrels, wild turkeys and waterfowl such as mallards and wood ducks. • Although there are oaks with simple, smooth-edged leaves elsewhere, shingle oak is the only species native to Michigan. • Bristle-tipped leaves reflect the link between shingle oak and the red/black oaks (pp. 111–115). Shingle oak hybridizes with several of these species, producing offspring that have leaves edged with small lobes or bristles. Two of the most common hybrids are **Q. x *runcinata*** (offspring of shingle oak and northern red oak, p. 112) and **Q. x *leana*** (offspring of shingle oak and black oak, p. 111). Hybrids with scarlet oak (p. 115) are much rarer.

ALSO CALLED: Jack oak, northern laurel oak.

SIZE AND SHAPE: Symmetrical trees 35–65' [116'] tall; young crowns pyramidal, rounded with age.

TRUNKS: Straight, 12–32" [44"] wide; **bark light grayish-brown,** with low, broad, scaly ridges; wood light reddish-brown, coarse-grained, decay resistant.

BRANCHES: Tough, wide-spreading; twigs slender, dark green to brown, soon lustrous and smooth; **pith 5-pointed** in cross-section; buds shiny, light brown, about ⅛" long, pointing outward, clustered at branch tips.

LEAVES: Alternate, simple, deciduous; blades yellow at first, **lustrous, dark green and hairless with raised veins above,** paler and **soft-hairy beneath,** leathery, **smooth- or slightly wavy-edged, 5–7" long, bristle-tipped** (or with a spine scar); leaves yellow, tan or red-brown in autumn.

FLOWERS: Tiny, yellowish, without petals; unisexual with male and female flowers on the same tree; male flowers in slender, woolly-hairy, hanging catkins 2–2¾" long; female flowers usually 1–2 on slender, woolly stalks in axils of expanding leaves; flowers in May–June (with leaves).

FRUITS: Nuts (**acorns**) with dark brown, often striped, leathery shells, ½–¾" long, tips rounded with a small point, the **lower ⅓–½ seated in a cup** of hairy, reddish-brown scales **about ¼" deep;** seeds single, white, very bitter kernels; **acorns single or paired on stout, ⅜" long stalks,** remain in cup, **mature in second year.**

HABITAT: Floodplains, swamp forests, dry, upland woods, roadsides and edges of clearings.

ORIGIN: Native.

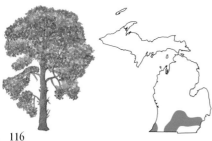

Key to Genera in the Birch Family (Betulaceae)

1a Female catkins tiny (about ⅛" long), egg-shaped, with distinctive reddish stigmas protruding from the tips; fruits large (⅜–½"), hard-shelled nuts within a sac or cluster of enlarged involucral bracts 1–2¾" long.........................*Corylus*, **hazelnut** (p. 121)

1b Female catkins larger (¼–¾" long), oblong to cylindrical; fruits small (⅛–⅜"), nutlets protected by scales or inflated bladders, borne in hanging clusters (catkins) 1⅛–6" long **2**

2a Nutlets in persistent, woody, cone-like catkins; pith 3-sided in cross-section .... *Alnus*, **alder** (key to species, below)

2b Nutlets not borne in woody "cones"; pith round or oval in cross-section.................................... **3**

3a Twigs and leaves often dotted with glands; nutlets tiny, winged, numerous, protected by small, 3-lobed scales in compact, elongating catkins .... *Betula*, **birch** (key to species, below)

3b Twigs and leaves not gland-dotted; nutlets wingless.. **4**

4a Bark smooth, pale or bluish-gray, over muscle-like ridges; leaf veins not forked; nutlets borne at the base of leafy, 2–3-lobed bracts in loose, elongated catkins .... *Carpinus*, **musclewood** (p. 120)

4b Bark shaggy, light brown, with rough lengthwise strips; leaf veins forked; nutlets enclosed in inflated bladders in compact catkins .... *Ostrya*, **ironwood** (p. 119)

Key to the Alders (Genus *Alnus*)

1a Branch-tip buds stalkless, covered by 3–5 unequal, overlapping scales; woody seed catkins equal to their stalks in length; nutlets broadly winged .... *A. viridis*, **green alder** (p. 126)

1b Branch-tip buds evidently stalked, covered by 2–3 equal scales; woody seed catkins longer than their stalks; nutlets narrowly winged or merely margined **2**

2a Seed catkins ⅝–1⅛" long, very sticky, in clusters of 2–5; leaves widest at or above midleaf, tip blunt or notched, usually with 5–6 veins per side .... *A. glutinosa*, **European alder** (p. 128)

2b Seed catkins ½–⅝" long, not sticky, in clusters of 3–10; leaves widest below midleaf, tip pointed, usually with 9–12 veins per side .... *A. incana* ssp. *rugosa*, **tag alder** (p. 127)

Key to the Birches (Genus *Betula*)

1a Mature bark yellowish-gray or pinkish to reddish- or blackish-brown; leaves usually with 8 or more pairs of prominent side-veins **2**

1b Mature bark whitish; leaves with 7 or fewer pairs of prominent side-veins **4**

2a Twigs and bark not smelling or tasting of wintergreen; mature bark pinkish; leaves with 6–10 veins per side .... *B. nigra*, **river birch** (p. 122)

2b Twigs and bark with the smell and flavor of wintergreen; mature bark yellowish-gray to dark reddish; leaves with 8–12 veins per side **3**

3a Mature bark shiny, dark reddish; leaves broadly pointed at the tip (sometimes slightly tapered), with 7–10 pairs of side-veins; found in swampy habitats
.... *B. murrayana*, **Murray birch** (p. 122)

3b Mature bark yellowish to bronze; leaves clearly tapered to a slender point, with 12–18 pairs of side-veins; found in moderately moist, often streamside habitats
.... *B. alleghaniensis*, **yellow birch** (p. 122)

4a Leaves broadly triangular, with a squared base and long, slender-pointed tip
.... *B. populifolia*, **gray birch** (p. 124)

4b Leaves variable in shape, often ovate or broadly elliptic; more abruptly tapered at the tip
.... **5**

5a Branches slender and drooping; mature bark peeling in long strands; leaves hairless beneath; introduced tree, escaped from cultivation
.... *B. pendula*, **European white birch** (p. 125)

5b Branches ascending; mature bark peeling in sheets; leaves hairy beneath (at least in vein axils when young) **6**

6a Leaves 1^1/$_8$–2" long (on fertile shoots), edged with relatively few coarse teeth (about 14 per side); a Eurasian escape occasionally found in wet habitats
.... *B. pubescens*, **downy birch** (p. 125)

6b Leaves 2–4" long, edged with many fine teeth (30+ per side); native species, growing in a wide range of habitats **7**

7a Leaves dotted with conspicuous resin glands; catkin scales with a long, rounded middle lobe *B. cordifolia*, **heart-leaved birch** (p. 123)

7b Leaves not conspicuously gland-dotted; catkin scales with a short, pointed middle lobe
.... *B. papyrifera*, **paper birch** (p. 123)

B. papyrifera, paper birch

Alnus viridis, green alder

THIS SLOW-GROWING TREE is too small to be of any commercial importance, but it produces extremely dense, hard, resilient wood that makes excellent tool handles, mallets and sleigh runners. Although it is also a very good fuel, it is almost impossible to split. The trunks have been used occasionally to make fence posts. • This attractive tall shrub or small tree, with its unusual fruit clusters, is cultivated as an ornamental in European parks and gardens. • The inconspicuous spring flowers are wind-pollinated. • The seeds, buds and catkins provide food for squirrels, grouse and various songbirds. • The genus name *Ostrya* is derived from the Greek *ostrua* or *ostuoes*, the name for a tree with very hard wood. The specific epithet *virginiana* means "of Virginia." The name "iron-wood" refers to the hard wood, but this name has also been applied to musclewood (p. 120) and to various other trees in other parts of the world. The fruit clusters resemble those of hops, hence the common name "hop-hornbeam."

ALSO CALLED: Hop-hornbeam, eastern hop-hornbeam, American hop-hornbeam, lever-wood, deerwood, rough-barked ironwood.

SIZE AND SHAPE: Trees 25–50 [74'] tall; crowns wide-spreading, rounded to cone-shaped; taproot.

TRUNKS: Straight, 6–12" [37"] in diameter; mature bark grayish-brown, **shaggy, with narrow, peeling strips** loose at both ends; wood light brown, fine-grained, very hard, tough, heavy.

BRANCHES: Long, slender; twigs pale green, finely hairy, becoming dark reddish-brown and hairless; buds greenish-brown, slightly hairy, about 1/8" long, **pointing outward**.

LEAVES: Alternate, simple, deciduous; 2 3/8–5" long, arranged **in 2 rows**, largest at twig tips; blades dark yellowish-green, soft, **sharply double-toothed**, tapered to a sharp point, with **straight veins forked near leaf edges;** leaves dull yellow in autumn, often persistent in winter.

FLOWERS: Tiny, greenish, without petals; uni-sexual with male and female flowers on the same tree; male flowers in dense, cylindrical, hanging catkins 1/2–2" long; female flowers 4–10 in loose, elongated catkins about 1/4" long; flowers in April–May (as leaves expand).

FRUITS: Hop-like, in **hanging, 1 1/8–2 3/8" long clusters of greenish to brownish, flattened-ovoid, 3/8–3/4" long, papery, inflated sacs,** each sac containing a 1/4" long nutlet; seeds single, inside **flattened nutlets about 1/4" long;** fruits mature in September, drop in winter.

HABITAT: Shady sites in well-drained, moderately dry forests.

ORIGIN: Native.

119

THIS SMALL, SHORT-LIVED TREE is not very important commercially, but it has exceptionally dense, strong wood. The wood is so hard that it is used to make levers, hammer handles and wedges for wood-splitting. It does not split or crack, so pioneers used it for making bowls and plates. Despite its toughness, however, the wood rots quickly when left in contact with soil. • This attractive, shade-tolerant species, with its scarlet to golden fall leaves, makes an excellent ornamental. Unfortunately, it is seldom used in landscaping. • Because of its smooth, blue-gray bark, musclewood is often confused with the true beeches of the genus *Fagus* (e.g., American beech, p. 104). Beech trees have very smooth trunks without muscle-like ridges, and their leaves are not double-toothed. • Birds and small rodents such as squirrels eat the buds, flower clusters and seeds, but browsing mammals seldom touch the twigs. In some regions, selective browsing by deer has created understories almost entirely of musclewood and other unpalatable species, severely limiting the replacement of overstory trees.

ALSO CALLED: Blue-beech, American hornbeam, ironwood, muscle-beech, smooth-barked ironwood, water-beech.

SIZE AND SHAPE: Small trees 10–35' [40'] tall; crowns low, flat-topped, bushy; roots shallow.

TRUNKS: Usually short and crooked, 4–12" [13"] in diameter, single or clumped, with **muscle-like ridges; mature bark slate gray, thin, smooth, tight;** wood heavy, hard, strong.

BRANCHES: Few, short, irregular, slender, zig-zagged, forming **flat sprays;** twigs greenish and hairy to reddish-brown or gray and hairless;

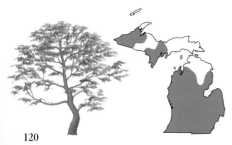

buds about 1/8" long, reddish-brown with pale scale edges, **pressed against the twig in 2 rows,** absent at twig tips.

LEAVES: Alternate, simple, deciduous, arranged **in 2 rows,** largest at twig tips; **blades 2–4" long, hairless and bluish-green above,** yellowish-green beneath, firm, **sharply double-toothed,** tapered to a sharp point, with **straight veins only slightly forked** (if at all); leaves red to golden in autumn.

FLOWERS: Tiny, greenish, without petals; unisexual with male and female flowers on the same tree; male flowers in dense, cylindrical, hanging catkins 1–1 1/2" long; female flowers hairy, in loose catkins 3/8–3/4" long; flowers in April–May (as leaves expand).

FRUITS: Ribbed nutlets 1/4–3/8" long, single in axils of green, 3-lobed, 3/4–1 1/8" long, leaf-like bracts that hang in clusters 4–6" long; seeds 1 per nutlet; nutlets mature in midsummer, some may persist into winter.

HABITAT: Rich, moist, shady **understory sites,** often near water.

ORIGIN: Native.

THE DELICIOUS EDIBLE NUTS of this tree have a flavor similar to European hazelnut or filbert (*C. avellana*). Some Native tribes preferred young hazelnuts to the harder, oilier mature nuts. Hazelnuts were eaten raw or prepared in a number of ways, including roasted in ovens (to reduce bitterness), cooked in cakes and desserts, ground to make nut butter and nut flour and dried for winter use. Crushed nuts mixed with bear fat, berries and meat provided tasty, high-calorie cakes or sausages—an early version of today's high-energy bars. • The male catkins of American hazelnut often develop a distinctive kink, caused by insect attacks. • **Beaked hazelnut (*C. cornuta*,** also called *C. rostrata*), shown in pink/dark green on the map, is a similar, slightly smaller (3–10' tall) shrub, identified by its smooth (hairless, without glands) leaf stalks and twigs and by the bristly, flask-shaped covering of fused bracts encasing each nut. Its nuts are also edible and were widely used by Native peoples. However, the bristly hairs on the husks act like tiny, irritating splinters in fingertips. Some people buried the nuts in wet mud for 10 days to rot away the prickles. Better yet, caches of husked nuts could be found in squirrels' nests.

ALSO CALLED: Hazelnut.

SIZE AND SHAPE: Tall, bushy shrubs 10–13' [34'] tall; crowns irregular; roots spreading, often suckering to form thickets.

TRUNKS: Usually clumped, 2–3" [4"] in diameter; bark smooth, gray.

BRANCHES: Alternate; twigs slender, brown, **glandular-hairy;** buds small, brown, round, with several finely hairy scales, absent at twig tips.

LEAVES: Alternate, simple, deciduous; blades leathery, dark green and hairless above, paler and soft-hairy beneath, oval to round, $1^1/2$–6" long, abruptly slender-pointed, rounded to notched at the base, **finely double-toothed,** straight veined, folded lengthwise in bud; **stalks soft-hairy, with gland-tipped bristles.**

FLOWERS: Tiny, without petals or sepals; unisexual with **male and female flowers on the same shrub;** male flowers 4-stamened, in **slender, hanging catkins** $1^1/2$–3" **long,** borne on **short, woody stalks** from side-buds on previous year's twigs; female flowers fewer, in **tiny, bud-like clusters about** $1/8$" **long,** tipped with **2 tiny, red threads (stigmas),** borne at the tips of leafy shoots; flowers develop in autumn and mature in March–April **(before leaves).**

FRUITS: Hard-shelled nuts, light brown, $3/8$–$5/8$" **long,** slightly flattened, surrounded by 2 hairy, broad, $3/4$–$1^1/4$" **long, leaf-like bracts with deeply cut edges** (the involucre); seeds 1 per nut; nuts single or in clusters of 2–4 (rarely 6) in August–September.

HABITAT: Relatively open sites in dry to moist woodlands and thickets.

ORIGIN: Native.

YELLOW BIRCH is an important source of hardwood lumber. The hard, golden to reddish-brown wood can be stained and buffed to a high polish. It has been used to make furniture, hardwood floors, doors, paneling, veneer, plywood, tool handles, snowshoe frames, sledges and railroad ties. In the 1700s, yellow birch was preferred over oak for building submerged parts of ships. • The aromatic, wintergreen-scented twigs and leaves make excellent tea. Trees can also be tapped in spring, and the sap can be boiled down to make syrup or fermented to make beer. • Never tear bark from living trees, as this can scar or even kill the tree. • **Murray birch (*B. murrayana*)**, shown in dark green on the map, is a new species that was recently discovered in Saginaw Forest, Washtenaw County. It was produced when **purpus birch (*B.* x *purpusii*,** a hybrid of yellow birch and bog birch, *B. pumila*) crossed with yellow birch. The resulting tree has larger pollen grains (with 112 chromosomes), larger stomata and larger, broader leaves than its parents. It also has dark reddish bark that peels like yellow birch bark. Careful examination of small "yellow birch" trees in swamps may reveal new populations of Murray birch. • Another native birch, **river birch (*B. nigra*)**, has tattered, pinkish bark, fewer leaf veins and no wintergreen scent. Its natural range extends to northwestern Indiana, and it is frequently planted in Michigan, so wild trees or garden escapes may eventually be found in southern Michigan.

ALSO CALLED: Swamp birch, curly birch, gold birch, hard birch, red birch, tall birch • *B. lutea.*

SIZE AND SHAPE: Trees 50–80' [114'] tall; crowns broad and rounded; roots shallow, wide-spreading.

TRUNKS: Straight, 24–40" [57"] in diameter; **young bark shiny reddish-brown,** with prominent **horizontal pores** (lenticels); **mature bark yellowish to bronze, tightly curling in papery shreds,** not peeling easily, eventually platy; wood hard, often wavy-grained.

BRANCHES: Large, spreading to drooping; twigs with a **moderate wintergreen fragrance** and

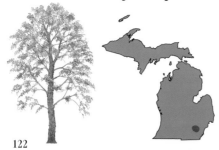

flavor, slender, shiny, with **dwarf shoots near the base;** buds brown, mostly hairy, flat-lying, about ¼" long, 5–7-scaled at twig tips, 3-scaled below, absent at twig tips; **scales 2-toned.**

LEAVES: Alternate, simple, deciduous; blades 2½–4½" long, deep yellowish-green above, paler beneath, with **8–12 straight veins per side, each ending in a large tooth with 2–3 smaller intervening teeth;** stalks short, grooved; leaves yellow in autumn.

FLOWERS: Tiny, without petals; unisexual with male and female flowers on the same tree; male flowers purplish yellow, in hanging catkins 2–4" long; female flowers greenish, in erect, cone-like catkins ½–¾" long; flowers form by autumn, mature in April–May (before leaves expand).

FRUITS: Small, flat, **2-winged nutlets** (samaras) in the axils of **3-lobed, hairy scales** about ¼" long, borne in **erect, cone-like catkins ¾–1½" long;** seeds 1 per nutlet; nutlets mature in autumn, gradually drop over winter.

HABITAT: Rich, moist, often shady sites in mixed hardwood forests and swamps and along streams.

ORIGIN: Native.

NATIVE PEOPLES used the tough, pliable bark of paper birch to make birch-bark canoes, sewing (with spruce roots) sheets of bark over white-cedar frames. Fir or pine resin was used for waterproofing. Birch bark also covered wigwams and provided material for baskets, cups and message paper. Strips of bark with lenticels were used as "sunglasses" to prevent snow blindness. • When several layers of outer bark are removed, the exposed inner bark soon blackens and dies. Exposure of large sections can kill the tree. • This sun-loving colonizer is more common and widespread now than it was 200 years ago, because cutting and burning have created many suitable sites. • Young paper birches resemble yellow birch (p. 122) but lack the distinctive wintergreen fragrance or flavor. • **Heartleaf birch** (**B. *cordifolia***, also called *B. papyrifera* var. *cordifolia* or mountain paper birch) is a very similar tree that is distinguished by its notched, conspicuously resin-dotted leaves (paper birch leaves have wedge-shaped to notched bases and inconspicuous or absent dots) and by the long, rounded (rather than short, pointed) middle lobe of its catkin scales. Some taxonomists include heartleaf birch and paper birch in the same species. Although the 2 species are different genetically, they can look identical. Heartleaf birch trees have been identified in northern Michigan, but if this species cannot be distinguished using field characteristics, perhaps it is best considered part of a broad paper birch complex.

ALSO CALLED: White birch, canoe birch, silver birch, spoolwood.

SIZE AND SHAPE: Trees 50–65' [107'] tall; crowns somewhat conical.

TRUNKS: Often leaning and clumped, 12–24" [70"] in diameter; young bark dark reddish, **thin, smooth,** with **horizontal pores** (lenticels); **mature bark white, peeling in large sheets,** eventually furrowed and almost black on lower trunk; inner bark orange; wood moderately hard, pale reddish-brown, odorless.

BRANCHES: Ascending to spreading, long and slender, with occasional short spur-like side-branches; **twigs slender,** dark reddish-brown, **with scattered, warty resin glands; buds resinous,** about 1/4" **long, with 3 brown-tipped, greenish scales,** absent at twig tips.

LEAVES: Alternate on long shoots, in 3s on short spurs, simple, deciduous; blades 2–3" long, dull green above, paler beneath, with **5–9 straight veins per side ending in large teeth with 3–5 smaller intervening teeth,** ovate, **widest below the middle,** slender-pointed; leaves yellow in autumn.

FLOWERS: Tiny, without petals; unisexual with male and female flowers on the same tree; male flowers brownish, in clusters of 1–3 hanging catkins 2 3/4–4" long; female flowers greenish, in erect catkins 3/8–1 1/2" long; flowers form by autumn, mature next April–May (before leaves expand).

FRUITS: Small, flat, broadly **2-winged nutlets** (samaras), about 1/16" long, **in axils of 3-lobed, usually hairy scales** within **hanging catkins 1 1/8–2" long;** seeds 1 per nutlet; nutlets mature in September–October, drop over winter.

HABITAT: Open, often disturbed sites and forest edges on a wide variety of substrates.

ORIGIN: Native.

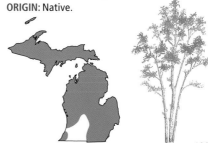

THIS EASTERN SPECIES was recently discovered in Michigan. In regions where it is common, gray birch wood has been used for firewood and for producing spindles, handles and other such items. • This small tree is occasionally planted as an ornamental. It is also sometimes grown in plantations as a nurse tree (to protect seedlings from heat and desiccation), but it soon interferes with young crop trees and must be cut. • Gray birch trees live about 50 years. A pioneer tree, it tolerates shade and thrives on dry, almost sterile soils. It can multiply rapidly to cover fields, burned areas and clear-cut sites.

Human activity often provides suitable habitat, and gray birch has been expanding west and north from its home range in northeastern North America. • White-tailed deer eat the twigs and buds in early spring. Ruffed grouse and small mammals eat the seeds, buds and young catkins. Many songbirds also feed on the seeds. • Gray birch trees usually have triangular black patches below each branch caused by the fungus *Pseudospropes longipilus*, which grows on excretions from the bark. • The species name *populifolia* means "with poplar-like leaves." Like the leaves of trembling aspen (p. 135), gray birch leaves tremble in the slightest breeze.

ALSO CALLED: Wire birch, fire birch, old field birch, swamp birch, white birch.

SIZE AND SHAPE: Small trees 12–40' [69'] tall; crowns narrow, open and irregular.

TRUNKS: **Often clumped and leaning,** 4–6" [23"] in diameter; young bark dark reddish-brown, thin, **smooth,** with **horizontal pores** (lenticels); **mature bark chalky white, peeling with difficulty in small plates;** wood light reddish-brown, light and soft.

BRANCHES: Often S-shaped with age; twigs dotted with warty resin glands, slender, **lacking wintergreen fragrance;** buds pale grayish-brown, often hairy, **gummy,** 3-scaled.

LEAVES: Alternate, simple, deciduous; blades 1½–2¾" long, shiny, rough and dark green above, smooth and paler beneath, with **6–9 straight veins per side** ending in **large teeth edged with smaller teeth, triangular,** square-based, **slender-tipped;** leaves yellow in autumn.

FLOWERS: Tiny; unisexual with male and female flowers on the same tree; **male flowers in single (usually) hanging catkins** 2½–4" long; female flowers in semi-erect catkins ½–1⅛" long; flowers form by autumn, mature the following spring (before leaves expand).

FRUITS: Small, flat, 2-winged nutlets, 1/16–1/8" wide, in the axils of hairy, 3-lobed scales; seeds 1 per nutlet; nutlets mature in autumn, drop in early winter.

HABITAT: Wet to mesic, sandy or gravelly soils, often in disturbed areas such as old fields.

ORIGIN: Native.

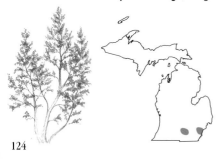

THE DURABLE WOOD of European white birch has been used for making skis, clogs and spindles, and as a source of cellulose and firewood. • Many cultivars of this small, graceful tree have been developed, including 'Laciniata,' which has deeply cut leaves on delicate, weeping branches. Unfortunately, birch trees are often attacked by bronze birch borer (*Agrilus anxius*) and by birch leaf miner (*Fenusa pusilla*). • In Europe, this fast-growing, sun-loving tree has been used as a nurse tree to protect young plantations of hardwood trees such as beech. • The leaves were used traditionally to make medicinal teas for treating urinary tract infections and kidney stones. The resin glands are sometimes used in hair lotions. • European white birch is often confused with gray birch (p. 124), but gray birch has leaves with longer, more slender points and more numerous teeth (18–47 vs. 9–28 per side). Also, gray birch has single (usually) or paired male catkins, densely hairy catkin scales and non-peeling bark. • A rarely cultivated species, **downy birch** (*B. pubescens*, sometimes included in *B. alba*) is occasionally reported to have naturalized in Michigan, but this claim has never been substantiated. Downy birch is the European counterpart of paper birch, distinguished by its resinous buds, small leaves (1¹/₈–2" long on fertile shoots), small female catkins (¹/₂–1¹/₈" long) and more stiffly erect branches.

ALSO CALLED: European birch, weeping birch, European weeping birch, silver birch • *B. verrucosa*.

SIZE AND SHAPE: Trees 30–50' [78'] tall; crowns open, broad to egg-shaped; roots shallow, weak.

TRUNKS: Usually clumped, up to 12" [50"] in diameter; **young bark thin, smooth, with horizontal pores** (lenticels); **mature bark bright chalky white,** peeling in **long strands,** eventually **blackened and furrowed near the trunk base;** wood yellowish-white, moderately hard.

BRANCHES: Spreading, with drooping tips; twigs reddish-tinged, **spindly, hairless, dotted with tiny resin glands;** buds 3-scaled.

LEAVES: Alternate, simple, deciduous; blades 1¹/₈–2³/₄" long, **hairless, with 5–9 straight veins per side ending in large teeth with smaller intervening teeth,** triangular to broadly oval, slender-pointed; stalks long, slender; leaves yellow in autumn, persist 3–4 weeks longer than leaves of native birches.

FLOWERS: Tiny, without petals; unisexual with male and female flowers on the same tree; male flowers in clusters of 2–4 hanging catkins 1¹/₂–3¹/₂" long; female flowers in stout catkins ³/₈–1¹/₈" long; flowers form by autumn, mature the following spring (before leaves expand).

FRUITS: Small, flat, **2-winged nutlets** (samaras) in axils of **sparsely hairy, 3-lobed scales** within hanging catkins ³/₄–1¹/₂" long; seeds 1 per nutlet; nutlets mature in autumn, drop over winter.

HABITAT: Open, usually well-drained sites, typically near vacant lots and homesteads.

ORIGIN: Introduced from Europe and Asia.

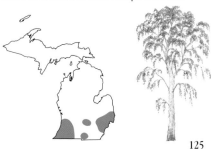

ALDER WOOD is moderately strong, but the trunks are too small to be of economic importance. Green alder has been used for firewood. • This species is more shade tolerant than other alders, so it often grows in forest understories. Green alder starts producing seed at 5–10 years of age, with heavy crops about every 4 years or so. Alder flowers are wind pollinated, so they appear early, before most other plants have developed leaves that would interfere with wind currents. Young alders also reproduce vegetatively by sending up basal sprouts. • Alder roots have clusters of nodules containing nitrogen-fixing bacteria, which convert atmospheric nitrogen into a form usable by plants. Alders therefore thrive on nutrient-poor sites, and when these shrubs die and decompose, they release stored nitrogen and enrich the soil for other plants. • Many birds and mammals eat alder buds, twigs and catkins. • The genus name *Alnus* is derived from a Celtic word meaning "neighbor of streams." The specific epithet *viridis* means "green" and refers to the bright green leaves. The earlier name, *crispa*, meaning "curly," is a reference to the leaf edges.

ALSO CALLED: Mountain alder, • *A. crispa*.

SIZE AND SHAPE: Tall shrubs or rarely small trees over 13' [28'] tall; crowns irregular to rounded.

TRUNKS: Usually clumped, up to 3" in diameter; **young bark smooth,** with large, pale **horizontal pores** (lenticels); inner bark reddish; mature bark reddish-brown to gray, becoming rough; wood reddish-brown, light, soft.

BRANCHES: Spreading; **twigs sticky,** somewhat hairy; **pith 3-sided** in cross-section; **buds stalkless,** with curved, sharp points and **overlapping, often reddish scales.**

LEAVES: Alternate, simple, deciduous; blades 1½–3½" long, bright shiny green above, paler and glandular beneath, with **6–9 prominent, straight veins per side,** ovate to oval, often slightly wavy-edged, with **small, sharp, single teeth, sticky when young.**

FLOWERS: Tiny, without petals; unisexual with male and female flowers on the same tree; male flowers in stalked clusters of slender, hanging catkins 2–3" long; female flowers in clusters of 3–5 **long-stalked, cone-like catkins** ³/₈–¹/₂" long; catkins form in autumn, persist over winter (female cones within buds), mature in May–June **(as leaves expand).**

FRUITS: Small, flat, **broadly 2-winged nutlets** (samaras) with wings equal to or wider than nutlet, in axils of 5-lobed, **woody scales in erect, persistent cones;** seeds 1 per nutlet; nutlets drop in late summer to autumn.

HABITAT: Mixed woods and riverbanks to dry uplands, often on rock, gravel or sand.

ORIGIN: Native.

TAG ALDER is too small to be of economic importance, but it does play an important ecological role in shading and stabilizing streambanks and enriching soil. • Native people and settlers extracted a dark dye from the bark for tanning and staining hides. The bark was also boiled to make medicinal teas for treating rheumatism, and it was applied to wounds as a poultice for reducing bleeding and swelling. Alder bark has astringent properties and contains salicin, a compound similar to aspirin. • This fast-growing, short-lived pioneer species readily invades land exposed by fire or clear-cutting. Tag alder cannot tolerate shade, so other trees and shrubs soon replace it. • This tree produces some of the earliest flowers each spring, which are eagerly sought by bees. The forked clusters of 3–4 toe-like catkins have been likened to turkey feet. • Sharp-tailed grouse and ruffed grouse eat alder buds, and cottontail rabbits, deer and moose browse the twigs. • The alternate common name "speckled alder" refers to the conspicuous pores dotting the bark. The names "gray alder," "hoary alder" and *incana*, which means "grayish" or "hoary," all refer to the pale undersides of the leaves.

ALSO CALLED: Speckled alder, gray alder, hoary alder, red alder, river alder, rough alder • *A. rugosa*.

SIZE AND SHAPE: Shrubs or small trees 5–25' [66'] tall; crowns open, broad, irregular; roots very shallow.

TRUNKS: Usually clumped, crooked, 1⅛–4" [12"] in diameter; bark dark reddish-brown, **smooth,** with conspicuous **pale orange, horizontal pores** (lenticels); inner bark reddish; wood reddish-brown, light, soft.

BRANCHES: Spreading, twisted; twigs zigzagged, hairy; **pith 3-sided** in cross-section; **buds reddish-brown, stalked, blunt-tipped, with 2–3 equal (not overlapping) scales,** absent at twig tips.

LEAVES: Alternate, simple, deciduous; blades 2–4" long, **dull, dark green above, paler green to hoary beneath,** thick, with **6–12 conspicuous, straight veins per side,** broadly ovate, with rounded to notched bases and short-pointed tips, **edges undulating and with sharp double teeth, never sticky;** leaves green in autumn.

FLOWERS: Tiny, without petals; unisexual with male and female flowers on the same tree; male flowers brownish, in stalked clusters of slender, hanging catkins 2–4" long; female flowers in clusters of 2–5 **short-stalked, cone-like catkins;** catkins form in autumn, persist over winter (with young female cones visible), mature in March–May **(before leaves expand).**

FRUITS: Small, flat, **narrowly 2-winged nutlets** (samaras) in axils of 5-lobed, **woody scales in** hanging, ⅜–⅝" **long cones that persist year-round;** seeds 1 per nutlet; nutlets drop in late summer to autumn.

HABITAT: Wet, open sites on shores and in depressions and wetlands.

ORIGIN: Native.

EUROPEAN ALDER was introduced to North America for producing charcoal, a key ingredient in gunpowder. In Scotland, this species was known as Scottish mahogany and was used to make fine furniture. Elsewhere, it was made into clogs, cart and spinning wheels, bowls, spoons, wooden heels and cigar boxes. Wood buried in bogs developed the color, but not the hardness, of ebony. Because of its ability to withstand rot in wet conditions, European alder was widely used in pumps, troughs, sluices and pilings. • Europeans traditionally used the bark for dying, tanning and dressing leather and for making fishing nets. The bark was also boiled to make a wash for treating inflammation, especially around the throat. In the Alps, peasants applied bags of heated alder leaves as a cure for rheumatism. • In eastern North America, European alder has been widely planted as an ornamental shade tree and as a companion tree for improving soil nitrogen in conifer plantations. • This fast-growing tree readily sends up suckers, especially when the parent plant is cut back. In some areas, European alder is an aggressive weed, displacing native trees and shrubs along streams and in wetlands.

ALSO CALLED: Black alder, European black alder.

SIZE AND SHAPE: Trees 30–50' [66'] tall; crowns rounded.

TRUNKS: Single or clumped, relatively straight, 8–12" [27"] in diameter; **young bark thin, smooth,** with large, pale **horizontal pores** (lenticels); inner bark reddish; mature bark dark brown, becoming rough; wood reddish-brown, light, soft.

BRANCHES: Spreading; **twigs often sticky,** somewhat hairy; **pith 3-sided** in cross-section; **buds stalked, blunt-tipped,** with 2–3 equal scales.

LEAVES: Alternate, simple, deciduous; blades 1½–3" long, smooth and dark green above, paler and finely hairy beneath, with **5–6 prominent, straight veins per side,** broadly ovate to almost round, widest above the middle, **blunt-tipped to notched,** coarsely **double-toothed, sticky when young;** leaves green to brown in late autumn.

FLOWERS: Tiny, without petals; unisexual with male and female flowers on the same tree; male flowers in stalked clusters of hanging catkins 2–4" long; female flowers in small clusters of **short-stalked, cone-like catkins ³/₄–1" long;** catkins form by autumn, mature in March–May (before leaves expand).

FRUITS: Small, flat, **narrowly 2-winged nutlets,** in axils of 5-lobed, **woody scales in sticky, ⁵/₈–1¹/₈" long cones that persist year-round;** seeds 1 per nutlet; nutlets drop in late summer to autumn.

HABITAT: Floodplains and swampy areas; rarely in drier, upland sites.

ORIGIN: Introduced from Europe.

Key to Genera in the Willow Family (Salicaceae)

1a Buds with a single scale; leaves typically lance-shaped to linear, more than 3 times as long as wide .... *Salix,* **willow** (key to species, below)

1b Buds covered by several overlapping scales; leaves ovate to round or triangular, less than 3 times as long as wide .... *Populus,* **poplar** (key to species, p. 132)

Key to the Willows (Genus *Salix*)

1a Twigs and leaves conspicuously contorted .... *S. matsudana,* **twisted willow** (p. 147)

1b Twigs and leaves relatively straight, not conspicuously contorted **2**

2a Leaves opposite to sub-opposite, purplish
.... *S. purpurea,* **purple-osier willow** (p. 149)

2b Leaves alternate, not purplish **3**

3a Leaf stalks with glands just below the blade **4**

3b Leaf stalks lacking glands near the blade **12**

4a Leaves linear to narrowly lance-shaped, more than 5 times as long as wide, widest below the middle.. **5**

4b Leaves lance-shaped to ovate-oblong, up to 4 times as long as wide, often widest at or above the middle **8**

5a Stipules well-developed and persistent, especially on young shoots
.... *S. nigra,* **black willow** (p. 141)

5b Stipules absent or slender, soon shed **6**

6a Branches slender, weeping, with long, hanging tips; seed catkins often 1–1¹⁄₈" long
.... *S. babylonica* **hybrids, weeping willows** (p. 142)

6b Branches stouter, sometimes hanging but not long-drooping; seed catkins usually more than 1¹⁄₂" long.. **7**

7a Mature leaves essentially hairless, glossy, dark green above; branchlets brittle-based, easily broken.. *S. fragilis,* **crack willow** (p. 147)

7b Mature leaves silvery-silky, dull green above; branchlets not brittle-based
.... *S. alba,* **white willow** (p. 142)

8a Leaves whitish beneath, with a conspicuous dull waxy bloom...................................... **9**

8b Leaves green above and below, without a notable waxy bloom.................................... **11**

9a Flowers and fruits produced in late summer–autumn; young leaves hairless; mature leaves leathery, edged with gland-tipped teeth
.... *S. serissima,* **autumn willow** (p. 143)

9b Flowers and fruits produced in spring to early summer...**10**

10a Leaves about twice as long as wide, reddish and translucent at first, with a resinous, balsam-like fragrance ....*S. pyrifolia*, **balsam willow** (p. 145)

10b Leaves 3–4 times as long as wide, neither translucent nor fragrant when young ....*S. amygdaloides*, **peachleaf willow** (p. 150)

11a Leaves usually 3–6 times as long as wide, with a long, slender point, pale green and shiny beneath; twigs and young leaves not fragrant when crushed ....*S. lucida*, **shining willow** (p. 143)

11b Leaves about 1½–3 times as long as wide, more abruptly pointed, only slightly paler beneath; twigs and young leaves aromatic, with fragrant resin ....*S. pentandra*, **bayleaf willow** (p. 151)

12a Leaves silky-satiny beneath, with dense hairs; leaf edges down-rolled **13**

12b Leaves hairless or with a few scattered hairs on the lower surface; leaf edges various, rarely down-rolled...**14**

13a Leaves 2–8" long, crowded on branches; small branches few, flexible, shiny ....*S. viminalis*, **basket willow** (p. 139)

13b Leaves 1½–4" long, scattered or well-spaced on branches; small branches numerous, brittle, often coated with a waxy bloom..................................... *S. pellita*, **satiny willow** (p. 140)

14a Leaves smooth-edged or with irregular, rounded teeth...**15**

14b Leaves with distinct, regular teeth **16**

15a Capsules on visible slender stalks that are at least twice as long as the pale, yellowish scales, borne in loose catkins, appearing with the leaves; branchlets wide-spreading; leaves dull green with raised veins beneath (especially when young) ....*S. bebbiana*, **Bebb's willow** (p. 153)

15b Capsules on short stalks that are obscured by dark brown scales, forming dense catkins, appearing before the leaves; branchlets not wide-spreading; leaves shiny green above, relatively smooth beneath ....*S. discolor*, **pussy willow** (p. 152)

16a Mature leaves mostly 1½–3 times as long as wide, abruptly sharp-pointed ....*S. myricoides*, **blueleaf willow** (p. 145)

16b Mature leaves narrower, mostly 4–8 times as long as wide **17**

17a Branches slender, weeping, with long, hanging tips; seed catkins often 1–1⅛" long ....*S. babylonica* hybrids, **weeping willows** (p. 142)

17b Branches stouter, sometimes hanging but not long-drooping; seed catkins usually more than 1½" long **18**

18a   Mature leaves hairless or with just a few hairs on the veins beneath **19**

18b   Mature leaves hairy, at least on the lower surface **25**

19a   Leaves very narrow and linear, 2–6" long, $^1/_8$–$^1/_2$" wide, edged with widely spaced teeth; tall colonial shrubs, often forming thickets on floodplains
....*S. interior*, **sandbar willow** (p. 144)

19b   Leaves wider relative to their length, usually lance-shaped, edges wavy or closely toothed; tree/shrub form various **20**

20a   Leaves on young and non-flowering shoots lacking stipules or young leaves soon shedding their stipules **21**

20b   Leaves on young and non-flowering shoots with noticeable, persistent stipules.................. **24**

21a   Leaves narrowly egg-shaped, tapered to a long, slender tip; buds pointed
....*S. amygdaloides*, **peachleaf willow** (p. 150)

21b   Leaves narrower, lance-shaped to linear, tipped with a sharp to slightly tapered point; buds rounded **22**

22a   Branches hanging, "weeping"; leaves linear, finely sharp-toothed, with hairy stalks
.... *S. babylonica*, **hybrids, weeping willows** (p. 142)

22b   Branches not "weeping"; leaves lance-shaped, sharp-toothed, stalks hairless **23**

23a   Leaf stalks mostly $^1/_8$–$^1/_4$" long; leaf blades finely toothed, usually with a few hairs on the veins beneath....................................... *S. petiolaris*, **slender willow** (p. 146)

23b   Leaf stalks mostly >$^1/_4$" long, sometimes with glands near the blade; leaf blades coarsely toothed, completely hairless .... *S. fragilis*, **crack willow** (p. 147)

24a   Leaves green above and beneath .... *S. nigra*, **black willow** (p. 141)

24b   Leaves green above, pale with a whitish bloom (glaucous) beneath
.... *S. eriocephala*, **heartleaf willow** (p. 148)

25a   Leaves woolly, edges smooth, wavy or irregularly blunt-toothed, often down-rolled; young branches with distinctive, lengthwise ridges just under the bark
.... *S. cinerea*, **large gray willow** (p. 152)

25b   Leaves silky hairy to hairless, edged with fine, gland-tipped teeth; twig wood lacking distinct ridges.. **26**

26a   Leaves rounded at the base; catkin stalks absent or $^1/_8$–$^3/_8$" long; catkin scales pale yellowish, soon shed .... *S. eriocephala*, **heartleaf willow** (p. 148)

26b   Leaves tapered to a wedge-shaped base; catkin stalks $^3/_8$–$1^1/_2$" long; catkin scales dark brown to blackish, persistent in fruit... *S. alba*, **white willow** (p. 142)

Key to the Poplars (Genus *Populus*)

1a Mature leaves white- or grayish-woolly beneath, edged with a few irregular teeth and/or 3–5 blunt, palmate lobes; leaf stalks nearly round, flattened only near the blade .... *P. alba*, **white poplar** (p. 133)

1b Mature leaves neither woolly beneath or lobed, edged with regular teeth; leaf stalks round or variously flattened...**2**

2a Leaf stalks round, often channeled above, usually shorter than the blade; leaf blades ovate, clearly longer than wide **3**

2b Leaf stalks flattened (at least near the blade), usually equal to or longer than the blade; leaf blades triangular to heart-shaped or rounded, about as long as wide; buds with or without fragrant resin **4**

3a Leaf blades ovate, rounded or squared at the base; buds sticky with fragrant resin ....*P. balsamifera*, **balsam poplar** (p. 136)

3b Leaf blades heart-shaped, notched at the base; buds not sticky-resinous ....*P. heterophylla*, **swamp cottonwood** (p. 138)

4a Leaves more or less triangular or 4-sided, edged with a definite translucent border created by callus-tipped teeth; buds sticky with fragrant resin; bark rough **5**

4b Leaves more or less round, without a translucent border, teeth blunt-tipped; buds neither sticky nor fragrant; bark smooth (rough near the trunk base with age) **6**

5a Leaves triangular, usually with 2–5 glands at the base of the blade, edged with coarse teeth ($^1/_{16}$–$^3/_{16}$"); capsules splitting into 3–4 parts; a native, open-crowned tree ....*P. deltoides*, **eastern cottonwood** (p. 137)

5b Leaves typically diamond-shaped (sometimes squared at the base), rarely glandular at the base, edged with fine teeth ($^1/_{32}$–$^1/_{16}$"); capsules splitting in half; an introduced, usually columnar tree...................................... *P. nigra*, **European black poplar** (p. 137)

6a Leaves edged with 20–30 fine ($<^1/_{32}$"), regular teeth, blades shorter than their stalks, essentially hairless .... *P. tremuloides*, **trembling aspen** (p. 135)

6b Leaves edged with 7–15 coarse ($^1/_{16}$–$^1/_{4}$"), wavy teeth, blades shorter than their stalks, conspicuously woolly beneath when young ....*P. grandidentata*, **bigtooth aspen** (p. 134)

WHITE POPLAR was among the first trees introduced to North America. It can withstand salt spray and was often used for shelters near the ocean. • Although still widely planted as an ornamental, this fast-growing tree may cause problems. The spreading roots raise sidewalks and clog sewers, and abundant suckers shoot up in undesirable places. White poplar can also be an aggressive weed, displacing native plants from natural environments such as dunes.
• North American poplars can divided into 4 main groups, called sections: 1) Leucoides, represented by swamp cottonwood (p. 138); 2) Tacamahaca or balsam poplars, represented by balsam poplar (p. 136) and balm-of-Gilead (p. 136); 3) Aigeiros or cottonwoods, represented by cottonwood (p. 137) and the introduced European black poplar (p. 137); 4) Leuce or aspen poplars, represented by trembling aspen (p. 135), bigtooth aspen (p. 134) and the introduced white poplar. Confusingly, some of the Tacamahaca are called cottonwoods, a

name usually applied to the Aigeiros. • White poplar often hybridizes with native species such as bigtooth aspen and trembling aspen, producing offspring with intermediate characteristics. Most (possibly all) spread of white poplar is vegetative, by suckering or sprouting from twig or root debris. • At first glance, vigorous shoots of white poplar might be mistaken for those of a maple, but the poplar is easily distinguished by its woolly (not smooth), alternate (not opposite) leaves.

ALSO CALLED: Silver poplar, silver-leaved poplar, European white poplar.

SIZE AND SHAPE: Large trees 50–80' [86'] tall; crowns broad, rounded; roots deep, forming colonies by suckers.

TRUNKS: Often forked, 24–48" [76"] in diameter; **young bark smooth,** greenish- to grayish-white with **dark, diamond-shaped pores** (lenticels); mature bark darker, black and deeply furrowed near the base; wood pale reddish-yellow, light, soft.

BRANCHES: Large, spreading, crooked; **twigs white-woolly; pith 5-pointed** in cross-section; buds densely white-hairy, $^1/_8$–$^1/_4$" long, pointed, 5–7-scaled, lowest scale directly above the leaf scar.

LEAVES: Alternate, simple, deciduous; blades 2–4$^3/_4$" long, **dark green above, densely white-woolly beneath,** broadly ovate and wavy-edged to round and **palmately 3–5-lobed** (maple leaf–like), irregularly coarse-toothed; **stalks flattened, woolly;** leaf scars 3-sided, with 3 vein scars.

FLOWERS: Tiny, without petals; unisexual with male and female flowers on separate trees (only female trees known in Michigan), borne in hanging catkins 1$^1/_2$–3" long; flowers in April–May (before leaves expand).

FRUITS: Tiny, pointed capsules in hanging catkins 4–6" long; seeds $^1/_{16}$–$^1/_8$" long, tipped with a tuft of silky, white hairs; capsules mature in May–June (with leaves).

HABITAT: Fields, fence lines and other disturbed sites; prefers warm, moist sites.

ORIGIN: Introduced from Europe and Asia.

THIS TREE'S WOOD is similar to the wood of trembling aspen (p. 135) and has become a major source of pulp. • Bigtooth aspen and trembling aspen are both important for revegetating recently cut or burned land, holding soil in place and protecting other, slower-growing plant species. These fast-growing, shade-intolerant pioneer trees typically live 75–100 years. Mature trees (more than 20 years old) produce abundant seed every 4–5 years. The catkins mature 4–6 weeks after flowering. Although aspen seeds live only a few days, they are very numerous and sprout quickly on bare ground. These species will not grow from cuttings, but if established trees are stressed or lose their main growing tip, they will send up suckers from their roots. • In spring, the whitish-downy twigs and buds make bigtooth aspen stand out among other trees. • Grouse, quail and purple finches eat the buds and catkins. Moose, elk, deer, beavers, muskrats and rabbits all eat the buds, bark, twigs and leaves. • The specific epithet *grandidentata* means "large-toothed," in reference to the leaves. Because of their flattened stalks, these leaves tremble at the slightest breeze.

ALSO CALLED: Large-toothed aspen, big-tooth poplar, popple.

SIZE AND SHAPE: Trees 50–65' [132'] tall; crowns short, rounded; roots very wide-spreading.

TRUNKS: Straight, 12–24" [33"] in diameter, self-pruning; **young bark smooth, olive to yellow-gray with diamond-shaped marks** about 3/8" wide; mature bark dark gray, furrowed near trunk base; wood pale, soft, straight-grained.

BRANCHES: Coarse, spreading to ascending; twigs relatively stout, greenish- to brownish-gray, downy to almost hairless, with orange pores (lenticels); **pith 5-pointed in cross-section; buds dusty brown, grayish-downy,** neither resinous nor fragrant, 1/4–3/8" long, 5–7-scaled, **lowest scale above the leaf scar,** tips pointing outward.

LEAVES: Alternate, simple, deciduous; **blades grayish-hairy at first,** soon hairless, dark green above, paler beneath, 2–5" long, **ovate to almost round,** usually short-pointed, **with 6–15 coarse, uneven, blunt teeth per side; stalks flattened,** usually shorter than blades; leaves yellow in autumn.

FLOWERS: Tiny, without petals; unisexual with male and female flowers **in hanging catkins on separate trees; catkins slender, 1 1/8–3" long,** with hairy bracts; flowers develop in April **(before leaves expand).**

FRUITS: Downy, pointed, 1/4" long capsules, numerous, in hanging catkins 3–6" long; seeds 1/16–1/8" long, tipped with a **tuft of silky, white hairs;** capsules mature in May–June (as leaves expand).

HABITAT: Well-drained, upland forests; largest on moist, fertile sites; scrubby on dry, poor sites.

ORIGIN: Native.

ASPEN WOOD is an important source of fiber for chipboard, oriented strand board and paper. The wood is also used for excelsior, matchsticks, chopsticks, crates and fences. • Trembling aspen usually reproduces vegetatively. It sends up suckers from spreading roots, producing groups of genetically identical trees (clones) that can include thousands of trees covering areas up to 200 acres. Some clones are believed to have originated from trees that colonized land exposed by retreating Pleistocene glaciers 9500–11,000 years ago, making the clones among the oldest and largest living organisms on earth.

• About 500 species of plants and animals use aspen. The bark and twigs are a preferred food of deer, moose, beaver and snowshoe hares. Birds feed on the buds and catkins. • Many parasites infect aspens. Heart-rot fungus (*Fomes ignarius populinus*) produces hollow trunks used by cavity nesters such as flying squirrels, woodpeckers, owls and some ducks.

• The trembling leaves of this tree gave rise to a number of Native names meaning "woman's tongue" or "noisy tree." • Trunks exposed to sunlight often produce a protective white powder that can be brushed onto skin as sunscreen. White-barked trees are sometimes mistaken for birches.

ALSO CALLED: Quaking aspen, aspen poplar, golden aspen, popple, small-toothed aspen.

SIZE AND SHAPE: Trees 40–80' [109'] tall; crowns short, rounded; roots shallow, wide-spreading.

TRUNKS: Straight or crooked, 10–24" [39"] in diameter, self-pruning; young bark smooth, **pale greenish-gray to almost white, with dark, diamond-shaped marks,** often whitish-powdery; mature bark dark gray and furrowed near trunk base; wood pale, light, soft, straight-grained.

BRANCHES: Slender, spreading to ascending; twigs slender, shiny, dark green to brownish-gray, with orange pores (lenticels); **pith 5-pointed** in cross-section; buds shiny reddish-brown, slightly resinous, **not gummy,** not fragrant, about ¼" long, 6–7-scaled, **lowest scale above the leaf scar.**

LEAVES: Alternate, simple, deciduous; blades dark green above, paler beneath, **broadly ovate to almost kidney-shaped,** short-pointed, 1⅛–2¾" **long, with 20–30 fine, uneven, blunt teeth per side; stalks flattened,** slender, usually **longer than the blades;** leaves yellow in autumn.

FLOWERS: Tiny, without petals; unisexual with male and female flowers in **slender, hanging** catkins 1½–3" **long, on separate trees;** flowers develop in March–April **(before leaves expand).**

FRUITS: Hairless, pointed, about ¼" long capsules, numerous, in hanging catkins up to 4" long; seeds ¹⁄₁₆–⅛" long, tipped with a **tuft of silky white hairs;** capsules split open in **May–June** (as leaves expand).

HABITAT: Moist to dry, upland habitats, on rocky, sandy, loamy and clayey soils.

ORIGIN: Native.

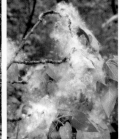

BALSAM POPLAR is often planted as a windbreak. This fast-growing pioneer tree usually lives about 70 years. It reproduces primarily by sending up sprouts from roots and stumps. Detached branches can also take root. • Balsalm poplar wood has a pleasant odor when burned, but logs are often "punky" with fungus. Wet balsam poplar is hard to split, but frozen logs (at 10°F or colder) split easily. • The bud resin was used traditionally in cough medicines and in antiseptic ointments for stopping bleeding. On wet spring days, the fragrance of the resin pervades the air around balsam poplar stands. • Balsam poplar hybridizes with several other poplars. A cross with eastern cottonwood (p. 137) yields **Jack's hybrid poplar** (*P.* x *jackii*, also called *P.* x *gileadensis*). • The resin from **balm-of-Gilead** has been used for centuries in herbal medicine. In Eurasia, balm-of-Gilead refers to evergreen trees (*Commiphora* spp.) in the incense-tree family (Burseraceae). These are the source of commercial balm-of-Gilead resin. In North America, this name has been applied to balsam fir (p. 64), to a heart-leaved form of *P. balsamifera* (previously called *P. candicans*) and to a sterile female cultivar of Jack's hybrid poplar. This cultivar is sometimes grown for medicinal and horticultural uses.

ALSO CALLED: Hackmatack, tacamahac, balm poplar, rough-barked poplar, balm tacamahac, liard, eastern balsam poplar, balsam, bam, hamatack • *P. tacamahacca.*

SIZE AND SHAPE: Trees 50–80' [128'] tall; crowns narrow, irregular; roots shallow, spreading.

TRUNKS: Straight, 12–24" [52"] in diameter, self-pruning; **young bark smooth, greenish-brown,** usually with dark markings; **mature bark dark gray, furrowed;** wood pale, light, soft.

BRANCHES: Few, ascending; twigs orange-brown,

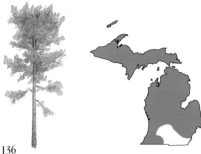

gray with age, stout, with large orange pores (lenticels); **pith 5-pointed** in cross-section; **buds shiny orange-brown, sticky with a fragrant resin,** pointed, $^1/_2$–1" long, 5-scaled, lowest scale above the leaf scar.

LEAVES: Alternate, simple, deciduous; blades firm, **glossy, dark green above, silvery green to yellowish-green beneath (often brown-stained),** oval, tapered to a point, 2$^3/_8$–6" long, edged with blunt teeth and with 2 warty glands at the base; **stalks 1$^1/_8$–1$^1/_2$" long, round** (not flattened); leaves yellow in autumn.

FLOWERS: Tiny, without petals; unisexual with male and female flowers in slender, **hanging catkins on separate trees;** male catkins 2$^3/_4$–4" long; female catkins 4–5" long; flowers in April–May **(before leaves expand).**

FRUITS: Numerous egg-shaped capsules about $^1/_4$" long, in hanging catkins 4–6" long; seeds brown, $^1/_{16}$" long, numerous, tipped with a **tuft of silky, white hairs;** capsules split open in **May–June** (as leaves expand).

HABITAT: Moist, low-lying sites such as ravines, river valleys and lakeshores.

ORIGIN: Native.

EASTERN COTTONWOOD (*P. deltoides* ssp. *deltoides*) is found from the Atlantic Coast inland to Iowa and Texas, whereas the **plains cottonwood** (*P. deltoides* ssp. *monilifera*) ranges west across the Great Plains to British Columbia, Wyoming and New Mexico. Plains cottonwood has minutely hairy (rather than hairless) buds, pale yellow (rather than reddish-brown) twigs and leaves with 10–30 (rather than 40–50) teeth and 1–2 (rather than 3–5) basal glands. • The wood is soft, weak and tends to warp, but it has been used for construction timbers, chipboard, plywood, crates and excelsior, as well as in the production of methanol. • This amazingly fast-growing tree can reach 100' in height in 30 years. Unfortunately, it is not suitable for city landscaping. Moisture-seeking roots often raise sidewalks and clog drainage pipes, and brittle branches litter the ground. • Hybrids between cottonwood and the distinctly columnar **European black poplar** (*P. nigra*), or Lombardy poplar, shown in pink/dark green on the map, are widely cultivated. One of these, **Carolina poplar** (*P.* x *canadensis*), is grown in plantations for wood and bark fiber and as a fast-growing shade tree. The protein-rich leaves of hybrid poplars are fed to chickens, sheep and cattle. The leaf concentrate contains as much protein as meat but is faster and cheaper to produce. Eventually, poplars could provide food for both humans and livestock.

ALSO CALLED: Necklace poplar, big cottonwood, common cottonwood, liard, Carolina poplar, eastern poplar.

SIZE AND SHAPE: Trees 65–100' [148'] tall; crowns broad (open grown) to narrow (in forests); roots usually shallow, spreading, not suckering.

TRUNKS: Short (open grown) to long (in forests), 24–60" [103"] in diameter, sometimes massive; young bark smooth, yellowish-gray; mature bark dark gray, furrowed; wood light, soft, fine-grained.

BRANCHES: Typically ascending at 45°; **twigs stout, vertically ridged below buds,** with sparse linear pores (lenticels); **pith 5-pointed** in cross-section; **buds shiny,** yellowish-brown, fragrant, **resinous,** pointed, 1/2–3/4" long, 5–7-scaled, **3-sided at twig tips, pointing outward below.**

LEAVES: Alternate, simple, deciduous; blades firm, shiny, green above, paler beneath, **rounded-triangular,** 2–43/4" long, **warty glands** at the base of the blade; leaf edges with **callus-tipped teeth; stalks slender, flat,** 2–3" long; leaf scars 3-lobed, with fringed upper edges; leaves yellow in autumn.

FLOWERS: Tiny, without petals; unisexual with male and female flowers in **slender, hanging catkins on separate trees;** male catkins reddish, 2–4" long; female catkins 6–8" long; flowers in April–May **(before leaves expand).**

FRUITS: Egg-shaped, pointed capsules 1/4–1/2" long, in loose, hanging catkins 6–10" long; seeds 1/16–1/8" long, tipped with **silky white hairs; capsules split into 3–4 in late May–June** (as leaves expand).

HABITAT: Moist, warm sites, usually on flood-plains or on sand dunes near lakes.

ORIGIN: Native.

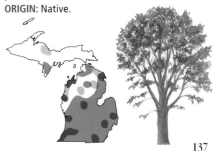

STRAIGHT TRUNKS FREE OF BRANCHES for over half their length make swamp cottonwood a desirable timber tree, though it is usually too scarce to be of economic importance. Also, the wood is soft and light, about half the weight of oak, and is therefore used in expendable articles such as crates, boxes and excelsior. • Swamp cottonwood reaches its northern limit in Michigan. With only 4 known populations remaining, it is one of the state's rarest trees. • This short-lived tree produces seed at about 10 years of age and heavy crops each subsequent year. Fluffy parachutes carry the tiny seeds on the wind and help seeds float on water to new sites. Like most poplars, swamp cottonwood has tiny, short-lived seeds with limited food reserves. To germinate, seed must land on wet, exposed mineral soil soon after it has been released. • Despite its common name, swamp cottonwood is not a true cottonwood. Cottonwoods belong to the Section Aigeiros, but swamp cottonwood is a member of the Section Leucoides. This distinctive group has dry (rather than sticky, resinous) buds and relatively large leaves with cylindrical (rather than flattened) stalks. • Swamp cottonwood usually reproduces vegetatively by sending out shallow roots with numerous suckers. This can produce large colonies of clones, composed of hundreds of shoots of a single tree.

ALSO CALLED: Swamp poplar, black cottonwood, downy poplar, balm-of-Gilead.

SIZE AND SHAPE: Trees 65–100' tall; crowns narrow, open, irregular; roots wide-spreading and suckering.

TRUNKS: Straight, 24–36" in diameter; young bark woolly-hairy, lightly furrowed; mature bark dull brown, furrowed or shaggy with long, narrow plates peeling from both ends; wood pale, light, soft, straight-grained.

BRANCHES: Short, spreading; twigs stout, **white-woolly at first,** becoming shiny, dark brown to gray, with large pores (lenticels); pith orange,

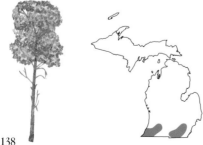

5-pointed in cross-section; buds reddish-brown, **more or less hairy,** about 1/4" long, **scarcely if at all sticky.**

LEAVES: Alternate, deciduous, simple; **blades white-woolly when young,** dark green above, paler beneath, **hairy on veins and lower blade, broadly ovate, 4–8" long, blunt-tipped or only slightly pointed, notched to rounded at the base,** edged with fine, blunt, incurved teeth; **stalks round** or slightly flattened near the tip, hairless, 2³/8–3¹/2" long.

FLOWERS: Tiny, without petals; unisexual **with male and female flowers on separate trees,** borne on ¹/8–¹/4" long stalks in hanging catkins in the axils of **fringed bracts; stamens 12–20;** stigmas on elongated styles; flowers in March–May **(before leaves).**

FRUITS: Reddish-brown, egg-shaped **capsules 1/4–1/2" long, on stalks ³/8–1/2" long,** in loose catkins 1–2³/8" long; seeds tiny, reddish-brown, tipped with a **tuft of silky, white hairs;** capsules split into 2–3 parts in spring **(with leaves).**

HABITAT: Swamps, often around the edges of buttonbush openings or woodland pools.

ORIGIN: Native.

BASKET WILLOW has been cultivated since ancient times as a source of "osiers" or withes. Its large shoots, which can be up to 12' long, were used in Europe to make large agricultural baskets and temporary fencing ("hurdles"). • This willow was introduced to many parts of North America as a small, fast-growing ornamental shade tree and as a source of long, slender branches for basket weaving and wickerwork. For quantity and quality, young basket willow shoots are still considered the best source of wicker for furniture and baskets. • Willow seeds are dispersed by wind and water. Basket willow often grows near flowing water, and its seeds are readily carried to new locations by rivers and streams. However, seeds must reach a suitable landing place quickly. Germination or death usually occurs 1–2 days after a seed is released. • The specific epithet *viminalis* means "bearing withes" and refers to the traditional use of this species in wickerwork. • Basket willow could be mistaken for satiny willow (p. 140), but the latter has a whitish, waxy film on its young branchlets. Also, the new branches of satiny willow are less stiffly erect than those of basket willow.

ALSO CALLED: Silky osier, common osier, osier willow.

SIZE AND SHAPE: Trees or shrubs to 40' tall; crowns spreading; roots shallow.

TRUNKS: Single or few; bark smooth, usually with raised pores (lenticels); wood soft, straight-grained, tough, odorless.

BRANCHES: Erect; **twigs yellowish-green** (usually) to reddish-brown, hairy at first, soon shiny, **long, slender, flexible; buds 1-scaled,** pressed to twigs.

LEAVES: Alternate, simple, deciduous; **blades dull green above, densely silky-satiny beneath, linear, 2–8" long,** 1/4–1/2" wide, with **smooth, down-rolled edges;** stalks 1/8–3/8" long, with swollen bases; stipules lance-shaped, glandular-toothed, soon shed; leaf scars V-shaped, with 3 vein scars.

FLOWERS: Tiny, without petals, in axils of small, **black, long-hairy bracts;** unisexual with male and female flowers forming catkins on separate trees; male flowers with 2 stamens; **catkins erect,** 3/4–1 1/8" **long, short-stalked,** appear April–May (before leaves expand).

FRUITS: Silvery, short-hairy, about 1/4" long, short-stalked capsules in dense, hanging catkins 1 1/2–2 3/8" long; seeds tiny, green, silky white-hairy; capsules split in half in summer.

HABITAT: Streambanks and riverbanks.

ORIGIN: Introduced from Europe and Asia.

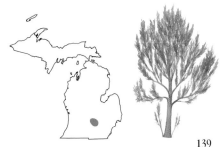

MOST WILLOWS generate good seed crops almost every year, but in some parts of its range, satiny willow produces few or no male plants. In these areas, reproduction is almost entirely by vegetative means such as suckering and fragmentation, rather than by seed.

• Because of their rapidly spreading and branching root systems, many willows are important in controlling erosion, especially along streams and rivers. These very fast-growing trees and shrubs can reproduce by sprouting from roots and stumps. They also grow easily from cuttings and broken branches.

• The species name *pellita* means "clad in skins," probably in reference to the "furry" undersurface of the leaves. • Satiny willow is a northern species that is very rare in Michigan. An essentially hairless variation, the form *psila* (*psila* means "smooth"), has been found around Lake Superior. It is characterized by dull blue-green leaves with hairless lower surfaces. • Satiny willow could be confused with Russian-olive (p. 209), because both trees have thick, similarly shaped leaves with smooth edges, dark green upper surfaces and silvery lower surfaces. Russian-olive, however, has shiny, silvery scales on its twigs, fruits and lower leaf surfaces. Also, its fruits are berry-like drupes, rather than tiny capsules in catkins.

ALSO CALLED: Silky willow.

SIZE AND SHAPE: Small, shrubby trees or tall shrubs 10–15' tall; roots shallow and spreading.

TRUNKS: Few; wood light, odorless, tough.

BRANCHES: Twigs brittle, yellowish-brown to dark reddish-brown, often with a waxy, bluish-white coating; buds covered with 1 scale, pressed to twigs.

LEAVES: Alternate, simple, deciduous; blades dark green and hairless above (often reddish when young), satiny white-hairy with a prominent midvein beneath and many parallel, impressed side-veins, thick, narrow, 1¹/₂–4" long, ¹/₄–¹/₂" wide (sometimes to 5" long, 1" wide), tapered at both ends, with smooth to slightly wavy, down-rolled edges; stalks ¹/₈–³/₈" long; stipules small or absent.

FLOWERS: Tiny, without petals, in axils of dark brown or blackish, long-hairy bracts; unisexual with male and female flowers in catkins on separate trees; male flowers 2-stamened, forming catkins ³/₄–1¹/₈" long; catkins erect, short-stalked, above small bracts; flowers in May–June (before or as leaves expand).

FRUITS: Pointed, ¹/₈–¹/₄" long, densely white silky-hairy, essentially stalkless capsules in dense catkins 1¹/₈–2" long; seeds tiny, green, with silky white hairs; capsules split open in June–July.

HABITAT: Riverbanks, lakeshores and depressions in rock outcrops.

ORIGIN: Native.

THIS COMMON TREE is North America's largest native willow. It is our only tree willow with leaves that are fairly uniformly green on both surfaces and with conspicuous stipules on fast-growing shoots in late summer. • Black willow has little commercial value, but it has been used locally for construction timbers and fuel and for making wicker baskets and furniture. During the American Revolution, the wood of black willow (and of other willows) was made into fine charcoal, which was then used to make gunpowder. • The branches of black willow have brittle bases and are easily broken by wind, on moist ground, they often take root and grow into new trees. This form of vegetative reproduction is especially effective along rivers and streams, where flowing water can carry branches great distances and establish colonies in new locations. Black willow cuttings can be embedded in riverbanks to control erosion. • The tiny, fluffy seeds disperse in wind and water, and they grow readily on moist, sunny sites. However, they must germinate within 24 hours of falling or die. • The species name *nigra* means "black" and refers to the blackish bark of mature trees.

ALSO CALLED: Swamp willow.

SIZE AND SHAPE: Trees or tall shrubs 35–65' [114'] tall; crowns broad, irregular; roots dense, spreading.

TRUNKS: Usually single, occasionally leaning and forked into 2–4 trunks, 12–40" [121"] in diameter; mature bark dark brown to blackish, flaky to stringy, deeply furrowed; wood light, soft, fine-grained.

BRANCHES: Spreading, slender; twigs pale yellowish-brown to reddish- or purplish-brown, ridged lengthwise below leaf scars, **tough and flexible but brittle-based; buds 1-scaled,** sharp-pointed, flat-lying, about 1/8" long.

LEAVES: Alternate, simple, deciduous; **blades uniformly green above and below, thin, 2–6" long,** typically **tapered to an abruptly curved (scythe-like) tip,** rounded to wedge-shaped at the base, **fine-toothed;** stalks 1/8–3/8" long, hairy, usually with glands near the blade; **stipules large, persistent,** fine-toothed; leaves yellow in autumn.

FLOWERS: Tiny, without petals, in axils of pale yellow, hairy, deciduous bracts; unisexual with male and female flowers in catkins on separate trees; male flowers with 3–7 (usually 6) stamens; catkins 3/4–2" long, **on leafy shoots 3/8–11/8" long;** flowers in April–June **(as leaves expand).**

FRUITS: Light brown, hairless capsules about 1/8" **long,** in loose, hanging catkins 3/4–3" long; seeds tiny, green, silky-hairy; capsules split open in June–July.

HABITAT: Moist to wet habitats on floodplains and in swamps and low meadows.

ORIGIN: Native.

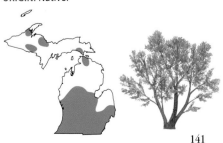

THE SILVER GRAY LEAVES of this attractive shade tree often sweep the ground. White willow is the most common willow in Europe and one of the most frequently planted in North America. Unfortunately, it is plagued by many diseases and insects. Also, its fallen leaves and branches often litter the ground, and its rapidly spreading roots can clog drainage pipes. • White willow wood does not split, so it has been used to make clogs, carvings, and balls and mallets for croquet and cricket. • White willow trees are often pollarded to produce tufts of straight shoots suitable for weaving. • Large willows with pendulous branches are called weeping willows. The true **weeping willow** (*S. babylonica*) is not hardy in the northern U.S., but hybrids of *S. babylonica* and *S. alba* (**weeping willow, *S.* x *sepulcralis***) and of *S. babylonica* and *S. fragilis* (**Wisconsin weeping willow, *S.* x *pendulina***) occasionally grow wild here. Also, *S. alba* frequently crosses with *S. fragilis* to produce **hybrid crack willow** (***S.* x *rubens***). This hybrid is probably more common than either parent. • A popular cultivar of *S. alba*, **golden weeping willow** (***S. alba* var. *vitellina* 'Pendula'**), has flexible, hairless, yellow twigs, and leaves with hairless upper surfaces.

ALSO CALLED: Golden willow, common willow, European white willow, French willow.

SIZE AND SHAPE: Trees or shrubs 50–80' [133'] tall; crowns broad; roots deep, spreading.

TRUNKS: Straight, 24–48" [96"] in diameter; mature bark light brown to dark gray, corky, furrowed; wood light, even, resilient.

BRANCHES: Stout, ascending; **twigs greenish-brown to yellow, slender, flexible but brittle-based, often hanging; buds 1-scaled,** hairy, flattened.

LEAVES: Alternate, simple, deciduous; blades bright to grayish-green above, whitish with a waxy bloom beneath, **silky-hairy (especially when young), lance-shaped,** tapered at both ends, 1½–7" long, with **fine, gland-tipped teeth;** stalks hairy, often glandular near the blade; stipules small, soon shed; leaves yellow in autumn.

FLOWERS: Tiny, without petals, in axils of **small, greenish-yellow, hairy bracts** that are soon shed; unisexual with male and female flowers in catkins on separate trees; male flowers with 2 (sometimes 3) stamens; **catkins erect, 1⅛–2" long, on shoots ⅜–1½" long, with 2–4 small leaves;** flowers April–June **(as leaves expand).**

FRUITS: Hairless, ⅛–¼" long, **essentially stalkless capsules** in stalked catkins 1½–2⅜" long; seeds tiny, green, tipped with a tuft of silky hairs; capsules split open in May–June.

HABITAT: Open, moist to wet sites along streams and in disturbed areas.

ORIGIN: Introduced from Europe and central Asia.

THIS ATTRACTIVE NATIVE WILLOW is often planted as an ornamental.
• Many animals, such as moose, deer, squirrels, rabbits and porcupines, feed on the leaves, buds, catkins and bark of shining willow.
• The species name *lucida*, "shining," refers to the shining leaves and the lustrous twigs. • The leaves of shining willow resemble those of **autumn willow** (*S. serissima*), shown in dark green on the map, and peach-leaf willow (p. 150), but autumn willow has a white, waxy coating on its lower leaf surfaces, and peachleaf willow has less glossy leaves with prominent, pale midveins. Yet another similar species, bayleaf willow (p. 151), is distinguished by its rela-

tively short-pointed leaves, its yellow-green (rather than green to brownish) female flowers and its consistently 5-stamened male flowers. • In our state, willows are the only alternate-leaved woody plants with flat-lying buds each covered by a single scale. American sycamore (p. 82) also has single bud scales, but its buds stick out from the twigs. • A hairy variety, *S. lucida* var. *intonsa*, is sometimes encountered. It is distinguished by the persistent reddish hairs on its leaves and twigs. The specific epithet *intonsa* means "not shaved."

ALSO CALLED: Yellow willow.

SIZE AND SHAPE: Small trees or tall shrubs 10–20' [74'] tall; crowns broad.

TRUNKS: Short, small, usually <8" [41"] in diameter; young bark smooth; mature bark brown, irregularly furrowed; wood light, soft.

BRANCHES: Upright; **twigs shiny yellowish- to chestnut brown, rusty-hairy at first,** soon hairless, slender; **buds 1-scaled,** pale brown, flat-lying.

LEAVES: Alternate, simple, deciduous; blades reddish and **rusty-hairy when young, shiny, dark green** and hairless when mature, **shiny but paler beneath,** lance-shaped, slender-pointed, 1½–6" long, with rounded or wedge-shaped bases, edged with **fine, gland-tipped teeth;** stalks ¼–½" long, **glandular near the blade; stipules glandular-toothed,** semicircular, sometimes absent.

FLOWERS: **Tiny,** without petals, in the axils of small, yellowish, thinly hairy bracts (shed before capsules ripen); unisexual with male and female flowers in catkins on separate trees; male flowers with 3–6 stamens; **catkins erect, ½–2" long, on leafy shoots** ⅜–1" long; flowers in May–June **(as leaves expand).**

FRUITS: **Pale brown, hairless capsules** about ¼" long, **on stalks** ¹⁄₁₆" long, in catkins ½–2" long and ⅜–½" wide; seeds tiny, silky-hairy; capsules split in half in June–July.

HABITAT: Wet sites on shorelines and floodplains and in ditches and various wetlands.

ORIGIN: Native.

SANDBAR WILLOWS are relatively small and their wood is light and soft, so these shrubs have little economic value. However, the wood was often used to smoke fish, meat and animal skins, and was also used to make snowshoes and bows. The tips of willow twigs were sometimes chewed to separate the fibers and then used as toothbrushes. • Some tribes used the flexible twigs and bark of sandbar willow to make rope, string and baskets. Bark fibers were woven together to make bags, blankets and clothing. Finely shredded inner bark provided absorbent padding for diapers and sanitary napkins. • This fast-growing pioneer species spreads quickly over newly exposed sandbars and alluvial flats by sending up shoots from its extensive shallow roots. In this way, it forms dense thickets that stabilize the soil and prepare the way for later species such as alders, poplars and other willows. • The species name *exigua*, "meager," refers to the extremely narrow leaves. The earlier name, *interior*, referred to sandbar willow's mainly interior (rather than coastal) distribution. • This species varies greatly over its broad North American range, which extends from Alaska to Mexico. It can be considered either a single species with many varying forms or a group of numerous, difficult-to-distinguish species.

ALSO CALLED: Basket willow, coyote willow, narrowleaf willow, slenderleaf willow, pink-barked willow, rope plant, silver willow • *S. exigua* ssp. *interior, S. interior.*

SIZE AND SHAPE: Tall shrubs 5–25' [52'] tall; crowns rounded; roots shallow, spreading, often suckering to form **extensive colonies.**

TRUNKS: Numerous, 2–6" [8"] in diameter; bark thin, smooth, with raised pores (lenticels), furrowed with age; wood soft, straight-grained, tough, odorless.

BRANCHES: Slender, erect; twigs yellowish- to

reddish-brown, hairless with age, slender, flexible; **buds 1-scaled**, flattened, absent at twig tips.

LEAVES: Alternate, simple, deciduous; blades deep yellowish-green, paler beneath, lacking a waxy bloom, **linear, 2–6" long, tapered at both ends,** edged with **irregular, widely spaced, gland-tipped teeth** (rarely toothless); stalks ⅛–¼" long; stipules tiny, soon shed; leaf scars V-shaped, with 3 vein scars; leaves yellow in autumn.

FLOWERS: Tiny, **unisexual** with male and female flowers in catkins on separate trees, in axils of small, **pale yellowish bracts** that are **soon shed**; male flowers with 2 stamens; **catkins on leafy branches 1⅛–4" long;** flowers in April–June **(after leaves)** and sometimes again in midsummer.

FRUITS: Slender, **lance-shaped capsules** about ¼" long, silky-hairy at first, often hairless with age, short-stalked, in **nodding catkins ¾–2⅜" long;** seeds tiny, tipped with a tuft of silky white hairs; capsules mature in summer.

HABITAT: Native, riverbanks, **floodplains** and beaches.

ORIGIN: Native.

THE SPICY ODOR OF BALSAM WILLOW is especially strong on the young, glandular-toothed leaves and bruised twigs or buds. This fragrance can last for decades (sometimes over 100 years) in dried, properly stored specimens. In herbaria, the scent is sometimes detectable some distance away from the cabinet where the plants are stored. The common name refers to this balsam-like fragrance. • Balsam willow is recognized in winter by its shiny reddish twigs and buds. • The specific epithet *pyrifolia* means "pear leaves," a reference to the shape and texture of the mature leaves. • **Blueleaf willow (*S. myricoides*,** also called *S. glaucophylloides* and bayberry willow), shown in pink/dark green on map, is another tall willow with hairless capsules in the axils of dark brown to blackish scales. Like balsam willow, blueleaf willow has reddish-tinged young leaves, but these are not translucent and they do not have a balsam-like fragrance. Mature blueleaf willow leaves have a relatively heavy, white, waxy coating on their lower surfaces, and dried plants usually turn black. Blueleaf willow grows on sandy or gravelly sites on dunes and sandy shores along the Great Lakes. • In Michigan, both of these willow species are usually shrubs less than 10' tall.

ALSO CALLED: *S. balsamifera.*

SIZE AND SHAPE: Shrubs or small trees to 6–12' [15'] tall, with a **balsam-like fragrance;** crowns spreading; roots shallow.

TRUNKS: Clumped, up to 3¹/₂" in diameter; bark smooth, thin, grayish-brown with age; wood soft, straight-grained, tough, odorless.

BRANCHES: Erect; twigs fuzzy, yellowish-green in spring, soon **purplish-brown, shiny and hairless; buds 1-scaled,** ¹/₈–³/₈" long, shiny, **reddish-purple,** flat-lying.

LEAVES: Alternate, simple, deciduous; **blades thin, reddish, translucent and somewhat hairy when young, firm to leathery and hairless when mature,** deep green above, paler with a **waxy bloom and fine net-veins beneath,** about 2–4" long, pointed, rounded to notched at the base, edged with **fine, blunt, gland-tipped teeth;** stalks ¹/₄–³/₄" long, sometimes glandular near the blade.

FLOWERS: Tiny, yellowish, without petals; **unisexual with male and female on separate trees,** in axils of **white-hairy, dark reddish-brown** bracts; male flowers with **2 yellow anthers less than ¹/₃₂" long;** flowers in catkins ³/₄–2³/₈" long, borne **on short, leafy branchlets,** in May–June **(with leaves).**

FRUITS: Hairless, dark orange, **lance-shaped capsules** ¹/₄–³/₈" long, **tipped with tiny styles;** capsules on stalks about ¹/₈" long, in **dense catkins 2–3" long;** seeds tiny, with silky white parachutes; capsules split open in early summer.

HABITAT: Wet sites such as bogs, swamps and ditches; occasionally on rock outcrops.

ORIGIN: Native.

THIS COMMON WILLOW is sometimes browsed so heavily by deer that it never reaches over 3' in height. • Slender willows can provide low-quality fuel. The branchlets were sometimes used to make baskets, hence the alternate name "basket willow." • The bitter-tasting inner bark of most willows contains salicin, a compound similar to acetylsalicylic acid (ASA). Willow-bark extracts have been used for centuries to relieve pain and combat fevers. • Willow flowers provide nectar and pollen for bees each spring. • Willow leaves and twigs are often deformed by large, round blisters or pimple-like growths. These are galls created by flies, wasps, aphids and other insect parasites. Each insect produces a particular type of gall on a specific part of the plant. When females deposit their eggs in the leaf or twig, the tree responds by producing a tumor-like growth. When the eggs hatch, the insect larvae grow and develop inside the gall, fed and protected by its tissues, until they finally emerge as adults. Occasionally, galls are caused by fungi. The cone-like galls at the tips of willow twigs are created by the willow pine-cone gall midge (*Rhabdophaga stobiloides*). • Slender willows with more or less permanently hairy leaves have sometimes been called *S.* x *subsericea*, but these are now included in *S. petiolaris*.

ALSO CALLED: Meadow willow, basket willow, stalked willow • *S. gracilis*.

SIZE AND SHAPE: Low to medium shrubs 3–23' [34'] tall; crowns broad; roots shallow.

TRUNKS: Clumped, 2–3" [4"] wide; young bark grayish-green to chestnut brown, smooth; mature bark dark brown, scaly; wood light, soft.

BRANCHES: Upright; twigs yellowish-green to olive-brown and hairy when young, hairless and nearly black with age, long, slender; **buds 1-scaled,** pressed to twigs.

LEAVES: Alternate, simple, deciduous, **pointing upward, often overlapping;** blades reddish and hairy when young, **shiny, green and usually hairless when mature,** paler with a **whitish bloom beneath, thin, linear-lance-shaped,** pointed at both ends, 1 1/2–4 3/4" long, **finely glandular-toothed** (at least above the middle); stalks yellowish, 1/8–3/8" long; **stipules absent.**

FLOWERS: **Tiny,** without petals and sepals; **unisexual with male and female flowers** in catkins **on separate trees,** in axils of hairy bracts; male flowers 2-stamened, in catkins 3/8–1 1/8" long; **catkins loosely flowered, on short, leafy shoots, often forming long series,** flowers in May–June **(with leaves).**

FRUITS: Silky-hairy, slender-beaked capsules 1/8–1/4" long, on hairy stalks about 1/8" long, in catkins 1/2–1 1/2" long; seeds tiny, silky hairy; capsules split open in late May–June.

HABITAT: Marshy ground on shores and in swamps, ditches and other low, open sites.

ORIGIN: Native.

CRACK WILLOW is one of the largest willows in the world, but it is not economically important. It is sometimes cut for firewood, and in colonial times, it was imported for making high-quality charcoal to use in cannon powder. In Scotland, the attractive wood has been used in boat finishing. • The specific epithet *fragilis* means "brittle" or "fragile" and refers to the brittle branches. Branch fragments often litter the ground after windy weather and soon root in moist soil. Streams carry twigs to new locations, helping to spread the species. • Crack willow is widely planted as an ornamental. It commonly escapes to grow wild, but pure specimens are rare. Hybrids between crack willow and white willow (p. 142), called hybrid crack willow, are much more common and display characteristics of both parents. • Crack willow branches and twigs spread at an angle of 60–90°, whereas those of white willow spread at 30–45°. • Crack willow can be confused with black willow (p. 141). Black willow leaves are narrower, with abruptly curved tips, green (not whitish) lower surfaces, finely (not coarsely) toothed edges and large, persistent stipules. • A more recent escape, **twisted willow** (*S. matsudana* **cv. Tortuosa** or corkscrew willow), also grows wild in several states. Twisted willow is easily recognized by its curiously contorted and curled leaves and twigs.

Photo, bottom left: *S. matsudana*

ALSO CALLED: Brittle willow, snap willow.

SIZE AND SHAPE: Multi-stemmed trees 50–80' [116'] tall, like gigantic shrubs; crowns open, spreading; **roots reddish,** often conspicuous on eroded shores.

TRUNKS: Several, up to 72" [98"] in diameter; mature bark dull, dark gray, deeply furrowed, narrow-ridged; wood soft, reddish, tough, fine-grained.

BRANCHES: Long, ascending to spreading; **twigs yellowish, greenish or dark reddish-brown, shiny, slender, stiff, brittle-based; buds reddish-brown, 1-scaled,** gummy, flat-lying, 1/8–1/4" long.

LEAVES: Alternate, simple, deciduous; blades green above, paler with a whitish bloom beneath, lance-shaped, 2 3/4–8" long (larger on rapidly growing shoots), tapered at both ends, **edged with coarse (10–17 per inch), irregular, gland-tipped teeth;** stalks usually with prominent glands near the blade; stipules tiny or absent.

FLOWERS: Tiny, without petals, in the axils of **small, pale yellow to yellowish-green, hairy bracts** (soon shed); unisexual with male and female flowers in catkins on separate trees; male flowers with 2 (sometimes 3–4) stamens; **hanging catkins 3/4–2 3/8" long, on leafy shoots 3/8–2" long;** flowers in April–June **(as leaves expand).**

FRUITS: Hairless, lance-shaped capsules 1/8–1/4" long, in catkins 2–3" long; seeds tiny, silky-hairy; capsules split open in May–July.

HABITAT: Wet sites on streambanks, lakeshores and roadsides, also in wet woodlands and pastures.

ORIGIN: Introduced from Europe and Asia Minor.

147

HEARTLEAF WILLOW typically has silvery galls (lower photo) caused by small insects. In the past, these galls were steeped to make a medicinal tea for stimulating urination and relieving fluid retention.
• The species name *eriocephala* is derived from the Greek *erion*, "wool," and *kephale*, "head," in reference to the woolly seed catkins.
• Willows are easily recognized as a group, but individual species are often difficult to identify. For one thing, many trees may not have all the features necessary to make a positive identification. In cases where fruit characteristics are important for identification, immature trees and male trees are especially troublesome. Many species flower before the leaves develop, so it may be difficult to find both catkins and leaves at the same time. Also, the leaves can vary greatly with age and habitat. For example, leaves on young, vigorous shoots may be much larger and hairier or less regularly toothed than those on mature trees. To further complicate matters, willows often hybridize, producing offspring with intermediate characteristics. • Heartleaf willow is a highly variable, complex species. Some taxonomists consider it a single species with many variable forms, while others treat it as a group of similar species that are difficult to tell apart.

ALSO CALLED: Diamond willow, Missouri River willow, Missouri willow, erect willow, yellow willow • *S. rigida, S. cordata.*

SIZE AND SHAPE: Shrubby trees or tall shrubs 5–15' tall; crowns spreading.

TRUNKS: Clumped, 3–6" in diameter; mature bark thin, gray to black, scaly; wood light, soft.

BRANCHES: Upright; **twigs yellowish-green and downy when young, reddish-brown and hairless with age; buds 1-scaled,** reddish-brown, flat-lying.

LEAVES: Alternate, simple, deciduous; **blades** reddish and white-hairy when young, hairless and dark purplish-green above when mature, silvery-whitish beneath with reddish hairs along some veins, stiff, oblong-lance-shaped, rounded to notched at the base, 2–6" long, finely glandular-toothed; stipules glandular-toothed, 1/4–3/4" long, persistent; leaves deep red and veiny in autumn.

FLOWERS: **Tiny,** without petals, in axils of dark brown, crinkly-hairy bracts 1/16" long; unisexual with male and female flowers in catkins on separate trees; male flowers 2-stamened, in catkins 3/8–1 1/8" long; catkins stalkless or (usually) **on leafy shoots up to 3/8" long,** often numerous in long series, flowers in April–May **(as or slightly before leaves expand).**

FRUITS: Brown **(reddish when young),** hairless or hairy, **lance-shaped capsules about 1/4" long, on stalks 1/16" long** (stalks longer than bracts); **capsules crowded and spreading in catkins 3/4–3" long;** seeds tiny, silky-hairy; capsules split open in summer.

HABITAT: Streambanks, floodplains, shores, ditches and swamps.

ORIGIN: Native.

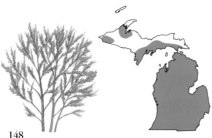

THE MOSTLY OPPOSITE LEAVES of this species are unique among our willows.
• Purple-osier willow has been widely planted and has escaped cultivation in many, widely separated locations. It is hardy as far north as southern Lake Superior.
• This attractive willow has been cultivated since ancient times as a source of withes for making baskets. Its striking purplish shoots can be woven with branches from other willows to produce contrasting patterns and trims. Many willows produce strong, slender, flexible withes ideal for weaving. • Most willows grow readily from cuttings, and thousands of offspring can be propagated from an individual tree. This property is particularly useful for preserving individual trees that have desirable attributes. Some willows have been perpetuated for centuries in this way, each genetically identical to the original parent tree. • Willow bark has been used for years to relieve pain, inflammation and fever. It contains salicin, from which acetylsalicylic acid (ASA) was derived. Both of these compounds are named after the genus *Salix*. • The generic name *Salix* is derived from the Celtic words *sal*, "near," and *lis*, "water," in reference to the usual habitat of most willows.

ALSO CALLED: Purple willow.

SIZE AND SHAPE: Shrubs or shrubby trees up to 20' [37'] tall; crowns spreading.

TRUNKS: Clumped; young bark smooth; wood light, soft, odorless.

BRANCHES: Upright to ascending, 3 4" [5"] in diameter; twigs yellowish-green to **dark purple,** hairless, slender, flexible; **buds essentially opposite, 1-scaled, purplish,** small, flat-lying, ¼–½" **long** on sprouts.

LEAVES: Essentially **opposite** (at least near twig tips), simple, deciduous; **blades dull green and often purplish above** with **prominent pale midveins,** paler with a **whitish bloom beneath,** essentially hairless, lance-shaped, usually **widest above the middle,** ¾–2⅜" long, smooth-edged or with fine gland-tipped teeth near the tip; stalks ¹⁄₁₆–⅛" long.

FLOWERS: Tiny, without petals; unisexual with male and female flowers in catkins on separate trees, in axils of small, hairy, blackish bracts (sometimes pale centered and/or becoming hairless); male flowers 2-stamened, with filaments (and sometimes anthers) fused; **catkins ¾–1⅛" long, often paired,** stalkless or on short, leafy shoots, flowers in spring **(before leaves expand).**

FRUITS: Densely short-hairy, egg-shaped, plump, stalkless capsules ⅛" **long,** in catkins ¾–1⅛" **long;** seeds tiny, silky-hairy; capsules split open in summer.

HABITAT: Low, wet sites near streams and pools and on wet, sandy shores.

ORIGIN: Introduced from Eurasia.

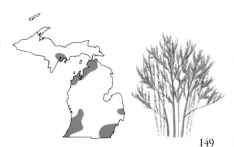

LIKE MOST WILLOWS, PEACHLEAF WILLOW has little commercial value. Its drooping branch tips make it popular for landscaping. It is rarely cut for timber but is sometimes used for firewood or as a source of charcoal. The tannin-rich bark produces a pale brown dye. • The dense, tenacious roots of peachleaf willow have saved many streambanks from erosion. • Willows provide food and shelter for many birds and mammals. Deer and moose browse on the leaves and twigs, while squirrels and rabbits eat the tender shoots and bark. The early-blooming flowers can be an important source of spring nectar for bees. • The specific epithet *amygdaloides* comes from the Greek *amugdalos*, "almond," and *öides*, "resembling," in reference to the almond-shaped leaves of this species. • Peachleaf willow can be confused with black willow (p. 141), but black willow has smaller, narrower leaves with curved tips and pale green (not waxy whitish) lower surfaces. Also, black willow has brittle-based branches, hairy young leaves and large, persistent stipules. • Peachleaf willow and shining willow (p. 143) have similar leaves, but the lower surfaces of shining willow leaves are shiny and pale green.

ALSO CALLED: Peach willow.

SIZE AND SHAPE: Trees or tall shrubs **15–65'** **[111']** **tall;** crowns narrow, irregular to rounded.

TRUNKS: Often leaning in open sites, usually single, occasionally in clumps of 2–4, up to 12–16" [43"] in diameter; young bark reddish or yellowish, smooth; mature bark grayish-brown, with flat, shaggy, interlacing ridges; wood light, soft, fine-grained.

BRANCHES: Ascending, often nodding at the tips; twigs yellowish- to reddish-brown with lighter pores

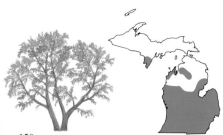

(lenticels), **slender, flexible; buds shiny brown, sharp-pointed, 1-scaled,** flat-lying, ¹/₈" long.

LEAVES: Alternate, simple, deciduous; **blades reddish and sparsely hairy when young,** dark green to yellowish-green and hairless when mature, **whitish with a waxy bloom beneath,** thin, with a **prominent midvein, lance-shaped, slender-pointed,** unevenly rounded at the base, 2–6" long, **fine-toothed;** stalks usually lack glands; stipules usually absent.

FLOWERS: Tiny, without petals; unisexual with male and female flowers in catkins on separate trees, in the axils of **deciduous, pale yellow, hairy bracts,** on leafy shoots; male flowers with 3–7 (typically 5) stamens, in catkins 1¹/₈–2³/₈" long; flowers in April–May **(as leaves expand).**

FRUITS: Reddish or yellowish, hairless, short-beaked, lance-shaped capsules about ¹/₄" long, in loose catkins 1¹/₂–3¹/₂" long; seeds tiny, tipped with a tuft of silky hairs; capsules split open in June–July.

HABITAT: Moist, open sites on floodplains and lakeshores and around marshes.

ORIGIN: Native.

BAYLEAF WILLOW was introduced to North America as a hardy ornamental shrub whose fragrant leaves were sometimes used to flavor food. It is still cultivated and is especially popular in regions with acidic soils. Bayleaf willow can be grown in most of the northern U.S. • Willows have been cultivated since at least the time of ancient Greece and Rome. Many species are highly valued in landscaping and are easily propagated from cuttings. • The specific epithet *pentandra* comes from the Greek *penta*, "five," and *andron*, "male," and refers to the 5-stamened male flowers. • This species could be confused with shining willow (p. 143), but the leaves of shining willow have long, slender, tapered tips, whereas those of bayleaf willow are relatively short-pointed. • Bayleaf willow is also very similar to autumn willow (p. 143), a native shrub that can reach 13' in height. However, the leaves of autumn willow have whitish lower surfaces with a thin, waxy bloom. Also, the tiny bracts of autumn willow catkins are hairy from base to tip, whereas those of bayleaf willow have hairless tips.

ALSO CALLED: Laurel willow.

SIZE AND SHAPE: Small trees or tall shrubs up to 25' tall; crowns broad.

TRUNKS: Usually clumped, often leaning; mature bark gray-brown; wood light, soft.

BRANCHES: Upright to spreading; twigs shiny reddish-brown, slender; **buds 1-scaled, yellow,** flat-lying.

LEAVES: Alternate, simple, deciduous; **blades shiny, dark green above** with yellow midveins, **green or slightly paler beneath,** hairless, **fragrant, ovate,** with pointed tips and rounded to wedge-shaped bases, 1¹/₂–4" long, edged with gland-tipped teeth; stalks with glands near the blade; stipules small, glandular.

FLOWERS: Tiny, without petals; unisexual, with male and female flowers in catkins on separate trees; male flowers with 4–9 (usually 5) stamens; catkins 1¹/₈–2³/₈" long, on **short, leafy shoots** in the axils of **deciduous, pale yellow, hairy bracts with hairless tips,** flowers in

May–June **(as or slightly after leaves expand).**

FRUITS: Hairless, yellow-green capsules about ¹/₄" **long,** on stalks ¹/₁₆" long in catkins 1³/₈–2³/₄" long; seeds tiny, green, silky-hairy; capsules split open in June–July.

HABITAT: Moist sites such as riverbanks, dunes and low fields; prefers acidic soils.

ORIGIN: Introduced from Europe and Asia.

151

THE FUZZY, immature catkins of this well-known willow have been likened to the soft paws or toes of a cat, hence the name "pussy willow." Pussy willow catkins are the first willow catkins to appear each year and are recognized as a sign of spring. Catkin-bearing branches from female shrubs are often gathered for use in bouquets. Male pussy willows (upper photo) should not be collected, because they will open and shed their pollen in the house. If bud-bearing twigs are brought indoors in late winter and set in water, they can be "forced" to produce pussy willows early. • Pussy willow is sometimes planted as a hardy, fast-growing ornamental shrub. • An occasional European escape, **large gray willow** (*S. cinerea*, also called gray willow or pussy willow), shown in dark green on the map, resembles native pussy willow, but its branches have distinctive long, prominent ridges on their wood. The bark must be stripped away from mature (at least 2–3-year-old) branches before these ridges can be seen. • Willow catkins provide important food for bees and other insects in early spring. Pollen and nectar in the catkins attract insects, which in turn pollinate hundreds of the tiny willow flowers.

ALSO CALLED: Tall pussy willow, glaucous willow, pussy feet.

SIZE AND SHAPE: Trees or tall shrubs **6–25' [47']** **tall;** crowns rounded; roots shallow.

TRUNKS: Few, clumped, 4–8" (17") in diameter; mature bark gray-brown, furrowed; wood light, soft.

BRANCHES: Upright, rather stout; twigs dark reddish-brown with pale pores (lenticels), shiny, sometimes with a waxy bloom, becoming hairless; buds 1-scaled, reddish-purple, 1/4–3/8" long, flat-lying.

LEAVES: Alternate, simple, deciduous; **highly variable, blades reddish-hairy at first,** becoming **green and hairless above** with hairless (or persistently few-haired) **undersides coated in a waxy bloom,** oblong to elliptic, 1 1/8–4" long, wedge-shaped at the base, **smooth-edged to irregularly toothed or almost wavy-edged** (especially above midleaf); stalks green, 1/4–1/2" long; stipules large on vigorous shoots.

FLOWERS: Tiny, without petals; unisexual with male and female flowers in catkins on separate trees; male flowers 2-stamened, in 3/4–1 1/2" long catkins; **catkins densely hairy,** stalkless or on short, bracted shoots, in axils of dark brown, white-hairy, 1/16–1/8" long bracts, in April–May **(before leaves expand).**

FRUITS: Minutely gray-hairy capsules 1/4–1/2" long, long-beaked, with styles <1/16" long, hanging in dense catkins 2–3 1/2" long; seeds tiny, tipped with a tuft of silky hairs; capsules split open in late May–June.

HABITAT: Low, wet sites including ditches, wet meadows, swamps and shores.

ORIGIN: Native.

THE WOOD OF BEBB'S WILLOW has been used for baseball bats and wickerwork. It was also once used to make charcoal for gunpowder. • Fungal infections often produce attractive reddish-orange to brown patterns in the pale wood of various willows. Peeled and sanded, such "diamond willow" branches are used to make walking sticks, lampposts, furniture and rustic plaques and clock faces. • A pioneer species, Bebb's willow is often among the first woody plants to appear after a fire. It can live about 20 years. • This widespread species is one of the most common willows in North America. It is abundant from coast to coast across the northern U.S. • Bebb's willow is an important source of food and shelter for many birds and mammals. Moose, beavers, muskrats and hares eat the twigs and bark, while grouse and grosbeaks feed on the buds and leaves. • The specific epithet *bebbiana* honors Michael Schuck Bebb (1833–95), an American botanist who studied willows. • Bebb's willow has extremely variable leaf forms and twig hairiness among varieties, within one plant and among plants of different ages. Several weakly defined varieties have been described. Raised, netted veins on the lower surfaces of young leaves often help to identify this species.

ALSO CALLED: Beaked willow, long-beak willow, diamond willow, gray willow.

SIZE AND SHAPE: Trees or tall shrubs 10–25' [31'] tall; crowns broad, rounded.

TRUNKS: Clumped, 2³/₈–6" [11"] in diameter; young bark reddish-brown to gray; mature bark grayish-brown, furrowed; wood light, soft, tough.

BRANCHES: Upright to spreading; twigs reddish-purple to orange-brown with pale pores (lenticels), eventually hairless; **buds 1-scaled,** shiny brown, blunt, flat-lying.

LEAVES: Alternate, simple, deciduous; blades silky-hairy and sometimes reddish when young, **dull green above when mature, whitish with a waxy bloom, hairy and prominently net-veined beneath,** often widest above midleaf, ³/₄–3" long, smooth- to wavy-edged, may be irregularly glandular-toothed toward the base; stipules tiny, soon shed, larger and persistent on vigorous shoots.

FLOWERS: Tiny, without petals; unisexual with male and female flowers in catkins on separate trees; male flowers 2-stamened, in catkins ³/₈–1¹/₈" long; catkins in the axils of **yellowish or straw-colored (often reddish-tipped), sparsely hairy, ¹/₁₆–¹/₈" long bracts** on leafy, ¹/₄–³/₄" long shoots, in May–June **(as leaves expand).**

FRUITS: Finely gray-hairy, long-beaked, about ¹/₄" **capsules on ¹/₈" stalks in loose catkins,** ³/₄–2³/₄" **long;** seeds tiny, tipped with a tuft of silky hairs; capsules split open in June–July.

HABITAT: Low-lying, moist to wet sites in swamps, forests, thickets and ditches and along shores.

ORIGIN: Native.

153

Key to Genera in the Rose Family (Rosaceae)

1a Leaves compound, divided into leaflets
....*Sorbus*, **mountain-ash** (key to species, see below)
1b Leaves simple, not divided into leaflets **2**

2a Fruits fleshy drupes .... *Prunus*, **cherry, plum, peach** (key to species, p. 155)
2b Fruits fleshy pomes **3**

3a Branches usually thorny; fruits containing 1–5 bony, seed-like stones
..................................*Crataegus*, **hawthorn** (discussion and key to species, pp. 157–159)
3b Branches lacking thorns; fruits otherwise **4**

4a Pith 5-pointed in cross-section; fruits dark reddish-purple to blackish, berry-like, usually 10-seeded, borne in elongated clusters
....*Amelanchier*, **serviceberry** (pp. 188–189)
4b Pith round in cross-section; fruits green or yellow to reddish, apple-like, containing 2–5 papery or leathery compartments that are easily opened to expose the seeds, borne singly or in small, rounded clusters **5**

5a Young leaves folded in bud, expanding from lengthwise pleats; short, pointed, thorn-like side-branches often present; mostly native species
....*Malus*, **crabapple** (key to species, p.160)
5b Young leaves expanding from rolled edges; side-branches not thorn-like; introduced fruit trees **6**

6a Young leaves with up-rolled edges gradually revealing the upper leaf surface; twigs hairless; fruits broad-based, with many grit cells in the flesh.......... *Pyrus*, **pear** (key to species, p. 160)
6b Young leaves with down-rolled edges gradually revealing the lower leaf surface; fruits round, lacking grit cells...................................... *Malus*, **apple, crabapple** (key to species, p. 160)

Key to the Mountain-ashes (Genus *Sorbus*)

1a Twigs and leaf/flower stalks densely white-woolly (at least at flowering time); leaves usually permanently hairy beneath; winter buds with silky, white hairs, not sticky
.... *S. aucuparia*, **European mountain-ash** (p. 177)
1b Twigs, leaves and flower stalks essentially hairless (sometimes with a few sparse hairs); winter buds hairless, gummy... **2**

2a Leaflets usually 3–5 times as long as wide, tapered to a long, slender point, broadest below the middle; fruits 3/16–1/4" in diameter
.... *S. americana*, **American mountain-ash** (p. 175)
2b Leaflets usually 2–3 times as long as wide, more abruptly pointed, broadest near the middle; fruits 5/16–1/2" in diameter................................... *S. decora*, **showy mountain-ash** (p. 176)

Key to the Cherries, Plums and Peaches (Genus *Prunus*)

1a Branches usually with rough thorns, not tipped with buds; leaves edged with prominent, outward-pointing teeth; fruits large, slightly oblong drupes (plums) **2**

1b Branches lacking thorns, tipped with buds; leaves edged with very fine, oblique teeth; fruits smaller, round drupes (cherries) **6**

2a Flowers and fruits usually solitary; leaves widest above the middle; mature fruits dark blue to almost black **3**

2b Flowers and fruits in round clusters of 2–5; leaves widest at or below the middle; mature fruits red to yellow, $3/4$–$1^1/8$" long **4**

3a Branches unarmed or somewhat thorny; fruits $3/4$–$1^1/8$" long, juicy and sweet
.... *P. domestica*, **garden plum** (p. 170)

3b Branches rather thorny; leaves $3/4$–$1^1/2$" long; fruits $3/8$–$1/2$" long, inedible
....*P. spinosa*, **blackthorn** (p. 170)

4a Leaf teeth rounded, some gland-tipped; sepals usually with glands
.... *P. nigra*, **Canada plum** (p. 169)

4b Leaf teeth sharp, not gland-tipped; sepals without glands **5**

5a Fruits red to yellow; leaves widest above midleaf, abruptly narrowed to a sharp, slender point; flowers $1/2$–1" across .... *P. americana*, **American plum** (p. 168)

5b Fruits dark purple; leaves widest at or below midleaf, broadly pointed or gradually tapered to a narrow point; flowers about $3/8$" across
.... *P. alleghaniensis*, **Alleghany plum** (p. 168)

6a Flowers and fruits in elongated clusters **7**

6b Flowers and fruits in small, rounded, usually tassel-like clusters **8**

7a Leaves leathery, edged with incurved teeth, brownish-hairy beneath along the midrib; sepals pointed, usually longer than wide, smooth-edged or with inconspicuous, irregular, gland-tipped teeth, persisting at the base of the fruit
.... *P. serotina*, **wild black cherry** (p. 161)

7b Leaves thinner (not leathery), edged with straight teeth, hairless beneath; sepals blunt, usually wider than long, conspicuously glandular-toothed, soon shed
.... *P. virginiana*, **chokecherry** (p. 162)

8a Flowers and fruits stalkless, usually single or paired **9**

8b Flowers and fruits distinctly stalked **11**

9a Leaves woolly beneath, oval to egg-shaped, widest at or above midleaf, less than $2^3/4$" long; fruits slightly hairy cherries .... *P. tomentosa*, **Manchu cherry** (p. 165)

9b Leaves hairless beneath, round to oblong lance-shaped, 2–6" long; ovary and fruits velvety or woolly **10**

10a Fruits peaches, 2–3" across, with a deeply pitted stone; leaves lance-shaped to oblong-lance-shaped, 3–6" long; flowers pink, 1–1³/₈" across .... *P. persica*, **peach** (p. 164)

10b Fruits apricots, <2" across, with a smooth stone; leaves round to broadly ovate, 2–4" long; flowers pink, ³/₄–1¹/₈" across .... *P. armeniaca*, **apricot** (p. 164)

11a Flowers rarely more than ⁵/₈" across, petals ³/₁₆–¹/₄" long; fruits less than ⁵/₈" in diameter **12**

11b Flowers ³/₄–1¹/₈" across, petals ³/₈–⁵/₈" long; fruits ⁵/₈–1" in diameter **13**

12a Flower and fruit clusters tassel-like, naked at the base (without leafy bracts); petals hairy beneath; cherries bright red; leaf blades usually more than twice as long as wide
.... *P. pensylvanica*, **pin cherry** (p. 163)

12b Flower and fruit clusters with a short, branched central stalk, leafy-bracted at the base; petals hairless; cherries nearly black; leaf blades less than 1¹/₂ times as long as wide .... *P. mahaleb*, **Mahaleb cherry** (p. 165)

13a Leaves soft and rather droopy, somewhat hairy beneath; calyx lobes smooth-edged, constricted below the base; mature leaves hairy beneath on the midvein, with glands on the stalk just below the 2³/₈–4³/₄" long blade; fruits sweet
.... *P. avium*, **sweet cherry** (p. 166)

13b Leaves firm, ascending, hairless; calyx lobes glandular-toothed, not constricted below the base; mature leaves hairless, with glands on the edge of the 1¹/₂–3¹/₂" long blade (not on the stalk); fruits sour .... *P. cerasus*, **sour cherry** (p. 167)

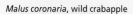

Malus coronaria, wild crabapple

Hawthorns (Genus *Crataegus*)

When it comes to taxonomic problems, few groups are thornier than the hawthorns. The shrubs and small trees in this large, complex group have been classified and reclassified over the years. The number of named species in North America has ranged from a few dozen in the 1800s to over 1200 by 1925.

Much of the confusion with hawthorns stems from their tendency to hybridize, producing offspring with intermediate characteristics, and from their ability to produce seed without fertilization (apomixis). Some species are relatively static and clearly defined, while others are highly variable and difficult to characterize. Also, many species are very similar to one another and can only be distinguished when specimens are of excellent quality. In many cases, both fruit and flower characteristics are needed to correctly identify a species. Trees with neither flowers nor fruits usually cannot be identified to species, even by experts.

The following suggestions may help you with hawthorn identification:

- Whenever possible, examine both flowers and fruits from the same tree (never from two trees that just look the same).

- When trees are in flower, look for last year's fruits on the ground.

- Anther color is based on fresh flowers with unopened anthers.

- Stamen, style and sepal characteristics can often be determined by carefully examining remnants on the tips of fresh fruits. The number of styles is usually the same as the number of nutlets (unless some ovaries failed to mature).

- Leaves of flowering branches can differ from leaves on vegetative shoots, and both may need to be considered in combination with several other factors. The "lobes" of hawthorn leaves are very shallow compared to other groups (e.g., oaks, pp. 106–116) and sometimes approach coarse double teeth.

Because of the identification difficulties associated with hawthorns, and the large number of taxa found in the state, not all species are discussed in detail in this guide. Instead, 10 of the most widely recognized species are described in detail, and an additional 15 species are discussed briefly. These 25 species represent 14 series (groups of closely related species). These 14 series can be distinguished using the following key, based on the work of Phipps and Muniyamma (1980).

Key to the Series of Michigan Hawthorns (Genus *Crataegus*)

1a Leaves mostly deeply lobed, with main veins extending to both lobe notches and lobe tips **2**

1b Leaves toothed or shallowly lobed, with main veins extending to lobe or tooth tips only **3**

2a Flowers with 1 style; fruits containing 1 stone (rarely 2–3); anthers red .... Series Oxyacanthae (*C. monogyna*, **oneseed hawthorn;** *C. laevigata*, **English hawthorn,** p. 178)

2b Flowers with 3–5 styles; fruits containing 3–5 stones; anthers pale yellow .... **Series Cordatae** (*C. phaenopyrum*, **Washington hawthorn,** p. 180)

3a Leaves 2–3 times as long as wide, narrowly wedge-shaped at the base, finely toothed and sometimes also shallowly lobed; thorns long and slender **4**

3b Combination of leaves and thorns not as above **5**

4a Leaves glossy, dark green, finely toothed and only slightly lobed; flower clusters lacking dense hairs; fruits with 2–3 styles and stones .... **Series Crus-galli** (*C. crus-galli*, **cockspur hawthorn,** p. 181)

4b Leaves dull to slightly glossy, regularly shallow-lobed; flower clusters with dense, short hairs; fruits with 3–5 styles and stones .... **Series Punctatae** (*C. punctata*, **dotted hawthorn,** p. 182)

5a Thorns relatively short (<$1^1/8$"); fruits blackish, stones with a cavity on the lower surface .... **Series Douglasianae** (*C. douglasii,* **black hawthorn,** p. 179)

5b Plants without the above combination of characteristics **6**

6a Leaves relatively small (<$1^1/2$" long), about as wide as long (triangular, circular) or diamond-shaped, usually with distinct lobes, rarely broadest above midleaf and scarcely lobed; leaf stalks often with a few glands; flowers <$5/8$" across; thorns $1^1/4$–$3^1/8$" long, thin when long; ripe fruits typically dull red, round and $5/16$–$3/8$" across .... **Series Rotundifoliae** (*C. chrysocarpa*, **fireberry hawthorn;** *C. dodgei,* **Dodge's hawthorn;** *C. irrasa*, **Blanchard's hawthorn;** *C. margarettiae,* **Margaret's hawthorn,** p. 184)

6b Leaves either clearly longer than wide, or if broad then >2" long when mature **7**

7a Mature fruits round, about $5/16$–$1/2$" across, pink to mauve or crimson, coated with a waxy white bloom; both green and ripe fruits often present; persistent sepals at fruit tips strongly elevated .... **Series Pruinosae** (*C. pruinosa*, **frosted hawthorn,** p. 186)

7b Mature fruits red, without a waxy white bloom, or large (>$5/8$") fruits occasionally with a bloom; persistent sepals only slightly elevated (if at all) **8**

8a Mature fruits at least ³/₈" long, round to ellipsoidal; mature leaf blades broad, >2" long
.... **9**

8b Mature fruits generally <³/₈" long; mature leaf blades generally <2" long **11**

9a Flowers ⁷/₈–1¹/₈" across; fruits >⁵/₈" across, with a whitish, waxy bloom
.....................................**Series Dilatatae** (*C. dilatata*, **broadleaf hawthorn**, p. 187)

9b Flowers smaller; fruits without a waxy bloom **10**

10a Mature leaves firm, with stout stalks and hairy lower leaf surfaces; anthers whitish, on
relatively short stalks (filaments); thorns relatively slender .... **Series Molles**
(*C. mollis*, **downy hawthorn;** *C. submollis*, **Quebec hawthorn**, p. 187)

10b Mature leaves relatively thin, with slender stalks and essentially hairless lower leaf surfaces;
anthers pink to red, on relatively large stalks (filaments); thorns relatively stout
.... **Series Coccineae** (*C. pedicellata*, **scarlet hawthorn;** *C. pringlei*,
Pringle's hawthorn; *C. holmesiana*, **Holmes' hawthorn**, p. 186)

11a Fruit stones with cavities on the lower side; leaves hairy beneath; thorns stout or absent; young
growth with conspicuous coral red buds; flower clusters densely hairy; fruits glossy scarlet,
often succulent ....**Series Macracanthae**
(*C. succulenta*, **fleshy hawthorn;** *C. calpodendron*, **pear hawthorn**, p. 183)

11b Plants without the above combination of characteristics **12**

12a Shrubs moderately thorny; ripe fruits usually dull red, sometimes more or less succulent; leaves
various ....**Series Brainerdianae** (*C. brainerdii*, **Brainerd's hawthorn;** *C. colae*,
Cole's hawthorn; *C. pinguis*, **fatty hawthorn**, p. 184)

12b Shrubs extremely thorny, with many stout thorns; ripe fruits usually bright red and rather dry;
leaves thin **13**

13a Flower clusters clearly bracted when the flowers mature; sepal edges with glandular teeth; leaves
elliptic; thorns often long and slender
.............................**Series Intricatae** (*C. intricata*, **Copenhagen hawthorn**, p. 180)

13b Flower clusters with few noticeable bracts when flowers mature; sepals usually smooth-edged;
leaves elliptic to triangular-egg-shaped; thorns stout, of various lengths, sometimes absent
...**Series Tenuifoliae** (*C. flabellata*, **fanleaf hawthorn;** *C. macrosperma,* **bigfruit
hawthorn**, p. 185)

Key to the Apples and Crabapples (Genus *Malus*)

1a Flowers brightly rose-colored (fading to white), with red or pink anthers; leaves pleated lengthwise in bud, sharply toothed and often more or less lobed when mature, soon hairless; branches usually thorny; mostly native species (except **M. *floribunda*, Japanese flowering crabapple,** p. 173) **2**

1b Flowers whitish or pale pink, with yellow anthers; leaves rolled lengthwise in bud, never lobed; branches not thorny; introduced species **3**

2a Flower bases, fruit and fruit/flower stalks woolly-hairy; leaves always hairy beneath .... **M. *ioënsis*, prairie crabapple** (p. 172)

2b Flower bases, fruit and fruit/flower stalks hairless or sparsely silky-hairy; leaves usually hairless .... **M. *coronaria*, wild crabapple** (p. 172)

3a Leaves blunt-toothed, rounded or notched at the base, more or less woolly beneath; leaf stalks, young twigs and calyx lobes woolly; apples 2¹/₄–4¹/₂" in diameter .... **M. *pumila*, common apple** (p. 174)

3b Leaves sharp-toothed, wedge-shaped at the base, nearly hairless beneath; leaf stalks, young twigs and calyx lobes various; crabapples about ³/₈" in diameter .... **M. *baccata*, Siberian crabapple** (p. 173)

Key to the Pears (Genus *Pyrus*)

1a Fruits green to brown or yellow, tipped with a persistent calyx .... **P. *communis*, common pear** (p. 171)

1b Fruits brown, without a persistent calyx or with only fragments remaining **2**

2a Leaves 2–3" long, essentially hairless, edged with rounded, scalloped teeth; styles 2–3 .... **P. *calleryana*, ornamental pear** (p. 171)

2b Leaves about 2" long, woolly beneath when young, edged with blunt, forward-pointing teeth; styles 5 .... **P. *longipes*, Algerian pear** (p. 171)

M. pumila, common apple

P. communis, common pear

WILD BLACK CHERRY wood is easily worked and polishes beautifully. It is considered equal in quality to black walnut, with a rich, red color similar to mahogany. Black cherry was once very popular in furniture and in frames for engravings and etchings. It has also been used in cabinets, paneling, veneers, interior trim, musical instruments and tool handles. Because of its early popularity, this tree is now scarce in much of its range. • In 1629, wild black cherry became one of the first trees introduced to English horticulture from North America. • Wild black cherry fruits can be eaten raw or used in jelly, syrup, wine, juice and pies. • The leaves and inner bark were once used in tonics, sedatives and cough syrups. **Caution:** All parts of this tree except the cherry flesh contain hydrocyanic acid. Wilted leaves have poisoned cattle, and children have died from chewing on twigs. • The cherries provide food for many game birds, songbirds and small mammals. Chipmunks and deer mice cache the pits, which are poisonous to humans. White-tailed deer eat the fresh green leaves in spring but may be poisoned by wilted leaves in autumn. • The crisped scales of the bark have been likened to burned potato chips.

ALSO CALLED: Black chokecherry, rum cherry, cabinet cherry, timber cherry, wine cherry.

SIZE AND SHAPE: Trees or tall shrubs 50–80' [138'] tall; crowns spreading, rounded; tap-rooted to spreading.

TRUNKS: Straight (in forests) to twisted (open grown), 12–32" [71"] in diameter; young bark dark reddish-brown to almost black, smooth, with conspicuous horizontal pores (lenticels); **mature bark rough with outcurved, squared scales,** reddish-brown beneath; wood reddish-brown, fine-grained, hard.

BRANCHES: Few, arched with drooping tips; twigs slender (some side-shoots short and stubby), reddish-brown, **smelling of bitter almonds when broken; buds chestnut brown,** often greenish-tinged, 1/8–1/4" long, pointing outward slightly.

LEAVES: Alternate, simple, deciduous; **blades thick, waxy, dark green above,** paler beneath with **fine, white (eventually rusty) hairs on both sides of the lower midvein,** 2–6" long, widest near midleaf and tapered to both ends, edged with **fine, incurved teeth;** stalks usually with **2 red glands near the blade.**

FLOWERS: White, cupped, on 1/4" long stalks, bisexual; petals 5; sepals 5; flowers hang in narrow, elongated, 4–6" long clusters at the tips of short, new, leafy shoots in May–June (as leaves expand fully).

FRUITS: **Reddish to blackish cherries** (drupes) with dark purple flesh, juicy, about 3/8" across, with **persistent sepals at the base;** seeds single, within a 1/4" stone; cherries hang in elongated clusters of 6–12, mature in August–September.

HABITAT: Well-drained, often disturbed sites such as fence lines and forest edges; persisting and becoming quite large in forests.

ORIGIN: Native.

CHOKECHERRY fruits are edible raw, but even fully ripe fruits can be rather astringent. Green chokecherries cause severe puckering and even choking, hence the common name. Usually, chokecherries are cooked and used to prepare syrups, sauces, preserves, wines and jellies, especially when mixed with pectin-rich apples. • **Caution:** All parts of this tree except the cherry flesh contain poisonous hydrocyanic acid, which gives the bark and leaves an unpleasant, bitter-almond smell when crushed. Although the cherry stones contain this toxin, Native peoples have been eating chokecherries, stones and all, for centuries. Sun-dried cakes of pulverized chokecherries were an important food in some cultures. Drying and/or cooking may reduce toxicity. • Native peoples and settlers used chokecherry bark and roots to make sedatives, blood-fortifying tonics, appetite stimulants and medicinal teas for treating coughs, tuberculosis, malaria, stomachaches and intestinal worms. • Chokecherry grows prolifically from sprouting stumps and root suckers. This fast-growing, light-loving, short-lived tree quickly invades logged land, abandoned farms and exposed streambanks, stabilizing soil and reducing erosion. • Game birds and more than 25 songbird species eat and disperse chokecherries.

ALSO CALLED: Eastern chokecherry, Virginia chokecherry, chuckley-plum, common chokecherry, red chokecherry, sloetree, wild cherry.

SIZE AND SHAPE: Small trees or tall shrubs 10–35' [67'] tall; crowns rounded or irregular; roots spreading, **often forming thickets** from suckers.

TRUNKS: Often twisted and/or inclined, 2–6" [19"] in diameter; **bark dark gray-brown, smooth or finely scaly,** with prominent lenticels when young; wood light brown, fine-grained, hard, heavy.

BRANCHES: Slender, ascending; twigs smooth, reddish- to grayish-brown, **strong-smelling** when crushed; buds ⅛" long (¼–½" at branch tips), with **dark brown, pale-edged scales.**

LEAVES: Alternate, simple, deciduous; blades deep green above, paler beneath, thin, hairless, usually **widest at or above midleaf, abruptly sharp-pointed,** 1½–4¾" long, edged with **small, slender, sharp teeth;** stalks with 1 to several **glands near the blade.**

FLOWERS: White, saucer-shaped, about ⅜" across, bisexual; petals 5, round; sepals 5; flowers on stalks about ¼" long, in **cylindrical, 2–6" long clusters** of 10–25, **hanging from the tips of short, new, leafy shoots,** in May–June **(before leaves expand fully).**

FRUITS: Shiny, **deep red or black cherries** (drupes), rarely yellowish, ¼–⅜" across, with tiny persistent sepals at the base; seeds single, within a stone; cherries hang in **elongated clusters,** ripen July–September.

HABITAT: Exposed areas and open woodlands, on substrates ranging from rich, wet soil to rock outcrops.

ORIGIN: Native.

THESE LITTLE CHERRIES are edible but sour. Mashed and strained, they make excellent jellies and cold drinks. • **Caution:** The leaves, bark and stones are toxic. • Pin cherry can live about 40 years, and once mature, it usually produces abundant fruit each year. The stones remain viable for decades on the ground, waiting for the proper conditions (fluctuating temperatures and light exposure) to trigger germination. • Pin cherry wood is seldom used, except as firewood. • This attractive shrub is sometimes planted as an ornamental, but it spreads quickly via suckers from underground runners. Because of this tendency, pin cherry is sometimes planted to stabilize soil. After fire, this shrub grows rapidly, reducing erosion and improving conditions for the establishment of other species. It soon disappears under a forest canopy. • The heavy, succulent fruits depend on animals (mainly birds) for dispersal and propagation. The name "bird cherry" refers to the popularity of the fruits among songbirds. • The clusters of small, round, shiny fruits have been likened to clusters of glass-headed pins stuck into a pincushion, hence the name "pin cherry."

ALSO CALLED: Bird cherry, fire cherry, wild red cherry, hay cherry, pigeon cherry.

SIZE AND SHAPE: Small trees or tall shrubs 15–35' [45'] tall; crowns narrow, rounded; roots spreading, forming colonies from suckers.

TRUNKS: Straight, 6–10" [12"] in diameter; **mature bark shiny reddish-brown,** smooth, peeling in thin horizontal strips, with conspicuous, **orange-powdered, horizontal pores** (lenticels); wood light brown, soft, porous.

BRANCHES: Slender, ascending when young, horizontal with age; twigs reddish, slender, sour-smelling when bruised or broken; **buds** 1/16–1/8" **long,** rounded, **several clustered at twig tips.**

LEAVES: Alternate, simple, deciduous; blades shiny green, hairless, thin, **lance-shaped, slender-pointed,** rounded at the base, 1 1/2–6" long, edged with **tiny, uneven, incurved teeth;** stalks with **glands near the blade;** leaves bright red to purplish-red in autumn.

FLOWERS: White, 3/8–1/2" across, bisexual; petals 5, round, about 1/4" long, **hairy at the base;** sepals

5; flowers on 3/8–3/4" long stalks, in tassel-like clusters (umbels) of 2–7, in May–early June (as leaves expand).

FRUITS: Bright red cherries (drupes), about 1/4" **in diameter,** hanging on slender stalks in **small, flat-topped clusters;** seeds single, within a round stone; cherries ripen July–September.

HABITAT: Open woodlands or recently disturbed sites such as roadsides and recently burned areas, usually in sandy soil.

ORIGIN: Native.

THE PEACH has been cultivated since ancient times for its sweet, juicy fruits. Many varieties have been developed, including the freestone peach, favored for its thick fruits with flesh that separates readily from the stone. Clingstone peach fruits do not separate readily, but the firmer flesh makes excellent preserves. Nectarines have hairless, usually smaller fruits. • The large, juicy fruits are delicious raw, but they can also be cooked in pies, cakes and cobblers, preserved by drying, freezing and canning, and used to flavor beverages, desserts and confections. • **Caution:** Although peach flesh is edible, the rest of the tree, including the kernel within the stone, is toxic. The roots, leaves and kernels were historically used in medicines, but their virtue was attributed to their high hydrocyanic acid content. • Some peaches are planted for their flowers, and various cultivars have single or double corollas in colors ranging from red to white. • The heavy fruits limit dispersal, but wild peach trees occasionally spring up from discarded pits near roads, trails and rivers. • Many *Prunus* species have been brought to North America, and some occasionally escape from cultivation. **Apricot (*P. armeniaca*)** is a rare European escape, distinguished from peach by its smaller, white to pink-tinged flowers, smaller fruits, smooth stones and broader (sometimes almost round) leaves.

SIZE AND SHAPE: Small, spreading trees up to 35' tall; crowns broad and rounded.

TRUNKS: Short, often crooked, up to 12" in diameter, usually marked with horizontal streaks; bark dark reddish-brown, smooth at first, rough with age.

BRANCHES: Spreading; twigs dark reddish-brown to green, smooth, long, slender, with short spur-shoots.

LEAVES: Alternate, simple, deciduous; blades shiny green, paler beneath, **3–6" long, lance-shaped,** slender-pointed, rounded to wedge-shaped at the base, finely saw-toothed, often **with sides upcurved from the midvein;** stalks short, with small glands near the blade.

FLOWERS: Usually **pink, 1–1³/₈" across,** bisexual; petals 5, rounded; sepals 5; **flowers single** (sometimes paired), in April–May **(before leaves expand).**

FRUITS: Velvety, yellowish to pink peaches (drupes), round, slightly grooved, up to 4" across and soft-fleshed in cultivation, **2–3" across** and firmer in the wild; seeds single, within a somewhat flattened, **deeply sculpted stone;** peaches single on **very short stalks,** mature in July–August.

HABITAT: Open, often disturbed sites on roadsides, in thickets and near abandoned homes.

ORIGIN: Introduced from Eurasia.

THIS HARDY CHERRY was originally brought to North America as a stock plant, to provide a strong base for grafting more delicate garden cherries. It was also often planted in hedges. Today, Mahaleb cherry is usually cultivated for its prolific, perfumed flowers and dark red, fragrant wood. All parts of this attractive tree, leaves, flowers, fruits, bark and wood, are aromatic. The wood has been used to produce cabinets, woodenware (dishes, utensils, etc.), walking sticks and pipe stems. • Unlike most species in the genus *Prunus*, Mahaleb cherry has bitter-tasting, inedible fruits. Nevertheless, the seeds are readily dispersed by birds and other animals, and Mahaleb cherry now grows wild in many parts of the U.S. and Canada. • Mahaleb cherry resembles pin cherry (p. 163) but is distinguished by its relatively broad leaves, hairless petals and deep red to black fruits. • **Manchu cherry** or Nanking cherry (**P. *tomentosa***), shown in pink/dark green on the map, is usually a shrub with stalkless flowers and fruits and finely sharp-toothed leaves, similar to those of a peach tree. Unlike the peach, Manchu cherry has pink blossoms, and its leaves are woolly underneath (rather than hairless). As the name suggests, Manchu cherry originated in eastern Asia.

ALSO CALLED: Perfumed cherry, St. Lucie cherry.

SIZE AND SHAPE: Small trees or tall shrubs up to 33' tall; crowns broad and rounded.

TRUNKS: Short, often crooked, up to 8" in diameter; bark dark gray, thin; wood dark red, aromatic.

BRANCHES: Widely spreading, numerous; twigs glandular-hairy, with short spur-shoots.

LEAVES: Alternate; blades shiny, dark green above, pale and hairy beneath, **broadly egg-shaped to almost round, 1–3" long,** abruptly sharp-pointed at the tip, usually notched at the base, finely toothed; stalks with **1–2 glands near the blade;** shed in autumn.

FLOWERS: White, about ¹/₂" across, with a **strong, sweet fragrance, stalked;** petals ¹/₅–¹/₃" long; sepals hairless; borne in short, branched **clusters of 4–10 with a main central stalk, on leafy spur-shoots,** in late April–early May.

FRUITS: Dark red to black, juicy **cherries** (drupes), **bitter,** round to egg-shaped, ¹/₅–¹/₄" (¹/₂") across; seeds single, in rounded stones; borne in small, branched clusters, mature in July–August.

HABITAT: Open, often disturbed sites along roads, on rocky banks and abandoned home sites, and bordering woodlands.

ORIGIN: Introduced from Eurasia.

SWEET CHERRY has large, luscious fruits—the common, commercially available cherries. This popular *Prunus* species has been cultivated in North America for over a century and many varieties are grown in orchards across the continent. In 2003, 26 million pounds of sweet cherries were produced in Michigan. The cherries are larger and sweeter and keep longer than those of most other species. They are delicious fresh from the tree. • The strong, hard wood takes a polish well. In Europe, it has been used in interior finishing and for making furniture, musical instruments and small household items. • Unlike many other cherries, sweet cherry does not produce suckers. • Occasionally, sweet cherry escapes and grows wild. Next to humans, birds are its most important dispersal agent. Many birds, including grouse, thrashers, robins and cedar waxwings, enjoy eating the cherries. At other times of the year, white-tailed deer and rabbits can damage trees by eating the leaves and twigs. • The specific epithet *avium*, from the Latin *avis* or "bird," refers to the popularity of the fruits among birds. • 'Bing cherry' is the name for the most widely grown cultivar of sweet cherry. It was developed in 1875 by Ah Bing, a Chinese nursery worker in Oregon.

Upper photo: *P. avium*, double-flowered cultivar

ALSO CALLED: Mazzard cherry, gean, Bing cherry.

SIZE AND SHAPE: Trees up to 35' [38'] tall; crowns cylindrical to pyramidal.

TRUNKS: Tall and reaching 24–30" [33"] in diameter in the wild, shorter and smaller in orchards; **bark reddish-brown, smooth, with conspicuous horizontal pores** (lenticels), sometimes peeling; wood yellowish-red, strong.

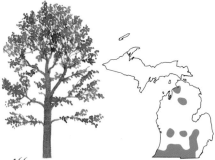

BRANCHES: Stout, spreading; twigs reddish-brown under a grayish film, smooth; buds shiny, brown, some **clustered at tips of short spur-shoots.**

LEAVES: Alternate, simple, deciduous; blades dull dark green above, paler and **hairy on veins beneath,** 2³/₈–4³/₄" long, widest above midleaf, pointed, with sharp, gland-tipped, double teeth; **stalks** ³/₄–1¹/₂" long, with 2 glands near blade.

FLOWERS: White, ³/₄–1¹/₈" across, bisexual; petals usually 5 (more in double-flowered cultivars); **sepals 5, hairless;** flowers in **tassel-like clusters** (umbels) of 1–5 on leafy spur-shoots in May (before or as leaves expand).

FRUITS: Dark red to almost black (sometimes yellow), fleshy **cherries** (drupes), **round to heart-shaped,** ¹/₂–1" across, hanging on slender, ³/₄–1¹/₈" long stalks, in small, flat-topped clusters on spur-shoots; seeds single, within round stones; cherries ripen June–July.

HABITAT: Open, often disturbed sites along fence lines and roads and in woods.

ORIGIN: Introduced from Asia Minor.

SOUR CHERRY is widely grown in orchards across North America. Some double-flowered cultivars are grown as ornamentals, but usually this species is cultivated for its fruit. In 2003, Michigan produced 154 million pounds, or 68%, of the sour cherries grown in the U.S. The tart, juicy cherries are sweetened and baked in pies and cakes, mashed and boiled to make jams and jellies, or canned in syrup. • Sour cherry can reproduce vegetatively by sending up numerous shoots (suckers) from underground runners. However, it usually escapes cultivation and spreads to new regions as seeds. Birds often swallow the hard, protective stones and deposit them, undigested, in new sites. • Game birds, songbirds, raccoons and foxes all eat the cherries, and rabbits and white-tailed deer browse on the leaves and twigs. • The specific epithet *cerasus* is a Greek word meaning "cherry tree." It is also the name of the town, Cerasus of Pontus, in the region where this cherry originated. • Sour cherry can be confused with sweet cherry (p. 166), but sweet cherry leaves have hairs on the undersides of the veins and glands on the stalks just below the blades. Also, sweet cherry fruits are larger, sweeter and more deeply colored.

ALSO CALLED: Pie cherry, mazzard cherry, morello cherry.

SIZE AND SHAPE: Small trees up to 35' [68'] tall; crowns usually broadly rounded; roots shallow, spreading.

TRUNKS: Short, soon branched, up to 35" [38"] in diameter; bark grayish.

BRANCHES: Stout; twigs with stubby spur-shoots; buds shiny reddish-brown, **some clustered at the tips of short spur-shoots,** pointing outward.

LEAVES: Alternate, simple, deciduous; **blades dark green, lustrous, hairless beneath** (when mature), firm, elliptical to ovate, widest above the middle, 1¹/₂–3¹/₂" long, tipped with a blunt point, edged with double or single, rounded teeth and with a gland on the blade near the stalk; stalks usually less than ³/₄" long, lacking glands.

FLOWERS: White, ³/₄–1¹/₈" across, bisexual; petals 5; **sepals 5, hairless;** flowers in small, flat-topped clusters of 2–5 at tips of leafy spur-shoots, in May (before or as leaves expand).

FRUITS: Bright red cherries (drupes), juicy, round, ³/₈–³/₄" **across,** in small, flat-topped clusters at the tips of leafy spur-shoots; seeds single, within a round stone; cherries ripen July.

HABITAT: Open, often disturbed sites such as fence lines, roadsides and woodland borders.

ORIGIN: Introduced from southern Europe, but probably from Asia Minor originally.

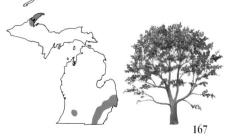

167

AMERICAN PLUM wood is hard and attractive but is not commercially valuable because of the tree's small size. • This small, attractive tree grows quickly but doesn't live long. It is cultivated in orchards, parks and gardens across North America for its beautiful, fragrant flowers and edible fruits. Hundreds of large-flowered cultivars have been developed. • The fruits have tough, sour outer skins, but their sweet, juicy flesh is delicious, making excellent jams, jellies, preserves and pies. The plums can also be halved and dried like prunes, or puréed, spread in a thin sheet and dried as fruit leather. • **Caution:** All parts of this tree except the flesh and skin of the plums contain toxic hydrocyanic acid. • **Alleghany plum** (*P. alleghaniensis*), shown in pink/dark green on the map, can grow to 15' in the mountains of West Virginia, but disjunct populations in Michigan (which are classified as a rare endemic variety, var. *davisii*) seldom exceed $6^1/_2$' in height. Alleghany plum resembles American plum, but it has smaller flowers and fruits (both about $^3/_8$" across), slightly hairy sepals and ovate, more broadly pointed leaves. Also, it prefers dry sites in oak and pine stands.

ALSO CALLED: Wild plum, brown plum, red plum, yellow plum.

SIZE AND SHAPE: Trees or tall shrubs 20–30' [35'] tall; crowns broad; roots spreading, with suckers often forming thickets.

TRUNKS: Short, 5–8" [11"] in diameter; young bark smooth, with horizontal pores (lenticels); mature bark reddish-brown to gray-brown or nearly black, rough with plates; wood reddish-brown, hard, strong.

BRANCHES: Spreading, somewhat thorny with spine-like dwarf twigs; twigs reddish- to grayish-brown, with a **bitter-almond scent;** buds grayish, $^1/_8$–$^3/_8$" long, with 2-colored, chestnut to grayish-brown scales.

LEAVES: Alternate, simple, deciduous; blades dark green above, paler beneath, lance-shaped to oval, $1^1/_2$–$4^1/_2$" long, **edged with fine, sharp, slender-pointed teeth** often tipped with a callus or bristle (not a gland); stalks often with **2 glands near the blade.**

FLOWERS: White, $^1/_2$–1" across, saucer-shaped, **very fragrant,** bisexual; petals 5, $^3/_8$–$^1/_2$" long; flowers on stalks $^3/_8$–1" long, in flat-topped clusters of 2–4, in late April to early June **(before or as leaves expand).**

FRUITS: Yellow to red plums (drupes) with a thin, waxy bloom, $^3/_4$–$1^1/_8$" long, yellow-fleshed; seeds single, within a flattened stone; plums **single or 2–4 together,** mature August–September.

HABITAT: Rocky or sandy soils in moist woods and along streams, roads and fence lines.

ORIGIN: Native.

CANADA PLUM is often planted as an ornamental for its beautiful, fragrant spring blossoms and its attractive, edible fruit. The cultivar 'Princess Kay' has showy double flowers. • The skins of the plums are usually tough and astringent, and the flesh can also be very sour, especially when still firm. After the first frosts, the fruits become soft and juicy. They can be eaten fresh, stewed to make jelly or jam, puréed to make juice or baked in pies. • **Caution:** Children have died from eating too many plums without removing the stones. As with other plums, all parts of this tree except the skin and flesh of the fruits contain toxic hydrocyanic acid. • Canada plum seems to prefer basic soils, but it is not restricted to calcareous regions. • White-tailed deer, black bears, foxes, bobcats, raccoons, muskrats, squirrels, small rodents and large birds all feed on the succulent fruits. • Plum trees often harbor an aphid that is deadly to potatoes, so gardeners should avoid planting plums and potatoes together. • The specific epithet *nigra*, "black," refers to the dark, almost black bark of the branches.

ALSO CALLED: Red plum, black plum, wild plum, horse plum.

SIZE AND SHAPE: Straggly trees or tall shrubs 20–35' [51'] tall; crowns irregular, flat-topped; roots shallow, spreading, usually forming thickets from suckers.

TRUNKS: Short, crooked, 5–10" [16"] in diameter, often clumped; young bark dark reddish-brown to blackish with gray horizontal pores (lenticels), soon splitting and curling; mature bark gray-brown, rough with thick, outcurved scales; wood reddish-brown, heavy, hard, fine-grained.

BRANCHES: Upright, crooked, somewhat thorny with **spine-like dwarf twigs;** twigs green to dark reddish-brown, with a **bitter-almond scent;** buds reddish- to grayish-brown, hairless, 1/8–3/8" long, flat-lying, absent at twig tips.

LEAVES: Alternate, simple, deciduous; **blades dull dark green above,** paler beneath, with prominent veins, broadly oval, 2¼–5½" long, abruptly slender-pointed, with **rounded, mostly gland-tipped, double teeth; stalks stout, with 1–2 large, dark glands** near the blade.

FLOWERS: White, turning pinkish, saucer-shaped, ½–1⅛" **across,** fragrant, bisexual; petals 5; sepals 5; flowers on reddish, 3/8–3/4" long stalks, in flat-topped clusters of 2–5 on year-old twigs, in late April–early June **(before or as leaves expand).**

FRUITS: Red, scarlet or yellow plums (drupes) **without a waxy bloom,** ¾–1⅛" **long,** thick-skinned, yellow-fleshed; seeds single, within flattened stones ¾–1" long; plums single or 2–4 together, ripen August–September.

HABITAT: Moist, open woodlands, thickets and pastures and along fence lines.

ORIGIN: Native.

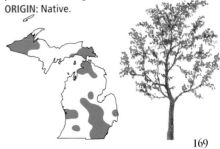

THE GARDEN PLUM has been cultivated in Eurasia for many years. British and French settlers brought it to North America, and it is now widely grown as a fruit tree. Many varieties with improved fruits have been developed. Cultivars with showy, double (10-petaled) flowers are planted as ornamentals in parks and gardens. • Plum wood is hard and takes a polish well. In Europe, it has been used to make cabinets and musical instruments. • Ripe plums are delicious fresh from the tree. They also make excellent jams, preserves, pies and fruit leather. The prunes commonly available in grocery stores are made from these large, firm, readily dried plums. • **Blackthorn** or sloe (***P. spinosa***), shown in dark green on the map, is another introduced shrub that occasionally escapes from cultivation to form spreading thickets. It was brought to North America from Europe and northern Asia for planting as an ornamental and in hedgerows. Blackthorn is very similar to the garden plum, but is a smaller, spinier tree with smaller ($3/4$–$1^1/2$") leaves and smaller ($3/8$–$1/2$"), inedible fruits. Blackthorn fruits have been used to flavor and color gin, and the strong, hard wood makes excellent walking sticks and tool handles.

ALSO CALLED: European plum, Damson plum.

SIZE AND SHAPE: Small, bushy trees or tall shrubs to 25' tall; crowns rounded, open; roots spreading, usually forming thickets from suckers.

TRUNKS: Short, up to 12" in diameter; mature bark grayish to almost black; wood reddish-brown, hard, fine-grained.

BRANCHES: Many, usually thorny with **spine-like dwarf twigs;** twigs reddish, often hairy.

LEAVES: Alternate, simple, deciduous; blades dark green above, **paler, prominently veined and hairy beneath,** oval, rounded to broadly pointed at the tip, $1^1/2$–$2^3/4$" long, **thick, edged with coarse, irregular saw-teeth.**

FLOWERS: White, saucer-shaped, $3/4$–1" across, bisexual; petals 5; sepals 5; flowers **single or in pairs** (sometimes 3s) in April.

FRUITS: Dark blue to nearly black plums (drupes), somewhat egg-shaped, $3/4$–$1^1/8$" **long,** juicy; seeds single, within a large stone; plums mature in July–November.

HABITAT: Roadsides, fence lines, old orchards.

ORIGIN: Introduced from Europe and southwestern Asia.

FOR CENTURIES, people have used and propagated pears. Today, cultivars of the original Eurasian species are grown across North America. Usually, pear trees are heavily pruned to improve fruit production and make harvesting easier, so they rarely reach their full height. • This long-lived, slow-growing tree produces fruit each year, but heavy crops are often followed by a year with low production. • Common pear wood is very hard and fine-grained. It has been used to make drawing instruments, rulers, tool handles, carvings and wood engravings. It also makes excellent fuel. • Small mammals, deer and cattle eat the fruit, especially when it has ripened and dropped. The seeds are dispersed via animal droppings and discarded pear cores. • Like domestic trees, wild-growing pears have edible fruits, but they are usually smaller (less than 2¼" long), drier and grittier. • **Ornamental pear** (**P. *calleryana***, also called Callery pear or Bradford pear), shown in light pink on the map, is often planted along streets in southern Michigan. It is distinguished by its heart-shaped leaves, 2–3 (not 5) styles and small (³/₈" wide), round fruits without persistent sepals. This rare escape originated in China. • Trees with leaves like ornamental pear, but with 5 (not 3) styles and with slightly larger (to ⁵/₈" wide) fruits, are an even more obscure species, **Algerian pear** (**P. *longipes***), shown in dark pink on the map. This African tree is a rare escape in Michigan.

SIZE AND SHAPE: Trees or shrubs to 30' [35'] tall; crowns round to cylindrical; roots spreading, often suckering to form thickets.

TRUNKS: Straight, up to 12" [23"] in diameter; mature bark dark brown to blackish, with small, squared scales; wood reddish-brown, fine-grained, hard.

BRANCHES: Short, stout, ascending, often with **spine-like spur-shoots;** twigs reddish-brown to olive brown, with yellow pores (lenticels); buds chestnut brown to grayish, hairy.

LEAVES: Alternate, simple, deciduous; **blades thick and leathery, hairless** (when mature), **shiny, dark green above,** paler beneath, sharp-pointed, **rounded at the base,** 1–3" long, finely blunt-toothed, **twisted in bud; stalks often equal to or longer than blade;** leaves yellow in autumn.

FLOWERS: Showy, fragrant, pink fading to **white, about 1–1³/₈" wide,** bisexual; sepals 5, hairy; **anthers 20–30, purple;** flowers in flat-topped clusters on spur-shoots in April–May (as leaves expand).

FRUITS: Fleshy pears (pomes) with gritty stone cells in the pulp, firm at first, juicy when ripe, **widest toward the tip and bearing old sepals, tapered to the base** (stalk), ³/₄–4¹/₂" long; seeds in leathery chambers in a core; pears hang near branch tips when ripe in October–December.

HABITAT: Fields, fence lines, disturbed sites and woodland edges.

ORIGIN: Introduced from Eurasia.

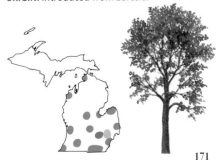

THIS SLOW-GROWING, short-lived tree is sometimes cultivated for its showy flowers, spicy fragrance and dense growth form. In 1897, its beautiful blossom was declared the official state flower of Michigan. • Crabapple wood has been used to make tool handles, spear and harpoon shafts and even some of the working parts in gristmills. Interesting patterns and colors in the wood are exploited in carvings and furniture.
• Although it produces only small fruit, wild crabapple is very hardy, so the trunks are used as stock for grafting more productive but less hardy apple varieties. • Wild crabapple fruits are usually cooked and sweetened to reduce their tartness. Rich in pectin, they are often mixed with other fruits to improve jelling. They also give a special scent to preserves. Wild crabapple cider is delicious. • Native peoples stored crabapples to use through the winter, and then made syrup or cider from leftover apples in spring. • **Prairie crabapple** (*M. ioënsis*, also called *Pyrus ioënsis*), shown in pink/dark green on the map, is a rare species that may have been introduced by Native peoples from regions to the west. Unlike wild crabapple, it has woolly-hairy leaves, flower stalks and outer sepals, but small ($3/4$–$1$$1/2$"), tart fruits.

Photo, center left: *M. coronaria* cultivar

ALSO CALLED: Sweet crabapple, American crabapple, garland-tree • *M. glabrata, P. coronaria*.
SIZE AND SHAPE: Small trees or tall shrubs 15–25' [28'] tall; crowns broad, irregular; roots spreading, often forming thickets from suckers.
TRUNKS: Short, crooked to straight, 6–8" [8"] in diameter; mature bark gray to reddish-brown, scaly; wood hard, strong, flexible, fine-grained.
BRANCHES: Spreading, crooked, with many **thorn-like spur-shoots;** twigs red-brown with flaky grayish skin, grayish-woolly at first;

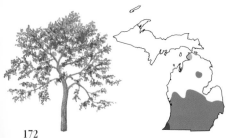

buds **bright red, hairy,** about $1/8$" long ($1/8$–$1/4$" at twig tips), flat-lying.
LEAVES: Alternate, simple, deciduous; blades shiny bright green above, paler beneath, woolly at first, **hairless when mature,** ovate to long-triangular, $1$$1/8$–4" long, rounded or notched at the base, **coarsely toothed at the tip to almost lobed at the base, folded lengthwise in bud;** stalks slender, often with 2 glands near the middle.
FLOWERS: Showy, delicate, fragrant, pink fading to white, $3/4$–2" across, bisexual; **sepals hairless on the outer surface,** woolly inside; **anthers pinkish, 10–20;** flowers in **clusters of 2–6 on leafy dwarf shoots** in late May–June **(after leaves expand).**
FRUITS: Green to yellowish-green, **waxy apples (pomes),** $3/4$–$1$$1/2$" **across,** fragrant; crabapples remain hard; mature by September–October, may persist through winter.
HABITAT: Roadsides and fence lines, and in the understory of deciduous woodlands.
ORIGIN: Native.

MANY CULTIVARS of Siberian crabapple and other domestic crabapples have been developed. These small trees are widely planted as ornamentals for their spectacular, lightly fragrant flowers, attractive fruit and dense branches. The flowers may be single or double (with extra petals) and may have red, purple, pink or white petals. The abundant fruits often remain on the tree well into winter, providing food for birds. Types with different leaf colors and with weeping or columnar forms are also available for landscaping.

• This small, hardy tree can live more than 100 years. Bud production for the next year's blooms begins in early summer, so any pruning should be done soon after the tree finishes flowering in spring. • Siberian crabapple has been crossed with some apple species to produce hardier cultivars. • Other cultivated crabapples and their hybrids can be expected to become naturalized in Michigan. Commonly planted candidates include **Japanese flowering crabapple** (*M. floribunda*), **pearleaf crabapple** (*M. prunifolia*) and **tea crabapple** (*M. hupehensis*). Unfortunately, identification of species is often difficult. • Crabapple fruits look tasty, but they are usually too tart and seedy to eat raw. They do, however, make lovely, deep red jelly with a rich apple flavor and fragrance. • The specific epithet *baccata* means "bearing berries."

ALSO CALLED: Flowering crabapple • *Pyrus baccata*.

SIZE AND SHAPE: Small, wide trees 20–35' tall; crowns broadly domed.

TRUNKS: Short; wood hard, reddish-brown.

BRANCHES: Spreading; **twigs hairless.**

LEAVES: Alternate, simple, deciduous; **blades lustrous green above, hairless when mature,** 1¹/₈–3" long, relatively narrow, slender-pointed at the tip, rounded to wedge-shaped at the base, finely toothed; stalks hairless; leaf scars with 3 vein scars; leaves yellow in autumn.

FLOWERS: White, 1–1³/₈" **across,** bisexual; petals relatively narrow and widely spaced; sepals long and slender, hairless when mature, soon shed; **anthers yellow;** ovary single; flowers in **showy, few-flowered clusters, in April–May** (as leaves expand).

FRUITS: Yellow or red apples (pomes) about ³/₈" **long, without tiny, persistent sepals at the tip,** hairless when young; crabapples hang on long, slender stalks, mature in October.

HABITAT: Fields, thickets, clearings and along railroad lines.

ORIGIN: Introduced from Siberia and northern China.

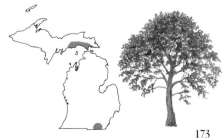

173

APPLE WOOD is solid and fine-grained. It has been used to make furniture, bowls, tools and carvings. It also makes excellent firewood, and its sawdust is used for smoking meat. • Thousands of cultivars have been developed from the common apple and from Siberian crabapple (p. 173). Apple trees are usually propagated by grafting cuttings, because trees grown from seed often produce inferior fruit. • The common apple was first cultivated in Greece at the time of the first Roman empire under the emperor Augustus (63 BC–14 AD). By 1000 AD, at least 30 varieties had been developed. Today, it is one of the most popular fruits in North America. • Apples are commonly eaten raw, but they are also juiced, dried, baked and stewed. The pectin-rich fruit makes excellent jelly, either alone or mixed with other fruits. • **Caution:** Apple flesh is delicious, but the small seeds are toxic and can prove fatal in large quantities. The almond-like fragrance is produced by cyanide-like toxins. • Most wild apple trees probably originate from cores discarded by people. • The taxonomy of the common apple is confusing. Most of the scientific synonyms listed below are currently used in some floras. *M. sylvestris* now usually refers to European crabapple.

ALSO CALLED: Wild apple, paradise apple • *M. sylvestris, M. domestica, M. communis, Pyrus pumila, P. malus.*

SIZE AND SHAPE: Small, widely spreading trees, up to 40' [43'] tall; crowns low, broadly domed.

TRUNKS: Short, up to 36" [43"]; mature bark dark brownish-gray with flaky plates; wood red-brown, hard.

BRANCHES: Spreading, crooked, with stubby (not thorn-like) spur-shoots; twigs and buds hairy.

LEAVES: Alternate, simple, deciduous; blades dark green above, **lightly to densely hairy beneath, untwisting from bud,** elliptic to ovate, 1½–4" long, abruptly pointed, rounded at the base, edged with **fine, sharp teeth;** stalks hairy; leaves yellow in autumn.

FLOWERS: Showy, pink fading to white, 1⅛" across, bisexual; **sepals hairy on the outside; anthers yellow,** numerous; **flowers in small clusters** on spur-shoots, in April (after leaves expand).

FRUITS: Large, 2¼–4½" in diameter, green, yellow or red, juicy **apples** (pomes), indented at both ends, tipped with a cluster of tiny **persistent sepals;** seeds dark brown, shiny, in small, leathery chambers in a core; apples mature and drop in autumn.

HABITAT: Along roadsides, in clearings and near the edges of woods.

ORIGIN: Introduced from Eurasia.

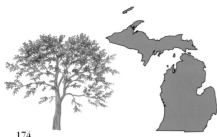

AMERICAN MOUNTAIN-ASH is a relatively slow-growing, short-lived tree that is sometimes cultivated for its attractive flowers, fruits and leaves. The moderately light, close-grained, weak wood has no commercial value. • The fruits (fresh or dried) contain iron and vitamin C. They are also acidic and rich in tannins, however, and should be eaten in moderation. Fruits gathered after the first frost are bittersweet and can be made into jelly, jam, marmalade or juice. Mountain-ash "berries" have also been used to make wine and to flavor liqueurs. Some tribes dried the fruits and ground them into meal. • The fruits have mild laxative, diuretic, astringent and digestive effects, so they were sometimes eaten with hard-to-digest foods. The Algonquians prepared a mild stimulant by boiling American mountain-ash twigs, new white spruce twigs, wintergreen leaves and elderberry flowers. • Grouse, cedar waxwings, grosbeaks, thrushes, squirrels and bears feed on the fruits. • American mountain-ash can be confused with related species. The leaflets of showy mountain-ash (p. 176) are slightly wider, and its flowers appear about a week later. European mountain-ash (p. 177) has hair on its buds and leaf undersides.

ALSO CALLED: American rowan-tree, dogberry, catberry, pigberry, roundwood, rowanberry, service-tree • *Pyrus americana.*

SIZE AND SHAPE: Trees or shrubs 12–35' [57'] tall; crowns open, **narrow, rounded.**

TRUNKS: Short, 4–10" [20"] in diameter; young bark pale gray with horizontal pores (lenticels), thin, smooth, fragrant; mature bark reddish-brown, slightly scaly; wood pale, soft, fine-grained, weak.

BRANCHES: Spreading, slender; twigs dark reddish- to grayish-brown, becoming **hairless; buds dark, shiny, gummy, essentially hairless,** ³/₈–¹/₂" long with narrow, curved tips.

LEAVES: Alternate, deciduous, **positioned on edge and arching;** compound, **pinnately divided into 9–17 leaflets;** leaflets dull green, paler beneath, thin, lance-shaped to narrowly oblong, 2–2³/₄" (rarely 4") long, **3–5 times as long as wide, taper-pointed, finely sharp-toothed, short-stalked,** roughly paired; leaflets often drop before main stalk (rachis); leaves clear yellow in autumn.

FLOWERS: White, tiny, bisexual; petals 5, widest above middle, about ¹/₈" long; sepals 5, fused in bell-shaped calyxes; stamens 15–20, anthers yellow; flowers on hairless stalks in **showy, many-branched, flat-topped or rounded, 2–8" wide clusters** (corymbs), in May–July (after leaves expand).

FRUITS: Bright orange-red, berry-like pomes (like tiny apples) ³/₁₆–¹/₄" across, with thin flesh; seeds shiny, chestnut brown, 1–2 per fruit; pomes in **branched, flat-topped clusters,** mature in September–October, **may persist through winter.**

HABITAT: Moist, shady sites near swamps and lakes; drier uplands such as rocky hillsides, thickets and coniferous forests.

ORIGIN: Native.

SHOWY MOUNTAIN-ASH can be cultivated as an ornamental, but European mountain-ash (p. 177) is more widely used in landscaping. • Birds are the main dispersers of mountain-ashes. The fleshy fruits provide important winter food for many birds and small mammals, persisting on branches above the snow when other fruits are scarce. If both native and introduced mountain-ash species are available, birds apparently eat the fruit of the native species first. Rising populations of cedar waxwings in urban areas reflect the popularity of mountain-ashes in landscaping. Flocks of tipsy birds are sometimes reported when the birds eat the small pomes after the tasty fruits have fermented. • The specific epithet *decora*, "handsome and comely," refers to the showy fruits and flowers of this attractive tree. • Showy mountain-ash is so similar to American mountain-ash (p. 175) that it was once classified as a variety of that species. American mountain-ash has narrower leaflets, smaller fruits and flowers, and an early flowering period (10–12 days ahead of showy mountain-ash). • At one time, taxonomists included the genera *Sorbus* and *Malus* in the genus *Pyrus*.

ALSO CALLED: Northern mountain-ash, dogberry, northern-ash dogberry, northern-ash, showy northern-ash • *Pyrus decora*.

SIZE AND SHAPE: Small trees or tall shrubs to 35' [58"] tall; crowns short, rounded.

TRUNKS: Straight, 4–8" [8"] in diameter; **young bark light grayish-green to golden brown with conspicuous, horizontal pores** (lenticels), thin, smooth; mature bark becoming slightly scaly; wood pale brown, close-grained, moderately light, soft, weak.

BRANCHES: Coarse, ascending; twigs reddish-brown to grayish, **thin-skinned,** hairless; **buds dark reddish-brown, gummy,** 3/8" long, with **hairy-edged inner scales.**

LEAVES: Alternate, deciduous, **horizontal, 4–6" long** (rarely to 10"); compound, **pinnately divided into 13–17 sub-opposite leaflets** on a central stalk (rachis); **leaflets bluish-green, paler beneath,** firm, hairless with age, **oblong to oblong-elliptic,** 2–3 times longer than wide, blunt or **abruptly short-pointed, finely sharp-toothed,** 1 1/8–3" long; leaflets often drop before rachis.

FLOWERS: White, tiny, bisexual; petals 5, round, 3/16" long; sepals 5, tiny; stamens 15–20, anthers yellow; flowers numerous, on short, stout, hairy stalks in **dense, 2 3/8–6" wide, many-branched clusters** (corymbs), in June–July (after leaves expand).

FRUITS: Shiny, orange-red, berry-like pomes (like small apples), thick-fleshed, 5/16–1/2" **across;** seeds 1–2 per fruit, shiny, dark; pomes hang in showy clusters, mature in August–September, **may persist over winter.**

HABITAT: Rocky shores of lakes and streams.

ORIGIN: Native.

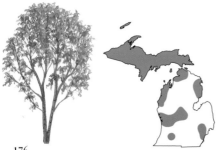

THIS FAST-GROWING ornamental is widely planted in gardens and parks and along streets. • The wood of European mountain-ash is relatively hard. It has been used for tool handles, spinning wheels and other wooden products. • Birds frequently carry mountain-ash seeds to new sites, and the trees can become pests in natural habitats near our towns and cities. • In Scandinavia, the bitter-tasting fruits were used, fresh or dried, to flavor sauces and game (especially fowl). The vitamin C–rich "berries" can be used to make delicious jellies. They have also been used in herbal remedies for diarrhea, hemorrhoids, scurvy and other ailments. • Scottish Highlanders planted this tree beside their homes for protection from witchcraft. • The generic name *Sorbus* was the classical Latin name for European mountain-ashes. The specific epithet *aucuparia* means "I catch birds" and refers to the bird-attracting fruits. European bird catchers often planted this tree to lure prey. The alternative common name "rowan-tree" comes from an old Scandinavian word meaning "red," in reference to the brilliant red fruits. • European mountain-ash is distinguished from native mountain-ashes by its hairier young twigs, downy-white, non-sticky buds and smaller, hairier leaves.

ALSO CALLED: Rowan-tree, dogberry • *Pyrus aucuparia.*

SIZE AND SHAPE: Trees or tall shrubs 15–40' [45"] tall; crowns open, rounded.

TRUNKS: Short, slender, up to about 10" [14"] in diameter; **young bark shiny, gray-brown with elongated, horizontal pores** (lenticels), thin, smooth; mature bark scaly; wood pale brown, fine-grained, hard.

BRANCHES: Coarse, spreading; twigs grayish, shiny, **hairy when young;** buds dark purple, **white-woolly,** ³/₈–¹/₂" long, **not gummy.**

LEAVES: Alternate, deciduous, compound, **pinnately divided into 9–17 sub-opposite leaflets** on a central stalk (rachis); leaflets green above, **whitish and hairy beneath, short-pointed** or blunt, **coarsely sharp-toothed** (except near the base), 1¹/₈–2" long; leaflets often drop before the rachis. ·

FLOWERS: White, tiny, bisexual; petals 5, round, ³/₁₆" long; sepals tiny, 5; stamens 15–20, anthers yellow; flowers numerous, on **hairy stalks in erect, flat-topped, 4–6" wide, many-branched**

clusters (corymbs), in May–June (after leaves expand).

FRUITS: Orange-yellow to scarlet, berry-like pomes (like tiny apples), fleshy, ³/₈–¹/₂" **across;** seeds 1–2, shiny, dark brown, about ¹/₄" long; pomes hang in round-topped clusters, mature in September, **may persist through winter.**

HABITAT: Moist sites in woods and wetlands; also in disturbed areas such as roadsides and fence lines.

ORIGIN: Introduced from Europe.

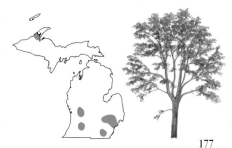

THIS ATTRACTIVE small tree was introduced to North America for its showy flowers. It is one of the most common trees in Great Britain, where countless miles of oneseed hawthorn were planted in the 17th and 18th centuries to produce tough, thorny, live-stock-proof hedges. • Hawthorn species are notoriously difficult to tell apart, but oneseed hawthorn is quite distinctive. It is the only species in Michigan with leaves cut more than halfway to the midvein, and the only one with single styles and single nutlets. However, oneseed hawthorn occasionally hybridizes with dotted hawthorn (p. 182), producing offspring with intermediate characteristics. • **English hawthorn** (*C. laevigata*, also called *C. oxyacantha* and quick-set hawthorn), shown in pink on the map, is a closely related species, also introduced from Europe. It is distinguished by its less deeply divided leaves with notches that scarcely extend halfway to the midvein. Also, its flowers usually have 2 styles and its fruits have 2 nutlets. Those with double and/or pink flowers are occasionally planted in Michigan and may escape to grow wild. • *Crataegus* was the traditional Latin name for hawthorn, derived from the Greek word *kratos*, "strength," in reference to the strong, hard wood. The specific epithet *monogyna* means "with a single pistil or gynoecium" and refers to the single-seeded fruits.

ALSO CALLED: English hawthorn, maythorn.

SIZE AND SHAPE: Trees or shrubs up to 25–35' [52'] tall; crowns broadly domed.

TRUNKS: Crooked, sometimes clumped, up to 12" [13½"] in diameter; mature bark dark gray to brownish, slightly scaly; wood heavy, hard.

BRANCHES: Many, crooked, spreading; twigs lustrous; **thorns shiny, gray, straight, ³/₈–³/₄" long, in leaf axils and at the tips of 1¹/₈–3" branchlets; buds round,** dark brown, often 2–3 together (1 producing a thorn).

LEAVES: Alternate, simple, deciduous; blades dark green above, paler beneath, firm, triangular to broadly ovate, ¹/₂–2" long, **cut more than halfway to the midvein into 3–7 lobes tipped with irregular sharp teeth;** leaves often persist into late autumn.

FLOWERS: Rose pink (cultivars dark red to white), unpleasant-smelling, ³/₈–¹/₂" across, bisexual; petals 5; sepals 5, bases fused in a tube; **flowers in branched, flat-topped clusters** (corymbs) on dwarf shoots in May–June.

FRUITS: **Bright red haws** (pomes, like small apples), thin-fleshed, rounded to ellipsoidal, about ¹/₄" wide, tipped with sepals and **1 protruding style;** seeds within **bony nutlets, 1 per fruit;** hips mature in September–October, **often persist through winter.**

HABITAT: Open, often disturbed sites in clearings and open woodlands and along roadsides and fence lines, especially on calcium-rich soils.

ORIGIN: Introduced from Europe and western Asia.

BLACK HAWTHORN is a mainly western species that is widespread from Alaska to California and east to Michigan, where it occurs in disjunct populations in the northern Great Lakes region. • The tasty-looking haws are edible but not very juicy. • Eye scratches from hawthorn thorns can be very dangerous and may even cause blindness. • Hawthorns are mainly dispersed by fruit-eating animals. The fleshy fruits provide food for many birds and small mammals. Cedar waxwings and ruffed grouse are especially fond of the haws and may eat these fruits throughout the winter, when most berries are covered by snow. Small mammals such as mice and voles usually wait to gather fallen haws from the ground. Hawthorn twigs and leaves, especially those of species with relatively few thorns such as black hawthorn, also provide food for browsing animals such as white-tailed deer and mule deer. • Dense tangles of thorny branches make ideal nesting sites for birds. • The specific epithet honors David Douglas (1798–1834), a Royal Horticultural Society collector best known for his work in the Pacific Northwest.

ALSO CALLED: Western hawthorn, Douglas's hawthorn.

SIZE AND SHAPE: Trees or shrubs to 20' [25'] tall, often forming thickets; crowns broad.

TRUNKS: Crooked, sometimes clumped, up to 12" in diameter; mature bark gray-brown, scaly; wood heavy, hard.

BRANCHES: Spreading, **sometimes thornless;** twigs lustrous, hairless; **thorns scattered,** stout, 3/8–1" long, straight or slightly curved; **buds round,** dark brown.

LEAVES: Alternate, simple, deciduous; blades dark green above, paler beneath, glossy and hairless when mature, ovate to broadly elliptic, mostly 3/4–1 1/2" long and 1/2–1 1/8" wide (sometimes up to 3" by 1 1/2"), edged with **coarse, gland-tipped teeth,** usually with **5–9 shallow, irregular lobes above midleaf.**

FLOWERS: White to pinkish, unpleasant-smelling, 3/8–1/2" across, bisexual; petals 5, soon shed; sepals 5, bases fused, tips silky-hairy and bent backward; anthers 10–20, white or pink; flowers in branched, **flat-topped clusters** (corymbs) **of 5–12 on dwarf shoots,** in June.

FRUITS: Dark reddish-purple to purplish-black haws (pomes, like small apples), succulent, short-ovoid, about 3/8" wide, tipped with tiny sepals and 5 protruding styles; seeds within bony nutlets, 3–5 per fruit; hips mature in September, **often persist through winter.**

HABITAT: Open, often disturbed sites around clearings and on shores, sand dunes, cliffs and rocky ridges.

ORIGIN: Native.

THIS SHOWY and desirable species for ornamental planting originated in the southern U.S. and was first planted in Michigan in hedges. With its large, white flowers in spring, shady canopy in summer, bright orange to scarlet leaves in autumn and bright red fruits in early winter, Washington hawthorn has been widely planted in parks and gardens across North America and Europe. This moderately hardy species is also one of the least susceptible to fire blight. Washington hawthorn is the only member of the Series Cordatae in Michigan. • Another small series, the Intricatae, is represented in Michigan by **Copenhagen hawthorn (*C. intricata*)**, shown in pink/dark green on the map, which broadly encompasses a complex including *C. bealii, C. diversifolia, C. foetida, C. meticulosa, C. rubella* and *C. wheeleri*. This unusually thorny group is noted for its bright red, rather dry fruits, which are tipped with sepals edged in glandular teeth. • Hawthorn trunks are usually small, but the hard, strong wood has been used for carving and lathe work and for making toothpicks, awls, pins and fishhooks. • Most people find the sweet-fetid scent of hawthorn flowers unpleasant. Many insects, however, find it delightful and are tempted to feed on the pollen and nectar, cross-pollinating the flowers in the process. • The specific epithet *phaenopyrum,* from the Greek *phanero,* "clearly visible," and *pyrus,* "a pear," likely refers to the pear-like leaves of these trees.

ALSO CALLED: Washington-thorn, red-haw, Virginia hedge thorn, Virginia heart-leaved thorn • *C. cordata*.

SIZE AND SHAPE: Small trees or tall shrubs 25–30' [36'] tall; crowns regular, oval to rounded, 20–30' across.

TRUNKS: Short, to 12" [16"] in diameter; bark thin, smooth, light brown, scaly with age.

BRANCHES: Upright, with numerous slender **thorns 1¹/₈–2" long;** twigs shiny brown; buds rounded, often 2–3 together (1 producing a thorn).

LEAVES: Alternate, simple, deciduous; blades dark, glossy green above, paler beneath, essentially hairless, ovate to **broadly triangular in outline, often 3–5 lobed, pointed, ³/₄–2³/₈" long and almost as wide, lobed and coarsely, irregularly toothed;** lobes 1–4 per side, largest at base, much smaller upward, **cut less than halfway to the midrib; veins ending at lobe tips and lobe bases;** stalks ³/₈–2" long, lacking glands; leaves bright orange to scarlet in autumn.

FLOWERS: White, ³/₈–¹/₂" across, bisexual; petals 5; sepals 5, short-triangular; **stamens about 20 with pale yellow anthers;** styles usually 5 (sometimes 3); **flowers numerous** in broad, hairless, multiple-branched clusters (cymes), in April–June.

FRUITS: Tiny, **shiny, bright scarlet haws** with thin, dry pulp, about ¹/₄" across, usually **shedding sepals from tips and leaving ends of nutlets clearly exposed** (almost exserted); seeds usually 5, 1 per nutlet; fruits mature in October–November, often persist until spring.

HABITAT: Fields and thickets.

ORIGIN: Native in the southeastern U.S.; probably escaped from cultivation in Michigan.

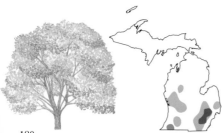

THIS HIGHLY VARIABLE SPECIES has been variously classified and reclassified over the years.
• Cockspur hawthorn is a fast-growing, short-lived tree that readily invades cleared land, but because it requires high light levels, it is soon shaded out when other trees become established. • The specific epithet *crus-galli* comes from the Latin *crus*, "shin or leg," and *gallus*, "cock," alluding to the sharp thorns that resemble rooster spurs. • The leaves described below are typical of flowering or fruiting shoots and are usually more than twice as long as wide. Leaves on vegetative shoots can be very different. Often they are elliptic to oblong and widest near the middle. Also, leaves on vegetative shoots may be somewhat lobed and can grow to twice the size of those on flowering shoots, reaching 2–3½" in length and 1⅛–3" in width. Such variability between vegetative and flowering branches is common in hawthorns. In some cases, the range of variation on a single tree or within a single population exceeds that between species. The larger leaves on short (flowering) shoots are usually the most useful for identifying hawthorns to species. • With its symmetrical trees (owing to layered branching) and glossy, unlobed leaves, cockspur hawthorn is one of the more easily identified species in this complex genus.

ALSO CALLED: Cockspur thorn • *C. bushii, C. fontanesiana, C. pyracanthoides, C. tenax.*

SIZE AND SHAPE: Trees or tall shrubs 20–25' [29'] tall; crowns broadly domed or depressed.

TRUNKS: Sometimes clumped, up to 10" [12"] in diameter; mature bark gray-brown, slightly scaly; wood heavy, hard.

BRANCHES: Numerous, crooked, **stiff, wide-spreading, horizontal;** twigs hairless; **thorns many, ³/₄–2³/₄" long,** straight or slightly curved; **buds rounded,** dark brown, often 2–3 together (1 producing a thorn).

LEAVES: Alternate, simple, deciduous; **blades glossy, dark green above,** dull and paler below, **leathery, ovate, widest above midleaf, with broad tips and wedge-shaped bases,** 1⅛–2" long, sharp-toothed (at least above the middle), **mostly unlobed;** stalks ⅛–½" long.

FLOWERS: White, unpleasant-smelling, ³/₈–½" wide, bisexual; petals 5, soon shed; sepals 5, slender, bases fused; anthers about 10, white, pale yellow or pink; flowers many, in **loose, hairless, flat-topped clusters** (corymbs) on dwarf shoots, in May–June.

FRUITS: **Green to dull red haws** (pomes, like small apples), **often dark-dotted,** rather hard, with thin, dry flesh, **short-egg-shaped to almost round, often 5-sided, about ³/₈" wide,** tipped with sepals and protruding styles; seeds in bony nutlets, 1–2 (sometimes 3) per fruit; fruits mature in September–October, **often persist through winter.**

HABITAT: Open, often disturbed sites such as pastures and open woodlands, on dry, rocky ground to wet sites.

ORIGIN: Native.

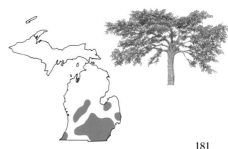

THIS ABUNDANT NATIVE TREE is one of the most common species in Michigan river bottoms and swamp forests. Dotted hawthorn is also one of the more easily recognized hawthorns. Its numerous horizontal branches and pale gray branchlets make it conspicuous in winter. In autumn, the dull, leathery, broad-tipped leaves and pale-dotted red to yellow haws identify this species. The leaves are always longer than wide, though they can vary greatly on the same tree. Leaves on vegetative shoots are often more lobed and much wider-tipped than those on flowering shoots. Sometimes the leaves on vegetative shoots are almost fan-shaped and have notched (rather than pointed or blunt) tips. • Many hawthorns are planted as ornamentals for their showy flowers, and the attractive clusters of fruit can add color to the winter landscape. When planted as a hedge, hawthorns can provide an impassable barrier of dense, thorny branches. However, these fast-growing trees can also become pests when they invade open areas such as pastures and parks. The long, sharp thorns are seldom appreciated along paths and fence lines and can be especially hazardous when unwanted trees must be removed. • The specific epithet *punctata*, "dotted," refers to the pale dots that speckle the haws of this species.

ALSO CALLED: Whitehaw.

SIZE AND SHAPE: Trees or shrubs to 25–35' [39'] tall, often in thickets; crowns open, broad.

TRUNKS: Mostly single, up to 12" [16"] in diameter, with **branched thorns**; mature bark brownish-gray, fissured; wood hard.

BRANCHES: Stiff, stout, wide-spreading, with **short, 3–9-leaved side-shoots;** twigs lustrous, hairless; **thorns slender, ³/₄–3" long, straight, slightly curved or branched; buds rounded,** often 2–3 together (1 producing a thorn).

LEAVES: Alternate, simple, deciduous; **blades dull green with impressed veins above,** paler and **slightly hairy beneath, firm,** elliptic-oblong to ovate, ³/₄–3" long, **widest and sharply single- or double-toothed above midleaf, often unlobed,** bases tapered.

FLOWERS: White, unpleasant-smelling, ³/₈–³/₄" across, bisexual; petals 5, soon shed; sepals 5, densely gray-hairy, slender, with fused bases; anthers about 20, pink, red or yellow; flowers many, in **loose, flat-topped clusters** (corymbs) on dwarf shoots, in May–June.

FRUITS: Dull red or orange-red, sometimes yellow (var. *aurea*), **pale-dotted haws** (pomes, like small apples), pear-shaped to **spherical, ³/₈–¹/₂" wide,** tipped with sepals and protruding styles, mellow-fleshed to scarcely succulent; seeds within bony nutlets, 3–5 per fruit; fruits mature in September–October, **often persist through winter.**

HABITAT: Rich to rocky sites in moist to wet woodlands, along roads and fence lines and on floodplains.

ORIGIN: Native.

THE HAWS OF FLESHY HAWTHORN are succulent and juicy when ripe, but sometimes they remain hard and dry until late in the season. All hawthorn haws are edible, but flavor and fleshiness can vary greatly with the species, habitat and time of year. Although haws are rich in pectin, they are often very seedy, so they are usually combined with other fruit to make jams, jellies and compotes. Some tribes mixed the flesh of haws with dried meat to make pemmican.

• The specific epithet *succulenta* means "with juicy flesh." • Fleshy hawthorn belongs to Series Macracanthae. According to ITIS (2003) and Voss (1985), the species for which this group is named, **C. macracantha**, is now included in *C. succulenta* as var. *macracantha*. • **Pear hawthorn** (**C. calpodendron**), shown in pink/dark green on the map, another species in the Macracanthae, is very similar to fleshy hawthorn but is distinguished by its woolly to silky-hairy young twigs and its larger (2–3¹/₂" long by 1¹/₂–3" wide), more prominently hairy, dull yellowish-green leaves. Pear hawthorn is also a smaller tree (at most 10–13' tall) with small (¹/₄–³/₈" long), shiny, orange-red, pear-shaped haws and few (if any), 1¹/₈–1¹/₂" long thorns. Pear hawthorn is widespread in southern Michigan. Its specific epithet *calpodendron*, "urn-tree," refers to the shape of the fruit.

ALSO CALLED: Succulent hawthorn • *C. macracantha*.

SIZE AND SHAPE: Trees or shrubs up to 20–25' [40'] tall; crowns broadly domed.

TRUNKS: Crooked, clumped, up to 26" in diameter; mature bark scaly; wood heavy, hard.

BRANCHES: Numerous, spreading; **twigs dark, lustrous, hairless** (or slightly hairy when young); **thorns glossy, blackish, strong,** 1¹/₈–1³/₄" (sometimes to 3") long; **buds rounded,** often 2–3 together (1 producing a thorn).

LEAVES: Alternate, simple, deciduous; **blades dark, lustrous green with impressed veins above,** paler and **finely hairy (at least on veins) beneath, firm,** broadly elliptic to ovate or diamond-shaped, 1¹/₈–2³/₈" (sometimes to 3") long, **finely sharp-toothed, shallowly 9–11-lobed above midleaf;** stalks usually glandless, grooved and winged near the blade.

FLOWERS: White, unpleasant-smelling, ³/₈–³/₄" across, bisexual; petals 5, soon shed; **sepals 5, glandular-toothed,** bases fused, tips bent backward or shed; anthers 10–20, white, pale yellow or pink; flowers in branched, **flat-topped** clusters (corymbs) on dwarf shoots, in May–June.

FRUITS: **Glossy, bright red haws** (pomes, like small apples), tipped with persistent sepals and protruding styles, **round,** ¹/₄–¹/₂" across; seeds within bony nutlets, 2–3 per fruit; fruits mature in September–October, **often persist through winter.**

HABITAT: Dry, rocky sites in fields and along fence lines, roadsides and beaches.

ORIGIN: Native.

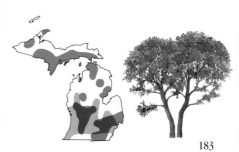

183

FIREBERRY HAWTHORN is one of 5 Michigan species in Series Rotundifoliae, which also includes **Dodge's hawthorn** (*C. dodgei* or *C. flavida*), **Blanchard's hawthorn** (*C. irrasa*), **Margaret's hawthorn** (*C. margarettiae* or *C. margaretta*) and **C. x immanis**. All 5 hawthorns are shrubby and typically have small, round leaves with delicate, glandular stalks. They also have numerous slender thorns, spherical fruits and clusters of a few small flowers that appear early in the year. • Members of the Series Brainerdianae are represented by 3 species in Michigan: **Brainerd's hawthorn** (*C. brainerdii*), shown in pink/dark green on the map, **Cole's hawthorn** (*C. colae*) and **fatty hawthorn** (*C. pinguis* or *C. scabrida*). Brainerd's hawthorn has red, mellow haws, and the toothed, lobed leaves are broad with wedge-shaped bases and abruptly pointed tips. Also, the nutlets in the haws have a shallow pit in the inner surface (not found in fireberry hawthorn stones). • Blanchard's hawthorn is found in northernmost Michigan, near Lake Superior. Dodge's hawthorn, Margaret's hawthorn and Brainerd's hawthorn are more widely distributed in the southern part of the state.

Bottom photos: *C. brainerdii*

ALSO CALLED: Round-leaved hawthorn • *C. aboriginum, C. brunetiana, C. faxonii, C. rotundifolia*.

SIZE AND SHAPE: Trees or shrubs to 20' tall, often forming thickets; crowns broad.

TRUNKS: Crooked, sometimes clumped; mature bark scaly; wood heavy, hard.

BRANCHES: Numerous, stout, usually thorny; twigs lustrous, smooth; **thorns shiny black, slender**, straight or slightly curved, 3/4–3" long; **buds round,** often 2–3 together (1 producing a thorn).

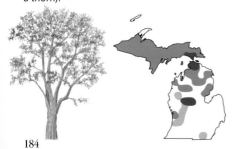

LEAVES: Alternate, simple, deciduous; blades usually dull yellowish-green, often with slightly impressed veins above, soon becoming hairless, firm, 3/4–3 1/2" long, **usually about as wide as long**, pointed to round-tipped, **edged to below midleaf with gland-tipped teeth and 7–13 shallow lobes; stalks slender, often with tiny glands** near the blade.

FLOWERS: White, unpleasant-smelling, 3/8–1/2" across, bisexual; petals 5, soon shed; sepals 5, edged with glands, fused at the base; anthers about 10, white or pale yellow; flowers in flat-topped, branched clusters (corymbs) on dwarf shoots, in May–June.

FRUITS: Hairy, deep red (rarely yellow) haws (pomes, like small apples), tipped with tiny sepals and protruding styles, round, about 3/8" wide; seeds within bony nutlets, 3–4 per fruit; fruits mature in August–October, **often persist through winter.**

HABITAT: Open, rocky, gravelly or sandy sites on shores, in open woodlands and along roads and fence lines.

ORIGIN: Native.

184

THE SPECIFIC EPITHET *flabellata*, "fan-shaped," refers to the shape of the leaves. • It is easy to determine if a tree is a hawthorn, but it is much more difficult, and sometimes impossible, to identify the species. *Crataegus* is a large, complex genus with over 1000 "species" described from North America alone. However, many of these taxa are hybrids or poorly defined varieties. • It has been suggested that the evolutionary diversification of North American species began when hawthorns invaded areas cleared for agriculture by Native peoples. These clearings opened new habitats where hawthorn species could spread and intermix. • Fanleaf hawthorn belongs to Series Tenuifoliae but forms a link with Series Rotundifoliae through its affinities with fireberry hawthorn (p. 184). These 2 species occupy the same geographical region, and fanleaf hawthorn may have contributed genes to fireberry hawthorn. • **Bigfruit hawthorn** (**C. macrosperma**), more widespread member of Series Tenuifoliae, can be distinguished by its early spring flowering. Many taxonomists include it in the species *C. flabellata*.

Bottom photo: *C. macrosperma*

ALSO CALLED: New England hawthorn • *C. densiflora, C. grayana*.

SIZE AND SHAPE: Trees or shrubs 15–20' tall, often in thickets; crowns broad.

TRUNKS: Crooked, clumped; mature bark scaly; wood heavy, hard.

BRANCHES: Numerous; twigs lustrous, hairless, slender; **thorns numerous, slender, straight or slightly curved, 2–2^3/$_8$" (sometimes 1^1/$_8$–4") long; buds rounded,** often 2–3 together (1 producing a thorn).

LEAVES: Alternate, simple, deciduous, **often bent backward;** blades hairless when mature, ovate to diamond-shaped or triangular (often nearly round on vegetative shoots), 1^1/$_8$–2" (sometimes to 3") long, tapered to a point, wedge-shaped or squared at the base, **edged with 7–13 pointed, sharply toothed lobes** (often with tips curved out or back).

FLOWERS: White, unpleasant-smelling, ^{1}/$_2$–^{3}/$_4$" across, bisexual; petals 5, soon shed; sepals 5, **slender, smooth-edged,** bases fused; anthers 10–20, pink; flowers numerous, in loose, **flat-topped** clusters (corymbs) on dwarf shoots, in May–June.

FRUITS: Crimson, thick-fleshed, juicy haws (pomes, like small apples), tipped with sepals and protruding styles, oblong to round, ^{3}/$_8$–^{1}/$_2$" across, sometimes slightly angled; seeds within bony nutlets, 3–5 per fruit; fruits mature in September–October, **often persist in winter.**

HABITAT: Open, often rocky, calcareous sites including clearings, pastures, streambanks and woodlands.

ORIGIN: Native.

POLYPLOIDY (having 3 or more sets of chromosomes) and apomixis (producing seed without fertilization) have contributed to the expansion of the genus *Crataegus* and to a good deal of taxonomic confusion. Through apomixis, even sterile hybrids can produce large groups of genetically identical plants with relatively stable characteristics, and these groups may eventually be described as species. In the long term, this lack of genetic diversity could become a weakness, but meanwhile, it allows one plant to produce hundreds or even millions of identical offspring. • Scarlet hawthorn belongs to Series Coccineae. Confusingly, the species for which the group was named, *C. coccinea*, has been variously reclassified as other species, including **Holmes' hawthorn** (*C. holmesiana*), **scarlet hawthorn** (*C. pedicellata*) and **Pringle's hawthorn** (*C. pringlei*), and as components of species in other series such as fireberry hawthorn (p. 184). • Members of Series Pruinosae have pinkish to purplish or crimson, waxy-coated fruits tipped with prominent, elevated sepals. **Frosted hawthorn** or waxyfruit hawthorn (*C. pruinosa*), for which the series is named, is identified by its leaves (>2" long, hairless, widest above the middle), anthers (20, white or pink) and sepals (smooth-edged).

Bottom photo: *C. pruinosa*

ALSO CALLED: *C. aulica, C. ellwangeriana.*

SIZE AND SHAPE: Trees or shrubs to 35' tall, highly variable; **crowns usually compact** and conical.

TRUNKS: Crooked, sometimes clumped; mature bark scaly; wood heavy, hard.

BRANCHES: Numerous, slender, spreading; twigs lustrous, hairless with age; **thorns smooth, shiny, stout, usually slightly curved,** $3/4$–$2^3/8$" **long; buds rounded,** dark brown, often 2–3 together (1 producing a thorn).

LEAVES: Alternate, simple, deciduous; blades

dark green and hairless above **(often rough-hairy when young), ovate to almost round, widest below midleaf,** $2^3/8$–$3^1/2$" **long, broad-based, edged with sharp, double teeth and 7–11 shallow lobes;** stalks $1/3$–$4/5$ as long as the blade, often glandular.

FLOWERS: White, with a sweet but unpleasant smell, $1/2$–$3/4$" across, bisexual; petals 5, soon shed; sepals 5, **glandular-toothed,** fused into a tube at the base; anthers 10–20; flowers numerous, in branched, **slender-stalked, flat-topped clusters** (corymbs) on dwarf shoots, in May–June.

FRUITS: Bright red, thick-fleshed, often juicy haws (pomes, like small apples), tipped with tiny persistent sepals and protruding styles, **spherical,** $3/8$–$1/2$" across; seeds within bony nutlets, 3–5 per fruit; fruits mature in autumn, **often persist through winter.**

HABITAT: Open, often disturbed sites such as pastures, fence lines; also in moist woods and along streams.

ORIGIN: Native.

MANY PARTS OF HAWTHORN TREES have been used in medicine. Dried leaves or flowers have been administered in capsules, teas and tinctures for treating heart and circulatory problems. Studies have shown that hawthorn dilates blood vessels, thereby improving circulation, increasing oxygen supply to the heart and stabilizing blood pressure. Hawthorn may also strengthen the heart by making it pump harder. Extracts have been used to treat moderate congestive heart failure, heart arrhythmia and mild angina, but more often hawthorn is recommended for preventing future heart problems. Some studies suggest that hawthorn may be effective in controlling or even lowering cholesterol, triglyceride and blood sugar levels. High doses also slow the central nervous system, and extracts have been used as a sedative for treating insomnia. • A smaller (10–20' tall) member of Series Molles, **Quebec hawthorn** (*C. submollis*, also called *C. champlainensis*), in dark green on the map, resembles downy hawthorn but is readily distinguished by its flowers (with 10 anthers) and its pear-shaped fruits. Its presence in Michigan is unclear, but it should occur on the Upper Peninsula. • The Series Dilatatae has questionable status in Michigan. It is represented by 1 species, **broadleaf hawthorn** (*C. dilatata*), shown in dark pink on the map, collected from a single site in 1929.

ALSO CALLED: Red hawthorn.

SIZE AND SHAPE: Trees or shrubs up to 25–30' [33'] tall, often forming thickets; crowns broad.

TRUNKS: Crooked, up to 24" [31"] in diameter; mature bark brownish-gray, slightly scaly; wood heavy, hard.

BRANCHES: Numerous, slender, spreading; twigs reddish-brown and silky-hairy when young, smooth and gray with age; **thorns few, reddish-brown, straight, slender,** 3/4–23/8" **long; buds rounded,** often 2–3 together (1 producing a thorn).

LEAVES: Alternate, simple, deciduous; **blades densely short-hairy above and woolly beneath when young,** dark green, hairless above and slightly hairy beneath when mature, **widest at or below midleaf,** 11/2–3" **long and almost as wide, sharply double-toothed or with 9–11 sharp-toothed lobes.**

FLOWERS: White, unpleasant-smelling, 3/4–1" across, bisexual; petals 5, soon shed; sepals 5, **woolly, glandular-toothed,** fused at the base; **anthers 20, white or pale yellow;** flowers in showy, hairy-branched, flat-topped clusters (corymbs) on dwarf shoots, in May–June.

FRUITS: Bright red haws (pomes, like small apples), usually thick-fleshed and mellow, **hairy** (at least near the ends), tipped with sepals and protruding styles, **round,** 3/8–1/2" across; seeds in bony nutlets, usually 5 per fruit; fruits mature in autumn, **often persist through winter.**

HABITAT: Fence lines, roadsides open woods and well-drained hillsides.

ORIGIN: Native.

THE FRUITS OF DOWNY SERVICEBERRY are rather dry and flavorless, but Native peoples used them to make a pudding, said to be almost as good as plum pudding. • Squirrels, chipmunks, skunks, raccoons, black bears and at least 40 bird species eat and disperse the fruits. Deer browse on the twigs and leaves. • "Serviceberry" is a variation of an earlier name, "sarvissberry," from "sarviss," a transformation of *Sorbus* (mountain-ash). "Downy" refers to the silvery-hairy young leaves of this species. The inclusion of "shad" in some common names alludes to the shad fish migration, which coincides with the blooming of this shrub. • It is easy to identify the genus *Amelanchier*, but identifying the species is much more difficult and sometimes impossible. Taxonomic problems stem from a combination of hybridization, polyploidy (having 3 or more sets of chromosomes) and apomixis (producing seed without fertilization). For example, serviceberries often produce fertile triploid offspring, i.e., plants with 3 sets of chromosomes. Most serviceberries hybridize freely and produce relatively fertile intermediate offspring. Even the most distinctive species can blend together in a continuous series of shrubs with intergrading characteristics. • Only 2 of Michigan's serviceberries are described in this guide. Most species never reach tree size.

ALSO CALLED: Downy juneberry, Allegheny serviceberry, apple shadbush, common serviceberry, shadblow.

SIZE AND SHAPE: Small trees or shrubs to 35' [63'] tall; crowns irregular, narrow.

TRUNKS: Usually **clumped,** 4–12" [25"] in diameter; **bark bluish-gray, thin, smooth,** slightly fissured with age; wood heavy, hard, reddish-brown.

BRANCHES: Slender; twigs greenish to purplish when young, ridged lengthwise below leaf scars; buds slender, **twisted, pointed,** 1/4–1/2" long,

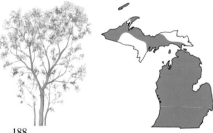

approximately 5-scaled.

LEAVES: Alternate, simple, deciduous; **blades densely whitish-woolly beneath and folded when young,** dark green and hairless above when mature, paler beneath with a **few hairs on the veins,** oval, thin, 2–4" long, sharp-tipped, with **about 25 regular, sharp teeth and fewer than 12 prominent veins per side; stalks finely hairy,** slender, 3/4–1 1/8" long.

FLOWERS: White, bisexual; petals 5, strap-like, 3/8–1/2" long; sepals 5, in a bell-shaped calyx; flowers on silky-hairy stalks in axils of slender, reddish, silky-hairy bracts, forming **showy, branched clusters** (racemes) at branch tips in April–May **(as leaves begin to expand).**

FRUITS: Dark reddish-purple, berry-like but dry pomes (like tiny apples), 1/4–1/2" across; tipped with persistent sepals; **lowermost stalks about 1/2" long;** seeds hard, 5–10 per pome; pomes ripen and drop in June–August.

HABITAT: Dry sites in fields, woodlands and clearings; occasionally in rich, swampy sites.

ORIGIN: Native.

SERVICEBERRIES seldom grow large enough to produce wood of commercial importance, but their hard, heavy trunks have been used to make tool handles, walking sticks and other small articles. • The sweet, juicy fruits are edible and rich in iron and copper. They can be eaten fresh from the tree, served with milk and sugar, added to pancakes, muffins and pies, or made into jellies, jams and preserves. Native peoples dried the small pomes like raisins or mashed and dried them in cakes. Often the dried fruits were mixed with meat and fat to form pemmican, a lightweight, high-energy food that could support winter travelers for long periods if the diet was supplemented with vitamin C (usually in the form of rose hips or spruce tea) to prevent scurvy. • The twigs have a faint bitter-almond scent. • This hardy, attractive shrub, with its showy flower clusters and edible, bird-attracting fruits, is often planted in gardens and parks. • The species name *laevis*, "smooth," refers to the hairless leaves and flower clusters. • Smooth serviceberry is very similar to downy serviceberry (p. 188) and is sometimes considered a variety of that species. Often the two grow together.

ALSO CALLED: Smooth juneberry, Allegheny serviceberry, juneberry.

SIZE AND SHAPE: Trees or shrubs 6–35' [60'] tall; crowns irregular, narrow.

TRUNKS: Often clumped, up to 20" [22"] in diameter; **bark thin, smooth, gray,** with dark vertical lines; wood heavy, hard.

BRANCHES: Slender; twigs purplish, hairless, ridged lengthwise below leaf scars; **buds narrowly egg-shaped, pointed, 1/4–1/2" long, twisted,** approximately 5-scaled.

LEAVES: Alternate, simple, deciduous; **blades coppery red, hairless and folded when young,** dark green when mature, paler beneath, essentially hairless, thin, oval to elliptic, 1 1/8–3" long, abruptly pointed, with **about 25 sharp teeth and 10 or fewer veins per side; stalks hairless,** slender, 3/8–1 1/8" long.

FLOWERS: White, bisexual; petals 5, strap-like, 3/8–3/4" long; sepals 5, about 1/8" long, bent backward in a bell-shaped calyx; **flowers on hairless, 3/8–1 1/8" long stalks** in axils of slender, ephemeral bracts, forming **showy, elongated,** **drooping clusters** (racemes), in April–May **(when leaves are at least half grown).**

FRUITS: Dark reddish-purple to black, berry-like, fleshy, juicy pomes (like tiny apples), 1/4–3/8" wide, tipped with sepals; **lowermost stalks 2–4" long;** seeds hard, 5–10 per pome; pomes ripen and drop in July–August.

HABITAT: Coniferous or mixed woodlands, clearings, fence lines and roadsides, usually on well-drained sites.

ORIGIN: Native.

THIS ATTRACTIVE, fast-growing tree has been culti-vated as an ornamental since the 1800s and is widely planted in both the U.S. and Europe. Trees live about 100 years and begin to flower profusely at a young age, producing showy clusters of nodding, bell-shaped flowers each spring. One variant, var. *vestita*, is valued for its beautiful pale pink flowers. In autumn, the unusual brownish fruits and yellow leaves add an interesting touch to parks and gardens. • Mountain silverbell grows well in full sun to light shade, and thrives on rich, well-drained, acidic to neutral soil. It can be propagated by seed or by layering. • Silverbell wood has little value. When a tree does reach saw timber size, it can be used for lumber, paneling and cabinets. • The acidic fruits are sometimes chewed for their refreshing quality and have been suggested as a possible candi-date for pickling. • Mountain silverbell is a southern species that barely reaches southern Illinois and Ohio. However, it is often cultivated well north of its natural range and occasionally escapes to sheltered sites. • The name *Halesia* honors the English physiologist Stephen Hales (1677–1761). • This small genus, with 3 species in the eastern U.S. and one in China, demonstrates a link between woody plants in North America and north-eastern Asia.

ALSO CALLED: Silver-bell tree, snowdrop-tree, opossumwood, calico-wood • *H. carolina* var. *monticola*, *H. monticola* (misapplied).

SIZE AND SHAPE: Medium trees about 35–80' tall; crowns rounded.

TRUNKS: Usually clumped, straight, 4–12" in diameter; bark reddish-brown, thin, with broad, scaly ridges, shed in large plates; wood light brown, soft, fine-grained.

BRANCHES: Stout, upcurved; twigs with dense, **star-shaped hairs** when young, smooth and dark green to grayish-brown with age;

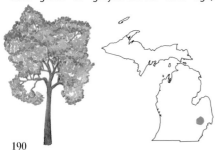

pith chambered; buds pinkish to dark red, hairy, pointed, about ⅛" long.

LEAVES: Alternate, deciduous, **simple; blades downy with white, star-shaped hairs when young,** deep yellow-green and hairless above with age, paler and hairy beneath, papery, oblong to elliptic, 3–7" long, often broadest above the middle, finely saw-toothed; stalks hair-like, ⅜–1⅛" long; leaves yellow in autumn.

FLOWERS: White (rarely pinkish), **bell-shaped,** ½–1⅛" across, bisexual; **petals 4,** broad, fused, ½–1" long; sepals about ¼" long, fused in a cone with 4 spreading lobes; **stamens 8–16,** with **filaments fused into a tube;** flowers hang on slender, ⅜–¾" long stalks, **in small, umbrella-shaped clusters** (umbels) of 2–5 on year-old wood, in April–May.

FRUITS: Dry, dark brown, **pod-like berries with 4 conspicuous lengthwise wings,** oblong, 1–2" long, with a long, slender tip; seeds 4; fruits mature in autumn, **persist into winter.**

HABITAT: Moist woods and streambanks.

ORIGIN: Introduced from the southeastern U.S.

THE DECAY-RESISTANT WOOD of black locust was once used for railroad ties, fence posts, stakes and pilings and was exported to England for shipbuilding. Unfortunately, locust borer beetles (*Megacyllene robiniae*) often spoil the wood. Although it can be used as firewood, black locust wood tends to flare and throw sparks. • This species was introduced to Europe from North America in the early 1600s and is now naturalized across the continent. • Cattle and humans have been poisoned by the toxic inner bark and leaves. Some tribes used the poisonous wood in arrows. Although the seeds are toxic to humans, many animals such as rabbits, squirrels, pheasants and mourning doves eat them with impunity. • Like most members of the pea family, this tree has root nodules containing nitrogen-fixing bacteria. Black locust has been used to reforest waste areas such as mine spoils, where few other trees could survive. Its root suckers produce dense colonies that help prevent erosion. The strong root networks have even been used to support dikes.

• **Clammy locust (*R. viscosa*)**, shown in pink/dark green on the map, is another ornamental from the southern U.S. that may occasionally escape from cultivation in Michigan. Unlike black locust, it has pink, odorless flowers and sticky twigs, leaf stalks and pods.

ALSO CALLED: False acacia, common locust, white locust, yellow locust.

SIZE AND SHAPE: Trees 30–50' [96'] tall; crowns open, irregular; roots wide-creeping, suckering.

TRUNKS: Irregular, 12–24" [74"] in diameter; mature bark dark brown, deeply furrowed, scaly; **inner bark yellow;** wood yellowish-green, hard, heavy.

BRANCHES: Brittle, short; **twigs spiny,** reddish-brown, slender, **zigzagged; spines paired at each bud or leaf base/scar,** about ³/₈" long, largest on vigorous shoots; buds tiny, clustered (usually 3–4), embedded under leaf stalk bases.

LEAVES: Alternate, deciduous, 8–14" long; compound, **pinnately divided into 7–21 leaflets (with a terminal leaflet)** in pairs along a 8–12" long stalk; leaflets dull green, oval, ³/₄–2" long; leaf scars 3-cornered, with 3 vein scars.

FLOWERS: White with a yellow blotch on the upper petals, fragrant, pea-like, ¹/₂–1" long, bisexual; **flowers hang in loose, showy, 4–6" long clusters** near shoot tips, in May–June (about 1 month after leaves expand).

FRUITS: Reddish-brown to black, flattened, thin-walled, hairless pods (legumes), 2³/₄–4" **long,** clustered; **seeds dark, pea-like, hard,** about ¹/₈" long, 4–8 per pod; pods persist through winter.

HABITAT: Fence lines, roadsides, pastures and moist, open woodlands.

ORIGIN: Introduced from the southeastern U.S.; aggressively invades native vegetation, especially on sandy soils.

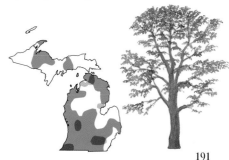

REDBUD reaches its northern limit in southern Michigan. The natural range of this beautiful tree is difficult to determine because it has been so widely planted and frequently escapes cultivation. • With its showy pink flowers in early spring, followed by a broad, shady canopy in summer, redbud is a lovely ornamental. Unfortunately, it is generally hardy only as far north as central Michigan. These small, well-formed trees are especially attractive when planted beside evergreens. Redbud grows rapidly under good conditions and begins to flower at about 5 years of age. Once mature, it blooms almost every year, and in cool weather, the spring flower display can continue for 3 weeks. • Redbud twigs produce a yellow dye when boiled in water. • On hot summer days, the broad leaves may curl and almost fold in half. This helps to reduce water loss and can also lower leaf temperature by reducing the surface exposed to sunlight. • The generic name *Cercis* comes from the Greek *kerkis*, "shuttle," which was thought to describe the shape of the pods. • Until recently, *Cercis* was considered a member of the pea family (Fabaceae or Leguminosae), in the subfamily Caesalpinoideae. This group is now recognized as a separate family, the cassia family (Caesalpiniaceae).

ALSO CALLED: Judas-tree, eastern redbud.

SIZE AND SHAPE: Small trees 12–25' [30'] tall; crowns low, spreading, flat or rounded.

TRUNKS: Short, straight, 4–12" [21"] in diameter; young bark grayish, smooth; mature bark scaly, reddish-brown; wood dark brown, hard, weak.

BRANCHES: Horizontal to ascending; twigs grayish to reddish-brown, slender, zigzagged, with 3 lengthwise ridges from each leaf scar; leaf buds dark reddish-brown, about 1/8" long, 5–6-scaled, sometimes with a tiny secondary bud at the base; **flower buds larger, rounded, clustered, stalked.**

LEAVES: Alternate, simple, deciduous; **blades glossy, dark green above,** paler beneath, **broadly heart-shaped,** thin, 2 3/4–4 3/4" long, with **5–9 prominent veins radiating from the stalk; stalks swollen near the blade;** leaves warm yellow in autumn.

FLOWERS: Deep to pale pink, pea-like, showy, about 3/8" **long,** bisexual; anthers 10, with filaments at the middle, splitting lengthwise; flowers on 3/8" long stalks in **abundant, 4–8-flowered, tassel-like clusters along branches** (not on new twigs) and **sometimes on trunks,** in April–May (before leaves expand).

FRUITS: Reddish-brown, flat, thin pods (legumes), tapered at both ends, 2–4" long, hanging in small clusters; seeds 10–12 per pod, shiny brown, flattened, about 1/4" across; pods mature in autumn and persist into winter.

HABITAT: Moist, fertile sites in forests, especially along rivers and streams.

ORIGIN: Native.

ALTHOUGH HONEY-LOCUST grows wild in southern regions, it has also been widely planted and occasionally escapes cultivation. Its native range is along major rivers north to Kalamazoo and Detroit, and in the lower reaches of the Huron River in southern Michigan. • The hard, heavy wood is easily polished but fairly brittle. It has been used for fence posts, furniture and occasionally lumber. The long, hard thorns were sometimes made into nails and pins. • Honey-locust pods have been used to make beer. They contain a sweetish substance that tastes like a mixture of castor oil and honey, hence the "honey" in the name. • The sweet flowers attract many bees. White-tailed deer, rabbits, squirrels and quail eat the seeds and the sweet pulp of the pods. Cattle also eat the seeds, pods and tender young plants. • Gardeners often prune young trees to form protective thorny hedges. Honey-locust is also considered an excellent lawn tree because the delicate foliage casts light shade. Cuttings from male-flowered branches grow into trees with pollen flowers only, so they do not produce fruit. Cultivars of a thornless variety, **thornless honey-locust** (***G. triacanthos* var. *inermis***), boast straight trunks and spreading canopies and are common in plantings along city streets.

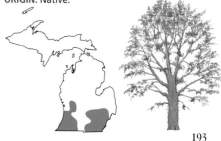

ALSO CALLED: Thorny-locust, sweet-locust, tree-thorned acacia.

SIZE AND SHAPE: Trees 50–80' [115'] tall; crowns broad, open; roots deep, spreading.

TRUNKS: Usually short, 24–40" [69"] in diameter, with **long (up to 12"), branched thorns;** young bark brownish, smooth, with horizontal pores (lenticels); mature bark dark gray, furrowed, scaly-ridged; wood reddish-brown, hard, heavy, resistant to decay.

BRANCHES: With reddish, smooth, forked thorns; twigs of 2 types: long, greenish- to reddish-brown, **zigzagged shoots, and very short leaf- and flower-bearing shoots; buds small, 3 or more one above the other,** absent at twig tips.

LEAVES: Alternate, deciduous, **6–12" long;** compound, **once or twice pinnately divided,** with 18–30 leaflets but **no tip leaflet;** twice-compound leaves have 4–7 pairs of branches on the main stalk (rachis); leaflets dark green above, paler beneath, oblong to lance-shaped, ³/₄–2" long; leaves yellow in autumn.

FLOWERS: Greenish-white, about ¹/₄" across; petals 5; unisexual (occasionally some bisexual) with male and female flowers on the same tree; male flowers in dense, 2–2³/₄" long clusters (racemes); female flowers few, in loose, 2³/₄–3¹/₂" long clusters; flowers in May–June.

FRUITS: Brownish, **leathery, flattened, spirally twisted pods (legumes), 6–18" long;** seeds bean-like, hard, about ³/₄" apart in pods, embedded in sweet pulp; pods mature by autumn, drop over winter without opening.

HABITAT: Open sites in moist, rich lowlands; also in disturbed areas and spreading from planted trees in hedgerows and homesteads.

ORIGIN: Native.

AT UP TO A YARD IN LENGTH, the leaves of Kentucky coffee-tree are by far the largest of any native tree in the state. It is easy to mistake leaf branches or leaflets for individual leaves. • Kentucky coffee-tree is often used in landscaping well beyond its natural range because it transplants easily and can tolerate urban conditions. • Wild animals rarely eat the bitter seeds, and cattle can become sick from drinking water contaminated with the leaves or fruits. **Caution:** The raw seeds are **poisonous**, but roasting may destroy the toxins. Some tribes reportedly ate the roasted seeds like nuts, and early settlers are said to have used ground roasted seeds as a coffee substitute. Hence the common names coffeenut and coffeetree. Others report that such names refer more to the coffee-like appearance of the "beans" than to historical uses. Given the bitterness and potential toxicity of these seeds, their use as a food is not recommended. • Kentucky coffee-tree is too uncommon to have commercial value, but the moderately heavy, decay-resistant wood has been used in cabinets, fence posts, railroad ties and general construction. • *Gymnocladus*, from the Greek *gymnos*, "naked," and *klodos*, "branch," refers to the relatively late emergence of the leaves in spring and the early leaf drop each autumn.

ALSO CALLED: Coffeenut.

SIZE AND SHAPE: Trees 50–80' [112'] tall; crowns narrow; roots widely spreading and suckering.

TRUNKS: Straight, 16–36" [54"] in diameter; mature bark dark gray, hard, with thin ridges of out-curled scale edges; wood reddish-brown, hard.

BRANCHES: Stout, widely spaced; **twigs coarse, knobbly,** grayish-brown, with orange pores (lenticels); **buds dark brown,** silky-hairy, 1/4–3/8" long, in **groups of 2–3 above leaf scars,** absent at twig tips.

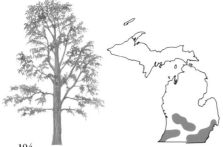

LEAVES: Alternate, early-deciduous; compound, **twice pinnately divided, with 3–7 pairs of branches (no terminal branches or tip leaflets) on a sturdy, 12–36" long central stalk** (rachis) that is easily mistaken for a slender twig; leaflets bluish-green, ovate, 1 1/2–2 3/8" long, pointed, short-stalked, seldom opposite, usually about 70; leaf scars large, heart-shaped.

FLOWERS: Greenish-white, soft-hairy, 1/2–3/4" across, 5-petaled; unisexual, usually with male and female flowers on separate trees; anthers 10, with filaments attached at the middle, splitting lengthwise; flowers in open, **many-branched, 2 3/8–4" (male) and 8–12" (female) long clusters** (panicles), in May–June (as or after leaves expand).

FRUITS: Dark reddish-brown pods (legumes), **leathery, becoming woody, flattened but thick, 4–10" long,** hanging on stout, 3/4–1 1/8" long stalks; seeds 4–7, dark brown, hard, slightly flattened, 3/8–3/4" across, embedded in sticky pulp; pods mature in autumn, **persist through winter.**

HABITAT: Moist woods with deep, rich soil, typically on river floodplains.

ORIGIN: Native.

THERE IS SOME CONFUSION about which *Aralia* grows in Michigan. In the past, Japanese angelica-tree was often misidentified as its North American cousin, **Hercules-club** or devil's-walkingstick (*A. spinosa*). Although both species are cultivated (*A. spinosa* rarely), apparently only the hardier *A. elata* is naturalized in Michigan. Japanese angelica-tree is distinguished by its stalkless (rather than short-stalked), regularly toothed (rather than remotely toothed) leaflets, its spreading leaf veins (which run to the tooth tips, rather than joining below the leaf edge) and its very broad (rather than elongated) flower clusters. • The tender shoots and young leaves are eaten as a springtime vegetable in East Asia. In Japan, this tasty treat, battered and fried tempura-style, is considered a delicacy. • **Caution:** The fruits are said to be **poisonous**. • In Asia, Japanese angelica-tree is considered a valuable medicinal plant. It is said to stimulate the central nervous system and is taken as a tonic for relieving physical and mental fatigue and depression. • The club-like branches and large leaves add a dramatic touch to gardens—likened to the lush look of a palm. Japanese angelica-tree is also resistant to pollution and produces large amounts of nectar for visiting insects and black "berries" for birds. It is also hardier, less weedy and less spiny than Hercules-club.

Bottom photos: *A. spinosa*

ALSO CALLED: Japanese aralia.

SIZE AND SHAPE: Prickly small trees or tall shrubs, up to 35' tall; crowns flat-topped; roots shallow, often sending up shoots to form thickets.

TRUNKS: Long, up to 4¹/₄" in diameter; bark straw-colored to dark brown, ridged, armed with yellowish prickles.

BRANCHES: Prickly, stout, club-like, few, upright to spreading; **twigs prickly, massive,** with a large pith; buds cone-shaped at twig tip, smaller and flat-lying below, few-scaled.

LEAVES: Alternate, deciduous, crowded near twig tips, **20–60" long,** 20–40" wide, **twice pinnately divided** into numerous paired branches and leaflets on a prickly main stalk (rachis); leaflets dark green, hairless, **sharply toothed, essentially stalkless,** ovate, about 1³/₄" long, often prickly underneath; **stalks with broad, sheathing bases;** leaf scars numerous, conspicuous, **narrowly crescent-shaped with a row of about 20 dots** (vein scars), almost encircling twigs; leaves purple, orange or yellow in autumn.

FLOWERS: Tiny, **creamy white,** bisexual; petals 5; stamens 5; **flowers numerous, in large, very broad clusters** (umbels) at branch tips, in July–August.

FRUITS: Fleshy, dark purple to black, egg-shaped, 5-ribbed, berry-like drupes, ¹/₄" long; seeds 2–5 per fruit, enclosed in flattened nutlets; drupes mature in early fall.

HABITAT: Prefers rich, moist, open sites.

ORIGIN: Introduced from eastern Asia; possibly escaped in Kalamazoo, Kent, Oakland and Washtenaw counties.

195

Key to Genera in the Cashew Family (Anacardiaceae)

1a Leaves with a single blade (simple) .... *Cotinus*, **smoketree** (p. 202)

1b Leaves pinnately divided into 7–31 leaflets (compound) **2**

2a Leaflets smooth-edged or with a few scattered teeth, contain allergenic oils that cause severe skin reactions; fruits smooth, whitish to yellowish berries in loose clusters
.... *Toxicodendron*, **poison-sumac** (p. 199)

2b Leaflets distinctly toothed, not highly allergenic; fruits fuzzy red berries in dense, pyramidal clusters .... *Rhus*, **sumac** (key to species, see below)

R. typhina, staghorn sumac

Key to the Sumacs (Genus *Rhus*)

1a Main axis of the leaf (rachis) winged; twigs hairless
.... *R. copallina*, **winged sumac** (p. 198)

1b Main axis of the leaf not winged; twigs velvety or hairless... **2**

2a Leaf stalks hairy; twigs velvety-hairy........................ *R. typhina*, **staghorn sumac** (p. 197)

2b Leaf stalks and twigs hairless... *R. glabra*, **smooth sumac** (p. 197)

WITH ITS STRIKING FORM, showy fruit clusters and brilliant autumn foliage, smooth sumac is sometimes planted as an ornamental. However, its spreading, suckering roots can be troublesome. • The wood of smooth sumac has been used for decorative finishing and novelty items. • The tannin-rich fruit, bark and leaves of sumacs were used to tan hides. The leaves and fruits were also boiled to make black ink, and the dried leaves were an ingredient in smoking mixtures. The milky sap has been used as a treatment for warts. • The fruits can be eaten as a trail nibble or gathered in larger quantities to make jelly. They can also be crushed and/or boiled and strained to make a lemonade-like drink. The fruits should not be boiled for too long or consumed in large quantities, because they contain tannic acid. • Sumac thickets stabilize

slopes and provide food and cover for many birds and mammals. • Smooth sumac can be confused with **staghorn sumac** (**R. typhina**, also called *R. hirta* or velvet sumac), but staghorn sumac has fuzzy leaves and twigs, brownish-hairy buds, and the hairs on its fruits are long and slender. These 2 species often hybridize to produce **pulvinate sumac** (**R. x pulvinata**), recognized by its finely hairy twigs and intermediate fruits.

SIZE AND SHAPE: Crooked trees or shrubs up to 15' [18'] tall; crowns rounded or flat-topped; roots shallow, spreading, usually **forming thickets from suckers.**

TRUNKS: Short, forked, 2–3" [4"] in diameter; bark thin, smooth with pores (lenticels); brown to gray; wood soft, brittle.

BRANCHES: Few, wide-spreading; **twigs stout,** smooth, with a whitish bloom, exuding **milky juice** when broken; **pith large;** buds whitish-hairy, absent at branch tips.

LEAVES: Alternate, deciduous; compound, **pinnately divided into 11–31 leaflets; central stalks reddish,** 7–15" long; leaflets dark green above, whitish beneath, lance-shaped to oblong, 2–5" long, slender-pointed, sharp-toothed, stalkless; leaf scars horseshoe-shaped, almost encircling the buds; leaves scarlet, orange or purplish in autumn.

FLOWERS: Yellowish-green, tiny; usually unisexual with male and female flowers on separate trees; petals 5; **stamens 5;** flowers in **dense, erect,**

4–10" long, cone-shaped clusters (panicles) at branch tips, in June (after leaves expand).

FRUITS: Scarlet, fuzzy drupes about ⅛" long, covered in **short, sticky hairs,** forming **dense, erect, cone-shaped clusters** at branch tips; seeds 1 per fruit, in a small stone; fruits mature in August, **persist through winter.**

HABITAT: Open, often disturbed areas, typically in dry to mesic sites, but can survive in a wide range of habitats.

ORIGIN: Native.

THIS ATTRACTIVE, hardy shrub, with its showy flowers and fruits, glossy summer foliage and scarlet autumn leaves, is a lovely but uncommon ornamental shrub. This fast-growing, short-lived tree thrives on sunny sites and can also tolerate heavy, alkaline soils. In the wild, it grows vigorously after fires, often spreading rapidly to form thickets from suckers. • The tart, red fruits can be nibbled as a trail snack or gathered to make a lemonade-like drink. • Shining sumac attracts many different animals. Grouse, quail, wild turkeys, pheasants and numerous songbirds eat the fruit; deer and rabbits browse on the twigs and eat the bark. • The sour red "berries" were sometimes chewed to prevent bedwetting and to heal mouth sores. The root tea is astringent and was also used to treat dysentery. • Shining sumac was an important source of copal resin. This transparent, slightly brownish substance was dissolved in turpentine and other solvents, producing a clear, highly valued varnish known as "copal varnish." The specific epithet *copallina* means "with copal gum." • Also known as "winged sumac," this species is easily identified by its winged leaf stalks and watery (rather than milky) sap. The alternate name refers to the distinctive winged main axis of the leaves.

ALSO CALLED: Winged sumac, dwarf sumac, black sumac, flameleaf sumac, mountain sumac, upland sumac, smooth sumac.

SIZE AND SHAPE: Small trees or shrubs, to 20' [33'] tall; crowns open, rounded; roots shallow, suckering.

TRUNKS: Short, up to 4" [9"] in diameter; bark light brown or gray, scaly; wood light brown, soft.

BRANCHES: Stout, often ridged and warty with age; twigs stout, greenish-brown to purplish-gray, **finely reddish-hairy**, soon hairless; **pith yellowish-brown, large;** buds densely hairy, without scales, round, about 1/8" across, absent at branch tips.

LEAVES: Alternate, deciduous, 6–16" long; compound, **pinnately divided into 7–21 leaflets; leaflets glossy, dark green and hairless above,** paler, dull and finely hairy beneath, 1 1/8–4" long, **stalkless, usually smooth-edged; central stalks with a wing** narrowed at each leaflet; leaf scars horseshoe-shaped around buds; leaves red to dark reddish-purple in autumn.

FLOWERS: Greenish-yellow, 1/8" wide, 5-parted; unisexual with male and female flowers on separate plants; flowers in **erect cone-shaped clusters (panicles) up to 6" long** at branch tips, in July–August (after leaves expand).

FRUITS: Dark red, berry-like drupes covered in sticky, red, glandular hairs, about 1/8" long; **in dense, erect to nodding, cone-shaped clusters;** seeds single, in small stones; fruits mature in late August–September, persist into winter.

HABITAT: Open, well-drained sites on hillsides, in clearings and along old lakeshores.

ORIGIN: Native.

IT IS VERY IMPORTANT to recognize poison-sumac, because most people develop severe skin reactions from contact with it. Those who have gathered sprays of the beautiful white fruits and dark glossy leaves for decorations have paid dearly for their mistake. **Caution:** If you touch this plant, wash your hands thoroughly with soap and warm water to remove the allergenic oil. Never use oil-based salves or liniments on your skin, because they can dissolve and spread the toxin.
• The allergenic oil in all parts of this shrubby tree can be picked up directly from the plant or indirectly from contaminated pets, clothing or other items. Smoke from burning plants also carries the oil and can cause severe reactions of skin, eyes and mucous membranes in the nose, mouth and throat. • Game birds and many songbirds eat the "berries" with impunity and disperse the seeds.
• Poison-sumac is distinguished from true sumacs (pp. 197–98), mountain-ashes (pp. 175–77) and elderberries (p. 242) by its smooth-edged (not toothed) leaves. Ashes (pp. 237–40) and common prickly-ash (p. 200) may have toothless leaves, but ash leaves are opposite (not alternate), and common prickly-ash has thorny branches. • Poison-sumac's persistent fruits facilitate year-round identification.

ALSO CALLED: Poison-sumach, swamp-sumac, poison-dogwood, poison-elderberry, poison-elder, poison-oak • *Rhus vernix*.

SIZE AND SHAPE: Small trees or tall shrubs 10–25' [31'] tall; crowns small, rounded.

TRUNKS: Slender, often branched from bases, 2³/₈–3" [5"] in diameter; bark gray, smooth, thin; wood moderately soft, weak.

BRANCHES: Moderately stout, spreading; twigs slender, drooping, dark green and hairy to mottled brownish-yellow and hairless, dotted with pores (lenticels); damaged twigs exude milky sap; **buds purplish-brown, hairy,** several-scaled, conical, ³/₈–³/₄" **long at branch tips,** smaller below.

LEAVES: Alternate, deciduous; compound, **pinnately divided into 7–13 leaflets,** often crowded in umbrella-like clusters at branch tips; central stalks 6–12" long, not winged; leaflets dark lustrous green, whitened beneath, **essentially hairless,** oblong to elliptic or ovate, 2–4" long, **short-stalked,** pointed, **smooth-edged** (sometimes wavy); leaf scars shield-shaped.

FLOWERS: Yellowish-green, tiny; unisexual with male and female flowers on separate plants; petals 5; **stamens 5;** flowers in **elongated, nodding, branched clusters** (raceme-like panicles) up to 8" long from leaf axils, in June–early July (after leaves expand).

FRUITS: Glossy, **whitish, pearl-like drupes,** dry, ¹/₈–¹/₄" across, in loose, arching to hanging clusters; seeds single, within stones; drupes mature in August–September, persist through winter.

HABITAT: Open, **swampy woodlands** and bog edges, often with tamarack (p. 68).

ORIGIN: Native.

THIS AROMATIC member of the citrus family has been used medicinally for many years. Chewed bark, leaves and fruits were packed around aching teeth to relieve pain, hence the common name "toothache-tree." Chewing is said to cause a tingling sensation in the mouth and to stimulate salivation. The berries and bark were also used to relieve rheumatism, spasms and convulsions and to stimulate circulation and perspiration. Rat studies suggest that alkaloids in the leaves may have anti-inflammatory, pain-killing and blood-pressure-lowering properties, but no human studies have been done. • There are no reports of harm from short-term, moderate use of prickly-ash, but this plant does contain anticoagulants (coumarins) that could interfere with some medicines. Pregnant and nursing women should avoid this plant. • The fragrant, lemon-scented bark and leaves can be used as a flavoring, recognized as safe by the FDA. • Common prickly-ash is an excellent, moderately shade-tolerant landscaping shrub. The thorny branches provide interest in winter; in the spring, trees are covered with chartreuse flowers. In summer, the lemon-scented leaves attract spectacular butterflies, and in autumn, the female trees produce attractive fruit clusters. • Prickly-ash is distinguished from ashes and sumacs by its spiny branches and leaf stalks. Locusts also have spines and compound leaves, but they have hidden buds, smooth leaf stalks and bean-like fruits.

ALSO CALLED: Toothache-tree, northern prickly-ash • *Xanthoxylum* (incorrectly spelled)

SIZE AND SHAPE: Tall shrubs or small trees, **4–10'** (sometimes to 26') tall; crowns rounded; roots often suckering to form colonies.

TRUNKS: Up to 6" wide; bark smooth to slightly furrowed, gray or brown with pale blotches; **wood yellow,** hard.

BRANCHES: Numerous; **twigs dark brown, hairy,** stiff, with a **citrus-like fragrance,** prickly with short (<³/₈"), stout, **paired spines** at leaf bases (rarely lacking spines); buds round, ¹/₈–¹/₄" long, woolly with reddish hairs.

LEAVES: Alternate, deciduous, dull green above, paler beneath, **hairy** (when young), **aromatic with tiny gland dots,** compound, **pinnately divided into 5–11 paired leaflets;** central stalks 4–8" long, prickly; leaflets oblong to elliptic or ovate, 1–2" long, **finely toothed** to wavy-edged, blunt-tipped; leaf scars kidney-shaped, with 3 dots (vein scars).

FLOWERS: Yellowish-green, <³/₁₆" **across;** unisexual with male and female flowers on separate plants; petals 5, fringed at tips; sepals absent; **stamens 5; flowers in branched, tassel-like clusters** in leaf axils, in April–May (before leaves expand).

FRUITS: Round, slightly fleshy pods (follicles), ³/₁₆" long, **bright red to brown, with lemon-scented gland dots,** splitting across the top; seeds shiny, black, 1–2 per pod; fruits mature in August–October.

HABITAT: Moist woodland, thickets and hedges.

ORIGIN: Native.

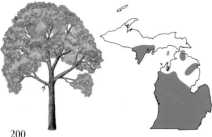

THIS UNUSUAL TREE, with its striking, rather tropical appearance, has been described as strange and gaunt. It is usually planted as a curiosity, but heavy, spreading branches and broad, thick leaves make castor-aralia an ideal shade tree for parks, golf courses and campuses. The trees provide interest throughout the year, with large leaves in spring that resemble those of sycamore or maple, showy white flower clusters in summer, large clusters of black fruits from autumn to midwinter (long after the leaves have dropped) and heavy, angular branches exposed in winter. An abundance of stout, yellow prickles on coarse branches and suckers clearly identify this unusual tree year-round. • A rarely seen variety from Japan, *K. septemlobus* var. *maximowiczii*, has deeply lobed leaves (cut at least ²/₃ of the way to the base, reminiscent of the tropical tree, schefflera. • The flowers attract many bees, and birds and squirrels quickly consume the fruit, thereby removing the litter problem. • Unfortunately, this excellent ornamental tree has the potential to become a pest. It produces large quantities of seeds that are apparently bird dispersed, and it has been documented to spread locally from cultivation. Once established, the trees have few or no pests in North America. Castor-aralia should be planted with caution near open fields and wetlands. • *Kalopanax* comes from the Greek *kalos*, "beautiful" or "handsome," and *panax*, "ginseng."

ALSO CALLED: Prickly castor-oil tree • *K. pictus*.

SIZE AND SHAPE: Large trees 40–90' tall; crowns broadly columnar to rounded; roots shallow, spreading, sending up suckers.

TRUNKS: Stout, up to 7–8' wide; bark dull dark gray, ridged, with large, spine-tipped warts (especially when young); wood heavy, brown to yellow, white or gray, ring-porous.

BRANCHES: Few, stout, heavy, wide-spreading, **prickly,** with stout, soft-tipped, yellowish to bright blue-green spines; **twigs stout, with spur-like side-branches;** buds 1–1¹/₂" long, sharp pointed, side buds widely spreading.

LEAVES: Alternate, simple, deciduous, **maple-leaf-like;** blades reddish at first, deep green with age, usually downy and prominently veined beneath, 5–10" across; **palmately cut** about ¹/₄–¹/₃ of the way to the center into **5 or 7 pointed lobes, irregularly sharp toothed; stalks hanging,** usually 5–8" long, often rough-hairy; leaves yellow or reddish when shed in late autumn.

FLOWERS: White, tiny; bisexual; petals 5; stamens 5; flowers numerous, 25–30 grouped in 1" **round heads** (umbels) on slender, white stalks about 4" long; **25–50 heads form large, rounded clusters 10–20" across** at branch tips, in July–August (after leaves expand).

FRUITS: Black drupes ¹/₈–¹/₄" **long,** tipped with slender style, containing 2 one-seeded stones; fruits mature in autumn, drop in December.

HABITAT: Open, often disturbed sites.

ORIGIN: Introduced from Japan, eastern Russia, Korea and China.

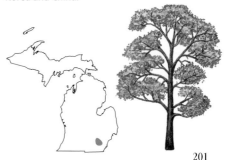

EUROPEAN SMOKETREE is often planted as an ornamental for its unusual feathery flower and fruit clusters and its beautiful fall foliage. Some popular cultivars have bright purple leaves throughout the growing season. • The name "smoketree" refers to the tree's airy plumes of tiny flowers and feathery fruit clusters. Their hazy appearance is due to an abundance of long, fluffy, green to pinkish hairs on the flower and fruit stalks. • European smoketree was introduced into America in the mid-1600s. This unusual, relatively pest-free species is recommended for specimen planting, shrubby borders and backdrops for other plants. The hardy, drought-tolerant trees grow best in full sun. Smoketrees can thrive in many conditions, including well-drained to wet, acidic to alkaline substrates with sandy, loamy or clay-rich soils. It is not considered a threat to native vegetation. • The roots and branches have been used to make an orange-yellow dye, but the color doesn't persist.

• **American smoketree** is a native species whose range (***C. obovatus***) extends north to Kentucky and Missouri. Although it is occasionally planted as an ornamental in Michigan, it is not naturalized. It has relatively large (3–6" long) leaves that are rounded and hairy (at least when young).

ALSO CALLED: Common smoke-tree, Asian smokebush, cloud tree, mist tree, Jupiter's beard • *Rhus cotinus*.

SIZE AND SHAPE: Shrubby trees 10–15' [17'] tall, with gummy, strong-smelling sap; crowns broad, rounded, bushy, to 12' across.

TRUNKS: Clumped, up to 8" in diameter; bark thin, gray to black; **wood yellow, fragrant** with strong-smelling, juicy sap.

BRANCHES: Spreading, drooping at tips with age; twigs exude fragrant, resinous sap when broken; buds reddish-brown, $\frac{1}{16}$" long, with several overlapping scales.

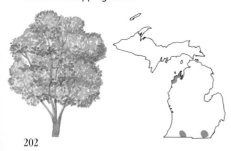

LEAVES: Alternate, deciduous, simple, with a **fragrance like orange peels; blades light green** (purple in some cultivars), broadly elliptical, $1\frac{1}{2}$–$3\frac{3}{4}$" long, tapered to a **wedge-shaped base, hairless, smooth-edged;** stalks slender, >1" long; leaf scars broadly triangular with 3 dots (vein scars); **leaves yellow to red or purple in autumn,** highly variable.

FLOWERS: Cream-colored to pink; unisexual (occasionally bisexual) with **male and female flowers on separate trees, mostly sterile,** developing **fluffy hairs that turn several shades of grayish-pink;** petals 5; flowers in airy, elongating, 6–8" long clusters (panicles), in May–June.

FRUITS: Brown, dry, oval but irregularly shaped drupes about $\frac{1}{8}$" long, on slender, fuzzy stalks with several reddish, hair-like branches at the base; seeds single; fruits bearing numerous **conspicuous fluffy hairs that turn several shades of grayish-pink,** in large, fluffy clusters, mature in August.

HABITAT: Disturbed areas.

ORIGIN: Introduced from Eurasia, from southern Europe to the Himalaya Mountains.

THIS IS OUR LARGEST native holly, but it rarely reaches tree size. These tall shrubs are often planted as ornamentals for their thick, green foliage and conspicuous, bright red berries. The attractive berries on winter branches are sometimes used in Christmas decorations. • **Caution:** The berries are **toxic** and can cause nausea, vomiting and diarrhea. Some herbalists valued this purging effect, which results from eating about 25 berries, because it was followed by a feeling of great lightness and well-being, with improved appetite

and digestion. The berries were also mixed with cedar-apples (the fleshy cones of eastern red-cedar, p. 74) and taken to expel intestinal worms. • Common winterberry leaves can be roasted until brown and then steeped in boiling water to make a pleasant-tasting hot drink. This was used as a substitute for black Oriental tea and was also said to act as a general tonic and to stimulate urination and sweating. Bark tea was used to treat fevers, liver problems and a variety of skin problems ranging from pimples to incipient gangrene. • Robins, mockingbirds, catbirds and bluebirds eat the fruit in late winter or early spring and spread the seeds. • The specific epithet *verticillata* means "whorled," a reference to the compact clusters of flowers and fruits in the leaf axils.

ALSO CALLED: Michigan holly, black-alder, striped-alder, white-alder, false-alder, fever-bush.

SIZE AND SHAPE: Tall shrubs or slender trees 10–15' [18'] tall; crowns rounded to oval; roots shallow.

TRUNKS: Short, up to 3" [3"] in diameter; mature bark thin, olive green to mottled bluish-gray, peeling in small pieces.

BRANCHES: Stout, numerous; twigs slender, olive brown to gray, finely ridged, with wart-like pores (lenticels); buds about 1/8" long, round.

LEAVES: Alternate, **deciduous**, simple; **blades thin to leathery**, dull dark olive green above with sunken veins, paler beneath with raised veins, **usually widest above midleaf**, 1 1/8–4" long, pointed, **wedge-shaped at the base, edged with fine, incurved teeth tipped in tiny bristles that often point upward** (perpendicular to leaf surface); stalks purplish, hairy, grooved; leaf scars small, with 1 large vein scar; **leaves turn black** with frost and drop.

FLOWERS: Yellowish- to greenish-white, tiny; unisexual (rarely bisexual) with male and female flowers on separate trees; petals 4–8, **smooth-edged, fused at the base;** sepals 4–8, **fringed with hairs;** flowers 1–3 (female) or 2–10 (male) on short stalks (shorter than adjacent leaf stalks), in May–July (before leaves expand fully).

FRUITS: Bright red to orange or rarely yellow, berry-like **drupes** with **smooth (not grooved) nutlets,** about 1/4" thick, in lower leaf axils; seeds 3–5 per fruit; drupes mature in September–October, persist into winter.

HABITAT: Swamps, wet woods, ditches and damp shorelines.

ORIGIN: Native.

MANY SOURCES REPORT that common mountain-holly "berries" were used by Native peoples for food, but details about the type of food and its preparation are lacking. Generally, this fruit is considered too sour for modern tastes. Descriptions range from spicy to extremely bitter. • **Caution:** The fruits are sometimes classified as **poisonous**. Some speculate that if the fruit was indeed used by Native peoples, it was probably for some evil purpose. • The buds and wood were used in medicinal teas to stimulate sweating and thus break fevers, hence the common name "feverbush." Branch tea, boiled to the consistency of syrup, was taken as a tonic. The stronger fruit was used to initiate vomiting and diarrhea and to expel intestinal worms. • Birds apparently eat the "berries" only when preferred foods are unavailable, but they may be wise to stay away. The bark was used to make bird lime, a sticky substance for ensnaring small birds. • *Nemopanthus*, from the Greek *nema*, "thread," *pous*, "foot," and *anthos*, "flower," alludes to the long, slender flower stalks. The specific epithet *mucronata*, "with a mucro or a short, sharp point," refers to the abruptly pointed leaves.

ALSO CALLED: Feverbush, catberry, wild holly, brick-timber • *N. mucronata*.

SIZE AND SHAPE: Tall shrubs or small trees, up to 15' [20'] tall; crowns rounded; roots spreading, often forming dense colonies.

TRUNKS: Up to 3" [4"] in diameter; bark thin, smooth, gray, with pale raised pores (lenticels).

BRANCHES: Numerous, of **2 types: long, slender shoots** with scattered leaves, and **short, stout side-shoots** with crowded leaves; twigs smooth, purplish, gray with age; buds small,

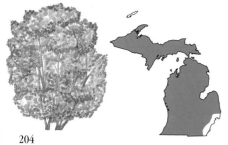

with a thick, slightly longer upper scale.

LEAVES: Alternate, simple, early deciduous; blades thin, hairless, dark green above, paler grayish-green beneath, ³/₄–2" long, usually **abruptly sharp-pointed, smooth edged** or with a few small, sharp teeth, finely net-veined; **stalks slender, reddish to purplish,** ¹/₄–³/₄" long; leaf scars triangular, with 1 vein scar.

FLOWERS: Yellowish- to greenish-white, small; unisexual (rarely bisexual) with **male and female flowers on separate trees; petals 4, slender, separate,** about ¹/₁₆" long; **anthers <¹/₃₂" long;** flowers single (sometimes 2–3), on thread-like, ³/₈–³/₄" long stalks from leaf axils, in May (before leaves expand).

FRUITS: Purplish-red to crimson (rarely yellowish) **berry-like drupes** ¹/₄–³/₈" long, on **slender, brittle stalks at least 1" long;** seeds in smooth-sided (sometimes faintly ribbed) nutlets, 4–5; drupes mature and drop in July–September.

HABITAT: Moist to wet sites, swamps, swales, woods and streambanks.

ORIGIN: Native.

JESUIT MISSIONARIES brought tree-of-heaven to England from China in 1751, and it was introduced to North America in 1874. • This hardy, smog-tolerant tree is widely planted as an ornamental. It grows rapidly (up to 6–10' per season) and thrives in even the poorest, driest soils, adding a splash of green to inhospitable city landscapes. Unfortunately, the leaves and male flowers have an unpleasant odor and the pollen can cause severe hay fever, so female trees are usually preferred. Also, the spreading roots can damage wells and drainage systems, and the wood is so brittle that snow, wind and even moderately heavy storms can bring down dozens of trees. • Escaped trees often

take over clearings, producing impenetrable thickets from root suckers. Once established, the thickets are hard to eliminate, so many people regard tree-of-heaven as a troublesome weed rather than a gift from above. • This species is featured in Betty Smith's *A Tree Grows in Brooklyn*, a story about a young girl inspired by a tree's determination to survive. • Tree-of-heaven has very bitter bark, wood and seeds. The small glands on the leaf lobes give off an unpleasant odor when rubbed, hence the alternative name "stinking-ash."

ALSO CALLED: Copal tree, ghetto palm, Chinese-sumac, stinking-ash • *A. glandulosa.*

SIZE AND SHAPE: Trees 30–40' [50'] tall; crowns broad, rounded; roots spreading.

TRUNKS: Often short and clumped, 12–40" [51"] in diameter; young bark greenish-gray; mature bark gray, thin, with irregular vertical lines; wood pale yellow, soft, weak.

BRANCHES: Few, stout, fragile; **twigs stout,** yellowish- to reddish-brown, with **prominent U-shaped leaf scars and pores** (lenticels); buds downy, hemispherical, 2–4-scaled, absent at branch tips.

LEAVES: Alternate, deciduous, ill-smelling; compound, **pinnately divided into 11–41 leaflets; central stalks 10–30" long,** with swollen bases; leaflets glossy, dark green, paler beneath, **2–6" long, with a gland-tipped lobe (sometimes 2) near the base,** slender-pointed, **stalked;** leaves clear yellow in autumn.

FLOWERS: Yellowish-green, about ¹⁄₄" across, 5-parted, unpleasant-smelling (especially males); unisexual with male and female flowers on separate trees (occasionally bisexual); flowers **in erect, pyramidal, 4–12" long clusters** (panicles) at branch tips, in June (after leaves expand).

FRUITS: Pale reddish- to yellowish-brown, **winged nutlets** (samaras), 1¹⁄₈–2" long, with a **seedcase at the center of a flat, spirally twisted wing;** seeds single; **samaras hang in dense clusters,** mature in October, persist into winter.

HABITAT: Open, usually disturbed sites such as empty lots, old fields and alleys.

ORIGIN: Introduced from northern China.

THIS SHORT-LIVED, slow-growing species is sometimes planted as an ornamental or hedge for its bright, shiny leaves and unusual clusters of persistent, buff-colored fruits. Common hop-tree is known to thrive well beyond its natural range and is hardy as far north as Lake Superior. This tree is fairly shade tolerant, but it flowers only in full sunlight. • The close-grained wood is fairly strong, but the trunks are too small to be of commercial use. • When bruised, all parts of the hop-tree give off a distinctive, citrus-like odor that is generally considered disagreeable, though some people find it pleasant. • In earlier days, when bad-tasting medicines were considered best, bitter-tasting hop-tree juice was sometimes given as a substitute for quinine. The fruits have been used in beer as a substitute for hops (*Humulus* spp.), hence the name "hop-tree." • The flowers smell like rotting flesh and attract carrion flies, which carry pollen from one tree to the next. The fruits are seldom eaten by wildlife, but the trees can provide shelter for birds in otherwise open areas. • *Ptelea* was the Greek name for elm. It was transferred to the hop-tree genus by Linnaeus because of the resemblance of the fruit to that of elms.

ALSO CALLED: Wafer-ash, stinking-ash, three-leaved hop-tree • *P. angustifolia.*

SIZE AND SHAPE: Small trees or tall shrubs 12–15' [17'] tall; crowns irregular, rounded.

TRUNKS: Short, 3–6" [8"] in diameter; **young bark shiny, reddish-brown, with prominent pores** (lenticels); mature bark grayish, rough, scaly; wood yellowish-brown, heavy, hard.

BRANCHES: Numerous, twisted, short; twigs yellowish- to **reddish-brown** with prominent pores (lenticels), **foul-smelling when bruised;** pith large, white; **buds woolly, rounded, tiny, sunken under leaf stalk bases,** absent at branch tips.

LEAVES: Alternate (mostly), deciduous; compound, **divided into 3 leaflets; leaflets glossy, dark green above,** paler beneath, **speckled with tiny, translucent glands** (visible in front of strong light), ovate to elliptic, 2–4½" long, sharp-pointed with wedge-shaped bases, smooth-edged or faintly toothed; leaf stalks 2³⁄₈–6" long; leaf scars horseshoe-shaped around buds.

FLOWERS: Greenish-white, foul-smelling, 4–5-parted; unisexual with male and female flowers on separate trees (occasionally bisexual); petals hairy, about ¼" long; flowers in 1½–3" wide, **repeatedly branched clusters** (cymes) at branch tips, in June (after leaves expand).

FRUITS: Buff-colored, **winged nutlets** (samaras) ³⁄₄–1" across, **with 2 seedcases surrounded by a flat, circular, net-veined wing; samaras hang in dense, stalked clusters,** mature in September–October, persist through winter.

HABITAT: Sandy sites in and around woodlands and along shorelines.

ORIGIN: Native.

AMERICAN BASSWOOD is one of our softest, lightest hardwoods, valued for use in hand carving and turnery. It has also been used for interior trim, veneer, plywood, cabinets, furniture, musical instruments, measuring sticks and pulp and paper. The odorless wood makes excellent food containers. • Native peoples and settlers soaked the inner bark in water to separate its tough fibers or "bass," which were then used to make ropes, nets, mats, shoes, clothing and thread. • Some tribes carved ritual masks on living trees, then split the masks away to hollow and dry the inside. If the tree survived, the mask was believed to have supernatural powers. • A hot bath with basswood (linden) flowers, followed by a cup of linden-flower tea, is said to soothe cold symptoms and enhance sleep. The flowers are also used in beauty products. • This fast-growing, moderately long-lived tree is an attractive ornamental with fragrant flowers, large leaves, excellent response to pruning and deep, spreading roots that make it wind-firm. • Easily damaged by fire and heavily browsed by deer and rabbits (its primary pest), American basswood often resprouts as clumps. • In North America, the native *Tilia* is called a "basswood," but in horticulture, other *Tilia* species are called "lindens" and in England, "lime-trees."

ALSO CALLED: American linden, whitewood, bee-tree, bast-tree, spoonwood • *T. glabra*.

SIZE AND SHAPE: Trees 60–80' [94'] tall; crowns regular, rounded; roots deep, wide-spreading.

TRUNKS: Straight, 16–50" [54"] in diameter; young bark pale, smooth; mature bark dark grayish-brown with blocky, narrow, flat-topped ridges; inner bark fibrous; wood pale reddish-brown, light, soft, uniform.

BRANCHES: Numerous, spreading and upcurved to ascending and arching; twigs yellowish-brown, hairless, zigzagged; **buds plump, asymmetrical, 2–3-scaled,** hairless, about ¼" long, in 2 rows, absent at twig tips.

LEAVES: Alternate, simple, deciduous; blades dull green, paler beneath with hairy vein axils, **heart-shaped, asymmetrical at bases,** abruptly slender-pointed, 3–7" long, palmately veined at base, edged with coarse, **sharp, gland-tipped teeth;** stalks almost half as long as blades; leaf scars semi-oval, raised, with 5–10 vein scars.

FLOWERS: Creamy-yellowish, about ½" across, fragrant, bisexual; petals 5; sepals 5; flowers hang in loose, branched clusters **(cymes) on slender, often persistent stalks from the lower midvein of prominent 4–5", strap-like bracts,** borne in axils of new leaves, in June–July (6–8 weeks after leaves expand).

FRUITS: Brown-woolly, round, nut-like capsules, about ¼" across, 1-seeded; **fruits hang in long-stalked clusters on strap-like bracts,** mature in September–October, persist through winter.

HABITAT: Cool, moist, rich woods, often near water and mixed with other hardwoods.

ORIGIN: Native.

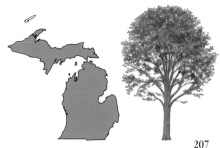

THIS HARDY TREE tolerates urban conditions well, and it has been planted since ancient times as an ornamental for its fragrant flowers, dense, deep green, neatly textured canopy and bright yellow autumn leaves. • In Saxon times, littleleaf linden was the dominant tree of many forests in England and Wales. Today, it is widely planted in North America, but in Europe the **common lime** (*T.* x *vulgaris* or *T. europaea*, a hybrid of *T. cordata* and another European species, *T. platyphyllos*, largeleaf lime) is preferred for landscaping. • The fine-textured, easily worked wood is ideal for carving and turning. Many of the intricate carvings of the famous English artist Grinling Gibbons (1648–1721) were made from this wood. Because linden wood does not warp, it is used for drawing boards and for the sounding boards and keys of pianos and organs. • The dried flowers are sometimes sold in health-food stores. They are used to make medicinal teas for stimulating sweating, enhancing resistance to infection and inducing sedation. • This shapely tree can become burred, sprouty and heavily branched with age. Some linden trees in English parks are more than 350 years old. • The specific epithet *cordata*, "heart-shaped," refers to the leaves.

ALSO CALLED: Small-leaved European linden, small-leaved lime.

SIZE AND SHAPE: Trees 40–50' tall; crowns pyramidal to round; roots deep, spreading.

TRUNKS: Straight, 15–30" in diameter; young bark pale, smooth; mature bark dark grayish-brown, with blocky ridges; wood light, soft, even-grained.

BRANCHES: Arching (typically) to spreading; twigs reddish-brown, soon hairless, **zigzagged;**

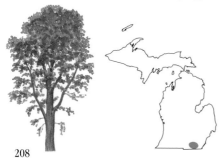

buds plump, asymmetrical, 2-scaled, greenish-red, in 2 rows, absent at twig tips.

LEAVES: Alternate, simple, deciduous; blades shiny, dark green, paler beneath, with rusty-hairy vein axils, **heart-shaped to nearly round, only slightly asymmetrical,** 1³/₈–3" long, edged with **coarse, sharp, gland-tipped teeth;** stalks hairless; leaf scars semi-oval, with 5–10 vein scars; leaves pale yellow to tan in autumn.

FLOWERS: Greenish-yellow, fragrant, star-shaped, about ¹/₂" across, bisexual; petals 5; sepals 5; flowers spreading to erect in branched, 5–8-flowered, **1–2" wide clusters (cymes)** on **slender stalks from midveins of 1³/₈–3" long, strap-like bracts,** in May–July (after leaves expand).

FRUITS: Grayish to pale yellow, rusty-hairy, nut-like capsules, faintly ribbed (if at all), about ¹/₄" long, 1-seeded, thin-shelled; capsules **hang in clusters from strap-like bracts,** mature in autumn, persist through winter.

HABITAT: Disturbed, open sites.

ORIGIN: Introduced from Europe; rare escape.

RUSSIAN-OLIVE is an attractive, silver-leaved shrub or small tree that is often planted as an ornamental. It is very hardy in cold climates, and it resists drought, tolerates city smoke and grows on salty soil. It can become a serious pest when it sends up suckers from spreading roots. Russian-olive commonly naturalizes in western North America but escapes much less frequently in the East. • Although the fruits are rather mealy, they are sweet and edible. In the Far East, they were used to make a type of sweet sherbet. • The nectar-rich flowers have a distinctive, heavy fragrance that some people find nauseating. • Another introduced species, **autumn-olive** (**E. *umbellata***), shown in pink/dark green on the map, is also called umbellate oleaster, Japanese silverberry and Asiatic oleaster. It is a tall shrub distinguished by the mixture of brown and silvery scales on its leaves and twigs; by the relatively long tube formed by its petals (longer than the sepals); and by its long-stalked red fruits. In recent years, autumn-olive has become a competitive invader in many parts of the state, especially in areas with nutrient-poor, sandy soils. • Without flowers or fruits, Russian-olive could be mistaken for a willow, but willows lack silvery scales on their leaves, have 3 vein scars in their leaf scars and have 1-scaled buds.

ALSO CALLED: Oleaster.

SIZE AND SHAPE: Small, slender trees or shrubs 15–35' [58'] tall; crowns dense, low, rounded.

TRUNKS: Often crooked or leaning, up to 30" [37"] in diameter; bark grayish-brown, thin, fissured, **shredding in strips.**

BRANCHES: Usually **spiny,** erect or hanging; **twigs densely silvery with tiny scales,** some reduced to leafless, spine-forming shoots; buds small, ovoid, several-scaled, silvery.

LEAVES: **Alternate,** in small clusters, simple, deciduous; **blades dull silvery-green above and beneath** with tiny scales and star-shaped hairs, leathery, narrowly oblong to lance-shaped, pointed, **1⅛–3" long, 3–8 times as long as wide;** leaf scars with 1 dash-like vein scar.

FLOWERS: **Yellow inside, silvery-scaly outside, fragrant,** bisexual or unisexual, **bell-shaped,** about ⅜" **long,** with a short, tubular nectary around the style; petals lacking; sepals 4; flowers short-stalked, 1–3 at the base of new growth, in June–July.

FRUITS: **Yellow to brownish, silvery-scaled, mealy, drupe-like "berries"** (enlarged hypanthium bases), elliptic-oblong, ⅜–¾" **long, tipped with sepals;** each contains a dry, smooth, about ¼" nutlet (achene) that encloses a single seed; fruits mature in autumn, often persist through winter.

HABITAT: Moist, open sites such as fields and riverbanks.

ORIGIN: Introduced from Eurasia.

209

BLACK TUPELO is Michigan's only native *Nyssa* species. This attractive shade tree is often planted as an ornamental for its interesting form, abundant, bird-attracting blue fruits and decorative leaves (shiny dark green in summer; golden to brilliant scarlet, often blotched with green, in autumn). Black tupelo reaches the northern limit of its range in southern Michigan but is planted as a hardy ornamental farther north. • This tree rarely reaches commercial size in Michigan, but in the past, its tough wood found many uses, especially when resistance to wear was important. Unusual items included pipes in a salt factory, hatters' blocks, pistol grips and even rollers for glass. Today the wood is considered suitable for making furniture (mostly hidden frames), paneling, boxes and crates. • The fruits are too sour for human tastes, but they are an important food for many animals. Foxes, wood ducks, wild turkeys, robins, pileated woodpeckers, brown thrashers, northern mockingbirds, thrushes, northern flickers and European starlings all eat the oil-rich drupes. White-tailed deer and beavers eat the twigs and leaves, and the flowers are an excellent source of nectar for bees. • The species name *sylvatica* means "of the woods."

ALSO CALLED: Blackgum, sourgum, pepperidge.

SIZE AND SHAPE: Trees 35–60' [65'] tall; crowns broadly elongated, often flat-topped.

TRUNKS: Straight, 4–16" [45"] in diameter; mature bark dark gray, with thick, irregular, blocky segments; wood fine-grained, hard, heavy, strong.

BRANCHES: Crooked, horizontal, often drooping with upturned tips; twigs reddish-brown with grayish skin, long and slender or short and dwarfed; **pith with hard, greenish crossbars** (in long-section); buds reddish-brown, hairy-tipped, 1/8–1/4" long, **pointing outward.**

LEAVES: Alternate, **clustered at shoot tips,** simple, deciduous; **blades shiny, dark green, whitened beneath, tough,** 2–43/4" long, **shape variable, generally widest above midleaf, abruptly pointed, tapered to a wedge-shaped base,** with smooth to slightly wavy edges (rarely irregularly coarse-toothed); stalks reddish; upper leaf surface golden to scarlet in autumn.

FLOWERS: **Greenish-white, inconspicuous,** tiny, unisexual (sometimes a few bisexual) with male and female flowers on separate trees; stalkless (female) or short-stalked (male); flowers in compact clusters (umbels), on hairy, 3/8–11/2" long stalks, in May–June (after leaves expand).

FRUITS: **Blue-black, plum-like drupes,** 3/8–1/2" **long,** with thin, oily flesh around a stone; seeds single within indistinctly 10–12-grooved stones; fruits stalkless, in **clusters of 1–3 on stalks 11/8– 21/4" long,** mature in October.

HABITAT: Usually moist to wet, wooded sites, often along the edges of lakes and wetlands, in sandy, acidic soil; rarely in drier upland forests.

ORIGIN: Native.

GLOSSY BUCKTHORN was introduced to our continent primarily as an ornamental. The cultivar 'Columnaris' (tall-hedge buckthorn) is popular in hedges and windbreaks. Glossy buckthorn is hardy throughout the state, and in some areas it has become a serious, aggressive invader of wetlands. • The hard wood has been used for making shoe lasts, nails and veneers. Its charcoal was once highly prized for making gunpowder. • Buckthorns were long ago credited with protective power against witchcraft, demons, poisons and headaches, but glossy buckthorn's true value, as a laxative, was not recognized until the 1300s. It might have been overlooked earlier because violent purgatives were then fashionable, whereas buckthorn is relatively mild. Today, herbalists recommend a tea of glossy buckthorn bark as a laxative. In Europe, the bark is often included in commercial laxatives. • The fruits mature over several weeks, so green, red and black fruits can occur at the same time. The unripe "berries" produce a green dye, and the bark gives a yellow dye. • Birds eat glossy buckthorn fruits, which are slightly **poisonous** to humans, usually causing vomiting. • A western species, **cascara buckthorn** (*F. purshiana*, also called *Rhamnus purshiana* or cascara), shown in pink/dark green on the map, has recently been found growing wild in Michigan. Cascara is distinguished by its finely toothed, short-stalked leaves with about 10–12 veins per side. Its inconspicuous flowers lack petals and the plants are often unisexual.

ALSO CALLED: European alder-buckthorn, European-alder, columnar buckthorn, fen buckthorn, arrow-wood, black-dogwood • *Rhamnus frangula.*

SIZE AND SHAPE: Small trees or shrubs to 20' [40'] tall; crowns rounded, open; roots spreading, suckering to form dense colonies.

TRUNKS: Short, up to 3" in diameter; bark thin, with conspicuous, pale, elongated pores (lenticels); inner bark yellow, with a fetid odor; wood fine-grained.

BRANCHES: Ascending at a narrow angle from the trunk; twigs brown to gray, **mottled with lenticels**, minutely hairy, brittle; **buds brown, hairy, lacking scales.**

LEAVES: Mostly **alternate**, simple, deciduous; blades glossy green, with **5–10 conspicuous, parallel veins per side**, elliptic to ovate and widest above midleaf, 1 1/8–3" long, 3/4–2" wide, abruptly pointed, **smooth-edged** or slightly wavy-edged; stalks stout, 2 3/8–4 3/4" long, with slender, ephemeral stipules; leaves yellow to red-tinged in autumn.

FLOWERS: Greenish-yellow, <1/4" across, bisexual; petals 5, <1/16" long, with notched tips; sepals 5, with fused bases; flowers on slender, unequal, 1/8–3/8" long stalks, in clusters of 1–6 (umbels) in lower leaf axils, in May–June (after leaves expand).

FRUITS: **Green to red to purplish-black, berry-like drupes,** about 1/4" across; seeds single within smooth, nutlet-like stones, **2–3 stones per fruit;** fruit clusters mature in July–September.

HABITAT: Moist to wet, typically disturbed sites in wetlands, ravines and low woods.

ORIGIN: Introduced from Eurasia and North Africa.

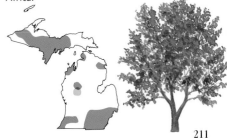

BUCKTHORNS cannot be categorized neatly as alternate- or opposite-leaved. Most have alternate leaves, but European buckthorn is more or less opposite-leaved. • This small tree's hardiness, spiny branches, insect resistance and responsiveness to pruning have made it a popular hedge plant. European buckthorn escaped from cultivation many years ago in North America and has been widely dispersed by birds. It is now an aggressive invader that is so common it often appears indigenous. • The extremely unpleasant-tasting fruits are somewhat **poisonous** to humans and have a strong laxative effect. In 1650, European buckthorn syrup, which contained cinnamon, nutmeg and aniseed to cut the bitter flavor of the fruits, was included in the British pharmacopoeia. In the 1800s, British children were given buckthorn syrup laced with ginger and sugar as a laxative. Buckthorn fruits are still recommended as a laxative and are listed in the U.S. National Formulary. • **Chinese buckthorn** (***R. utilis***), shown in dark green on the map, is a common escape in some areas. It resembles European buckthorn, but it has shiny, relatively long (about 3–3¾" long and more than twice as long as wide) leaves with 5–6 pairs of veins and its fruits have only 2 stones. • In autumn, introduced shrubs such as the buckthorn often stand out in sharp contrast to native plants, which shed their leaves promptly each fall.

ALSO CALLED: Common buckthorn, purging buckthorn, European waythorn, Hart's thorn, Carolina buckthorn.

SIZE AND SHAPE: Small trees or shrubs to 20' [61'] tall; crowns rounded; roots spreading, suckering to form dense colonies.

TRUNKS: Up to 14" in diameter; bark grayish-brown with elongated pores (lenticels), thin, smooth, peeling in curly-edged sheets; wood fine-grained.

BRANCHES: Stiff, often **spine-tipped; twigs rigid,** of **2 types:** long, smooth, rather angled shoots, and short, warty shoots with crowded leaf scars and/or thorn-like tips; buds hairless

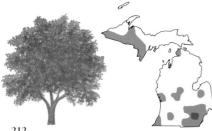

with blackish scales, flat-lying.

LEAVES: Mostly opposite, simple, late-deciduous; **blades dull dark green, hairless,** with 3–5 conspicuous, strongly upcurved veins per side, **minutely blunt-toothed,** broadly ovate to elliptic, **1⅛–3½" long,** with tips abruptly pointed, slightly folded and often curved back; stalks hairy, grooved.

FLOWERS: Greenish-yellow, <¼" across; functionally **unisexual with male and female flowers on separate plants; petals 4, lance-shaped, <¹⁄₁₆" long (male flowers) or <¹⁄₃₂" long (female); sepals 4, fused; flowers on thread-like, unequal stalks, in compact clusters (**umbels**), borne in leaf axils, in May–June (as leaves expand).

FRUITS: Green to red to purplish-black, berry-like drupes, about ¼" across; seeds single within grooved, nutlet-like stones, usually **4 stones per fruit;** fruits in dense clusters, mature in August–September.

HABITAT: Open, upland, typically disturbed sites such as abandoned lots, clearings, open woodlands and roadsides.

ORIGIN: Introduced from Europe.

Key to the Dogwoods (Genus *Cornus*)

1a Leaves alternate .... *C. alternifolia*, **alternate-leaf dogwood** (p. 214)
1b Leaves opposite.. **2**

2a Flowers tiny, in a compact cluster at the center, or 4 large, petal-like white bracts forming a flower-like cluster (pseudanthium); individual fruits stalkless, in a compact cluster at the end of a slender stalk, red when ripe
.... *C. florida*, **eastern flowering dogwood** (p. 217)
2b Flowers larger (about ¹/₈–¹/₄" long), in open, widely branched, flat-topped clusters (cymes), without obvious bracts; individual fruits clearly stalked, variously colored........ **3**

3a Upper leaf surfaces rough to the touch, with tiny, stiff, erect hairs; fruits white to bluish **4**
3b Upper leaf surfaces smooth to the touch, hairless or with soft, flat-lying hairs; fruits variously colored.. **5**

4a Leaves with 3–5 veins per side; pith of old twigs usually brown
.... *C. drummondii*, **roughleaf dogwood** (p. 216)
4b Leaves with 6–8 veins per side; pith of old twigs white
.... *C. rugosa*, **roundleaf dogwood** (p. 216)

5a Branchlets bright red to greenish, with pale pores; leaf veins 4–5 per side; fruits white with a brown, yellow-striped stone .... *C. sericea*, **red-osier dogwood** (p. 214)
5b Branchlets green, sometimes purple-streaked or -flecked; fruits bluish or white, with a pinkish stone.. **6**

6a Leaves with 6–8 veins per side; fruits blue
.... *C. rugosa*, **roundleaf dogwood** (p. 216)
6b Leaves with 3–4 (rarely 5) veins per side; fruits white
.... *C. racemosa*, **gray dogwood** (p. 216)

DOGWOODS typically have opposite leaves, but this species is an exception to the rule. • The strong wood has no commercial value, but because it resists abrasion and withstands friction, the wood was used to make bearings and parts for mills. • This dogwood and its cultivars are popular ornamental shrubs because of their profuse spring flowers, scarlet autumn leaves and purple, bird-attracting fruits. These small trees have an unusual shape owing to their distinct layers of horizontal branches, giving rise to the alternative name "pagoda dogwood." • Alternate-leaf dogwood is hardy throughout the state. It is not prone to serious diseases, but it is sometimes damaged by dogwood borer (*Synanthedon scitula*) and other insect pests. • The dry, bitter fruits provide food for grouse, pheasants, wild turkeys and squirrels. White-tailed deer browse the twigs and leaves. • **Red-osier dogwood** (*C. sericea*, also called *C. stolonifera*) is readily distinguished by its opposite leaves and white (rarely blue) fruits with yellow-striped stones. This common, widespread shrub is usually 3–10' tall with stems $1/2$–1" thick, but the state champion has a trunk diameter of 3" and measures 17' in height.

ALSO CALLED: Pagoda dogwood, green osier, blue dogwood, pagoda-tree.

SIZE AND SHAPE: Small trees or large, straggly shrubs 12–20 [25']' tall; crowns flat, layered.

TRUNKS: Short, 2–6" [9"] in diameter; young bark greenish- to reddish-brown, thin, smooth; mature bark shallow-ridged; wood reddish-brown, heavy, hard, fine-grained.

BRANCHES: Almost horizontal, with upcurved tips, **in tiers;** twigs shiny reddish-green to purplish, with pores (lenticels) and often with **1–2 side-branches longer than the central shoot;**

pith white; buds shiny chestnut brown, with 2 loose outer scales.

LEAVES: Alternate (sometimes semi-opposite on short shoots), **clustered at branch tips,** simple, deciduous; blades green and hairless above, grayish and minutely hairy beneath, oval, with **4–5 parallel side-veins arched toward the tip,** 2–5" long, tapered to a point, **smooth- or slightly wavy-edged;** stalks $3/8$–$2 3/8$" long; leaves red to yellow in autumn.

FLOWERS: White or cream-colored, small, 4-parted, bisexual; numerous, on jointed stalks, in **irregular, 2–4" wide, rounded to flat-topped clusters** (cymes), in May–June (after leaves expand).

FRUITS: Dark blue to bluish-black, berry-like drupes, about $1/4$" across, **on short, red stalks** in branched clusters; seeds single within egg-shaped stones; drupes mature in August–October.

HABITAT: Rich, moist sites in woodlands and cedar swamps; often on floodplains.

ORIGIN: Native.

ALTHOUGH GRAY DOGWOOD is often too small to be considered a tree, vigorous specimens can reach 15' in height. Gray dogwood is sometimes planted as a hardy ornamental, capable of tolerating a wide range of soil moisture conditions. It is easily transplanted and can be grown as a hedge or in dense masses. The shrubs are valued for their attractive, white, springtime flowers, followed by showy, red-stalked fruit clusters in late summer and autumn. • A similar species, **roundleaf dogwood (*C. rugosa*)**, shown in pink/dark green on the map, is a slightly smaller shrub (3–10' tall) with pale blue to grayish fruits and larger (2–5" long), broader (often almost round) leaves that have 7–10 (rather than 3–4) pairs of veins. • The rare shrub, **roughleaf dogwood (*C. drummondii*)**, grows along rivers and woodland borders in southeastern Michigan. Like gray dogwood, this species has leaves with only 3–4 (rarely 5) veins per side, but its upper leaf surfaces are distinctly rough-textured and the pith of its twigs is usually brownish rather than white. • Some of the names in this genus can be confusing. The specific epithet *racemosa*, "with racemes," refers to the panicle-like flower clusters that are somewhat longer than the broad cymes typical of this genus. The name *rugosa*, "wrinkled" or "rough," refers to the rough upper surface of the leaves. However, the common name roughleaf dogwood applies to *C. drummondii*, not *C. rugosa*.

ALSO CALLED: Northern swamp-dogwood, panicled dogwood, gray-stemmed dogwood • *C. foemina* ssp. *racemosa*.

SIZE AND SHAPE: Shrubs 3–15' [38'] tall; crowns rounded; roots spreading, often forming thickets.

TRUNKS: Short, up to 4" [6"] in diameter; young bark greenish to tan to gray-brown; mature bark gray, smooth.

BRANCHES: Numerous, paired; twigs slender, essentially **hairless,** more or less **2-ridged,** green to reddish at first, soon **light brown to gray with age;** pith white in new growth, **pale brown after 2–3 years;** buds small, scales meeting at edges (not overlapping).

LEAVES: Opposite, simple, deciduous; blades dark grayish green, **smooth to touch above,** paler, minutely hairy and often whitened by minute bumps (papillae) beneath, $3/4$–4" long, wedge-shaped at base, slender-pointed, **smooth-edged, with 3–4 weakly parallel, arching side veins;** stalks $1/4$–$1/2$" long; **leaves red to purplish** in autumn.

FLOWERS: White or cream-colored, small, strongly convex, ill-scented, 4-parted, bisexual; petals 4, curved backward; **calyx lobes <$1/32$" long;** stamens 4; flowers in loose, **$1 1/8$–$2 3/8$" wide, rounded to pyramidal clusters** (panicles) on hairy, reddish, $3/4$–1" long stalks, in May–July.

FRUITS: White (rarely pale gray to bluish), **berry-like drupes** about $1/4$" across, **on bright red stalks** in branched clusters; seeds single, within egg-shaped, **pinkish stones;** drupes mature in July–September.

HABITAT: Moist, open sites in wet woodlands and swamps and on shores and roadsides; sometimes in drier, sandy sites.

ORIGIN: Native.

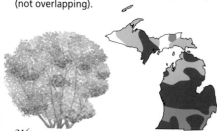

THIS FAST-GROWING, short-lived tree is popular in southern parks and gardens. With its beautiful spring flowers, showy, bird-attracting fruits and red autumn leaves, eastern flowering dogwood is one of our finest native ornamental trees, but its delicate flower buds are damaged by temperatures below −20°F. Sadly, dogwood anthracnose (*Discula destructiva*) is rapidly eradicating eastern flowering dogwood in some regions and was recently discovered in southwestern Michigan. • The hard, strong wood has been used for golf-club heads, tool handles, rolling pins, weaving shuttles, spindles, small wheel hubs, barrel hoops and engravers' blocks. • Some tribes used the roots to make a scarlet dye for coloring porcupine quills and eagle feathers. The bark also yields a red dye. • Dried, ground bark was used as a quinine substitute for treating fevers. A bark decoction was used to treat mouth problems, and the fibrous twigs were used as chewing sticks (early toothbrushes), said to whiten teeth. • The drupes are not poisonous but are bitterly inedible when raw. Occasionally, they have been mashed, seeded and mixed with other fruits in jams and jellies. • Many birds and small mammals eat the bitter fruits.

ALSO CALLED: Arrow-wood, bitter red-cherry, common dogwood, white cornel, dogtree, Florida dogwood, great-flowered dogwood, Virginia dogwood.

SIZE AND SHAPE: Small trees or tall shrubs 10–35' [55'] tall; crowns bushy, spreading, flat-topped; roots deep.

TRUNKS: Short, 4–12" [17"] in diameter; mature bark dark reddish-brown, deeply checked with 4-sided scales; wood white to brownish, tough, heavy and fine-grained.

BRANCHES: Spreading in more or less horizontal tiers; twigs greenish to reddish with white hairs and pores (lenticels); flower buds stalked, dome-shaped, at twig tips.

LEAVES: Opposite, usually 2–4 at branch tips, simple, deciduous; blades green above, grayish-green beneath, elliptic to oval, with **parallel veins arched toward the tip,** 2–6" long, narrow-pointed, **slightly wavy-edged;** leaves bronze to scarlet in autumn.

FLOWERS: Yellowish, tiny, 4-parted, bisexual; forming small, **dense 20–30-flowered clusters at the center of 4 white or pinkish, petal-like bracts,** each ³/₄–2" **long** and tipped with a reddish notch;

pseudanthia (clusters of flowers plus bracts) **resemble single, showy, 2–4" wide blooms;** flowers at branch tips in May–early June (before leaves expand).

FRUITS: Shiny, red, berry-like drupes ³/₈–¹/₂" long, tipped with persistent sepals, with thin, mealy flesh around a stone; seeds single within stones; fruits in **dense clusters of 3–6 or more on slender stalks,** undeveloped fruits often present, mature in August–October.

HABITAT: Moderately dry to moist sites in deciduous forests and ravines.

ORIGIN: Native.

THIS NATIVE TREE is too small to be commercially important. It is sometimes planted for its attractive autumn leaves and fruits, but European *Euonymus* species are more popular for landscaping.
• Eastern wahoo bark was used in folk medicine for many years as a tonic, laxative, diuretic and expectorant. Some Native tribes boiled the bark to make medicinal teas for treating problems of the uterus or eyes, and for applying to facial sores. Various extracts, syrups and medicinal teas have been used over the years for treating fevers, upset stomachs, constipation, lung ailments, liver congestion and heart problems. Dried root bark was taken to relieve dropsy (fluid retention). The seed oil was used to induce vomiting and evacuation of the bowels, and the whole fruits were said to increase urine flow. In 1917, bark and root extracts were reported to affect the heart much like digitalis, and wahoo became a popular heart medicine. By 1921, this species had been dropped as an official drug plant, although it remained in the U.S. National Formulary until 1947.
• **Caution:** The fruits, seeds and bark of this tree are considered poisonous. Children may be attracted to the brightly colored fruits.
• Many species of birds eat and disperse the seeds.

ALSO CALLED: Burning-bush euonymus, spindletree • *E. atropurpureus.*

SIZE AND SHAPE: Small trees or shrubs 10–15' [18'] tall; crowns rounded; roots spreading.

TRUNKS: Straight, often short or clumped, rarely up to 3" [3"] in diameter; bark greenish-gray, often streaked reddish-brown, thin; wood nearly white, hard, dense.

BRANCHES: Spreading; twigs greenish, smooth, **somewhat 4-sided,** often with corky ridges below the buds; buds green, reddish-tinged, 6-scaled, about 1/8" long, flat-lying.

LEAVES: Opposite, simple, deciduous; blades light green and hairless above, paler and **sparsely hairy beneath,** oblong-ovate to ovate or elliptic, 1 1/2–5" long, 3/8–2" wide, **abruptly pointed, finely sharp-toothed;** stalks about 3/8" long; leaves red in autumn.

FLOWERS: Purplish-maroon, about 1/4" across, bisexual; petals usually 4, wide-spreading; sepals usually 4, fused at the base; on slender stalks in branched, 3/4–1 1/2" wide, 5–18-flowered clusters (cymes); flower clusters on 3/4–2" long stalks from leaf axils, in June–July (after leaves expand).

FRUITS: Prominently 4-lobed capsules, pink to red or purplish when mature, 3/8–1/2" wide; **seeds 4, each enclosed in a fleshy, bright red aril;** capsules hang on slender stalks, **split across the bottom to release seeds** in September, **empty capsules persist into winter.**

HABITAT: Low, moist sites such as damp woods and streamside thickets.

ORIGIN: Native.

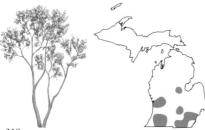

THE DENSE, HARD WOOD of this species was once favored by carvers. It has also been used to make toothpicks, spindles, skewers, pipe stems and high-quality, easily erased art charcoal. Tanners valued the bark for preparing fine leather for gloves. • The bark, leaves and fruits of European spindle-tree have provided herbalists and drug manufacturers with a strong laxative. Unfortunately, the medicine is rather too effective, causing drastic purging and pain in the colon. The U.S. Food and Drug Administration classifies this tree as dangerous. • European spindle-tree is planted as an ornamental for its red autumn leaves and fruits. • Two Asian horticultural species occasionally grow wild in woodlands and yards, and can be very weedy. **Winged burning-bush (*E. alata*)**, or winged euonymus, shown in pink/dark green on the map, is a tall (up to 23') shrub readily distinguished by the 2–4 conspicuous corky wings on its twigs and by its stalkless leaves, which turn bright red in autumn. **Japanese spindle-tree (*E. hamiltoniana*)**, or Hamilton's strawberry-bush, is similar to European spindle-tree, but its leaves are larger (4–5" long) and its flowers have purple (not yellow) anthers.

ALSO CALLED: European euonymus, skewerwood, prickwood • *E. europaeus.*

SIZE AND SHAPE: Small trees or tall shrubs up to 20' [45'] tall; crowns rounded; roots spreading.

TRUNKS: Straight, often short or clumped, up to 20" in diameter; bark greenish-gray, often reddish-streaked, thin; wood hard, dense.

BRANCHES: Spreading; twigs greenish, smooth, **somewhat 4-sided; buds loosely 6-scaled,** about ⅛" long, **plump, not flat-lying,** present at twig tips.

LEAVES: Opposite, simple, deciduous; **blades hairless,** green above, paler beneath, oblong-ovate to lance-shaped or elliptic, 1½–4½" long, **abruptly pointed, finely toothed;** stalks <1" long; **leaves red in autumn.**

FLOWERS: Greenish to yellowish-white, about ¼" across, bisexual; petals usually 4, wide-spreading; sepals usually 4, fused at the base; flowers on slender stalks in loose, branched, 3–7-flowered clusters (cymes) on ¾–2" long stalks from leaf axils, in June (after leaves expand).

FRUITS: Prominently 4-lobed capsules, yellow, pink or red- to purple-tinged when mature, ⅜–½" wide; **seeds 4, each enclosed in a fleshy, orange aril;** capsules hang on slender stalks, **split open across the bottom to release seeds** in September, **empty capsules persist.**

HABITAT: Low, moist sites on shores, in and around woods, in waste places and along roads.

ORIGIN: Introduced from Europe.

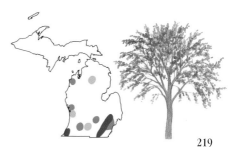

ALTHOUGH not widely grown as an ornamental, this shade-tolerant native shrub has been cultivated since 1640 for its attractive, dark green leaves, lightly fragrant flower clusters and distinctive, persistent fruits. The hanging clusters of unusual papery pods attract attention through much of the year. The pods, along with the striped, greenish branches, add interest in winter when the shrubs are leafless and loose seeds in the pods rattle in the breeze. Children sometimes like to crush the pods to hear them pop. • The spreading roots send up suckers that may form thickets in open areas. In gardens, this tendency can cause problems when shoots appear in unwanted places. Otherwise, this attractive shrub is relatively maintenance free. It transplants easily and can be grown from cuttings or seeds. • The genus name *Staphylea* is derived from the Greek *staphyle*, "bunch of grapes," in reference to the hanging clusters of flowers. The specific epithet *trifolia* describes the 3-parted leaves. • When fruits and flowers are absent, American bladdernut may be confused with common hop-tree (p. 206). However, these two species are easily distinguished by examining their leaves and branches, which are opposite in bladdernuts and alternate in hop-trees.

ALSO CALLED: Tall bladdernut.

SIZE AND SHAPE: Trees or shrubs to 20' [36'] tall; crowns rounded; roots spreading.

TRUNKS: Often clumped, up to 4" [6"] in diameter; young bark smooth, green, often with mottled stripes; mature bark gray to brown, becoming slightly ridged with pale, longitudinal stripes.

BRANCHES: Erect, rather stiff; twigs stout, greenish, almost ringed at nodes, somewhat striped; buds egg-shaped, 2–4-scaled, paired at stem tips.

LEAVES: **Opposite,** deciduous; compound, divided into **3 leaflets;** leaflets dark green and smooth above, paler and sparsely hairy beneath, 1 1/2–4" long, pointed, finely saw-toothed; tip leaflet long-stalked, side-leaflets essentially stalkless; main leaf stalk 1 1/8–4 3/4" long, with slender, ephemeral bracts at the base (2 stipules) and at the top (2 stipules below each leaflet); leaves green to pale yellow in autumn.

FLOWERS: **Greenish-white, narrowly bell-shaped,** about 3/8" long, bisexual, 5-parted; sepals nearly as long as petals; flowers **in nodding, branched, 1 1/8–4" long clusters** (racemes) at branch tips, in April–May (just before leaves expand fully).

FRUITS: **Inflated, thin-walled, veiny capsules with 3 pointed lobes, green to yellowish-brown, 1 1/8–2 3/8" long;** seeds yellow-brown, bony, 1–4 per chamber, **rattling in ripe capsules;** capsules hang on slender stalks, split open near tips in September, persist into winter.

HABITAT: Moist, rich sites on floodplains and hillsides, often in woods and thickets.

ORIGIN: Native.

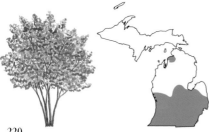

HORSECHESTNUT is a hardy, moderately fast-growing tree often planted as an ornamental. It lives 80–100 years and can tolerate urban conditions, but its broad, domed canopy requires considerable space. • Horsechestnut is the "spreading chestnut tree" that Henry Wadsworth Longfellow wrote about. The large, sweeping branches tipped with showy, erect flower clusters suggest enormous candelabras. • The fruits and seeds have been used for centuries to treat colds, whooping cough, fever, rheumatism, backache, nerve pain and sunburn. Today, horsechestnut-seed preparations are sold in Europe and the U.S. for reducing inflammation and pain associated with varicose veins, ulcers, hemorrhoids and phlebitis. • **Caution:** The seeds, leaves and bark contain aesculin, a **toxic alkaloid** that can cause vomiting, stupor, twitching and even paralysis. Some sources report that horsechestnuts have been used as horse fodder, but most say these fruits are poisonous to livestock.

• Horsechestnut trees produce good seed crops almost every year. The large, inedible fruits are generally shunned by wildlife, though squirrels occasionally eat the embryo stalks in the seeds.

• The name "horsechestnut" reflects the similarity between these seeds and the edible seeds of chestnuts (*Castanea* spp., p. 106). Be careful never to confuse them.

SIZE AND SHAPE: Trees 35–65' [77'] tall; crowns broad, rounded.

TRUNKS: Short, 12–32" [60"] in diameter; young bark dark gray-brown, smooth; mature bark fissured, scaly; wood pale, light, close-grained.

BRANCHES: Ascending, then downcurved and finally upcurved at the tips; **twigs stout,** reddish-brown with white pores (lenticels), **unpleasant-smelling when bruised; buds shiny, dark brown, sticky, $3/4$–$1^1/2$" long at twig tips,** smaller and paired below.

LEAVES: Opposite, deciduous; compound, **palmately divided into 5–9 (usually 7) stalkless leaflets at the tip of a long stalk;** leaflets yellowish-green, widest above midleaf, gradually tapered to the base, 4–8" long; leaf scars large, horseshoe-shaped; leaves rusty yellow in autumn.

FLOWERS: White to cream-colored, spotted with red and yellow, bell-shaped, $3/4$–$1^1/8$" long; unisexual and bisexual flowers in each cluster; petals 5, unequal; flowers **in showy, erect, 8–12" long, cone-shaped clusters** (panicles) **at tips of branches,** in June (after leaves expand).

FRUITS: Green to brown, spiny, leathery, round capsules, 2–$2^1/4$" across; seeds up to 2" across, 1–2 (rarely 3) per capsule, smooth, **satin-shiny, mahogany brown with a rough, pale end;** capsules hang in clusters, split lengthwise into 3 segments, drop in autumn.

HABITAT: Disturbed sites along fences and in woodlands.

ORIGIN: Introduced from southeastern Europe.

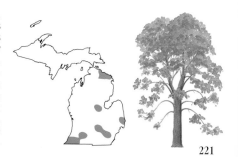

OHIO BUCKEYE is Michigan's only indigenous *Aesculus* species. This midwestern species reaches the northernmost limit of its range in the southern parts of the state. Ohio buckeye is sometimes planted as an ornamental shade tree, and adventive trees are occasionally found, usually on floodplains. • The weak, uniform wood is easy to carve and resists splitting, so it was ideal for making artificial limbs. It has also been used as a source of paper pulp and for making woodenware, crates and troughs for collecting maple sap. Ohio buckeye was once a valuable timber tree in the U.S., but because of its increasing rarity, it now has little commercial importance. • **Caution:** Most parts of this tree, including the large seeds, contain the **toxic alkaloid** aesculin. Perhaps because of its toxicity, Ohio buckeye is relatively disease- and insect-free, and its fruits are seldom harvested by wildlife. However, squirrels sometimes eat the soft, young "nuts." • The name "buckeye" refers to the seeds, which somewhat resemble the eyes of deer, and this species is the official tree of the state of Ohio.

• Horsechestnut (p. 221) is readily distinguished by its larger (4–8"), more numerous (usually 7), abruptly pointed leaflets and its sticky winter buds.

ALSO CALLED: Fetid buckeye.

SIZE AND SHAPE: Trees 25–50' [104'] tall; crowns broad, rounded.

TRUNKS: Straight, 6–14" [23"] in diameter; young bark gray, smooth; mature bark dark gray-brown, with thick, scaly plates; wood pale, light, close-grained.

BRANCHES: Slender, spreading to drooping, upcurved at tips; **twigs stout, reddish-brown, with orange pores** (lenticels), unpleasant-smelling when bruised; **buds** ¹/₂–³/₄" **long at twig tips, reddish, powdery-coated,** smaller and paired below.

LEAVES: Opposite, deciduous; compound, palmately divided into 5 (rarely 7) stalkless leaflets at the tip of a 4–6" long stalk; leaflets bright or yellowish-green above, paler and hairy beneath, lance-shaped, **widest above midleaf,** gradually tapered to base, 2¹/₂–6" long, unevenly sharp-toothed; leaf scars large, horseshoe-shaped; leaves yellow to orange in autumn.

FLOWERS: Pale greenish-yellow, narrowly bell-shaped, ¹/₂–1³/₈" long; unisexual and bisexual flowers in each cluster; petals 4, unequal, hairy; stamens 7, often twice as long as petals; flowers in **showy, erect, 4–6" long, cone-shaped clusters** (panicles) **at branch tips,** in April–May (after leaves expand).

FRUITS: Yellowish-green, spiny, leathery capsules ³/₄–1¹/₈" **across** (rarely to 2"); **seeds satin-shiny, dark reddish-brown** with a rough, pale end, ³/₄–1³/₈" **across, 1 (rarely 2–3) per capsule;** capsules split lengthwise into 3 segments, drop in September–October.

HABITAT: Moist, rich forests, especially on floodplains.

ORIGIN: Native.

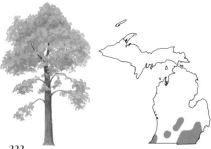

Key to the Maples (Genus *Acer*)

1a Leaves compound, divided into 3–5 leaflets .... *A. negundo*, **ashleaf maple** (p. 232)
1b Leaves simple **2**

2a Leaves deeply 3–5–lobed, otherwise smooth-edged or with a few coarse teeth, notches rounded **3**
2b Leaf variously lobed, edged with many sharp teeth, notches pointed at the base and often
toothed almost to the base **5**

3a Flowers with conspicuous petals, borne on ascending, hairless stalks in elongated, stalked
clusters; samaras with wings spreading at almost 180°; leaf juice milky
....*A. platanoides*, **Norway maple** (p. 226)
3b Flowers lacking petals, hanging on slender, hairy stalks in tassel-like clusters; samaras with
wings spreading at <120°, often almost parallel; leaf juice clear **4**

4a Leaves mostly 3-lobed with drooping edges, smooth- or wavy-edged or with a few irregular coarse
teeth, green or brownish and more or less hairy beneath ... *A. nigrum*, **black maple** (p. 225)
4b Leaves mostly 5-lobed with flat (not drooping) edges, edged with regular, coarse, pointed teeth,
pale and essentially hairless beneath .... *A. saccharum*, **sugar maple** (p. 224)

5a Leaves deeply cut into 5 or more coarsely toothed, relatively narrow lobes, with lobe bases
usually narrower than the upper lobe **6**
5b Leaves more shallowly cut into 3–5 parallel-sided to broadly triangular lobes, edged with
regular, coarse to fine teeth **7**

6a Flowers with conspicuous petals, borne in elongated, stalked clusters, appearing after leaves
unfold; samaras mature in mid- to late summer, wings spreading at <30°; leaves with coarse
single teeth .... *A. pseudoplatanus*, **sycamore maple** (p. 226)
6b Flowers lacking petals, hanging on slender stalks in tassel-like clusters, appearing long
before leaves; samaras mature in spring, wings spreading at about 90°; leaves with many
double teeth .... *A. saccharinum*, **silver maple** (p. 227)

7a Leaves narrowly triangular, longer than wide, with 2 small basal lobes and a large, coarsely
toothed central lobe .... *A. ginnala*, **Amur maple** (p. 231)
7b Leaves more rounded, usually about as wide as long, with 3 large lobes above midleaf and
sometimes 2 smaller basal lobes **8**

8a Buds 6–10-scaled; main lobe at leaf tip with roughly parallel sides; flowers in compact, tassel-like
clusters, appearing before leaves; samaras mature in spring ...... *A. rubrum*, **red maple** (p. 228)
8b Buds 2-scaled; main lobe at leaf tip triangular, gradually tapered from the base; flowers in
elongated, branched clusters, appearing after leaves; samaras mature in summer **9**

9a Young trunks grayish, not striped; leaves edged with coarse (5–8/in), single teeth; flowers in
erect, many-branched clusters .... *A. spicatum*, **mountain maple** (p. 229)
9b Young trunks green with pale stripes; leaves edged with fine (18–30/in), double teeth; flowers
hanging in simple, elongated clusters .... *A. pensylvanicum*, **striped maple** (p. 230)

FINE-GRAINED, DURABLE sugar maple wood polishes well and sometimes has a beautiful wavy or speckled (birdseye) appearance. It is highly valued for flooring, furniture, veneer, paneling, plywood, sports articles, musical instruments, tool handles, spindles, cutting blocks and other items that require hard wood. In the past, the wood was used for plows, wagons and early wooden railroad rails. • Settlers used potash-rich maple ashes as fertilizer. The ashes have also been used in soap and in pottery glazes. • "Sugaring-off" was an important part of pioneer culture. Sugar maple sap was gathered in pails each spring and boiled over wood fires to produce maple syrup or sugar. Many traditional sugar bushes remain, but large, modern-day operations use vacuum-plastic tubing to carry sap from trees to processing sites, where oil- or gas-powered evaporators reduce it to syrup in a multimillion-dollar industry. The sap contains 2–6% sugar, so 30–40 quarts are required to produce 1 quart of syrup. • Severe declines in some sugar bushes in parts of North America during the 1980s were caused by a combination of drought, extremely cold winters and severe defoliation. • Sugar maple is the most common tree in Michigan.

ALSO CALLED: Hard maple, rock maple, bird's-eye maple, curly maple, head maple, sugartree, sweet maple • *A. saccharaphorum.*

SIZE AND SHAPE: Trees 60–80' [87'] tall; crowns rounded, broad; roots shallow, wide-spreading.

TRUNKS: Straight, 20–60" [71"] in diameter; mature bark dark gray, irregularly ridged, sometimes scaly; wood light yellowish-brown, hard, heavy.

BRANCHES: Sturdy; twigs shiny reddish-brown, hairless, straight; buds brown, faintly hairy, **sharply pointed, with 12–16 paired scales,**

$^{1}/_{4}$–$^{3}/_{8}$" long at twig tips, smaller and paired below.

LEAVES: Opposite, simple, deciduous; blades deep yellowish-green above, paler beneath, hairless, 3–8" long, with **5 palmate lobes** (occasionally 3) separated by rounded notches, edged with a **few irregular, blunt-pointed teeth;** stalks 1$^{1}/_{2}$–3" long; leaves yellow to bright red in autumn.

FLOWERS: Greenish-yellow, small; functionally unisexual, often with male and female flowers in mixed clusters on the same tree; petals absent; sepals 5; **flowers hang on slender, hairy, 1$^{1}/_{8}$–2$^{3}/_{4}$" long stalks in tassel-like clusters** (umbel-like corymbs) at or near branch tips, in April–May (before or as leaves expand).

FRUITS: Green to brown **pairs of winged samaras, U-shaped, with spreading to almost parallel wings shorter than the slender stalks;** samaras $^{3}/_{4}$–1$^{1}/_{2}$" long; **seedcases plump;** samaras hang in clusters, mature and drop in September–October.

HABITAT: Fairly dry to moderately moist forests with soils ranging from rich to sandy.

ORIGIN: Native.

BLACK MAPLE has strong, straight-grained, uniformly textured wood that is sold as "hard maple," a term applied to both black and sugar maple (p. 224). It is used for furniture, fixtures, farm tools, spindles, veneer, plywood, flooring, dies and cutting blocks. • The sap from black maple trees can be collected and used to make syrup and sugar. • Like sugar maple, black maple saplings are shade tolerant and can survive for many years in the forest understory until new openings provide the light necessary for them to shoot up quickly and take their place in the canopy. • Black maple and sugar maple hybridize frequently, producing offspring with intermediate characteristics. Some taxonomists classify black maple as a variety or subspecies of sugar maple. Both maples are distinguished by their leaves and bark. Sugar maple leaves are flat, deep yellow-green and hairless, and their central lobes are rather square, with parallel sides. Black maple leaves are drooping and deep green with velvety lower surfaces, and their central lobes tend to taper from the base. Sugar maple bark is grayish with loose-edged plates, whereas black maple bark is blackish-gray and more deeply furrowed.

ALSO CALLED: Black sugar maple, hard maple, rock maple • *A. saccharum* ssp. *nigrum*.

SIZE AND SHAPE: Trees 65–100' [118'] tall; crowns broad, rounded.

TRUNKS: Straight, 20–25" [30"] in diameter; mature bark blackish-gray, with long, irregular, vertical ridges, sometimes scaly; wood pale yellowish-brown, heavy, hard.

BRANCHES: Sturdy; twigs dull yellowish- to reddish-brown, stout, straight; buds dark grayish-brown, hairy, with paired scales, about ¹/₄" long at twig tips, smaller and paired below.

LEAVES: Opposite, simple, deciduous, **appearing wilted;** blades dark green above, **densely brownish-velvety beneath,** 4–6" long, with **3 palmate lobes** (sometimes 5 indistinct lobes) separated by **open, shallow notches,** edged with a **few irregular, blunt-pointed teeth;** stalks hairy; leaves yellow to brownish-yellow (seldom red) in autumn.

FLOWERS: Yellowish, small, unisexual, with male and female flowers mixed or in separate clusters on the same tree; petals absent; sepals 5; **flowers hang on slender, hairy, ³/₄–2³/₄" long**

stalks, in tassel-like clusters (umbel-like corymbs) at or near branch tips, in April–May (before or as leaves expand).

FRUITS: Green to brown **pairs of winged samaras, U-shaped with slightly spreading to almost parallel wings about as long as the slender, hairy stalks;** samaras about 1¹/₈" long; **seedcases plump;** samaras hang in clusters, mature and drop in October.

HABITAT: Moist, fertile sites in bottomlands and on floodplains.

ORIGIN: Native.

THIS POPULAR ORNAMENTAL shade tree can grow in polluted urban sites with compacted, nutrient-poor soils. It is more resistant than native maples to insects and fungal diseases. Norway maple usually produces abundant seed, and it can become an aggressive invader of natural vegetation. • Many cultivars of this beautiful, hardy species have been developed. The cultivar 'Schwedleri' (Schwedler maple), with its purplish-red spring leaves and bright orange-red to purple autumn foliage, has been planted in North America for over a century. 'Crimson King' boasts rich maroon leaves and is also very popular. Norway maple keeps its leaves about 2 weeks longer than native maples in the autumn. • Norway maple can be confused with sugar maple, but Norway maple's dark green (rather than yellow-green) leaves have 5–7 (rather than 3–5), bristle-tipped (rather than blunt-pointed) lobes and turn only yellow (never red or orange) in autumn. • Another introduced European species, **sycamore maple** (*A. pseudoplatanus*), shown in dark green on the map, is also widely planted in the state, but it rarely escapes. Sycamore maple is distinguished by its thicker, more wrinkled leaves, with white-hairy veins and numerous coarse teeth.

SIZE AND SHAPE: Trees 40–65' [105'] tall; crowns dense, rounded, broad; roots spreading, relatively deep.

TRUNKS: Straight, 12–28" [58"] in diameter; bark very dark gray, with regular low, intersecting ridges, not scaly; wood pale, straight-grained, uniformly textured.

BRANCHES: Sturdy, ascending to spreading; twigs straight, purplish-tinged to reddish-brown, hairless, with prominent pores (lenticels) and **milky juice;** buds purplish to reddish, plump, blunt, with **4–8 fleshy, paired scales, about** ¼" **long at twig tips,** smaller and paired below.

LEAVES: Opposite, simple, deciduous, with **milky juice;** blades dark green, hairless, 3–6" long, 4–7" wide, with **5 (rarely 7) palmate lobes plus a few large, bristle-tipped teeth;** stalks long; leaves yellow to orange brown in autumn.

FLOWERS: Greenish-yellow, about ³/₈" across, bisexual or male; petals 5; sepals 5; **flowers in erect, rounded clusters** (corymbs) at branch tips, in April–June (before or as leaves expand).

FRUITS: Green to brown **pairs of winged samaras,** with wings spreading at almost 180°; samaras 1³/₄–2" long; **seedcases flat; samaras hang on slender stalks in clusters,** mature in September–October, often persist through winter.

HABITAT: Roadsides, vacant lots, hedgerows and thickets on a wide range of soils.

ORIGIN: Introduced from Europe and western Asia.

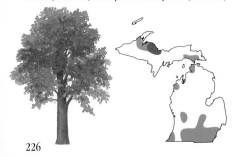

SILVER MAPLE has straight-grained, rather brittle wood, called "soft maple," that is usually used where strength is not important, for example, in inexpensive furniture, veneer, boxes, crates and pulp.

• Although not as showy as most maples in autumn, this handsome, fast-growing, hardy tree is widely planted as an ornamental. However, silver maple requires considerable space and usually produces abundant seed and leaf fall each year. Also, its brittle limbs break easily and its roots can spread aggressively to clog sewer pipes. • Several cultivars with deeply divided leaves have been developed and are propagated from cuttings. 'Laciniatum' or 'Wieri' (cutleaf silver maple) is especially popular. • Silver maple sap is only half as sweet as that of sugar maple (p. 224), but with patient boiling it yields a delicious pale syrup. • When felled, silver maple sends up vigorous shoots from dormant buds in the stump. Also, fallen branches can sprout roots and grow into new trees.

• Many birds and small mammals such as grosbeaks and squirrels eat the abundant seeds. Silver maple trees commonly have hollow trunks that provide dens for squirrels, raccoons and other mammals, nesting cavities for wood ducks and other birds, and hideouts for small children.

ALSO CALLED: Soft maple, white maple, silverleaf maple, river maple, swamp maple, water maple.

SIZE AND SHAPE: Trees 65–100' [125'] tall; crowns broad, rounded, open; roots spreading, usually very shallow.

TRUNKS: Short in open sites, taller in forests, 20–48" [88"] in diameter; young bark gray, smooth; mature bark gray, **often shaggy** with thin strips that peel from both ends; wood pale, hard, heavy.

BRANCHES: Sharply ascending, then arching downward to upturned tips; twigs shiny, hairless, unpleasant-smelling when broken; buds shiny, reddish, blunt, with 6–10 paired scales; flower buds plump, ringing the twigs.

LEAVES: **Opposite,** simple, deciduous; blades light green, **silvery white beneath,** 3–6" long, with **5–7 palmate lobes separated by deep, concavely narrowed notches, irregularly coarse-toothed;** stalks 3–4" long; leaves pale yellow to brown in October.

FLOWERS: Greenish-yellow or reddish, tiny; unisexual with male and female flowers in separate clusters on same or separate trees; petals absent; sepals 5; **flowers in dense, almost stalkless clusters** (umbels), in March–April **(long before leaves expand).**

FRUITS: Yellowish-green to brownish **pairs of winged samaras with wings spreading at 90°,** often only 1 per pair maturing; samaras $1^{1}/_{8}$–$2^{3}/_{4}$" **long; seedcases ribbed; samaras hang on slender stalks in clusters,** mature and drop singly in late May–early June (as leaves expand fully).

HABITAT: Moist to wet sites near streams, swamps and lakes.

ORIGIN: Native.

RED MAPLE is one of the first trees to flower each spring. It grows quickly and usually lives 100–150 years. • Red maple's straight-grained, uniform wood (called "soft maple") has been used for pulp and for making crates, furniture, cabinets, veneer and flooring. • Pennsylvanian colonists made a dark red ink by boiling the bark, which also yields brown or black dyes with different mordants. • This attractive, red-tinged tree is widely planted as an ornamental. Several cultivars have been developed that endure urban conditions. • Although red maple sap is only half as sweet as that of sugar maple (p. 224), it can be used to make syrup. • This widespread, variable species is very similar to silver maple (p. 227), especially when leafless, and the 2 species often cross-pollinate to produce a hybrid known as **Freeman's maple (*A.* x *freemanii*)**. The leaves of Freeman's maple turn blotchy red and yellow in autumn, and their notches are narrower than those of red maple but wider than those of silver maple. The samaras of Freeman's maple are similarly intermediate (1–1½" long). This widespread hybrid is found only occasionally in Michigan. Reports of silver maple from north of its usual range are often Freeman's maple.

Photo, bottom left: *A. x freemanii*

ALSO CALLED: Scarlet maple, soft maple, swamp maple, curled maple.

SIZE AND SHAPE: Trees 50–80' [179'] tall; crowns dense, long, rounded; roots shallow, wide-spreading.

TRUNKS: Short in open sites, often lower half branch-free in forests, 16–32" [71"] in diameter; young bark light gray, smooth; mature bark dark grayish-brown, scaly, with thin plates that peel from both ends; wood pale brown, heavy, hard, not strong.

BRANCHES: Ascending; twigs shiny, reddish, hairless, not unpleasant-smelling; buds shiny, reddish, hairless, usually with 8 paired scales, blunt, about ⅛" long at twig tips, smaller and paired below; **flower buds usually ring dwarf twigs**.

LEAVES: Opposite, simple, deciduous; blades light green, whitish beneath, 2–6" long, with **3–5 palmate lobes separated by shallow, sharp notches, irregularly double-toothed;** stalks 2–4" long; leaves bright red, orange or yellow in autumn.

FLOWERS: Red to orange, short-stalked, about ⅛" across; unisexual, usually with male and female flowers on separate branches on the same tree; petals 5; sepals 5; **flowers in small, tassel-like clusters** (umbels), in March–April **(long before leaves expand)**.

FRUITS: Red, reddish-brown or yellow **pairs of winged samaras with wings spreading at 50–60°, slender-stalked;** samaras ½–1⅛" long; **samaras hang in clusters,** mature and drop singly in late May–early June (4–6 weeks after flowering).

HABITAT: Cool, moist sites in low-lying forest swamps; sometimes on moderately dry upland sites.

ORIGIN: Native.

MOUNTAIN MAPLE is our smallest native maple, typically shrubby rather than tree-like. Although it has no commercial value, it is sometimes cultivated for its colorful leaves and fruits. • Mountain maple is very important for preventing erosion on streambanks and steep slopes. When spreading branches become buried in leaf litter, they put down roots and send up new shoots. This process (layering) can produce impenetrable thickets on recently cleared land. • Some tribes boiled the young twigs with a pinch of alum and used the solution to soothe eyes irritated by smoke. • Moose and deer eagerly seek new mountain maple growth. • Without flowers or fruits, this species might be confused with some of the viburnums. Mapleleaf viburnum (p. 246) is a similar shrub distinguished by its downy twigs and resin-dotted lower leaf surfaces. American highbush-cranberry (p. 246) has small, club-shaped glands on its leaf stalks near the blade. These viburnums have relatively short-stalked leaves (often with slender stipules) with more sparingly toothed blades than mountain maple. • Leafless maples could be confused with dogwoods, but the fruits (samaras) and finely hairy twigs identify them as maples.

ALSO CALLED: Dwarf maple, moose maple, low-moose maple, whitewood, whiterod, white maple.

SIZE AND SHAPE: Small, bushy trees or **tall shrubs 15–30'** [58'] **tall;** crowns uneven, rounded; roots very shallow.

TRUNKS: Crooked, often clumped, short, 2³/₄–4" [11"] in diameter; bark greenish-gray to reddish, thin, smooth or finely grooved; wood pale, soft, weak, fine-grained.

BRANCHES: Slender, ascending, few; **twigs velvety,** minutely gray-hairy, **yellowish-green to purplish-gray or pink;** pith brown; **buds red, gray-hairy, 2-scaled, stalked,** single at twig tips, paired below.

LEAVES: Opposite, simple, deciduous; blades deep yellowish-green, whitish-hairy beneath, 2–5" long, **irregularly saw-toothed,** with **3 prominent lobes above midleaf** and sometimes 2 small lower lobes; lobes separated by **wide, wedge-shaped notches;** stalks usually longer than blades, reddish; leaves red to yellow or brown in autumn.

FLOWERS: Pale yellowish-green, ¹/₄" across; bisexual, male or female, with all 3 flower types often present on the same tree; petals 5; sepals 5; flowers in groups of 2–4 along a central stalk, forming **erect, branched clusters** (panicles) 2³/₈–4" **long,** in late May–June (after leaves expand).

FRUITS: Scarlet to yellow or pinkish-brown pairs of samaras with **wings diverging at 90° or less;** samaras about ³/₄" long; **seedcases indented on 1 side; samaras hang in slender clusters,** mature in July–August, often persist into winter.

HABITAT: Cool, moist mixed woods, thickets, swamps and rocky ravines.

ORIGIN: Native.

THIS SHADE-TOLERANT TREE lives about 100 years. It is planted as an ornamental in North America and Europe for its beautiful leaves (the largest of our maples) and attractive winter bark. • Sometimes a tree will produce only male flowers one year and only female flowers the next. • Striped maple's soft, weak wood has no commercial value, but it is sometimes used as firewood. • Beavers and hares eat the bark of this tree, and the samaras provide food for songbirds, grouse and small mammals (mainly rodents). This shrub is a favorite food of deer and moose, hence another common name, "moosewood." In fact, the word "moose" originated from the Algonquian word *mousou*, or "twig-eater." • In winter, shrubby striped maples could be confused with American bladdernut (p. 220). Bladdernut also has striped bark and opposite branching, but its leaves are compound (trifoliate) and its fruits are 3-lobed, inflated capsules. Viburnums with opposite, 3-lobed leaves, such as American highbush-cranberry (p. 246) and mapleleaf viburnum (p. 246), may also resemble striped maple, but viburnum bark is not striped and the fruits are berry-like drupes.

ALSO CALLED: Moosewood, moose maple, whistlewood, goosefoot maple.

SIZE AND SHAPE: Trees or shrubs 13–35' [59'] tall; crowns uneven, rounded; roots spreading, shallow.

TRUNKS: Short, 4–8" [14"] in diameter; **young bark green with conspicuous whitish vertical stripes;** mature bark greenish-brown with darkened stripes; wood pale pinkish brown, light, fine-grained.

BRANCHES: Ascending, arching; twigs shiny, reddish-brown, hairless, rather stout; **buds red,**

hairless, 2-scaled, stalked, about ³/₈" long at twig tips, smaller, flat-lying and paired below.

LEAVES: Opposite, simple, deciduous; blades yellowish-green, hairless, **4–7" long, tipped with 3 palmate, shallow, slender-pointed lobes** (sometimes unlobed with rapid growth), **finely double-toothed;** stalks 1–3" long, grooved; leaves clear yellow in autumn.

FLOWERS: Bright greenish-yellow, bell-shaped, ¹/₄" across; unisexual (rarely bisexual) with male and female flowers in separate clusters on the same or separate trees; petals 5; sepals 5; flowers on slender stalks along a central axis, **in hanging clusters (racemes) 2–6" long,** in late May–June (after leaves expand).

FRUITS: Greenish **pairs of winged samaras with wings spreading widely at 90–120°;** samaras ³/₄–1¹/₈" long; **seedcases indented on 1 side; samaras hang on short stalks in elongated clusters** at branch tips, mature in late July–August, drop in autumn.

HABITAT: Cool, moist, deciduous woodlands; sometimes in drier pine-oak forests or in cedar swamps.

ORIGIN: Native.

THIS POPULAR ornamental tree is widely planted for its fragrant flowers, showy reddish samaras and spectacular autumn foliage. Amur maple is one of the few maples with perfumed flowers and one of the best trees for fall color. It makes a good patio shade tree and can be planted in groups to form borders, hedges, screens and backgrounds. Tree form, leaf characteristics and fruit color are all highly variable, so selection of desirable cultivars would seem appropriate, but few have been developed. • Amur maple is adapted to northern areas with relatively cool summers, and it tolerates dry conditions and partial shade. It even thrives in tubs along the streets of some cities. This hardy tree requires little maintenance, though occasionally weedy seedlings can be a problem. • Although Amur maple is usually shrubby, it can withstand heavy pruning and is often shaped into a tree form. Maples should not be pruned until the leaves are fully expanded, because the heavy flow of spring sap causes excessive "bleeding" if trees are pruned too early. • The species name *ginnala* is derived from the vernacular name for this species in its native range in eastern Asia.

SIZE AND SHAPE: Small trees or **tall shrubs 13–20'** [30'] **tall;** crowns rounded, shrubby and uneven when young; roots shallow.

TRUNKS: Usually clumped, sometimes pruned to a single stem, up to 23" in diameter; bark dark gray, scaly, fissured; wood pale, light, soft, weak.

BRANCHES: Slender, often wand-like and arching; twigs slender, yellowish-brown, hairless, somewhat angled; buds reddish-brown to tan, with hairy-tipped scales.

LEAVES: Opposite, simple, deciduous; blades glossy, deep green, paler beneath, essentially **hairless with age,** 1¹/₈–4" long, narrowly triangular, 3-lobed (rarely undivided or 5-lobed) with **2 short basal lobes and a large central lobe, notches wedge-shaped, with irregularly double sharp-toothed edges;** stalks slender, 1¹/₈–1¹/₂" long; leaves brilliant red (sometimes yellow or orange) in autumn.

FLOWERS: Pale yellow to creamy white, fragrant, about ¹/₄" long; petals 5, inconspicuous;

sepals 5; **flowers in drooping clusters** (corymbs) at branch tips, in May–June (as leaves expand).

FRUITS: Scarlet or pinkish-brown pairs of dry **samaras** with **inner edges of wings almost parallel;** samaras ³/₄–1" long, hairless; **samaras in hanging clusters,** mature in July–August, often persist into winter.

HABITAT: Yards, ditches, fence lines and other open, disturbed sites.

ORIGIN: Introduced from Manchuria and Japan.

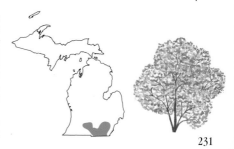

231

THIS HARDY, fast-growing tree can survive dry and extremely cold conditions, so it is widely planted as a shade and shelterbelt tree. Unfortunately, its weak, spreading branches are easily broken by wet snow, ice and wind. Ashleaf maple is shade-intolerant, growing rapidly for the first 15–20 years and living 60–75 years.
• Ashleaf maple trunks are usually too small and irregular to provide lumber, but the close-grained wood has been used occasionally for crates, boxes, paper pulp and firewood. • When sugar was scarce, settlers sometimes tapped this tree to make maple syrup, but ashleaf maple is the least productive maple for this purpose.
• The abundant seeds of female trees can be a nuisance in gardens, but they do provide important winter food for mice, squirrels and seed-eating birds such as evening grosbeaks. • The boxelder bug (*Boisea trivittata*) is a widespread pest that can occur in large numbers in urban areas where ashleaf maple is common.

• This maple could be mistaken for an ash (*Fraxinus* spp., pp. 236–240), but ash trees usually have more numerous (5–9), smooth-edged or regularly toothed leaflets. Also, ash leaf scar ends are well separated (not meeting), ash samaras are single with symmetrical wings and ash seedcases are smooth.

ALSO CALLED: Boxelder, western box-elder, Manitoba maple.

SIZE AND SHAPE: Trees 35–65' [110'] tall; crowns broad, uneven, open; roots widely spreading, mostly shallow.

TRUNKS: Usually short, 12–32" [67"] in diameter; young bark light grayish-brown, smooth; mature bark darker grayish-brown, with narrow, interlacing ridges; wood nearly white, soft, weak.

BRANCHES: Spreading, crooked; **twigs shiny or waxy-powdered,** brown to greenish-purple, smooth; buds dull red, finely white-hairy, blunt,

with 2–6 paired scales, about ¼" long at twig tips, flat-lying or hidden by leaf-stalk bases below.

LEAVES: Opposite, deciduous; compound, **pinnately divided into 3–5 leaflets** (sometimes 7–9 with rapid growth); leaflets yellowish-green above, grayish-green beneath, **2–4³/₄" long, irregularly coarse-toothed or shallow-lobed; leaf scars meeting around twigs;** leaves yellow in autumn.

FLOWERS: Pale yellowish-green, tiny; unisexual with **male and female flowers on separate trees; petals absent;** sepals 5; male flowers hang on hairy, thread-like stalks in loose bundles (umbels); female flowers short-stalked along a central axis in nodding clusters (racemes); flowers in April–May (as or before leaves expand).

FRUITS: Green to pale brown **pairs of winged samaras** with **wings usually spreading at <45°;** samaras 1⅛–2" long; seedcases wrinkled, elongated, pointed; **samaras hang in elongated clusters,** mature in autumn, may persist through winter.

HABITAT: Low, moist sites, often in disturbed areas, usually near water or on floodplains.

ORIGIN: Native.

Key to Genera in the Olive Family (Oleaceae)

1a Leaves pinnately divided into leaflets; fruits slender, long-winged samaras
....*Fraxinus*, **ash** (key to species, see below)

1b Leaves simple; fruits not samaras **2**

2a Leaves tapered to a wedge-shaped base and short (<³/₈") stalk; flowers white,
¹/₈–¹/₄" across, in 1–3¹/₂" long clusters; fruits berry-like drupes
....*Ligustrum*, **privet** (key to species, see below)

2b Leaves squared to notched at the base, with ³/₄–1¹/₈" long stalks; flowers deep purple to
(occasionally) white, about ³/₈" across, in 4–8" long clusters; fruits woody capsules
.... *Syringa*, **lilac** (p. 234)

Key to the Ashes (Genus *Fraxinus*)

1a Leaflets smooth-edged (sometimes with a few faint, irregular, blunt teeth); samaras with
cylindrical seedcases winged on the upper part only (not to the base) **2**

1b Leaflets regularly (sometimes faintly) toothed above midleaf; samaras various **3**

2a Wings extending about ¹/₃ of the way down the seedcases; leaflets 2³/₈–6" long, lower leaf
surfaces pale green, essentially hairless, dulled by many minute bumps
.... *F. americana*, **white ash** (p. 236)

2b Wings extending over halfway down the seedcases; leaflets 5–10" long,
lower leaf surfaces pale yellowish-green, soft-hairy, lacking minute bumps
.... *F. profunda*, **pumpkin ash** (p. 238)

3a Leaves divided into 5–9 leaflets, distinctly paler beneath; seedcases cylindrical,
winged on upper part only (not to the base), tapered to the base; calyx visible at the base of each
samara; uppermost side-buds close against branch-tip bud
.... *F. pennsylvanica*, **green ash** (p. 237)

3b Leaves divided into 7–13 leaflets, green above and below; seedcases flattened, winged to the blunt
base; calyx minute, not visible on each samara; uppermost side-buds clearly separated from
branch-tip bud...**4**

4a Twigs 4-sided, with 4 corky ridges; bark soft and velvety; leaflets stalked
.... *F. quadrangulata*, **blue ash** (p. 240)

4b Twigs round; bark firm and hard; leaflets stalkless.................... *F. nigra*, **black ash** (p. 239)

Key to the Privets (Genus *Ligustrum*)

1a Flowers about ¹/₈" long, basal tube equal to or shorter than lobes; leaves hairless; flower stalks and twigs
with tiny (about ¹/₁₆" long) hairs.....................................*L. vulgare*, **European privet** (p. 235)

1b Flowers about ¹/₄" long, basal tube at least twice as long as lobes; leaves with or without hairs;
flower stalks and twigs hairless or with longer (>¹/₁₆") hairs...**2**

2a Twigs, flower stalks, sepals and leaf midribs (beneath) hairy; filaments longer than flower tube;
leaves shed promptly in autumn ....*L. obtusifolium*, **border privet** (p. 235)

2b Twigs, flower stalks, sepals and leaf midribs essentially hairless; filaments shorter than flower
tube; leaves remain on trees well into winter
....*L. ovalifolium*, **California privet** (p. 235)

THIS TOUGH IMMIGRANT is one of the most commonly planted flowering shrubs in North America. Hundreds of cultivars have been developed. • Lilacs bloom for about 2 weeks in spring, but hot weather shortens the flowering period, and hot sun may fade the flowers. • The fragrance of lilac bouquets can fill a room. To make bouquets last longer, cut flowers just as they are starting to open and bash the woody stem ends with a hammer or immerse them in boiling water for a few seconds. Most such bouquets will last 7–10 days. • Lilac flowers can be eaten raw in fruit salads, crystallized with a coating of beaten egg whites and sugar or added to batter for fritters. • North America's oldest lilacs, found in New Hampshire and Michigan, are close to 300 years old. Their trunks are more than 20" in diameter and have an unusual, pronounced twist. • Another garden escape, **Japanese-tree lilac (*S. reticulata*)**, often reaches 15–25' in height. It is identified by the many raised horizontal pores (lenticels) on its twigs, the network of raised veins on the lower side of its leaves and its showy white flower clusters.

SIZE AND SHAPE: Shrubby trees or tall shrubs 10–25' [29'] tall; crowns rounded; roots spreading, often sending up suckers and forming thickets.

TRUNKS: Usually clumped, small [13"]; bark grayish, thin, flaky with age.

BRANCHES: Numerous; **paired twigs** olive green with **prominent pores** (lenticels), round, 1/4" or more thick, stiff, soon hairless; buds green or brown, hairless, broadly egg-shaped, with 3–5 pairs of fleshy scales, usually paired at twig tips.

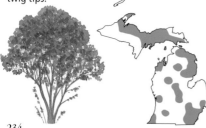

LEAVES: Opposite, simple, deciduous; blades dull dark green, paler beneath, **ovate to heart-shaped, 2–5" long,** pointed, smooth-edged, with squared or notched bases; stalks slender, 3/4–1 1/8" long; leaf scars with 1 horizontal vein scar; leaves yellow to brownish in autumn.

FLOWERS: Purple, pink or white, fragrant, about 3/8" across, bisexual; petals 4, widely spreading, bases fused in a 3/8" long tube; sepals 4, fused at the base, glandular-hairy; stamens 2; flowers in dense, conical, usually paired clusters (panicles) 4–8" long, at the tips of previous year's branches, in May (as leaves expand).

FRUITS: Green to brown, **leathery to woody,** hairless, flattened, **pointed capsules,** 3/8–1/2" long; seeds 4 per capsule; capsules mature in August, persist through winter.

HABITAT: Roadsides, waste places, abandoned farmsteads, old fields and shores.

ORIGIN: Introduced from southeastern Europe.

MANY CULTIVARS of this popular hedge plant have been developed, some with golden or variegated leaves. With their numerous, resilient twigs, these bushy shrubs take pruning and shaping well. Mazes of tangled, intertwining, leafy branches shoot out in all directions, hence the expression "mad as a privet hedge." • **Caution:** Children have been poisoned by eating the fruits, but no deaths have been documented. • The leaves and bark were boiled to make astringent, bitter, medicinal teas for treating stomach ulcers and diarrhea, and for stimulating appetite and improving digestion. • Two other privets, introduced from Japan, occasionally grow wild in disturbed sites in the state. **Border privet (*L. obtusifolium*),** shown in pink/dark green on map, has hairy twigs and its anthers are largely hidden within the flower and therefore much less conspicuous. It has larger flowers (about $1/4$" long) with large ($1/8$" long) anthers and petal lobes that are only about half as long as the flower tube (petals fused for $2/3$ their length). **California privet (*L. ovalifolium*),** shown in dark pink on the map, is distinguished by its hairless twigs and showy stamens, with anthers that project beyond the flower tip.

ALSO CALLED: Common privet, primwort, print, skedge, skedgewith.

SIZE AND SHAPE: Tall shrubs or small trees, 6–15' tall; crowns broad, rounded.

TRUNKS: Short, clumped; young bark thin, gray.

BRANCHES: Numerous, paired; twigs slender, greenish, **with tiny** (<$1/32$" long), **soft, curled hairs,** light brown to gray with age, sometimes becoming hairless; pith white; buds small, egg-shaped, with overlapping scales.

LEAVES: Opposite, simple, variably evergreen; blades dark green above, paler underneath, firm, moderately thick, **hairless,** elliptic to lance-shaped or ovate, $1^1/8$–$2^3/8$" long, **smooth-edged,** obscurely veined; stalks $1/8$–$3/8$" long; leaf scars elliptical; leaves long-lived, eventually shed before spring.

FLOWERS: White, showy, with a heavy fragrance, broadly funnel-shaped, $1/8$–$1/4$" across, **bisexual; petals 4,** about $1/8$" long, **fused for $1/2$ their length or less,** spreading at the tips; sepals 4, small, fused into unlobed cups; **stamens 2,** attached to the petals, **tipped with** $1/16$" **long anthers, shorter than the petals;** flowers **in dense,** $1^1/8$–$2^3/8$" **long, minutely hairy, branched clusters** (panicles) at branch tips, in June–July.

FRUITS: Lustrous, black, berry-like drupes, about $1/4$" across, **firm;** seeds 1–4 per fruit, each in a hard stone; drupes mature in August–September, often persist on shrubs until spring.

HABITAT: Dry to damp, often disturbed sites, in thickets and woodlands and on roadsides.

ORIGIN: Introduced from southern Europe and northern Africa.

WHITE ASH is the main source of commercial ash, a tough, shock-resistant wood highly valued for hockey sticks, baseball bats and tennis rackets. It is also used for tool handles, boats, barrels, casks, ladders and furniture veneer. In earlier days, plowing implements and airplane and automobile frames were made of ash wood. White ash also makes excellent fuel, comparable to oak and hickory. • This tree's slender, graceful shape, colorful autumn leaves and neatly patterned bark make white ash an attractive ornamental. • Some tribes used the bark to produce a yellow dye.

• Ash leaf juice has been recommended for soothing mosquito bites and bee stings. • In some parts of North America, white ash populations have undergone a progressive dieback called "ash yellows," probably triggered by climate-induced stresses that left trees more susceptible to insects or disease. • The emerald ash borer (*Agrilus planipennis*) was introduced in 2002 and already threatens to decimate North American ash trees. It has killed 10–15 million trees in Michigan, Ohio, Indiana and Ontario, and threatens to spread across the continent.

ALSO CALLED: American ash, Canadian white ash, Biltmore ash.

SIZE AND SHAPE: Trees 35–80' [118'] tall; crowns pyramidal; roots usually moderately deep.

TRUNKS: Straight, long, 20–40" [73'] in diameter; **mature bark grayish, with narrow intersecting ridges in regular diamond patterns;** wood light brown, straight-grained, heavy, hard.

BRANCHES: Long, stout, ascending to spreading; **twigs hairless,** shiny, stout, developing a waxy, grayish skin; **leaf scars large with a U-shaped top;** buds reddish-brown with a soft, granular surface, 2–6-scaled; **tip buds reddish-brown, broadly pyramidal,** 1/4–1/2" long, flanked by a **smaller bud on each side.**

LEAVES: Opposite, deciduous, 8–16" long; compound, **pinnately divided into 5–9 (usually 7) similar leaflets;** leaflets dark green above, **dull, whitish beneath, with tiny bumps** (papillae), essentially hairless, ovate to oblong, 2 3/8–6" long, on 1/4–1/2" long stalks, abruptly sharp-pointed, **smooth-edged or with a few rounded teeth;** leaf scars raised, U-shaped; **leaves yellow or bronze-purple in autumn,** leaflets shed singly.

FLOWERS: Purplish to yellowish, tiny; unisexual with male and female flowers on separate trees; petals absent; sepals minute; flowers in compact clusters along twigs, in May (before leaves expand).

FRUITS: Pale green to yellowish, **slender, winged nutlets** (samaras), 1–2" long, with a **long wing enclosing the upper** 1/3 **of each cylindrical seedcase;** seeds single; **samaras hang in long clusters,** mature in August–September, persist into winter.

HABITAT: Upland sites with well-drained soils, in beech-maple or oak-hickory stands.

ORIGIN: Native.

THE TOUGH WOOD of green ash is not as strong as that of white ash, but it is marketed under the same name and has been used for canoe paddles, baseball bats, tennis rackets, snowshoe frames, tool handles and picture frames. • Green ash bark produces a red dye, and the wood ashes provided potash. • A fast-growing, hardy tree, green ash is often planted as an ornamental (especially in the West), but it can become invasive in urban landscapes. • The abundant seeds provide important autumn and winter food for quail, wild turkeys, cardinals and finches, as well as for squirrels and other rodents. • *F. pennsylvanica* is a widely distributed and variable species. Often it is divided into two groups: the typical *F. pennsylvanica* with hairy leaflets, twigs and flower and fruit stalks, is called **red ash**, and the essentially hairless variety *subintegerrima* is called **green ash**. Red ash is most common in the East and green ash is the most common ash on and around the Plains, but both are the same species. • It is fairly easy to identify a tree as an ash, but much more difficult to determine which species. Ashes with hairy twigs include red ash, blue ash and pumpkin ash, whereas green ash, white ash, and black ash have hairless twigs.

ALSO CALLED: Red ash, rim ash, soft ash, swamp ash, water ash.

SIZE AND SHAPE: Shrubby to medium trees 35–50' [131'] tall, variable; crowns irregular, rounded; roots shallow.

TRUNKS: Usually straight, 12–24" [77"] in diameter; bark grayish-brown, often reddish-tinged, flaky, with **irregular, shallow ridges in diamond-shaped patterns;** wood light grayish-brown, straight-grained, heavy, brittle.

BRANCHES: Stout, ascending to spreading; **twigs stout, sometimes hairy; leaf scars large, with a straight top edge;** buds reddish-brown, hairy, 4–6-scaled, pyramidal, $1/8$–$3/8$" **long, slightly longer than wide at branch tips, with a smaller bud on each side.**

LEAVES: Opposite, deciduous, 10–12" long; compound, **pinnately divided into 5–9 (usually 7) leaflets;** leaflets yellowish-green above, paler beneath, oval, 3–6" long, taper-pointed, **shallow-toothed above the middle, borne on short, narrowly winged stalks;** leaf scars semicircular; leaves yellowish-brown in autumn, leaflets shed singly.

FLOWERS: Purplish to yellowish, tiny; unisexual with male and female flowers on separate trees; petals absent; sepals minute; flowers in **many-flowered, compact clusters along twigs,** in May (before or as leaves expand).

FRUITS: Pale green to yellowish, **slender, winged nutlets** (samaras), $1 1/8$–$2 3/8$" long, **with a long wing enclosing the upper $1/2$ or more of each cylindrical seedcase;** wings often with notched tips; **seeds single; samaras hang in long clusters,** mature in September, persist into winter.

HABITAT: Moist to wet soils on open floodplains and swamps, with other hardwoods.

ORIGIN: Native.

237

PUMPKIN ASH is native to the eastern U.S. but was not discovered in Michigan until 1992. • The wood of all ash species except black ash (p. 239) is sold as "white ash." Pumpkin ash has no commercial value because of its scarcity. Although the wood is inferior to that of white ash (p. 236), it has been used for crates, railroad ties, veneer, pulp and fuel. • Ash samaras are dispersed by wind and water. The seeds require exposure to cool, moist conditions for several months before they germinate. • Many small birds and mammals eat the seeds, and white-tailed deer browse on the twigs and leaves. Pumpkin ash snags provide nest sites and dens for cavity-dwelling birds and small mammals. • Gall gnats sometimes cause the male flowers of ash trees to develop abnormally into galls, which stay on the trees for several months. • The specific epithet *profunda* means "deep" or "profound" and refers to the swampy habitat of this species. • The leaves and fruits of pumpkin ash are distinctly larger than those of our other ashes. The leaves can grow to 18" long, with leaflets up to 10" long. The samaras average 2$\frac{1}{8}$" in length and $\frac{3}{8}$" in width.

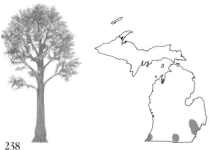

ALSO CALLED: *F. tomentosa*.

SIZE AND SHAPE: Trees up to 100' tall; crowns narrow, oval; roots spreading, shallow.

TRUNKS: Straight, single, usually **buttressed;** mature bark grayish, **with thin, intersecting ridges in regular diamond patterns;** wood grayish-brown, straight-grained, hard.

BRANCHES: Straight; **twigs downy,** grayish-brown, stout; **buds broadly pyramidal at branch tips;** bud scales paired, soft, **granular-textured**.

LEAVES: Opposite, deciduous, **8–18" long;** compound, **pinnately divided into 5–9 (usually 7) similar leaflets; central stalks woolly;** leaflets dark green above, **paler yellowish-green and soft-hairy beneath, 5–10" long,** lance-shaped to elliptic, taper-pointed, often unequal at the base, smooth-edged (or nearly so), **on wingless stalks** $\frac{3}{8}$–$\frac{1}{2}$" **long;** leaf scars broadly U-shaped.

FLOWERS: Tiny; unisexual with male and female flowers on **separate trees;** petals absent; sepals $\frac{1}{16}$–$\frac{1}{8}$" long; flowers in compact, many-flowered clusters, in early spring (before leaves expand).

FRUITS: Pale green to yellowish, **winged nutlets (samaras),** single, slender, often widest above the middle, **1$\frac{1}{2}$–3" long, with tiny sepal remnants at the base** and **a wing extending more than halfway down each thick, cylindrical seedcase;** wings round or notched at the tip; seeds single; **samaras hang in long clusters,** mature in autumn, persist into winter.

HABITAT: Deciduous swamp forests.

ORIGIN: Native.

BLACK ASH wood is much softer and heavier than that of white ash, but it has been used for interior trim, furniture, cabinets and veneer. The wood is also very flexible and can be permanently bent, so it was favored for snowshoe frames and canoe ribs. When soaked and pounded, the logs separate readily along their annual rings into thin sheets. Long strips from these sheets were used for making barrel hoops and for weaving baskets and chair seats. • This shade-intolerant tree can tolerate standing water for many weeks. Usually it grows in mixed stands with other moisture-loving trees such as black spruce, eastern white-cedar and silver maple. Pure stands are susceptible to attacks by emerald ash borer (*Agrilus planipennis*). • Black ash produces good seed crops at intervals of up to 7 years. Fallen seeds lie dormant for a season before germinating. • Hanging on branches through winter or buried under snow, the seeds provide important food for wild turkeys, grouse and small mammals. • This tree is easily recognized in winter by its soft, pale gray bark and blue-black buds. In most ashes, the tip bud is at least as wide as long, but in this species it is slightly longer than wide.

ALSO CALLED: Swamp ash, hoop ash, basket ash, brown ash, water ash.

SIZE AND SHAPE: Trees 35–65' [155'] tall; crowns narrow, open; roots very shallow, spreading.

TRUNKS: Slender, often bent, 12–24" [43"] in diameter; **young bark light gray, soft, corky-ridged, easily rubbed off by hand;** mature bark scaly; wood grayish-brown, coarsely straight-grained, heavy, tough.

BRANCHES: Coarse, ascending; **twigs stout, soon dull gray, hairless; leaf scars large, slightly notched at the top; buds blackish-brown, pointed,** 6-scaled; **tip bud pyramidal,** $^1/_4$–$^3/_8$" **long,** typically $^1/_8$–$^3/_8$" **above 2 smaller side-buds.**

LEAVES: Opposite, deciduous, **10–16" long;** compound, pinnately divided into 7–11 similar leaflets; leaflets dark green, **hairless except for reddish-brown fuzz at the base,** elongated-ovate, $2^3/_4$–$5^1/_2$" long, slender-pointed, **finely sharp-toothed, stalkless;** leaf scars large, rounded; leaves reddish-brown in autumn, drop as whole leaves.

FLOWERS: Purplish, tiny; mostly bisexual, sometimes unisexual, with 1, 2 or 3 flower types on a single tree; petals absent; sepals minute; stamens 2; flowers on hairless stalks in compact, branched clusters (panicles) along twigs and at branch tips, in May (before leaves expand).

FRUITS: Pale green to yellowish, **winged, slender nutlets** (samaras) 1–1$^3/_4$" long, with **broad, often twisted wings encircling flattened seedcases;** wings with round or notched tips; seeds single; **samaras hang in long clusters,** mature in August–September, sometimes persist through winter.

HABITAT: Open, cool, wet sites in **swampy woodlands** and along shores.

ORIGIN: Native.

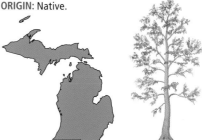

THIS UNUSUAL ASH reaches the northern limit of its range in Michigan and is rare in neighboring Wisconsin. • Blue ash is sometimes planted as an ornamental shade tree. It grows quickly and can live 125–150 years. • Although blue ash is now of little commercial value because of its scarcity, its wood, sold as "white ash," has been used in sporting goods, agricultural tools, furniture, flooring and interior trim. Blue ash wood is durable, though somewhat brittle, and it has distinctive rings of large pores, which are laid down each spring. • The species name *quadrangulata* means "4-angled" and refers to the 4 corky ridges on the twigs. This characteristic distinguishes blue ash from all other ashes. Another unique feature is the sticky sap from the inner bark, which turns blue when exposed to air, hence the common name. To produce a blue dye, the bark is chopped into pieces and steeped in boiling water. The mixture is then boiled down to concentrate the color. • The unusual scaly bark of blue ash is also distinctive. On older trees, the loose, hanging plates bring to mind the bark of shagbark hickory (p. 99).

SIZE AND SHAPE: Trees 35–65' [90'] tall; crowns narrow, rounded, often irregular.

TRUNKS: Straight, slender, 6–20" [33"] in diameter; mature bark grayish, shaggy with loose, scaly plates; **inner bark blue when exposed to air;** wood yellowish-brown, coarse-grained, hard, heavy.

BRANCHES: Spreading, short, stout; **twigs conspicuously 4-sided, with 4 corky ridges,** rusty-hairy; buds dark brown, hairy, 6-scaled, about ¹/₄" long; branch **tip bud slightly flattened,** with a **smaller bud on each side.**

LEAVES: Opposite, deciduous, **8–16" long;** compound, **pinnately divided into 5–11 similar leaflets;** leaflets dark yellowish-green, paler beneath, hairy in main vein axils or hairless, lance-shaped, 3–5¹/₂" long, taper-pointed, with asymmetrical bases, slender-stalked, coarsely toothed; leaf scars oval to crescent-shaped, with an upcurved line of bundle scars.

FLOWERS: Purplish, tiny, **bisexual;** petals absent; sepals minute, soon shed; flowers on hairless stalks, in compact, many-flowered, branched clusters (panicles) in April (before leaves expand).

FRUITS: Green to yellowish, **winged nutlets (samaras),** with a **broad, often twisted wing enclosing each flattened seedcase,** oblong-lance-shaped, 1–2" long; wings with rounded or (usually) notched tips; **bases lack sepal remnants;** seeds single; **samaras hang in loose clusters,** mature in September–October.

HABITAT: Low-lying, moist sites on floodplains and sandy beaches; occasionally on drier sites in limestone areas.

ORIGIN: Native.

Key to Genera in the Honeysuckle Family (Caprifoliaceae)

1a Leaves pinnately divided into 5–7 leaflets .... *Sambucus*, **elder** (p. 242)

1b Leaves with a single blade (simple) **2**

2a Leaves lance-shaped to egg-shaped, gradually tapered to a long, slender point
....*Lonicera*, **honeysuckle** (p. 243)

2b Leaves ovate to almost round, sometimes maple leaf–like, with 3 palmate lobes,
abruptly sharp-pointed or blunt .... *Viburnum*, **viburnum** (key to species, see below)

Key to the Viburnums (Genus *Viburnum*)

1a Leaves maple leaf–like, with 3 palmate lobes and palmate veins, smooth-edged or coarsely
toothed; outer flowers sterile, very showy, with greatly enlarged petals.. **2**

1b Leaves ovate, not lobed, regularly saw-toothed; outer flowers similar to inner flowers............... **4**

2a Flower clusters of outer and inner flowers all similar; lower leaf surfaces downy and resin-dotted;
fruits blue; shrubs rarely over 6' tall......... *V. acerifolium*, **mapleleaf viburnum** (p. 246)

2b Flower clusters with showy, enlarged outer flowers and much smaller inner flowers; lower leaf
surfaces thinly hairy, without resin dots; fruits red to orange; tall shrubs or small trees up to
15' tall **3**

3a Glands on leaf stalks mostly higher than wide, stalked, with rounded tops
.... *V. trilobum*, **American highbush-cranberry** (p. 246)

3b Glands on leaf stalks wider than high, sessile (not stalked), with concave tops
.... *V. opulus* var. *opulus*, **European highbush-cranberry** (p. 246)

4a Flower and fruit clusters with branches arising from the tip of a slender, 1/4–2" long stalk; leaf
stalks not grooved and winged; plants usually small (less than 13' tall) and shrubby................... **5**

4b Flower and fruit clusters stalkless or with short (<1/4") stalks, with branches arising directly
from the leaf axils.. **6**

5a Lower leaf surfaces with tiny star-shaped hairs (at least when young); winter buds naked;
stones 3-grooved .... *V. lantana*, **wayfaring-tree** (p. 245)

5b Lower leaf surfaces lacking tiny star-shaped hairs, sometimes with minute red-brown scales;
winter buds with 2 outer scales; stones not grooved .... *V. nudum*, **witherod** (p. 244)

6a Leaf tips abruptly narrowed to a tapered point; leaf stalks with wavy, often down-rolled wings
....*V. lentago*, **nannyberry** (p. 244)

6b Leaf tips blunt or slightly pointed; leaf stalks with or without wings
....*V. prunifolium*, **smooth blackhaw** (p. 244)

THE JUICY FRUITS of common elderberry have been be used to make jelly, jam, preserves and wines. The flowers can add fragrance and flavor to candy, jelly and vinegar. • **Caution:** The leaves, bark and roots of elders contain cyanide. Raw berries may cause vomiting, though cooking destroys the toxins. • Historically, the bark and leaves were used to "cleanse the system." Bark peeled downward was believed to stimulate bowel movements, whereas bark peeled upward would cause vomiting. No matter how you peel it, the bark usually acts both ways at once. • Flower clusters have been used to make healing salves, and hot flower tea is taken to stimulate sweating and relieve rheumatism and the symptoms of flu and colds. • In Europe, black elderberry (*S. nigra* ssp. *nigra*) has been shown to stimulate the immune system and prevent viruses from invading respiratory tract cells. An Israeli study of the drug Sambucol found that 20% of flu sufferers felt better within 24 hours, 73% improved in 2 days and 90% felt cured in 3 days. Sambucol has been found to inhibit many viruses, including herpes and even HIV. • **Red-berried elderberry** (*S. racemosa*, also called *S. pubens*), another widespread species, is found throughout the state. It is distinguished by its fewer (5–7, usually 5) leaflets and by the dark brown (not white) pith of its twigs. Its more elongated flower clusters develop in May–June (with the leaves) and the bright red, inedible fruits mature in early summer.

ALSO CALLED: American elder, white elder • *S. canadensis*.

SIZE AND SHAPE: Shrubs or small trees up to 13' [26'] tall, foul-smelling when bruised; crowns irregular; roots shallow, suckering to form thickets.

TRUNKS: Short, up to 2" [4"] in diameter; bark thin, gray to yellowish-brown, with raised pores (lenticels), furrowed with age.

BRANCHES: Opposite, few; twigs stout, essentially **hairless,** soft, **scarcely woody,** with widely spaced swollen joints; **pith large, white** (sometimes brown at edges); buds egg-shaped, 1/16–1/8" long, with paired, overlapping scales.

LEAVES: Opposite, deciduous, 4–12" long; **compound,** pinnately divided into **5–11 (usually 7) leaflets;** leaflets lustrous green above, paler beneath, 2–6" long, slender-pointed, rounded and slightly uneven at the base, **sharply toothed,** short-stalked; lowermost leaflets sometimes divided into 2–3 parts; leaf scars triangular with 5 vein scars, paired at branch tips.

FLOWERS: White, heavily scented, bisexual, 5-parted, star-shaped, about 1/8" across; flowers in **flat-topped, clusters** (cymes) **2–7" wide,** in July (after leaves expand).

FRUITS: Purplish black (rarely red, green or yellow) **berry-like drupes,** with red juice, about 1/4" across, on rose red stalks about 1/4" long, **in large, flat-topped clusters; seeds 3–5,** in small, yellowish stones; drupes mature in August–October.

HABITAT: Moist sites in woods, meadows and swamps and on stream banks and floodplains.

ORIGIN: Native.

THIS HANDSOME SHRUB is cultivated for its showy flowers and fruits. The fruits are most striking in late fall, when they stand out in contrast to the dark, glossy leaves. • A hardy Asian species originally from Manchuria and Korea, Amur honeysuckle is highly adaptable and seems able to thrive in a variety of environments, ranging from sunny urban high-stress sites to deep, shady forests. Amur honeysuckle has almost no insect or disease pests in North America, and it can tolerate many adverse conditions, including restricted root zones, drought, heat, salt spray and heavy browsing. Consequently, this fast-growing shrub has become increasingly aggressive, rapidly spreading into areas where it is not wanted and often displacing native plants from their natural habitats. In Michigan, Amur honeysuckle was first collected as a wild plant at East Lansing in 1963. Today it is classified as an exotic weed. • The berries attract squirrels and numerous songbirds, which then carry the seeds to new sites. • **Caution:** Although the fruits of some Asian honeysuckles are edible, most European species have poisonous fruits that cause digestive, nervous and heart disorders, and occasionally death. Unfortunately, some toxic fruits are sweet and pleasant tasting, so they present an even greater risk.

SIZE AND SHAPE: **Tall shrubs to 15' tall;** crowns broad, spreading, vase-shaped; roots shallow.

TRUNKS: Erect to spreading; bark relatively light brown with **low, interconnecting ridges, not peeling off in layers.**

BRANCHES: **Arched** to spreading, often in almost horizontal tiers; **twigs pale brown, striped** to lightly furrowed; buds paired.

LEAVES: **Opposite,** deciduous, simple; blades glossy, dark green, egg-shaped to broadly lance-shaped, **1¼–3¼" long, tipped with a long, slender point, tapered to the base,** downy on both surfaces (at least on veins), smooth-edged, short-stalked; green to chartreuse in autumn, appear early and drop late.

FLOWERS: **White** (ivory to cream with age), fragrant, bisexual, funnel-shaped, **2-lipped** with a broad 4-lobed upper lip and narrow lower lip, **½–¾" long, 2 per stalk;** petals 5, fused into a short tube at the base, spreading at tips; sepals 5, tiny, fused; stamens 5; **styles hairy;** stalks <¼" long, shorter than adjacent leaf stalks; **flowers in twin pairs** (4 per joint) from upper leaf axils in May–June.

FRUITS: Fleshy, **dark red berries, on very short stalks;** seeds few; berries mature in September, **persist into winter**.

HABITAT: Swampy to upland, open or wooded areas, often on disturbed sites and near settlements.

ORIGIN: Introduced from northeastern Asia.

THIS HARDY, FAST-GROWING shrub is often planted as an ornamental for its showy, fragrant flowers, attractive fruits and reddish winter twigs. It takes pruning well and can be shaped into a handsome hedge, but the root suckers can cause problems. • The fruits are edible and have a sweet, raisin-like flavor. The "berries" can be eaten straight from the branch or cooked and seeded to make jams and jellies. Often the sweet pulp is mixed with tart fruits in fruit stews and sauces. • Nannyberries provide food for wild turkeys, grouse, pheasants and many songbirds, which in turn disperse the seeds. • Nannyberry can be confused with **witherod** (**V. nudum** var. **cassinoides**, also known as *V. cassinoides*, wild raisin and possumhaw). Witherod is distinguished by its smooth- to wavy-edged or irregularly blunt-toothed (not sharp-toothed) leaves, unwinged leaf stalks, stalked flower clusters and golden to yellowish buds. • **Smooth blackhaw (V. prunifolium)** is a rare species of southern woodlands. It is very similar to nannyberry, but its leaves are blunt to broadly pointed (not slender-pointed), and the leaves on flowering branches are smaller (1–2" long). Also, its leaf stalks usually lack wings.

ALSO CALLED: Sweet viburnum, blackhaw, wild raisin, sheepberry.

SIZE AND SHAPE: Small trees or shrubs 10–25' [50'] tall; crowns irregular, broadly rounded; roots shallow, spreading, suckering.

TRUNKS: Slender, crooked, 4–8" [11"] in diameter, usually clumped; mature bark grayish-brown to reddish, with small, irregular scales; wood dark reddish-brown, hard, heavy, fine-grained.

BRANCHES: Few, arching, stout, tough; twigs becoming purplish-brown, slender, smooth, with round pores (lenticels), **unpleasant-smelling** when bruised; **buds slender, brownish-gray,** granular, lacking scales, with 2 immature leaves **visible,** bulbous-based and $1/2$–$1\frac{1}{8}$" long at branch tips, smaller below.

LEAVES: Opposite, simple, deciduous, with an **unpleasant odor** when bruised; **blades hairless,** lustrous, deep yellowish-green, slightly paler and **brown-speckled beneath,** ovate to oval, 2–4" long, abruptly tapered to a **slender point, edged with fine, sharp, incurved teeth; stalks grooved, clearly winged** with a narrow, irregular extension of the blade.

FLOWERS: Creamy white, pleasant-smelling, bisexual, $1/4$" across, 5-parted; numerous, in **round-topped, wide-branching clusters** (cymes); flower clusters stalkless, **2–5" across,** at branch tips, in late May–early June (as or after leaves expand).

FRUITS: Bluish-black, berry-like drupes with a whitish bloom, $1/4$–$1/2$" long, thin-fleshed, **on reddish stems, in open, branched clusters;** seeds single, in a black, flattened stone; drupes mature and drop in August–September.

HABITAT: Wet, rich sites near water, along forest edges, by roadsides and in thickets.

ORIGIN: Native.

THE VERY HARD WOOD of wayfaring-tree has been fashioned into mouthpieces for tobacco pipes. The flexible young branches were used as switches for driving livestock and as ties for binding kindling in the days before string. • This shrub is widely planted as an ornamental for its showy flowers (lasting about 2 weeks), attractive foliage (deep green in summer, purplish-red to scarlet in autumn) and attractive fruits (initially pinkish-white, becoming rose, red, purple and finally black). It is a tough, low-maintenance plant that resists most insects and diseases, tolerates dry soils and spreads readily via seeds and suckers. • The juicy "berries" attract many songbirds. Although the fruits are so astringent as to be inedible raw, they make wonderful jams and jellies. The fruit clusters, preserved by immersion in glycerin and boiling water, add color to dried flower arrangements. Mature fruits were once used to make ink. • The distinctive, dense, star-shaped hairs on the lower leaf surfaces help to protect the leaves from insects and disease and to conserve moisture in dry environments. • The name wayfaring-tree arose because of this shrub's commonness along lanes and byways in southern England.

ALSO CALLED: Wayfaring viburnum.

SIZE AND SHAPE: Small trees or large shrubs to 13' tall; crowns dense and rounded; roots spreading.

TRUNKS: Slender, usually clumped; mature bark grayish-brown, scaly.

BRANCHES: Wide-spreading, tough, thick; **twigs yellowish-gray with dense, star-shaped hairs; buds grayish,** with yellowish-white hairs, **lacking scales,** with **1–2 pairs of immature leaves visible;** flower buds large, wider than long, surrounded by 2 young leaves.

LEAVES: Opposite, simple, deciduous; blades dull, dark green above, **grayish with dense, star-shaped hairs beneath,** 2–5" long, prominently veined, **appearing wrinkled and leathery,** ovate, short-pointed to blunt-tipped, rounded to slightly notched at the base, sharp-toothed; stalks $3/8$–$1 1/8$" long, hairy; leaves deep red in autumn.

FLOWERS: Creamy white, sweet-smelling, 5-parted, $1/4$–$3/8$" across, bisexual; numerous, **in short-stalked, flat-topped, 2–4" wide clusters (cymes);** flower clusters with **star-shaped hairs,** at branch tips, in May–June.

FRUITS: Coral red to black, berry-like drupes, slightly flattened, about $3/8$" long, fleshy, **in flat-topped clusters;** seeds single, in a **flattened stone with 3 grooves on 1 side;** drupes mature August–September.

HABITAT: Roadsides, fence lines and deciduous woods and thickets.

ORIGIN: Introduced from Europe and western Asia.

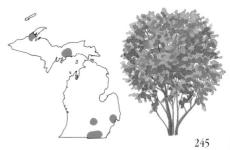

AMERICAN HIGHBUSH-CRANBERRY fruits are boiled and strained to make jellies and jams. The fruits smell a bit like dirty socks, but their flavor isn't bad. Lemon or orange zest helps eliminate the odor. • The "berries" make an excellent winter-survival food because they remain above the snow and are sweeter after freezing. Birds often eat them when other foods are unavailable. • The bark has been used to treat menstrual pains, stomach cramps, aching muscles, asthma, hysteria and convulsions. • **European highbush-cranberry (*V. opulus* var. *opulus*)**, also called Guelder-rose, shown in dark green on map, is a European introduction that frequently escapes cultivation. It is distinguished by its bristle-like leaf stipules, bitter fruits and the saucer-like glands at the tops of its leaf stalks. The popular cultivar 'Sterile,' or 'Roseum' (snowball), has very showy balls of enlarged flowers, all sterile. American and European highbush-cranberries intergrade and are often placed in the same species. • Another common viburnum, **mapleleaf viburnum (*V. acerifolium*)**, has 3-lobed leaves but is usually less than 6' tall and has less conspicuous flower clusters without showy sterile flowers. When not in flower, mapleleaf viburnum is distinguished by its downy, resin-dotted lower leaf surfaces and its distinctive blue fruits.

ALSO CALLED: Native highbush-cranberry, American cranberrybush, cranberry viburnum • *V. opulus* var. *americanum, V. opulus* ssp. *trilobum.*

SIZE AND SHAPE: Tall shrubs or small trees to 15' [25'] tall; crowns open, irregular; roots spreading.

TRUNKS: Upright, less than 4" [6"] in diameter; mature bark grayish.

BRANCHES: Few, arching; twigs thick, gray, hairless; buds plump, paired at branch tips, reddish, with 2 fused scales.

LEAVES: Opposite, simple, deciduous; blades dark green and hairless above, paler and smooth or thinly hairy beneath, **maple leaf–like,** 1½–4¼" long and wide, **deeply cut into 3 spreading, pointed lobes** (lobes sometimes poorly developed on leaves near branch tips), sparsely coarse-toothed (rarely smooth-edged); **stalks grooved,** with **1–6 club-shaped glands at the top** (near the blade) and 2 slender, thick-tipped stipules at the base.

FLOWERS: White, 5-parted, bisexual, of 2 types: **small, fertile flowers at the cluster center,** and **larger (½–1" wide), flat, sterile flowers around the outer edge;** flowers numerous, in **flat-topped, wide-branching, 2–6" wide clusters** (cymes); flower clusters on ¾–2" long stalks at branch tips, in late May–July (after leaves expand).

FRUITS: Juicy, red to orange, berry-like drupes, about ⅜" across; seeds single, within a flattened stone; **drupes hang in branched clusters,** mature in August–September, often persist into winter.

HABITAT: Moist, rich sites near water and in cool woodlands and ravines.

ORIGIN: Native.

NORTHERN CATALPAS are cultivated for their showy flowers and large, tropical-looking leaves. They respond well to pruning, but unfortunately, the weak branches often break during storms. • Catalpa wood is weak and light but slow to rot in soil. This fast-growing tree is sometimes grown in dense plantations to produce fence posts and telephone poles. Catalpa wood is also used occasionally in inexpensive furniture. • Northern catalpa flowers at about 15 years of age and produces large seed crops every 2–3 years. Bees and a variety of night-flying moths pollinate the beautiful flowers, producing conspicuous seedpods that are of little value to wildlife. • The genus name *Catalpa* was adapted from a Native name used by tribes in Carolina. The specific epithet *speciosa* means "beautiful" or "showy." • **Southern catalpa (*C. bignonioides*)** is often planted as an ornamental, but occasionally escapes to grow wild. It is a smaller, less hardy tree, with smaller, more numerous flowers, slenderer ($1/4$–$3/8$" thick) capsules and short-pointed leaves that have an unpleasant odor when crushed.

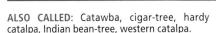

Photo, bottom left: *C. bignonioides*

ALSO CALLED: Catawba, cigar-tree, hardy catalpa, Indian bean-tree, western catalpa.

SIZE AND SHAPE: Trees 35–60' [63'] tall; crowns narrow to broad, rounded.

TRUNKS: Short, 8–16" [62"] in diameter; mature bark dark reddish-brown with large, irregular, thick scales; wood light brown, soft, coarse-grained.

BRANCHES: Stout, spreading; twigs stout, blunt-tipped; buds 6-scaled, $1/8$–$1/4$" long, absent at branch tips.

LEAVES: Opposite or whorled, simple, deciduous, **odorless;** blades firm, yellowish-green above, paler and soft-hairy beneath, with clusters of **dark, nectar-producing glands in vein axils, heart-shaped, slender-pointed, 4–12" long,** usually smooth-edged; stalks 4–$6^1/4$" long; leaf scars rounded, with a ring of vein scars; leaves blackened by first frost.

FLOWERS: White with yellow stripes and purple spots in the throat, bell-shaped, 2-lipped, showy, 2–$2^3/4$" across, bisexual; petals fused in a tube with 5 spreading, frilly lobes; sepals greenish-purple, fused, irregularly split; flowers in erect, branched, 4–8" long clusters (panicles) at branch tips, in June–July (after leaves expand).

FRUITS: Green to dark brown, **cylindrical pods 10–20" long,** about $1/2$" thick, hang in clusters of 1–3; **seeds numerous, flat,** $3/4$–$1^1/8$" **long, with 2 blunt, hair-tipped, papery wings;** pods mature in early autumn, **persist through winter,** split open lengthwise in spring.

HABITAT: Native in bottomlands; introduced along roads and forest edges and in fields.

ORIGIN: Native.

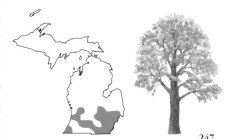

Silver Buffaloberry *Shepherdia argentea*   Oleaster Family

SILVER BUFFALOBERRY is a hardy shrub that tolerates very cold temperatures and drought. The dense, spiny branches make excellent hedges, and the spreading roots help to control erosion. • The bright red "berries" of this species are edible, but they are sour and almost unpalatable until after the first frosts. They are usually used to make jams, sauces and delicious jellies. The flavor has been likened to that of grapes, and some suggest using buffaloberries to make wine. • In the past, the fruits were often cooked with buffalo meat, hence the common name. Others say the name refers to the buffalo's own fondness for these berries. • Traditionally, the fruits were gathered by beating branches over a blanket. According to Native legend, this began when Old Man spotted some beautiful red berries in the water. Again and again he dove in but found nothing. Finally, nearly drowned, he lay exhausted on the shore and looked up to see the berries overhead. Old Man was so angry, he beat the bush with a club until all but one berry had fallen, and to this day, people beat the bushes for their berries. In some parts of the western U.S., two men could gather 30 bushels a day in this way.

• Buffaloberries are sometimes called soapberries, because they contain bitter, soapy substances (saponins) that foam in water.

ALSO CALLED: Thorny buffalo-berry, rabbit-berry, beef-suet tree, silver leaf, wild oleaster, wild olive-tree, bull-berry • *Lepargyrea argentea*.

SIZE AND SHAPE: Tall shrubs or small trees to 20' tall; crowns rounded; roots spreading, often suckering to form colonies.

TRUNKS: Short; mature bark dull gray, somewhat ridged, shedding in long strips; wood dark brown, soft, weak.

BRANCHES: Stiff, thorny, short; twigs stout, **often thorn-tipped,** covered with **dense, silvery,** star-shaped hairs; pith dark brown; buds covered with silvery hairs and reddish scales, about ⅛" long, with 1–2 pairs of scales.

LEAVES: Opposite, simple, deciduous; **blades silvery on both sides, with fine scales and star-shaped hairs,** leathery, oblong to lance-shaped, ¾–2³⁄₈" long, blunt-tipped, round to wedge-shaped at the base; stalks stout, about ⅛" long; leaf scars bean-shaped, with 1 vein scar.

FLOWERS: Yellowish green, inconspicuous; unisexual with **male and female flowers on separate shrubs;** petals absent; sepals 4; male flowers cupped, with 4-lobed calyx and **8 stamens;** female flowers broadly cupped, with an 8-lobed nectary; flowers in small clusters (umbels) in upper leaf axils, in April–June **(before leaves expand).**

FRUITS: Scarlet to orange, fleshy, berry-like drupes about ¼" long; seeds single, in tiny flattened nutlets; drupes single or in small clusters, mature in July–September.

HABITAT: Rocky limestone fields; riverbanks and canyons in western North America.

ORIGIN: Introduced from western North America.

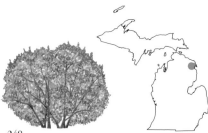

248

THIS ATTRACTIVE SHRUB has potential as an ornamental in low, moist to wet sites. It is easily propagated and tolerates a range of habitats. Buttonbush also produces a large amount of nectar which attracts numerous small butterflies. • In the past, bitter button-bush bark and twigs were used in remedies for kidney stones, gallstones, coughs, fevers, asthma and loss of appetite. Buttonbush was also used to treat malaria, probably because it resembles its relative, quinine tree (*Cinchona pubescens*), a known source of quinine. In the 1800s, some pharmaceutical companies marketed buttonbush extract as a tonic, fever-reducer, laxative and diuretic. In folk medicine, the bark was chewed to relieve toothaches and bark tea was used to wash inflamed eyes; leaf tea was taken to relieve cramps, fevers, coughs, kidney stones, palsy, pleurisy and toothaches; and the flowers and leaves were made into a fragrant syrup that was taken as a mild tonic and laxative. More recently, analysis of buttonbush glycosides failed to explain past uses, and its medicinal value is now considered doubtful. • **Caution:** The leaves are **poisonous** to livestock, but white-tailed deer are said to browse the foliage and young twigs. Waterbirds, especially mallards, and shorebirds feed on the seeds, and dense buttonbush thickets make excellent protected nesting sites.

ALSO CALLED: Honey-balls, globe-flower, pond dogwood, pin-ball, little snowball.

SIZE AND SHAPE: Tall shrubs or small trees 5–15' [35'] tall; crowns open, irregular; roots spreading, suckering.

TRUNKS: Clumped, often leaning, about 4" [11"] in diameter; mature bark dark brown to blackish, with broad, scaly ridges; wood pale red-brown, fine-grained, heavy, hard.

BRANCHES: Paired or in 3s; twigs reddish to yellowish, essentially hairless, with vertical pores (lenticels); pith large, yellowish; buds small, embedded in bark, absent at twig tips.

LEAVES: Opposite or in whorls of 3, simple, deciduous; blades glossy, dark green above, paler beneath, 2½–6" long, smooth-edged; stipules tiny, single; stalks stout, grooved; leaf scars small, semicircular; leaves drop over winter.

FLOWERS: Fragrant, **creamy white,** bisexual, funnel-shaped, about ¼" long, tipped with 4 small petal lobes, a **thread-like style and 4 stamens project from the mouth,** stalkless, numerous (100–200), mixed with club-shaped bracts **in dense, round heads ¾–1⅛" wide,** heads on upright stalks 1¼–2½" long, in July–August.

FRUITS: Reddish-green to **deep red-brown, narrowly pyramidal capsules,** about ¼" long, tapered to the base, in dense, **rough, ½–¾" balls;** seeds oblong, hanging, 2–4 per capsule; capsules split from the base into 1-seeded segments, in September–October.

HABITAT: Wet sites along streambanks and lakeshores and in swamps and thickets.

ORIGIN: Native.

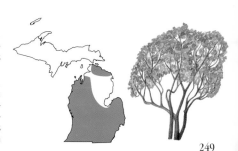

Appendix • Michigan Arboreta

Ann Arbor
Nichols Arboretum, University of Michigan

Augusta
W.K. Kellogg Experimental Forest

Battle Creek
Leila Arboretum

Berrien Springs
Andrews University Campus Arboretum

Burton
For-Mar Nature Preserve and Arboretum

Dearborn
Arjay Miller Arboretum

Decatur
Fred Russ Forest Experiment Station

East Lansing
Clarence E. Lewis Landscape Arboretum

Grand Rapids
Frederik Meijer Gardens

Hillsdale
Slayton Arboretum & Children's Garden

Midland
Dow Gardens

Niles
Fernwood Botanical Garden & Nature Preserve

Port Austin
Huron County Nature Center Wilderness Arboretum

Royal Oak
Detroit Zoological Park

Tipton
Hidden Lake Gardens

Acer saccharum, sugar maple

Some Michigan Herbaria • Appendix

Albion
Albion College

Alma
Alma College

Ann Arbor
University of Michigan

Berrien Springs
Andrews University

Bloomfield Hills
Cranbrook Institute of Science

East Lansing
Michigan State University

Flint
University of Michigan

Houghton
Isle Royale National Park

Kalamazoo
Western Michigan University

Mount Pleasant
Central Michigan University

Pellston
University of Michigan

Ypsilanti
Eastern Michigan University

A mounted and labeled herbarium specimen

Glossary

Page numbers indicate where terms are illustrated.

achene: a small, thin-walled, dry fruit containing a single seed (p. 256)

acorn: the hard, dry nut of oaks, with a single, large seed and a scaly, cup-like base (p. 256)

adventive: introduced but only locally established in the wild, if at all; compare "naturalized"

adventitious: growing from unusual places, e.g., roots growing from stems

aggregate fruit: a fruit produced by two or more pistils of a single flower, sometimes appearing to be dense clusters of many tiny fruits (e.g., a raspberry) (p. 256); compare "multiple fruit"

alternate: attached singly, neither paired nor whorled (p. 254); compare "opposite," "whorled"

angiosperm: a plant with ovules/seeds enclosed in an ovary/fruit; a flowering plant, member of the Magnoliophyta; compare "gymnosperm"

annual ring: the wood laid down in a single year, visible (in cross-section) as a ring because of alternating layers of earlywood and denser latewood (p. 15)

anther: the pollen-bearing part of a stamen (p. 19)

arboretum [arboreta]: a place where trees and other plants are cultivated for their beauty and for scientific and educational purposes (see appendix, p. 250)

aril: a specialized covering attached to a mature seed (p. 256)

armed: bearing prickles, spines or thorns (p. 254)

ascending: oriented obliquely upward (p. 14)

axil: the angle between an organ (e.g., a leaf) and the part to which it is attached (e.g., a stem) (p. 17)

axis [axes]: the main stem or central line of a plant or plant part

bark cambium: see "cork cambium"

bark: the protective outer covering of the trunks and branches of a woody plant, composed of dead, corky cells and produced by the cork cambium; in the broadest sense, bark includes all tissue from the phloem outward (pp. 15, 17)

bast: see "phloem"

berry: a fleshy fruit developed from a single ovary and containing one to several seeds (p. 257)

bisexual: with both male and female sex organs; also called "perfect"; compare "unisexual"

blade: the broad, flat part of an organ (e.g., of a leaf or petal) (p. 257)

bloom: a whitish, waxy powder on the surface of some leaves and fruits

board foot [board feet]: a cubic measure for lumber, equivalent to that of a board measuring 12 inches by 12 inches by 1 inch

bole: the section of a trunk below the crown (p. 14)

bract: a small, specialized leaf or scale (p. 255)

Compound leaves

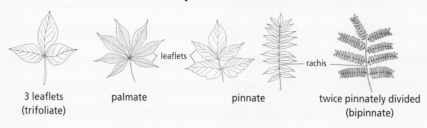

3 leaflets (trifoliate)

palmate

leaflets

pinnate

rachis

twice pinnately divided (bipinnate)

Simple leaves: lobes and teeth

teeth

palmately lobed

lobes

lobes

pinnately lobed

teeth

bud: an undeveloped stem, branch, leaf or flower, usually covered by protective scales (pp. 17, 258)

bur: a barbed or bristly fruit (or compact cluster of fruits) designed to stick to passing animals (p. 256)

callus: a small, firm thickening or protuberance

calyx [calyxes, calyces]: the outer (lowermost) circle of floral parts composed of separate or fused segments called sepals, which are usually green and leaf-like (p. 19); compare "corolla"

cambium: a thin layer of cells responsible for producing new xylem and phloem cells or new bark cells (see "cork cambium") and thereby controlling stem growth (p. 15)

canopy: see "overstory"

capsule: a dry fruit produced by a compound ovary and splitting open at maturity (p. 256)

carpel: the female unit of reproduction in a flower, formed from a modified leaf and consisting of a stigma, style and seed-bearing ovary; compare "pistil" (p. 256)

catkin: a dense spike or raceme of many small, unisexual flowers that lack petals but usually have a bract (pp. 255, 256)

chlorophyll: the green pigment that allows plants to manufacture carbohydrates through photosynthesis

ciliate: edged with cilia; fringed

cilium [cilia]: a tiny, eyelash-like structure, usually part of a fringe

clone: the offspring produced vegetatively (asexually) by a single individual

compound: composed of two or more smaller parts, such as leaves consisting of several leaflets (p. 252), flower clusters consisting of smaller groups, ovaries consisting of two or more carpels, or substances formed by the chemical union of two or more ingredients; compare "simple"

cone: a reproductive structure with overlapping scales or bracts arranged around a central axis, usually woody when bearing seeds and non-woody when bearing pollen (pp. 18, 255)

conifer: a cone-bearing shrub or tree

coniferous: cone-bearing (e.g., coniferous trees) or composed of coniferous trees (e.g., coniferous forests)

cork cambium: thin layer of living cells located on the inner side of the bark and responsible for producing new bark cells (p. 14)

corolla: the circle of floral parts second from the outside, composed of separate or fused segments called petals; usually conspicuous in size and color but sometimes small, reduced to nectaries or absent (p. 19); compare "calyx"

corymb: a flat- or round-topped, branched flower cluster in which the outer (lower) flowers bloom first (p. 255)

cotyledon: a leaf of the developing plant (embryo) within a seed; a seed leaf

Leaf shapes

needles   linear   linear-oblong   oblong   lance-shaped, widest above midleaf (oblanceolate)   lance-shaped (lanceolate)   ovate   ovate, widest above midleaf (obovate)

sheath   single teeth

elliptic   oval   round (orbicular)   heart-shaped (cordate)   broadly triangular (deltate)   triangular

double teeth

Glossary

cross-pollination: the transfer of pollen from the anthers of one flower to the stigma of another flower on a different plant; compare "self-pollination"

cross-section: a slice or fragment cut and viewed at right angles to the main axis; compare "long-section"

crown: the leafy head of a tree or shrub (p. 14)

cultivar: a cultivated plant variety with one or more distinct differences from the species; e.g., *Acer platanoides* is a botanical species, of which 'Crimson King' is a cultivar distinguished by maroon leaves

cuticle: a waxy layer covering the outer surface of a stem of leaf

cyme: a flat- or round-topped flower cluster in which the inner (upper) flowers bloom first (p. 255)

DBH: trunk diameter at breast height or diameter at 4½ feet from the ground (p. 14)

deciduous: shed after completing its normal function, usually at the end of the growing season; compare "persistent"

dehiscent: splitting open along slits or via pores to release seeds

dioecious: with male and female flowers or cones on separate plants (p. 255); compare "monoecious"

disjunct: separated, referring to plant or animal populations located a significant distance from all other populations of the same species

double-toothed: edged with large teeth bearing smaller teeth (p. 253); compare "single-toothed"

drupe: a fruit with an outer fleshy part covered by a thin skin and surrounding a hard or bony stone that encloses a single seed, e.g., a plum (p. 257)

dwarf shoot: see "spur-shoot"

earlywood: pale, relatively large-pored wood produced by rapid growth early in the growing season (p. 15); also called "springwood"

ellipsoid: a three-dimensional form in which every plane is an ellipse or a circle

embryo: an immature plant within a seed

endangered: threatened with immediate elimination through all or a significant portion of a region

evergreen: always bearing green leaves

extinct: a species that no longer exists anywhere

extirpated: formerly native to a region, now no longer existing there in the wild but still found elsewhere

family [families]: a group of related plants or animals forming a taxonomic category ranking below order and above genus

fertile: plants capable of producing viable pollen, ovules or spores; soil rich in nutrients and capable of sustaining abundant plant growth

fetid: with a strong, offensive odor

filament: the stalk of a stamen, usually bearing an anther at its tip (p. 19)

fleshy: succulent, firm and pulpy; plump and juicy

flora: the plants that are representative of a certain region or period; also a comprehensive treatise or list that includes all such plants

flower: a specialized shoot of a plant, with a shortened axis bearing reproductive structures (modified leaves) such as sepals, petals, stamens and pistils

follicle: a dry, pod-like fruit, splitting open along a single line on one side (p. 256)

fruit: the seed-bearing organ of an angiosperm, including the ripened ovary and any other structures that join with it as a unit (pp. 256, 257)

functionally unisexual: having both male and female parts (sometimes appearing bisexual), but with organs of only one sex maturing to produce reproductive cells

Leaf/branch attachment

thorns

whorled   spiralled   opposite   alternate   armed

generic name: the first part of a scientific name, denoting the genus to which the species belongs; e.g., *Abies* in *Abies balsamea*

genus [genera]: a group of related plants or animals constituting a category of biological classification below family and above species

germinate: to sprout

girdle: to remove a ring of bark and cambium around a trunk, thereby stopping the transport of water and nutrients and killing the tree

gland: a bump, appendage or depression that secretes substances such as nectar or oil (p. 259)

glandular-hairy: with gland-tipped hairs

glandular-toothed: with gland-tipped teeth (p. 259)

gymnosperm: a plant with naked ovules/seeds (i.e., not enclosed in an ovary); a conifer, a member of the Pinophyta; compare "angiosperm"

hardwood: a broad-leaved, deciduous tree (occasionally evergreen elsewhere) belonging to the angiosperms or Magnoliophyta; compare "softwood"

haw: the fruit of hawthorns, a small, berry-like pome containing 1–5 bony nutlets (p. 257)

heartwood: the darker, harder wood at the center of a trunk, containing accumulations of resin and other compounds and therefore unable to transport fluids (p. 14)

herbarium [herbaria]: a large collection of dried plant specimens that have been mounted, labelled and filed systematically (see appendix, p. 251)

husk: the dry, often thick, outer covering of some fruits (p. 256)

hybrid: the offspring of two kinds of parents (usually parents from different species)

hybridization: the process of creating a hybrid

hypanthium [hypanthia]: a ring or cup around the ovary formed by fused parts of the sepals, petals and/or stamens

imperfect: see "unisexual"

introduced: brought in from another region (e.g., Europe), not native

key: see "samara" (p. 257)

latewood: the relatively small-pored wood produced by slow growth toward the end of the growing season (p. 15); also called "summerwood"

layering: a form of vegetative reproduction in which branches droop to the ground, root and send up new shoots

leader: the uppermost shoot of a tree

leaf scar: the mark left on a stem where a leaf was once attached (pp. 17, 258, 259)

leaflet: a single part of a compound leaf (p. 252)

legume: a pod-like fruit characteristic of the pea family (Fabaceae or Leguminosae), typically splitting down both sides (p. 256)

lenticel: a slightly raised pore on root, trunk or branch bark (p. 17)

Cones and flower/fruit clusters

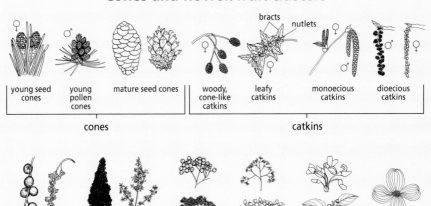

bracts nutlets

| young seed cones | young pollen cones | mature seed cones | woody, cone-like catkins | leafy catkins | monoecious catkins | dioecious catkins |

cones   catkins

racemes   panicles   corymbs   cymes   umbels   pseudanthium

Glossary

lobe: a rounded division, too large to be called a tooth (p. 252)

long-section: in full, "longitudinal section"; a slice or fragment cut and viewed parallel to the main axis; compare "cross-section"

membranous: in a thin, usually translucent sheet; like a membrane

midvein: the middle vein of a leaf (p. 259)

monoecious: with male and female parts in separate flowers or cones on the same plant (p. 255); compare "dioecious"

multiple fruit: a dense cluster of many small fruits, each produced by an individual flower (e.g., a mulberry) (p. 256); compare "aggregate fruit"

naked: exposed, not covered by scales, hairs or other appendages

native: indigenous to a region, having evolved there as part of an ecosystem over a long period of time; compare "naturalized," "introduced"

naturalized: well established in the wild, but originally introduced from another area; compare "adventive," "native"

nectar: the sweet liquid secreted by a nectary, usually serving to attract pollinators

nectary: a nectar-secreting gland, usually in a flower

net-veined: with a network of branched veins; also called "reticulate"

node: the point where a leaf or branch attaches to a stem; a joint (p. 258)

nut: a dry, thick-walled, usually one-seeded fruit that does not split open when mature (p. 256)

nutlet: a small, nut-like fruit (p. 255)

opposite: situated directly in front of one another (e.g., stamens opposite petals) or directly across from each other at the same node (e.g., leaves, branches) (p. 254); compare "alternate," "whorled"

ovary: the organ containing the young, undeveloped seed(s), located at the base of the pistil and maturing to become all or part of the fruit (p. 19)

overstory: the uppermost stratum of foliage in a forest, the forest canopy; compare "understory"

ovoid: a three-dimensional, egg-shaped form that is broadest below the middle

ovule: an organ that develops into a single seed after fertilization (p. 19)

palmate: with three or more lobes or leaflets arising from one point, like fingers of a hand (p. 252); compare "pinnate"

panicle: a branched flower cluster in which the lower blooms develop first (p. 255)

perfect: see "bisexual"

perianth: a flower's petals and sepals collectively

persistent: remaining attached after its normal function has been completed; compare "deciduous" (p. 257)

Fruits

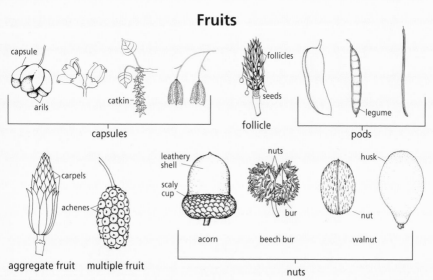

petal: a segment of the inner whorl (corolla) of the perianth, usually white or brightly colored (p. 19)

phloem: a thin layer of vascular tissue located between the bark and the wood, responsible for transporting nutrients (e.g., sugars) produced by the tree to its living tissues (p. 15); also called "bast"

photosynthesis: the process by which plants manufacture carbohydrates using chlorophyll, carbon dioxide, water and the energy of the sun

pinnate: with branches, lobes, leaflets or veins arranged on both sides of a central stalk or vein, feather-like (p. 252); compare "palmate"

pioneer species: a colonizer of sites in the early stages of succession (e.g., sites that have been burned, cleared or otherwise disturbed)

pistil: the female part of a flower, composed of single or fused carpels (p. 19)

pith: the soft, spongy centre of a stem or branch (pp. 17, 258)

pod: a dry fruit that splits open to release seeds (p. 256)

pollard: a tree with a small, dense crown produced by cutting branches almost back to the trunk; also to prune a tree in this severe manner

pollen: tiny, powdery grains containing the male reproductive cells that fertilize the ovule

pollen cone: a cone that produces pollen, i.e., a male cone (p. 255); compare "seed cone"

pollination: the transfer of pollen from male to female reproductive organs, leading to fertilization

pome: a fleshy fruit with a core (e.g., an apple); comprises an enlarged hypanthium around a compound ovary (p. 257)

pseudanthium [pseudanthia]: a compact cluster of tiny flowers and associated bracts resembling a single large flower (p. 255)

raceme: an unbranched cluster of stalked flowers on an elongated central stalk, in which the lowest flowers bloom first (p. 255)

rachis [rachises]: the main axis of a compound leaf or flower cluster (p. 252)

rare: existing in low numbers and/or in very restricted areas in a region

ray: a ribbon-like group of cells visible as a radial line in wood (viewed in cross-section), responsible for transporting water and nutrients across trunks or large branches

respiration: the act of taking in oxygen and producing carbon dioxide through oxidation

rib: a prominent, usually longitudinal vein

runner: a slender, prostrate, spreading branch, rooting and often developing new shoots and/or plants at its nodes or at the tip

samara: a dry, winged, one-seeded fruit that does not split open at maturity; may be single (e.g., ashes) or paired (e.g., maples) (p. 257); also called "key," especially for the ashes and maples

sap: the mineral- and sugar-containing solution that circulates through a plant via the xylem and phloem

Fruits

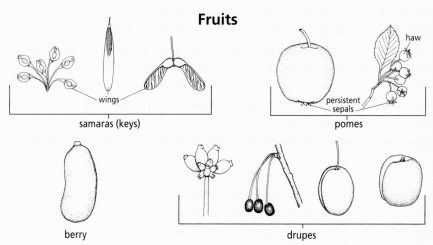

samaras (keys)

wings

pomes

haw

persistent sepals

berry

drupes

Glossary

sapwood: the paler, softer, outer wood of a trunk, still capable of transporting fluids (p. 15)

scale: a small, flat structure, usually thin and membranous (pp. 17, 18)

scar: the mark left on a stem by a fallen leaf, scale or fruit (pp. 17, 258, 259)

scurfy: covered with tiny scales

seasonality: the timing of biological events (e.g., leaf growth, flower development) during the year

seed: a fertilized ovule, containing a developing plant embryo along with nourishing tissue (usually) and a protective covering or seed coat (pp. 18, 256)

seed cone: a cone that produces seeds, i.e., a female cone (p. 255); compare "pollen cone"

self-pollination: the transfer of pollen from the anthers to the stigma of the same flower, or from one flower to another flower on the same plant; compare "cross-pollination"

sepal: a segment of the outer whorl (calyx) of the perianth, usually green and leaf-like (pp. 19, 257)

sexual reproduction: producing offspring through the union of female and male cells, as in the fertilization of the egg cell in an ovule by a pollen grain; compare "vegetative reproduction"

sheath: a tubular organ surrounding or partly surrounding some part of a plant (e.g., the base of a bundle of pine needles) (p. 253)

shrub: a perennial, woody plant, usually less than 15 feet tall and bushy with several small (typically less than 3 inches wide) main stems originating at or near the ground; compare "tree"

simple: in one piece, undivided; describes leaves not divided into separate leaflets (though sometimes deeply lobed); describes fruits derived from a single ovary; compare "compound"

single-toothed: edged with simple teeth, that is, teeth not bearing smaller teeth (p. 253); compare "double-toothed"

softwood: a needle-leaved, coniferous, normally evergreen tree (deciduous in larches) belonging to the gymnosperms or Pinophyta; compare "hardwood"

species [species], abbreviated **sp.** [spp.]: the fundamental unit of biological classification; a group of closely related plants or animals ranked below genus and above subspecies and variety

specific epithet: the second part of a species' scientific name, distinguishing that species from other members of the same genus; e.g., *balsamea* in *Abies balsamea*

spreading: diverging widely from the vertical, approaching horizontal (p. 14)

springwood: see "earlywood"

spur-shoot: a short, compressed branch, developing many closely spaced nodes (p. 258); also called a "dwarf shoot"

stamen: the male organ of a flower, usually comprising a pollen-bearing anther and a stalk called a filament (p. 19)

staminate: with stamens

sterile: lacking viable pollen, ovules or spores

stigma: the tip of the female organ (pistil) of a flower, designed to catch and hold pollen (p. 19)

stipule: a bract-like or leaf-like appendage at the base of a leaf stalk (p. 259)

stoma, stomate [stomata]: a tiny pore in the plant "skin" (epidermis), bounded by two guard cells that open and close the pore by changing shape; gas exchange takes place through a plant's stomata

stone: the tough, bony centre of some fruits (e.g., drupes), enclosing and protecting a seed

style: the narrow middle part of a pistil, connecting the stigma and ovary (p. 19)

subspecies, abbreviated **ssp.:** a naturally occurring, regional form of a species, often geographically isolated from other subspecies but still potentially

Twig parts

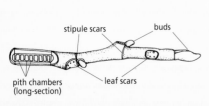

stipule scars

buds

pith chambers
(long-section)

leaf scars

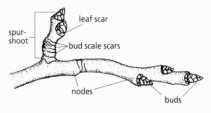

spur-shoot

leaf scar

bud scale scars

nodes

buds

interfertile with them; a ranking between species and variety in biological classification

succulent: fleshy, soft and juicy; also refers to a plant that stores water in fleshy stems or leaves

sucker: a vertical vegetative shoot growing from an underground runner or from spreading roots (p. 14)

summerwood: see "latewood"

synonym: an alternative name for a plant; usually a scientific name that has been rejected because it was incorrect or was misapplied

taproot: a root system with a prominent main root that extends vertically downward and bears smaller side roots (p. 14)

taxon [taxa]: a taxonomic group or entity (e.g., a genus, species or variety)

taxonomy: the orderly classification of organisms based on similarities and differences believed to reflect natural evolutionary relationships; also the study of these systems of classification

tepal: a sepal or petal, when these structures are not easily distinguished

terminal: located at the tip

threatened: likely to become endangered in a region unless factors affecting its vulnerability are reversed

tooth [teeth]: a small, often pointed lobe on the edge of a structure such as a leaf (pp. 252, 253, 259)

tree: an erect, perennial, woody plant with a definite crown reaching over 15 feet in height, and with a trunk (or trunks) reaching at least 3 inches in diameter; compare "shrub"

trifoliate: divided into three leaflets (p. 252)

trunk: the main stem of a tree or shrub, composed mainly of dead, woody cells covered by a thin layer of living tissues under a protective covering of bark (pp. 14, 15)

umbel: a round- or flat-topped flower cluster in which several flower stalks are of approximately the same length and arise from the same point, like the ribs of an inverted umbrella (p. 255)

understory: the lower stratum of foliage in a forest, located below the forest canopy; compare "overstory"

unisexual: with one set of sex organs only, either male or female; also called "imperfect"; compare "bisexual," "functionally unisexual"

variety, abbreviated **var.:** a naturally occurring variant of a species; ranked below subspecies in biological classification

vascular: pertaining to the conduction of substances such as sap or blood within the body of an organism; see also "vein," "xylem," "phloem"

vegetative reproduction: producing offspring from asexual parts (e.g., rhizomes, leaves) rather than from fertilized ovules (seeds); compare "sexual reproduction"

vein: a strand of conducting tubes consisting of xylem and phloem, especially if visible on the surface (e.g., on a petal or leaf) (p. 259)

vein scar: the mark left on a stem where a vein was once attached (p. 17)

whorl: a ring of three or more similar structures (e.g., leaves, branches or flowers) arising from one node

whorled: arranged in whorls (p. 254); compare "alternate," "opposite"

wing: a thin, flattened expansion on the side(s) or tip of an organ (e.g., on a fruit or twig) (pp. 18, 257)

wood: the tough, fibrous material forming the greater part of the trunks, branches and roots of trees and shrubs; composed mainly of cellulose and lignin

xylem: a vascular tissue, consisting mainly of tubes of hollow dead cells joined end to end, that conducts water and minerals and provides support; makes up the wood in trees and shrubs (p. 15)

Leaf parts

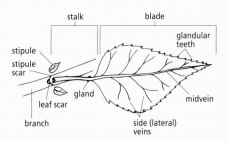

stalk   blade

stipule
stipule scar
glandular teeth
leaf scar   gland
branch
side (lateral) veins
midvein

References

Albert, Dennis A. 1995. *Regional Landscape Ecosystems of Michigan, Minnesota and Wisconsin: A Working Map and Classification*. 4th rev: July 1994. North Central Forest Experiment Station, USDA Forest Service, East Lansing, Michigan.

Allison, Bruce. 2005. *Wisconsin's Champion Trees*. Wisconsin Book Publishing, Verona, Wisconsin.

Barnes, B. V. and W. H. Wagner. 2004. *Michigan Trees*. University of Michigan Press, Ann Arbor.

Beck, A. and K. Renwald. 2001. *Tree and Shrub Gardening for Ontario*. Lone Pine Publishing, Edmonton, Alberta.

Blackburn, B. 1952. *Trees and Shrubs in Eastern North America*. Oxford University Press, New York.

Brickell, C., T. Cole and J. D. Zuk, eds. 1996. *Reader's Digest A–Z Encyclopedia of Garden Plants*. Reader's Digest Association, Montreal, Quebec.

Britton, N. L. and A. Brown. 1913. *An Illustrated Flora of the Northern United States and Canada*. Dover, New York.

Burns, Russell M., and Barbara H. Honkala [tech. coords]. 1990. *Silvics of North America: 1. Conifers; 2. Hardwoods*. Vol.2. Agriculture Handbook 654. U.S. Department of Agriculture, Forest Service, Washington, DC.

Campbell, C. S., F. Hyland, et al. 1975. *Winter Keys to Woody Plants of Maine*. University of Maine Press, Orono, Maine.

Chicago Botanic Garden. 1996. *Trees*. Pantheon Books, New York.

Core, E. L. and N. P. Ammons. 1958. *Woody Plants in Winter*. Boxwood Press, Pittsburgh.

Couplan, F. 1998. *The Encyclopedia of Edible Plants of North America*. Keats Publishing, New Canaan, Connecticut.

Crellin, J. K. and J. Philpot. 1989. *Herbal Medicine Past and Present. Volume II: A Reference Guide to Medicinal Plants*. Duke University Press, Durham, North Carolina.

Dickmann, D. I. and L. A. Leefers. 2003. *The Forests of Michigan*. University of Michigan Press, Ann Arbor.

Douce, G. Keith, David J. Moorhead and Charles T. Bargeron (project coords.). 2005. *Invasive and Exotic Species* website at http://www.invasive.org/weeds.cfm, a joint project of the University of Georgia's Bugwood Network, USDA Forest Service and USDA APHIS PPQ. Accessed April 2005.

Duke, J. A. 1997. *The Green Pharmacy*. Rodale Press, Emmaus, Pennsylvania.

Duncan, W. H. and M. B. Duncan. 1988. *Trees of the Southeastern United States*. University of Georgia Press, Athens, Georgia.

Edlin, H. 1978. *The Tree Key: A Guide to Identification in Garden, Field and Forest*. Charles Scribner's Sons, New York.

Elias, T. S. 1989. *Field Guide to North American Trees*. Grolier Book Clubs, Danbury, Connecticut.

Endangered Species Program, Michigan Department of Natural Resources. 2000. *Michigan's Special Plants*. Michigan State University Extension: 21, Lansing, Michigan.

Erichsen-Brown, C. 1979. *Use of Plants for the Past 500 Years*. Breezy Creeks Press, Aurora, Ontario.

Farrar, J. L. 1995. *Trees in Canada*. Fitzhenry and Whiteside, Markham, Ontario.

Fernald, M. L. 1950. *Gray's Manual of Botany*. American Book Company, New York.

Flint, H. L. 1983. *Landscape Plants for Eastern North America*. John Wiley and Sons, New York.

Foster, S. and J. A. Duke. 1990. *Field Guide to Medicinal Plants: Eastern and Central North America*. Houghton Mifflin, Boston.

Gleason, H. A. and A. Cronquist. 1991. *Manual of Vascular Plants of the Northeastern United States and Adjacent Canada*. New York Botanical Garden, Bronx, New York.

Gorer, R. 1976. *Trees and Shrubs: A Complete Guide*. David and Charles Publishers, Vancouver, BC.

Grieve, M. 1931. *A Modern Herbal*. Jonathan Cape, Harmondsworth, Middlesex, England. Republished in 1976 by Penguin Books.

Grimm, W. C. 1962. *The Book of Trees*. Stackpole, Harrisburg, Pennsylvania.

Grimm, W. C. 1966. *Recognizing Native Shrubs*. Stackpole, Harrisburg, Pennsylvania.

Harlow, William H. and Ellwood S. Harrar. 1969. *Textbook of Dendrology*, 5th ed. McGraw-Hill, New York.

Holmgrem, N. H. 1998. *Illustrated Companion to Gleason and Cronquist's Manual*. New York Botanical Garden, Bronx, New York.

Hosie, R. C. 1969. *Native Trees of Canada*. Canadian Forest Service, Queen's Printer, Ottawa, Ontario.

Hottes, A. C. 1952. *The Book of Trees*. De La Mare, New York.

Hutchens, A. R. 1991. *Indian Herbalogy of North America*. Shambhala, Boston.

Hyams, E. 1965. *Ornamental Shrubs for Temperate Zone Gardens*. A. S. Barnes and Co., New York.

ITIS. 2003. *ITIS Integrated Taxonomic Information System*. U.S. Department of Agriculture, http://www.itis.usda.gov/. Accessed April 2005.

Johnston, A. 1987. *Plants and the Blackfoot*. Lethbridge Historical Society, Lethbridge, Alberta.

References

Kartesz, J. T. and C. A. Meacham 1999. *Synthesis of the North American Flora*. North Carolina Botanical Garden, University of North Carolina, Chapel Hill, North Carolina.

Kershaw, L. J. 2001. *Trees of Ontario*. Lone Pine Publishing, Edmonton, Alberta,

Lacey, L. 1993. *Micmac Medicines: Remedies and Recollections*. Nimbus, Halifax, Nova Scotia.

Lauriault, J. 1992. *Identification Guide to the Trees of Canada*. Canadian Museum of Nature, Ottawa, Ontario.

Little, E. L. 1980. *The Audubon Society Field Guide to North American Trees: Western Region*. Alfred A. Knopf, New York.

Little, E. L. 1996. *The Audubon Society Field Guide to North American Trees: Eastern Region*. Alfred A. Knopf, New York.

Lust, J. 1974. *The Herb Book*. Bantam, New York.

Medsger, O. P. 1966. *Edible Wild Plants*. Collier-Macmillan, Toronto, Ontario.

Michigan Botanical Society. 2005. *Big Tree Database for Michigan*. Michigan Botanical Society website at http://michbotclub.org/big_trees/searchable_database.htm. Accessed April 2005.

Mitchell, A. and J. Wilkinson. 1982. *The Trees of Britain and Northern Europe*. Wm. Collins, Sons and Co., London.

Mitchell, A. 1987. *The Guide to Trees of Canada and North America*. Prospero Books, Kansas City, Missouri.

Mozingo, H. 1987. *Shrubs of the Great Basin*. University of Nevada Press, Reno.

Naegele, T. A. 1996. *Edible and Medicinal Plants of the Great Lakes Region*. Wilderness Adventure Books, Davisburg, Michigan.

Otis, C. H. 1965. *Michigan Trees*. University of Michigan Press, Ann Arbor.

Peattie, D. C. 1953. *A Natural History of Western Trees*. Houghton Mifflin, Boston.

Peattie, D. C. 1966. *A Natural History of Trees of Eastern and Central North America*. Houghton Mifflin, Boston.

Peirce, A. 1999. *The American Pharmaceutical Association Practical Guide to Natural Medicines*. Stonesong Press, New York.

Peterson, L. A. 1977. *A Field Guide to Edible Wild Plants of Eastern and Central North America*. Hougton Mifflin, Boston.

Petrides, G. A. and O. Petrides. 1992. *A Field Guide to Western Trees*. Houghton Mifflin, Boston.

Petrides, G. A. and J. Wehr. 1998. *Eastern Trees*. Hougton Mifflin, Boston.

Phillips, R. 1978. *Trees of North America and Europe*. Pan Books, London

Phillips, D. H. and D. A. Burdekin. 1992. *Diseases of Forest and Ornamental Trees*. MacMillan, London.

Phipps, J. B. and M. Muniyamma. 1980. A taxonomic revision of *Crataegus* (Rosaceae) in Ontario. *Canadian Journal of Botany* 58: 1621-1699.

Preston, R. J., Jr. 1989. *North American Trees*. Iowa State University Press, Ames, Iowa.

Rabeler, R. K. 1998. *Gleason's Plants of Michigan*. Oakleaf Press, Ann Arbor.

Reader's Digest. 1981. *Field Guide to the Trees and Shrubs of Britain*. Reader's Digest Association, London.

Reader's Digest. 1986. *Magic and Medicine of Plants*. Reader's Digest Association, Montreal, Quebec.

Rehder, A. 1951. *Manual of Cultivated Trees and Shrubs Hardy in North America*. Macmillan, New York.

Reznicek, A. A., E. G. Voss, et al. 2004. *Online Atlas of Michigan Plants*. University of Michigan, Ann Arbor. http://herbarium.lsa.umich.edu/website/michflora. Accessed April 2005.

Rosendahl, C. O. 1955. *Trees and Shrubs of the Upper Midwest*. University of Minnesota Press, Minneapolis.

Smith, N. F. 1995. *Trees of Michigan and the Upper Great Lakes*. Thunder Bay Press, Lansing, Michigan.

Soper, J. H. and M. L. Heimburger. 1982. *Shrubs of Ontario*. Royal Ontario Museum, Toronto, Ontario.

Spangler, R. L. and J. Ripperda. 1977. *Landscape Plants for Central and Northeastern United States, Including Lower and Eastern Canada*. Burgess Publishing, Minneapolis.

Stokes, D. W. 1981. *The Natural History of Wild Shrubs and Vines: Eastern and Central North America*. Harper and Row, New York.

Tekiela, S. 2002. *Trees of Michigan: A Field Guide*. Adventure Publications, Cambridge, Michigan.

Trelease, W. 1931. *Winter Botany*. Dover, New York.

Viertel, A. T. 1970. *Trees, Shrubs and Vines*. Syracuse University Press, Syracuse, New York.

Voss, E. G. 1972. *Michigan Flora. Part I: Gymnosperms and Monocots*. University of Michigan Herbarium, Ann Arbor.

Voss, E. G. 1985. *Michigan Flora. Part II: Dicots (Saururaceae–Cornaceae)*. University of Michigan Herbarium, Ann Arbor.

Voss, E. G. 1996. *Michigan Flora. Part III. Dicots Concluded*. University of Michigan Herbarium, Ann Arbor.

Index

Index

Index

Index

Index

Index

Index

Index

Index

271

About the Author

An avid naturalist since childhood, Linda Kershaw focused on botany at the University of Waterloo, earning her masters degree in 1976. Since then she has worked as a consultant and researcher in northwestern Canada and as an author and editor in Edmonton, while pursuing two favorite pastimes—photography and illustrating. Linda hopes that her books will help people to appreciate the beauty and fascinating history of plants and to recognize the intrinsic value of nature's rich mosaic.